*A Philosophy
of the
Christian Religion*

A Philosophy
of the
Christian Religion

by

EDWARD JOHN CARNELL, TH.D., PH.D.,
Professor of Apologetics, Fuller Theological Seminary

WM. B. EERDMANS PUBLISHING COMPANY
Grand Rapids   **Michigan**

Set up and printed, December, 1951
Second printing, August, 1954
Reprinted, April, 1960
Reprinted, September, 1964
Reprinted, September, 1970

PHOTOLITHOPRINTED BY GRAND RAPIDS BOOK MANUFACTURERS, INC.
GRAND RAPIDS, MICHIGAN
1970

Preface

It is the universal conviction among Christians that a consistent venture in the religious life must lead a person step by step from lower to higher commitments. Religion starts whenever an individual is willing to name a value for which to live and die; religion reaches its perfection with faith in the person of Jesus Christ.

Stages in the religious life may be compared to the rocks on which small boys hop when crossing a stream. Because the stones are so far apart, it is necessary that the lads either keep jumping from one to the next or fall into the water. There is no third course of action.

It is quite true that a person may elect not to arouse any religious interest at all. He may refuse to become articulate about the highest values in life. That is his responsibility. But once he *does* venture, he must either sustain momentum or fall into the creek.

The purpose of this volume is to trace through a set of typical value options in life. Reasons will be suggested in each case why one *must* move on from the lower to the higher on the one hand, and from the higher to faith in the person of Christ on the other. Christianity is a coherent religion. It never asks the heart to trust values which the reason is obliged to discard as contradictory. *No value commitment is completely satisfying until the complete man is satisfied.*

Whether this book succeeds in this ambitious venture, only investigation can determine. The rational connections seem sufficient to me; I can only hope that they will seem sufficient likewise, to others.

Edward John Carnell

Table of Contents

Part I

EMERGENCE OF A PROBLEM

1

The Human Venture

T HE law of self-preservation is so deeply engrained in our
nature that it is impossible for man to engage in any
conscious activity without seeking his own well-being.
Whether we eat or drink, or whatever we do, we do it all in
the name of what we think will augment the sum total of our
own happiness. A preferring-unhappiness man is a contradiction in terms. Or, rather, he is man who unconsciously finds
his own brand of well-being through commitment to what
he pretends is a form of unhappiness. In no case does he
break the rule that in every action we overtly or covertly pledge
obedience to the canons of personal interest and preference.

But what of the man who sacrifices his own life for the good
of another? Does he not break this rule? The answer is no.
Life is more than physical survival. Happiness at times is
increased when we commit ourselves to those choices which
in the end may issue in our own physical destruction. There
are invisible data which we must reckon with: honesty, justice,
courage, charity. If we betray ourselves by turning aside
from these, we decrease our happiness; for we sense with a
perfect intuition that the best within us is accented only when
we are faithful to these unseen, yet always seen, vitalities.
When Private Rodger Young gave his life for the men he
marched among, therefore, he did it knowing that it would
be far less desirable to live as a coward than to die as a friend.
He stabilized self-love and self-security by jeopardizing his
physical survival.

I. Freedom and Values

That which men choose when seeking an increase of happiness is known as a *value*. Nothing mystical about it, a value is simply anything which we prize or esteem. Values comprise the very stuff of satisfaction, the magnetic power which draws a free man into commitment.

While it is true that both man and the brute share self-preservation, and thus both seek for values which stabilize well-being, only man has the power of reflecting about reflection, thinking about thought. In short, man is *free*. Whereas the lower animal remains relatively content within the framework of zones laid down by nature, man complements his natural necessity through free, creative activity. The confines of natural necessity are examined and assessed by each generation, with the hope that pressure points may be relieved and chafing edges smoothed down. There is no conceivable outer limit to the ways freedom may manipulate natural bonds to yield a more predictably reliable quantity of security.

Since each generation leaves a deposit of gain and loss behind it, therefore, it is self-evident why only man, not the brute, writes and appreciates history. Only those free enough to make history are interested in examining history. History is the sum total of the facts (or the account of the facts) which comprise the responses of free men to creative possibilities. The herd knows none of the distinctive traits which define individuality; consequently, it leaves no cultural pattern behind it. Individuality is possible only when soul is compounded with freedom, for freedom converts the monotony of physical survival into the tingling, challenging adventure of creative living. Freedom transforms the assignment of living into a pleasurable excursion through adventurous waters.

A. *Reefs and Shoals*

Existing is but the continuity of an organism in time and space; living is sparkling, creative freedom. While one need only survive to exist, one must create to live. The free, creating individual has something to live *for*. Values catch his attention, arrest his interest, tap his resources. Freedom has reconnaissance powers: Like a powerful jet plane zooming over the land at supersonic speed, freedom is able to appraise value alternatives with a quick sweep. Freedom commands an army of vassals. Memory corrals the past, vision harnesses the present, and anticipation projects the future. Played according to the rules, life can be a very pleasant game.

Yet, life is more than a game. It is a serious venture. Unless care is taken in the employment of freedom, a person may either internally decay through atrophy, or be crushed by powerful outside forces. The atrophy is a disease which infiltrates the heart whenever the zest for living is lost, as illustrated in the case of any despondent person. Whoever has no interest in things is consciously or unconsciously yielding to the virus of disconcern and carelessness. And the outside forces are those powers which array themselves against the soul in retaliation for a commitment ill chosen. Just as there is an unmistakable warmth when one finds a value which joins itself cordially to the inner expectations, so there is a bitter recoil when a commitment frustrates or repels our expectations. It is not enough just to be creative, therefore. Unless the potentialities of freedom are disciplined and channeled, they can be as much a cause of grief as they can be a source of contentment.

Our days are brief. In fact, they are too brief. For this reason few find the clue to life soon enough to benefit them maximally in their quest for security. Like the pebbles which bank the ocean shores — infinite in number and endless in variety — so also is the field of value options: Who can number them? Yet, we are on the run. We are in the race. There seems to be neither time nor leisure to canvass the wisdom of those value decisions which draw us deeper and deeper into life's commitments. We feel like the boy told to take whatever he wished from a sporting goods store, but that he must run at top speed while making his selections: There is more in sight than either time or opportunity will permit him to take. The factors of life are complex, the mind confused.

But we are committed. As Pascal long ago pointed out in his *Wager,* we are already in the race. "Yes, but you must wager: this is not voluntary, you are embarked. Which will you take then?" If there were opportunity to reverse the gears of time, this problem would not have arisen. The fact is, however, that we have already been born; we now live in this world; our destiny is currently being shaped. Having been catapulted into existence without covenant or consent, it is only our option either to begin creative living or prematurely to introduce death in our members. As exercise is to the body, so creative freedom is to the spirit: Take away the activity and the health vanishes.

A remarkable characteristic of values and interests is their power to unite themselves with the fabric of our hearts. Through passionate commitment the individual joins himself to the object of his affection. The heart of the fair maiden is not simply a fact "out there" in the world of things. The young man identifies himself with the heart of his beloved, until his own person is one with hers. Roots grow so deeply within him that his own life begins to flicker and die when that of the beloved vanishes. The individual *is* the totality of his value commitments, for without interest there is no life. To live *is* to strive, to hope, and to die for the worth-while.

The stakes are high, the gaming dangerous. The stake is the gaining or losing of the self, and the game is the choosing between options which seem to shade off into one another — even though life-and-death issues lay concealed beneath their outer cloaks. Happy is the man who has fought and won in this game, for he has gained himself; while greatly to be pitied is the one who has risked all on a venture, only to find the dissatisfaction of emptiness gnawing away at the heart. Wanting both time and opportunity to make amends, his loss is inward, essential, and perpetual. Wretched is that creature in the county home with neither strength to create for the future nor consolation from memory that past opportunities were wisely used.

Despondency sometimes seeks relief through death. Yet, is *this* decision unattended by risk? Dare we presume in ad-

vance that thorny boughs will not reach low to tear our flesh
with their slashing swords? Death *may* be worse than life.
The prudent general will surrender his forces to the enemy,
rather than retreat through unknown waters where worse
terrors may lurk. Indeed, all will learn the meaning of death
in due time. When we must, we shall die. But until the implications of death are known, one cannot be sure but what
despondency in time is better than despondency in eternity.
"The fear of death is more to be dreaded than death itself."[1]

The tabloid mind may cavalierly rant about the "meaningless universe" and the "ultimate emptiness" of everything —
even gaining his university salary through such performing.
But neither he nor his hearer can entertain that doctrine in the
innermost recesses of the heart. Something inside cries out
against the conclusion that a purpose-seeking man has been
hatched by a purposeless universe. The urge may be ill founded;
it may have to be disqualified. Yet, there it is: Our heart tells
us that there *are* destinies at stake in this life. We cannot
eradicate *this* voice. Wisdom dictates, therefore, that before
one decides whether or not this witness is trustworthy, a tho-
rough investigation be conducted; lest through either over-
sight or default an everlasting loss in the soul be sustained.

Decisions affecting the whole individual may be made only
after an examination of the whole of relevant facts in the universe. In this game of life and death no clue should be by-
passed until it first has been processed by the searching heart.
The more a man can successfully bind himself to the universe
over against him, the more he is able to release the surging
wells of creative potentiality within him. Living takes on
dignity, faith, and hope when freedom is persuaded that it is
truly dealing with ultimate reality.

One may view the matter of cosmic support from the heart's
point of view, in which case *religion* emerges; or he may view
it from the perspective of the inquiring mind, and *philosophy*
emerges. Still, both disciplines testify to the potentialities of
freedom.

---

1. *Publilius Syrus* (Lyman tr.), Maxim 511.

B. *Complications*

The heart quickly inquires: What *ought* I to do? The question is pitched on the level of the normative, and this is proper. If there are values which control our destinies, it is imperative that happiness-seeking individuals pursue them.

But defining the normative is more easily said than done. *De gustibus non est disputandum.* This is the first complication: In matters of tastes there is no disputation. Some men like spinach, others do not. Some collect stamps, others throw them away. This is the problem: Are values simply matters of personal taste?

This is only the beginning of sorrows, however. A more serious complexity stems out of the *qualitative* nature of values. Mathematics is the perfect science because it lives and moves and has its being in quantitative relations, relations which value interests can not by any sleight of hand be reduced to. Quantities are measured, bottled, and classified almost entirely independent of the evaluating individual himself. Quantities of goods may be bought, sold, and shipped by the pound or boatload. *Qualitative* relations will not yield that easily, however. It is one thing to measure the rays of the setting sun, but it is quite another to conclude meaningfully that the sun itself exemplifies beauty.

It may appear that there is no other alternative at this juncture than to digress into an extended study of the nature and types of values. By what other means may we solve the problem of how we can meaningfully speak of normative qualitative relations? Well, one possibility is to examine the axioms which guide men in actual living. Somehow we *do* manage to convert the qualitative into significant meaning, even though this meaning does not enjoy the precision of quantitative relations. Whether or not the axiologist can discover the mechanics of how it happens, it is a fact of our experience that we *are* in possession of certain intuitively perceived axioms which guide us in this business of living. Perhaps if we are sufficiently devoted to these primitive guides, we may find solvents for the more difficult situations.

When men hastily choose values which they must later regret, society properly denominates them *foolish*. This fact suggests the first self-evident truth in value relations: *Foolishness
is to axiology as inconsistency is to logic.* Whereas wisdom
is tested by consistency, values are judged by their power to
increase or decrease happiness. When a man rushes into a
burning house and rescues his collection of cigar bands, while
allowing his own children to perish in the flames, he is properly
branded a fool. He is juxtaposing himself — a seeker after
happiness — with a decision which can only result in the long
run in the decrease of that happiness. He elects something he
will later regret.

The mention of the long run implies the second axiom.
*Foolishness can be detected by patiently juxtaposing the in-
trinsic power of a value with what the individual expects from
it.* The foolishness of quitting high school and contracting
for employment in the local foundry can be exposed by placing
the value of the job side by side with what the individual — in
the long swing of events — expects to get out of that position.
"You will regret this rash act" is the conclusion the prudent
counsellor hands to the anxious high school boy. The freedom
of man permits him to evaluate a commitment in terms of its
full theoretical implications. The dog may lap up all of its
water at once, but the soldier rations it out carefully; for he
knows that the supply is scant and the desert trail long. It is
the foolish man who squanders on present satisfactions, only
to suffer regret in the end. Wisdom looks to the ends. *Res-
pice finem.*

There is probably no sadder word in the language than *regret*. Disraeli's observation of the cycle of life is sadly only too
true. "Youth is a blunder; manhood a struggle; old age a
regret."[2] Regret is freedom's looking back on an irretrievably
lost opportunity. Freedom may span the movement of time,
but it cannot reverse time, for time moves in one direction. It
is but ours so to make our decisions one moment that we have
no occasion to regret them the next. Regret may be mild or

---

2. *Coningsby*, Book III, Chapter I.

desperate, depending on how great is the loss. The condemned prisoner regrets all, for he has lost all. He has lost *himself*.

Wise men order their life in such a way that the passage of time confirms the prudence of the course they elect. By first of all knowing themselves, they can predict what values will sustain them without regret. Wise men enjoy a peace which attends skillful commitment.

II. Our Contemporary Peril

In hours of peril an important discipline must be developed. Because the time in which all may be gained or lost is so brief, while the awareness of what it involved is so clear, it is difficult for one to collect his nerves to act with deliberateness. And yet there is no time when greater caution should be taken than during the stress of emergency or tragedy. A rash decision when the fire is first detected may make the difference between a lifetime of happiness and a lifetime of regret.

Our contemporary culture is beset by frayed and ragged nerves. Advances in technology have catapulted us into a state of constant danger. Individual and collective security have been taken for granted hitherto. Now the very foundations of our culture may be destroyed almost without notice. It appears there will be no opportunity for attrition in the next conflict, for the winner will take all.

The sweep hand on the clock is lashing us on to decisions in areas where we would ordinarily sue for delay. Swift action is called for in this hour of contemporary peril, as all is at stake. If the father has but five minutes to decide whether to pay a ransom for his child or see the little one die, he must decide at once. He must waive the luxury of going through the files on the psychology of kidnappers to learn whether thugs do or do not mean their threats. If he delays, the child may perish.

Out of a reckoning with peril the third axiom emerges. *In extremity one chooses what is dearest to him.* A quick decision must be made. And regret will be the least if the *dearest* is saved, though all else may be lost. The miscellanies of life are but furniture for the most precious values.

The prospect of danger forces men to take quick inventory of what is most valuable. The dearest is that which is most intimate and most satisfying when juxtaposed beside the innermost essence of our own person. The dearest stands the test of time. When the flood waters carry away our home and gear, for example, we breathe a sigh of thanksgiving when we are told that all the children are safe and sound. We miss the house; we love the children.

A. *The Handbook*

There is a grave risk involved in making any decisions during times of peril. Unquestionably. But there is no other option than to decide. There may be only probability to guide the contemporary man, but there is little probability but what all will be lost if we do not swiftly venture. The hydrogen bomb will see to that.

Danger and simplicity go nicely together. Observe the lesson of the word *exit*. It is concise, intelligible, appropriately colored, and conspicuously displayed. One may pay little attention to it during times of tranquility. But there it is, ready to guide and assist when the cry of *fire!* rings through the great auditorium and anxious eyes look for an escape. When the smoke begins to roll and piercing screams fill the air, the trapped have no time to decode a complicated tome. They want salvation, and they want it given with simplicity.

Modern man, like a soldier facing the enemy, will have his predicament eased somewhat if he has a codified handbook telling how to conduct himself in times of emergency. A graded scale of value commitments is needed, so that with one sweep of the eye a man can determine exactly what course of action to follow in the hour of peril. What ought one to commit himself to in this contemporary uncertainty? What is worthwhile? What is fundamental and enduring? These are pivotal questions. If the dearest and the most lasting can be de-

fined, the heart will find relief; for the ultimate will then serve
as a standard by which to classify the peripheral.

B. *Day of Grace*

The spirit of prudential discernment does not always strive
with man, for the delicate balance of values in life is easily
upset. There are moments when man is free to evaluate one
ultimate over against another with a genuine (though never
absolute) freedom from prejudice. The child is open for teaching; the philosophy student in college is docile. But this
nimbleness in freedom does not long remain, for philosophical
ultimates intoxicate, blind, overpower. A plausibly stated
philosophy of reality has a siren-like ability to draw the hearts
of men into its vortex, until the resulting commitment is so
strong that blindness to any other option results. The fanaticism of a communist illustrates this perfectly. One moment
he is only a dissatisfied member of a social minority, casting
about for moorings; while the next he is so overwhelmed by
the promises of communism that he sees nothing worth living
and dying for, save this political-economic program.

Man has his day of grace. For this reason he must treasure
his freedom as he would his own life. A misplaced commitment may not always be covered by an easy retraction. Freedom itself blends in with the commitment until a blindness
to one's own predicament results. Men begin innocently by
just toying with sex, for example. Then they commence to
subordinate other values to it. Finally, the urge for sexual
satisfaction develops into an obsession under the power of
which men will cheat, steal, and kill. We have our day of
grace. The sober man can evaluate the place of drink in the
hierarchy of values, but the man overpowered by drink cannot,
since he is only able to see the option through the eyes of one
already committed in its favor.

The lesson to be learned is that one must develop a critical
self-restraint, lest a fanaticism displace the clarity and objectivity which form the very stuff of a balanced life. Riots are

instigated by those obsessed individuals who allow minor values to become ultimates. They sacrifice the enduring on the altar of the perishing.

If modern man has yet a clear vision with which to see and understand, he may properly rejoice, for the day of grace remains. Only he who is girded about with balance and maturity can scythe through our contemporary forest of uncertainty to bring us to the clearing of hope and faith. Now is the day of salvation. Western culture yet survives. Let us thus, with Milton, resolutely seek

The golden key
which opes the palace of eternity.

II

A Familiar Option

FAMILIARITY breeds contempt. Men are aware of this truth. Many of our most precious possessions in life are often neglected because they are either too close to us or are too easy to obtain. We frequently cross continents to locate hidden treasures, only to learn that the largest and purest diamonds lie right in our own back yard.

Contempt for the familiar is destroyed whenever the things hitherto taken for granted are suddenly snatched away from us. A perfect illustration of this is health. It is presumed upon until it is lost. Then, suddenly, we offer kingdoms for its return.

I. Christianity

When careful inventory is taken of the foundations upon which Western culture rests, none has been more Gibraltar-like through the ages than Christianity. Even the immense contribution made by the Greeks has been refined and purified by the Hebrew-Christian world view. Yet, our familiarity with Christianity tends to encourage contempt. Perhaps in our contemporary impasse, an hour when the pillars of our culture are being shaken by the Samsons of communism, we may again sense that if the values which Christianity supports are lost, all is lost.

A. *Point-blank*

There is something very strange about Christianity. Whereas the great philosophic systems are fortified by immense arguments to justify both their procedure and their goal, the Scriptures start off point-blank to discuss some of the profoundest topics conceivable to man: God, creation, the relation between time and eternity, the nature and destiny of man. The procedure seems almost naive in our eyes, we are so used to proceeding along other lines of method.

But this is only the first strange thing about Christianity. The Biblical witness likewise earns an easy contempt for itself by the relentless way it so arranges its propositions that guilt in the inner man is made one of the first topics of inquiry. This is opposite the procedure salesmen are taught to follow when peddling their wares to homes or to industry. They must first compliment and praise; then their client will feel more inclined to purchase the product. Scripture, however, first of all engages men as guilty sinners. It *condemns* the ego. The Bible is surely *not* the world's best seller because it outlines a congenial way to win friends and influence people.

Exhibit A is Jesus Christ. He is the master teacher of morality because of the skillful way he so phrased his questions and answers that guilty hearts were exposed. He drew men out to act on his words. When he finished speaking, men either repented or they were hardened, some even taking up stones to destroy him. Those who resorted to such violence presumed that by destroying the accuser they would snuff out the accusation. They overlooked the simple principle that it was their own heart which condemned them. A perfect instance of this methodology is found in Matthew 21:23-27:

> And when he entered the temple, the chief priests and the elders of the people came up to him as he was teaching, and said, 'By what authority are you doing these things, and who gave you this authority?' Jesus answered them, 'I also will ask you a question; and if you tell me the answer, then I also will tell you by what authority I do these things. The baptism of John, whence was it? From heaven or from men?' And they argued with one another, 'If we say, "From heaven," he will say to us, "Why then did you not believe him?" But if we say, "From men," we are afraid of the multitude; for all hold that John was a prophet.' So they answered Jesus, 'We do not know.' And he said to them, 'Neither will I tell you by what authority I do these things.'

The progression of this argument is extremely interesting. As long as the discussion was kept formal and academic, the chief priests and elders were delighted to parley with Christ. But when the center of gravity shifted from Christ's to their *own* moral condition, they sheepishly bowed out of the discussion. Since personal pride was now at stake, the issue was no longer simply academic. Christ was finally crucified, but it did not occur to those who condemned him that the real cause of their violence was their own intolerance over having their inner prides and pretensions brought to the light. "For every one who does evil hates the light, and does not come to the light, lest his deeds should be exposed." (John 3:20)

B. *Mounting Charges*

A striking peculiarity of philosophy is the way it avoids any serious fraternizing with the Biblical records. One would need the proverbial lamp of Diogenes to find a modern, influential philosopher who has this foundation of Western culture at heart when his presuppositions are drawn up. Witness the monumental work, *The Library of Living Philosophers,* for example. If one will scan the indexes with an eye to such terms as "Jesus Christ," the "Trinity," "sin," and "Scripture," he will notice the peripheral place that the Christian documents enjoy in shaping modern philosophical presuppositions. Is there a principle of sufficient reason at work here? Does academic rigor in Western culture *require* the negating of the very foundations which we hitherto supposed were the supports of our culture?

Hardly has the floor been thrown open for discussion but what the chairman is obliged to rap for attention, so enthusiastic are the philosophers in calling out fundamental reasons why their independence from the Biblical records is justified.

1. FAITH. The first speaker reflects the unanimous opinion of the rest when he asserts that philosophy is grounded in knowledge, while Biblical religion turns on faith. So, that is that. In Jamesean terms, faith belongs to the tender-minded,

knowledge to the tough-minded. Before this issue is laid to rest, however, two observations must be made.

First, faith is not a stranger in the world. Faith is simply commitment or trust. It is just believing in what one is assured is veracious, valuable, or engaging. Freedom wanders aimlessly if it has nothing to which it may become committed. The philosopher does not pass beyond faith, therefore. He has faith in himself, his method, rationality, the existence of other minds, and a host of other objects and relations. Faith is the foundation of all social relations. We trust the banker, the engineer, our wife. Now suppose (for the sake of examining Christianity as a problem of thought) that a *personal God* is the ultimate being, and that one has truncated truth while he remains unfamiliar with God; would anything other than trust in this God be a conceivably satisfying binder between time and eternity? In unloading faith, hence, one had best proceed with care. He may covertly be depriving himself of an indispensable condition for good philosophy itself.

Second, and perhaps more to the point, a straw-man opponent is attacked when faith and knowledge are antipathetically related. The Bible is a system of propositions which address the reason as decisively as any other faculty in man. Knowledge is the light which clarifies the nature of things to which man ought to be committed. Reason tests, segregates, orders, and classifies. Proper commitment does not follow through until the whole man is convinced of the reasonableness and coherence of a value proposition. Knowledge describes and orders the alternatives, separating the worthy from the unworthy, the good from the bad, the true from the false, so that the heart may have an unambiguous place to rest.

Philosophy presupposes that reason guides the wise man into life, and Christianity does not gainsay this. Reason stands guard over the heart, warning it of the consequences which follow if this or that commitment is decided upon. Men are under obligation to sharpen their reason in order that they might reduce the plus-minus threshold of possible error which attends all decision. But man is not fully a man until he *commits* himself to what the understanding finds is worthy of commitment. Without faith in what reason gains, the gain itself is fruitless.

2. AUTHORITY. A further reason why the Biblical flower is often born to blush unseen is the spirit of authority and finality in which it speaks. "Thus says the Lord Jehovah of hosts" is a framework of dogmatic utterance which appears to run counter to the mood of tentativity and the spirit of constant revision in modern thinking. In reflecting upon this matter, one cannot disavow that the Bible *does* presume to speak the mind of God with finality. But does this fact cancel out our interest in investigating it? That is the issue.

First, it is impossible *not* to trust in authorities. The individual who disclaims all expressions of authority simply makes himself his final authority. He implicitly trusts the proposition that there are none in whom he may rest. To trust no one is but a way of announcing self-trust. When this is seen, the problem is no longer whether it is good or bad to trust authority, *but rather which authority is it best to trust?*

Second, in both the laboratory and the research library we have faith in anyone who meets two general criteria: He must be credible and trustworthy in his own person, and he must exhibit an access to the relevant data by speaking of things which, when tested by competent critical norms, sustain our expectations. If this credible individual be oneself, the man across the street, or God, one should follow exactly the same rule. One *must* submit to an authority — there is no other option. And wisdom dictates that one give himself to that which leaves him with the least disappointment, frustration, or regret. If one rules out the possibility of *God* as being a worthy authority whom man may trust, therefore, he does so on personal or moral, but not logical, grounds. If God is trustworthy, it would be irrational not to trust him.

Third, when matters pertaining to ultimates are in question there are very good antecedent reasons why God (if it so be that there is a God) *is* the best ground of trust. Suppose, for the sake of the question, that God does exist. And suppose that this God is the sovereign creator of heaven and earth, holding the meaning of all things in the eternal repository of his own wisdom; who could be in a better position to know the beginning from the end? Would there be a more thinkably perfect authority to rest in than God? Of course, the investigator will have to test carefully that it is *God* who claims to speak. All pretenses to revelation must be put through a scrutinizing test. Such testing, done in an honest effort to gain fellowship with the true God, is as wholesome to the individual as it is pleasing to God. But the point is that God *may be* the clue to our contemporary predicament. If the inventor of a machine is an authority on the subject of that machine, *a fortiori* is not God rightfully entitled to be the supreme authority?

If investigation proves (with Nietzsche) that God is dead, the fact would yet remain that *if there were a God*, he would be our best authority. If the one who knows all cannot be trusted, then how much less can anyone else? Hence, if (as a problem of thought) a man *prefers* non-God as his trust, he evidences great axiological foolishness. A child who is a lonely orphan by necessity is to be pitied. But if the child *chooses* non-father, he is playing the fool.

3. OBSCURITY. Since the philosophic-scientific mind identifies symbolic precision with truth, it understandably experiences a certain amount of impatience with the text of the Bible. Whereas a work in philosophy blushes with embarrassment until the major terms employed are adequately defined for the reader, the Scriptures commence from the beginning simply using, but (apparently) not defining their profoundest concepts. Note the first verse in the Bible: "In the beginning God created the heavens and the earth." Neither here, nor in the context, is a formal, Aristotelian definition given of any of the difficult terms which are so casually employed: "Beginning," "God," "heavens," "earth." In contrast to Aristotle or Spinoza certain sections of Scripture read like a child story book.

One can easily sympathize with the one who is troubled about revelation as an option. There is probably no greater curse in all of human discourse than ambiguity of terms. As a consequence of slovenly thinking, misinformation abounds everywhere. It is not accidental that both philosopher and scientist seek to define their terms carefully, for the area in which they work is exceedingly complex. But does it follow that the Scriptures, in failing to pursue this pattern, cannot commend themselves to the mind of a thinking investigator? Perhaps, and perhaps not. The question must be investigated.

First, it is well to preface this subject of definitions by pointing out an ambiguity in the concept of definition itself. We have suggested thus far that the Biblical writers are uninterested in definitions. This admission must be taken provisionally, for (it will shortly be seen) they use a form of definition too profound for either Aristotle or Spinoza to appreciate; yet a form quite adequate for the man on the street suffering from a broken heart or a lonely spirit.

There is no absolute pattern which one must abide by in formulating definitions. To define is to communicate to others the limits of the terms one is employing. And here, if anywhere, the end justifies the means; for the purpose in defining is to edify, not entertain. One is interested in communicating concepts to others. There is only one fundamental rule which the communicator must obey: *Does the hearer understand the meaning of your concepts?* All other rules are clarifications of this one. One may communicate meaning by tapping a stick on the table, making signs with his fingers, blowing horns, emitting smoke signals, or using any other of an endless number of outlets. There is no *essential* difference between the word or the smoke; each is a vehicle to communicate meaning. I can define my smoke pattern either by looking up the matter in a smoke-talk dictionary (if any), or by resorting to some other device. I can say that the smoke pattern means what I intend to communicate when I now tap my foot ten times. Or, I can lead the inquirer out to the pasture and say that the smoke means *that* (pointing out the object with the index finger). If the inquirer grunts assent that he understands, I may go back to my smoke making. Meaning has been communicated.

Second, economy in social relations generally dictates that one employ the *connotative* or Aristotelian-type of definition as the simplest way to announce how a term is being employed. An example of this is the following: "Man is a sentient being qualified to worship God." The species (man) is subsumed under a higher genus (sentient being), while the differentia (qualified to worship God) sets this species apart from other species of the same genus.

But the connotative definition does not exhaust the possible alternatives. An equally effective, though less commonly used, form is the *denotative.*

> The second method for indicating the meaning of a word may be called *denotative defining,* and the result which it yields is a *denotative definition — one which attempts to give meaning to a name by indicating examples or citing specimens of objects of which it is the name.* . . . A denotative definition simply attempts to clarify the meanings of certain words by indicating *a representative part of their denotation.* Thus we might say 'the word *skyscraper* means denotatively (or indicates) what is denoted by the names *Woolworth Building, Empire State Building, Chrysler Building, R. C. A. Building,* etc.,' or 'the word *steamship* means denotatively what is denoted by the names *Ile de France, Queen Mary, Deutschland,* etc.'[1]

Thus, one could denotatively account for the word *miracle* by listing all of the miracles in the Bible, providing this represents the extent to which he wishes his term to refer. This will not *prove* miracles true, of course. Definitions only clarify terms; they do not make things real.

Third, suppose that one were to define *God.* What then? Philosophers have long failed to find a connotative definition of God, for how can the highest genus be subsumed under anything? But what of the denotative type? Since there is only one specimen to which the name may be applied, no list

---

1. Frye and Levi, *Rational Belief,* (New York: Harcourt, Brace and Company, 1941), p. 135.

can be drawn up beyond that name which we already start with: God. Is this satisfactory: "I mean by the term *God* what is denoted by the following: *God*"? This obviously gets one nowhere. To elicit a sympathy with what the Biblical writers were faced with, this fact must be pointed out. They were interested in leading people to *God*.

Suppose, further, that one had the job of so arranging his terms that in the end the reader would become acquainted with the *person* of God, rather than merely understanding the meaning of the *term*, God. How would one proceed with this assignment? God surely would be defined only when he was personally known. God is not a term; he is a person. To know God is to have fellowship with him.

A difficult matter suddenly becomes clear and simple when artificially erected stumbling blocks are turned out of the way. How does the child succeed in defining *father*? Easily. "I mean by the term *father* all that is suggested by the story I am going to tell you about my father. The term will become clear as the story goes on." So, the tale commences. Father is one who brings home food; the one who carries the children in his arms; the one who laughs and plays with the family behind the apple tree in the yard. "This is how I am using the term *father*." And so it suddenly becomes clear to us. *Father* is the carrying-children-in-arms one, the playing-behind-the-apple-tree one. He is the food-getting one, the tire-fixing one. The story is completed, and we quickly understand the meaning of the term *father*. But what is more, we begin to know the individual personally. What is objectionable about telling stories to define terms?

Because they sought to introduce men to this same childlike knowledge by acquaintance, the Biblical writers elected to tell a story about God's covenantal dealings with man, rather than give a glossary of formal terms. And as the story unfolds, the meaning becomes increasingly clear. God is the one who creates and sustains; God is the one whom Abraham served; God is the father of Isaac and Jacob; God is the one who led the children of Israel; God is the Father of Jesus Christ; God is the one who comforted and guided the apostles; God is the one who is head of the church. The terms used to convey the stories of God's dealings are rich in themselves. God is El Shaddai, Jehovah, Immanuel, Most High, Shiloh, Branch, Star, Strength of Israel, Light, Rock, Keeper, Fountain, etc.

Actually, the Biblical definition of God begins with the very first verse in Scripture, for at that point the narrative starts to tell the story of how God is related to the world. And the definition is not completed until the end of the book of Revelation. As each book unfolds and the significance of God's covenantal dealings with men becomes richer, the meaning of the *person* of God so eclipses the meaning of the *term*, God, that finally one basks in perfect fellowship, crying: "What is in a name? God by any other name would be as sweet." Names can only suggest to us what is denoted in God's person and act. The sovereign, creating author of heaven and earth is *El Shaddai*. The one who graciously delivers from Egypt is *Jehovah*. The incarnate God as savior is *Jesus*.

Suppose, thus, that the Bible *is* God's word for man. Could there be any finer way to define God than to proceed along the way of telling a story? Would the pages of Scripture be improved if they clarified the *term*, God, but left his *person* unknown? Children love stories. That is the key to the success of the sale of juvenile books, for tingling little tales have a rich way of making things clear. The stories worm their way into the heart through adventure, challenge, and intrigue, until finally the stories belong to the child. The child means by the term *Little Black Sambo* all that is expressed in the story of a small boy's pretty clothing and umbrella, the threatening tigers, and the mountain-high plate of hot pancakes. Sambo is the weeping-behind-the-tree one, the owning–crimson–slippers one. In like manner, the child in Sunday School often knows little or nothing about the genus and differentia which give formal meaning to the term, Jesus; but he may know Jesus personally in his heart. And is not this the thing that counts?

If the child knows his father as the toy-mending and finger-bandaging one, so that the term *father* denotes all that is en-

tailed in such relations, is not the Biblical method of bringing
men into a personal acquaintance with God both acceptable and
satisfying? Aristotle and Spinoza define the *term,* God, for
us, but the Bible defines *God.* God is (at least) the sum total
of what is denoted by his covenantal history. God is the near-
one, the creating-one, the healing-one, the fatherly-one, the
coming-one. In sum, regardless what one may think of the
actual system structurized in the Bible, he cannot gainsay that
an effective means of defining terms has been employed.

4. THE AESTHETIC. Philosophy has always had its best eye
on the ideal of converting the totality of reality into dialectically necessary relations. Plato banished the poet from the
Republic as a teller of untruth. Only rational relations could
be tolerated in a realm ruled by the philosopher-king. And the
ideal of science is hardly different. Science is at its best when
qualitative relations are reduced to quantitative. The poet
is banished from the physics laboratory, too. Impatience
mounts, therefore, when both philosopher and scientist detect
the prominent place of the aesthetic in Biblical revelation.

> For ye shall go out with joy,
> And be led forth with peace:
> The mountains and the hills
> Shall break forth before you into singing;
> And all the trees of the field
> Shall clap their hands.[2]

Formally analyzed, this text does not seem to mean what it
says. How can hills break forth into singing, when they have
no throat? Or the trees clap their hands, when they are devoid
of fleshly appendages?

One of the most interesting experiments in the history of
philosophy was the attempt by the Pythagoreans to reduce all
relations in the universe to mathematics. *All is number,* was
the guiding presupposition. But the experiment miserably
failed. And the reason is that though the physical world may
be ordered according to perfect geometry and mathematics,
man may not. Man spoils the symmetry of the picture. He

---

2. Isaiah 55:12.

is not a unity of mathematical relations, nor is he simply rationality. He is somewhat this, somewhat other things. He weeps, laughs, and thinks, while numbers do not. And the whole person performs each act, for man is not a Trojan horse formed of nicely separable, discrete parts.

It seems plausible to destroy everything save quantitative relations, in the name of preserving truth for man; but the fallacy is that the whole man sees whole truth only when the quantitative issues in the qualitative. There can be no final separation between intellect and emotions, for they are part of the one whole man. We are drawn into intellectual activities only when non-rational vitalities are stimulated within us. Thus, mathematical relations are beautiful to the physicist, and material properties beautiful to the chemist. It is this artistic fringe which preserves living from complete impoverishment. Imagination is the basis of the hypothesis; but imagination goes beyond the fact and extends to the possible. And in the realm of the possible the heart beats fast. Out of the possible come beauty and depth, challenge and adventure. The green trees become waving umbrellas, the white clouds lazy sailboats, and the winding road a silky ribbon before us. The stamp collector is handling more than atoms in a mass. He is dealing with relations which call up thrilling experiences of abiding joy. He champs at the bit to mount a mint block of stamps, freshly received.

A great piece of art is immortal because it embodies an abiding human experience. Art is give and take. Mathematical proportions form the basis of art, but beauty emerges only when the receiving heart takes this symmetry and lines it up with that aesthetic intuition which is the timeless possession of all men. Unless there is a coincidence between the *rationes aeternae* of the heart and the symmetrical proportions of an art piece, immortality will be wanting. A mathematically perfect score of music may be emotionally vapid. It will not wear well if it is deficient in depth perception.

Man is carried away rhapsodically by the thundering harmonies of a great symphony orchestra (while the dog is not) because he discovers in the experience a counterpart to the mysterious environment of spirit in the heart. The heart leaps the barrier of time and knits itself to the heart of the composer himself.

When the Scriptures interlard poetic insight with formal, doctrinal consistency, therefore, it should be observed that such a procedure is what we should expect if the *whole* man is being addressed. In the midst of the history of the birth of Christ, for example, Luke here and there interjects poetic utterances which make the passage live for the inquiring heart.

'My soul magnifies the Lord,
and my spirit rejoices in God my Savior,
for he has regarded the low estate of his handmaiden.
For behold, henceforth all generations will call me blessed.'[3]

Man is not simply *nous*. He is not a Bessie or a Mark III (the famous electronic computing machines). He happens to be a complexity of intellect, emotions, and will — plus a lot more. Whole truth must satisfy the whole man. When the Bible reaches down into the treasures of aesthetics, calling forth rich emotional experiences within man, thus, it does so quite conscious of the fact that the most lasting and abiding joys in life are never so purely rational that they engage only the mind. The lasting pleasures are whole pleasures: friendship, love, devotion to truth, devotion to goodness. The Bible remains a monument to living literature, and is read by men of every stratum of life, because it has captured the abiding experiences of the race. And it has compounded these experiences with a plausible system of thought which engages the reason congenially. Shall we so quickly scorn the vitalities which excite our inner person?

Jehovah is my shepherd;
I shall not want.
He maketh me to lie down
In green pastures.[4]

---

3. Luke 1:46-48.
4. Psalm 23:1-2.

The Psalmist may have been banished from Plato's Republic on the ground that he does not express truth accurately, but he will never be banished by the common man who is not so spoiled by philosophy as to evaluate himself in the shallow dimension of *nous* only. The heart knows a depth of insight which, *while it may never be separated from rational consistency,* is yet not univocally identified with such consistency.

II. In the Balances

A. *Crux: Perspective*

Wisdom is characterized by wholeness. The foolish man acts partially, for he does not relate what he does to the entire picture of things. Consequently, he is frequently beset by the haunting, gnawing plague of regret. Foolishness is rash, quick to choose, easily persuaded; while wisdom is sagacious, long-ranged, stable, foresighted. The wise man conducts himself in the present with an eye to the future, esteeming future tranquility as too valuable a possession to be crucified on the cross of present gratification. He realizes that regret is an admission of faulty judgment, faulty prescience. King Herod, the enflamed ruler, rashly promised the whirling, well proportioned daughter of Herodias whatever of his kingdom she might wish, only to be very sorry for what he had done when the full implications of the vow were perceived. "And the king was sorry." (Matthew 14:9) The king was a fool, for he did not use freedom fully.

In sum, if wisdom is characterized by full perspective coherence, folly is known by its partiality. The partial is the enticing, the now, the immediate. But the partial destroys abiding security by assuring the choosing individual of far more than it can ever effectively make good. Cheating may promise an immediate satisfaction, for example; but its long-term effect is to rot away the interior walls of the moral self. Wisdom knows that it is more profitable to receive a lower grade in a course and enjoy a solid moral experience. The grade will be forgotten with the passage of time, while moral fibre will either build up or destroy the individual himself.

In evaluating the Biblical claims as an answer to our contemporary predicament, hence, wisdom must abide and partiality vanish. Scripture must be judged as a system, as a whole; otherwise it will seem naive or inadequate. Suffering, for example, is an offense to partiality. But whole perspective sees in suffering a *conditio sine qua non* for the acquisition of all worth-while things. If we must suffer for righteousness' sake to gain *mortal* life (for the man without self-discipline is soon dissipated), shall we gain *immortal* assurance through any other means? The apparent artlessness of the Biblical system stems out of the fact that it presupposes (but refuses to discuss) that in whole perspective coherence, and in it alone, lies adequate truth. Instead of announcing its middle premises, therefore, it simply warns what will be the lot of those who reject its proposed course. The Bible never argues with men that they ought to act wisely. It presupposes this. It simply seeks to show how freedom is to be directed if whole happiness is to be secured.

> The inwardness of true religion, as opposed to the multiplied observances and ceremonies of contemporary Judaism, represented by the Scribes and Pharisees; righteousness as judged in the sight of God, not by the correctness of the outward act or word, but by the inward motive and the state of the heart, and demanding therefore at every point a more exacting standard; humility of spirit, as opposed to self-righteous complacency: the single eye which makes the whole body full of light; and, summing up the whole, the losing of one's life to find it, dying to selfish desires and egoistic cravings, to find our true self in that wider life which is at once the service of man and the service of God: this is obviously a spiritual gospel which is bound up with no future event but is verifiable here and now.[5]

In judging the Scriptures, therefore, it is only fair to apply wisdom to wisdom. Things should be evaluated in the light of what they claim to accomplish. Just as the automobile must be judged for its mobility, durability, and proportions,

---

5. A. Seth Pringle-Pattison, *Studies in the Philosophy of Religion,* (London: Oxford, 1930), p. 161.

and not whether it would serve as an anchor on an ocean-going vessel, so also the Bible should be tested in the light of relevant criteria. Does it lead men into commitments which they must later regret? Is its system such as we should expect would proceed from the mind of a holy, omniscient Being? Is it internally consistent? Can I accept its implications with all my faculties? Christians in all ages have tasted and found that the Lord is good. But each man must eat for himself; the act cannot be done vicariously. One may find upon examining the Biblical system that he *cannot* believe that the mind of God is therein contained; and in this case he should abide by his conscience in the matter. But his conscience cannot become a guide until it has first applied whole coherence in a searching way. Conscience must have data to work with.

Evaluating the Biblical witness is an extremely difficult task, in any case. It addresses men as sinners, and who can bear this? It speaks of values we ordinarily seek after only under pressing conditions, and who is interested in this? It sets forth the hope of eternal life; but are we not too busy enjoying this life to fret ourselves in preparation for another? One world at a time!

But haste thee not! Dare we put hand over our heart and declare that we are *not* sinners? Dare we say with sober tongue that we care *not* for peace and joy? Dare we laud our measly mortal days and preach that we are *not* moved at the thought of endless life? It is characteristic of juvenility to skip blithely over the profound and lasting; but the aged seek these vitalities alone. The youth are vivacious and unbridled, drinking of life's fullness and esteeming peace of conscience, submission before God, and the removal of death's fear as values with Sunday School hues — not to be taken seriously. The youth are often too drunken with their own free potentialities to understand what the limits of human creativity are. The aged have empirically discovered that both our days and our strength are limited. They are weary and exhausted from having expended themselves. Sweet and enduring, therefore, are the values of love, friendship, peace, and joy. These *give* strength; they do not sap it away. Happy is that boy or girl who can so order his youth that he anticipates senility!

B. *Yes, but. . .*

The trouble with whole perspective coherence is not theory, but practice — so runs the easy, but quite challenging, objection. Since man can never know the future fully, how, then, can he be responsible for conducting himself as if he did? The realization of *full* perspective coherence is an impossibility. Under all circumstances we judge from a finite perspective and according to personal interests. How can we ever infallibly know how to conduct ourselves one day so that we will be free from all regret the next?

The objection is partially convincing because it is partially true. But it is profoundly false, nevertheless. The partial persuasion rests on the very obvious datum that the free person happens to be just plain man, not God. And only God knows the future exhaustively. Man does not even know the present, let alone the infinity of the future. But the error lies in the fact that men *must* act — there is no other option. And the course attended by the least dissatisfaction is to apply to the best of one's ability a principle which ideally would exclude all risk. And this principle is whole perspective coherence. When a student enrolls in college, for example, he employs as best he can what, ideally applied, would leave him completely without frustration. Regardless how many blind spots there may be in planning a college career, how many unknown factors making up the future equation, he *must* venture. Worthwhile things just will not wait. The courses of study must be elected.

If the objection were valid, therefore, one could decide nothing, not even to object; for even the objection itself is not unattended by the risk of unknown factors. But the fact is that we *must* act. The principle holds whether we are registering for a philosophy course or plotting the meaning of the universe itself. And since we must act, prudence dictates that it is better to apply a perfect standard imperfectly than to venture nothing at all.

C. *The Bilateral Factors*

When Socrates weighed the arguments for immortality in the *Phaedo,* he was always interested in two things. *First,* he wanted to know where he would be taken if he *went along with* a suggested hypothesis. Will I be led into difficulties by pursuing this path? Or are difficulties cleared away through such a choice? *Second,* he wanted to know where he would be taken if he *denied* the hypothesis. Do problems mount or diminish by the denial? The reason for this divided question is that in lieu of perfect insight men must live by the rule of probability. And probabilities emerge when alternative options are matched, compared, contrasted, and balanced over against each other. Before a wise girl accepts or rejects a suitor, she will carefully consider what is involved in both acceptance and rejection. Her wooer may be deficient in ideal characteristics, but he is at least a man and that is something in his favor. The person who waits for perfection in life is waiting still. Whenever the perfect is missing, wise men follow Plato in accepting a *second best* as the rule of their life.[6]

The positive delineation of Christianity, found both in the Scriptures and in the endless volumes of commentary on them, is so well known to Western culture that one would hesitate to use up more valuable paper printing the story again. We have been briefed by critics of many stripes on the multitudinous difficulties into which we are led when we seek to accept the Christian world view. Hardly a stone has been left unturned

---

6. "As is familiar to all students, Plato has the category of the second best, which he uses in all kinds of circumstances. Failing the best, we should avail ourselves of the second best. Such are books as compared to the spoken word; such is the spoken word as compared to the unspoken word. Such are written laws as contrasted with the rule of reason. They are second best because they involve a compromise with the limitations of human nature; and this compromise Plato was willing to make." Raphael Demos, *The Philosophy of Plato,* (New York: Charles Scribner's Sons, 1939), pp. 26-27.

in this labor. A demolition of Biblical Christianity is often considered an integral part of a university course in philosophy of religion. And if there is any respect for Scripture left after this, a contempt through familiarity swallows it up. Since we can purchase a copy of the New Testament in a five and ten cent store, we are little apt to perceive that the future of Western culture may turn on what men do with the data that lie between its two covers. Many wise men hitherto have believed that man's only hope is found in Jesus Christ. It may be they were nearer the truth than the skeptical philosopher who, while enjoying the fruits of a Christian culture, teaches his students a complete moral relativism which neither he nor they can live by.

But there is a conspicuous paucity of literature which lays bare what is left if we leave Christianity in favor of another option. Few who reject an objective system of morals are bold enough to announce the bitter implications which necessarily flow from such a rejection. And yet the most effective way to restore a lost appreciation is to imagine what one is left with if a value in question is destroyed. For example, the child may be careless about her ragged old doll. But she quickly reverses her attitude either when a neighbor child tries to take the doll away or when it is suddenly discovered that this happens to be the only doll available. It is simply the old question of supply and demand.

The Christian philosopher is persuaded in the depths of his heart that Christianity is by-passed by the contemporary mind more on the grounds of personal contempt than of Christianity's inability to unravel present problems. Since men simply are not thirsty for the water of life, they do not drink. If this hypothesis should prove true, one may conclude that modern man's predicament stems out of a want of appetite, not a want of food and drink. The heart cannot be filled until it realizes its antecedent emptiness.

For what is more consistent with faith than to acknowledge ourselves naked of all virtue, that we may be clothed by God; empty of all good, that we may be filled by him; slaves

to sin, that we may be liberated by him; blind, that we may
be enlightened by him; lame, that we may be guided; weak,
that we may be supported by him; to divest ourselves of all
ground of glorying, that he alone may be eminently glorious,
and that we may glory in him?[7]

The purpose of the following chapters is so to arouse an
appetite for Christianity, that the hungry man will return to
the Biblical sources and find food and drink for himself. It
is not an attempted demonstration of Christianity in the conventional sense. The nearest that proof will be enjoyed is in
the establishing of a dialectic of despair as the alternative to
the Christian option. But in the last analysis there is no proof
of any pudding apart from the eating. If the Christian philosopher can arouse an appetite on the one hand, plus showing that
there *is* pudding on the other, he has discharged the full
responsibilities of his office. He cannot (nor would he want to)
make a man eat.

---

7. John Calvin, *Institutes of the Christian Religion* (Dedication).

Part II

THE LOWER IMMEDIACIES

III

The Siren Voice of Pleasure

WHERE shall we begin? Well, why not evaluate that force which is first to engage the growing mind? Why not commence with pleasure? Hedonism is a plausible starting point in any case, for the lure of pleasure haunts every man from adolescence to the grave. Furthermore, we have the benefit of help if we start here — and chiefly that of King Solomon.*

I. Mirth's Easy Glory

At just the mention of the moral relaxation found in wine, women, and song, a power of eagerness and longing surges up within us. No sales talk is required to draw us into *this* engagement. Rather, it is the experience of every man that he inclines by nature toward the luring, the exciting, the morally risqué. Our problem is to resist, to throttle off momentum, to deviate from this path. In fact, we are already committed to pleasure. Yet, we have an uneasy feeling as we embark on the voyage.

A. *Solomon's Great Experiment*

If ever a person threw both himself and his resources into the labor of finding whole perspective values, it was King Solomon. He had the acumen to recognize the alternatives, plus the financial resources to undergird his commanding authority. He occupied the rare position of being able to put values to an empirical test, for at his meanest nod armies moved. And in the book of Ecclesiastes there is a picture of the soaring spirit of Solomon, seeking some place to rest. In the entire corpus of religio-philosophical literature it would be

* See footnote, page 182.

difficult to discover a more disciplined search for values. Something within Solomon, some power of self over the self, taught this wise king that man possesses depths of vital resources which are not easily satisfied within him. With all the gaudy splendor about him, Solomon was yet uneasy with himself. He felt that there was a *more* in life, and he meant to locate it. Since the happiness of his own person was at stake, he prepared to pay whatever price might be levied for the gain of ultimate security. What else mattered if he himself was unhappy?

Interestingly enough the first option he put to the test was *mirth*. "I said in my heart, Come now, I will prove thee with mirth; therefore enjoy pleasure." (Ecclesiastes 2:1) Who can read this without entertaining both interest and sympathy? If the lure of pleasure in the heart is not reality, what then is? Flesh and wine exhibit their own *prima facie* claim to finality. Their shimmering sparkle is sufficient advertising. And yet Solomon quickly recoiled from his systematic venture into hedonic indulgence, discrediting the option as deceiving. "Behold, this also was vanity. I said of laughter, It is mad; and of mirth, What doeth it?" *(2:1-2)*

There is something enticing (almost irritating) about this Biblical experiment, however, for one has a feeling that a page in the argument has been torn out. Solomon is clear when he describes both what he was searching for and what he actually found out; but he is very unclear as to the reasons for his conclusions. He announces no middle premises. The reader is given clues, as it were, and then he is left to draw his own inferences.

If the problem is not too hard, however, — and this one is not — a good teacher does well *not* to tell too many answers. The geometry instructor who passes out answer books along with the questions is an accomplice in the softening of the student's own spirit. In the maieutic art (which Socrates followed so effectively) the purpose is to give birth to knowledge in the reader or hearer, not impart a finished product to be memorized by rote. When the student agonizes through a problem for himself, he develops the muscles of his own person in the process. The solution becomes part of himself. And surely Solomon is seeking the same thing: He wishes the reader to mediate the solution through his own person. And a cursory reflection upon the elements in the problem shows actually how easy this mediation is.

B. *Immediacy*

If pleasure is defined as anything which makes a man happy, then obviously every individual is a hedonist by trade, for no man so hates his own flesh as to seek unhappiness deliberately. If one is to make it mean anything, therefore, the hedonic ideal must of necessity be limited. And when the process of peeling away is completed, the irreducible element left is *immediacy*. Pleasure is immediate satisfaction, however broadly conceived. Pleasure is that which sustains the individual during the actual engagement. The seeker after pleasure never postpones, never suffers, for self-denial is entertained only when spirit delays present possession in favor of future prospect.

Instantaneity, accessibility, and intensity give initial plausibility to pleasure. Self-denial is not the course which we choose by nature. Our first — though hardly our purest — inclination is to give in, to let go, to indulge. The immediate is real; it is gratifying. For this reason it naturally seems to merit a higher place in the hierarchy of values than the things which are not seen. Why exchange the real values of the here and now for the presumed values of eternity?

One can appreciate why immediate satisfaction is a plausible ultimate in life when he recalls that the masses of the people generally gravitate in the direction of hedonism. The *Pax Romana* was no accident. It came through the skillful deploying of centers of power, plus a generously distributed quantity of bread and circuses. There is nothing essentially new about the welfare state, therefore. The politician realizes that the masses greatly enjoy the path of least resistance.

A proof of the lure of immediacy is the way pleasure over-powers even those most set on conquering it. One may think of King David, for example, a man of great spiritual stature and a prototype of Jesus Christ. His consistent ways in up-rightness and self-sacrifice remain exemplary for all genera-tions. From the time of his musical triumphs in the court of King Saul till the hours when he penned the sublime utterances of the Psalms, he deliberately tried to shun the intrigue of the immediate whenever it conflicted with higher values. And yet fleshly immediacy reduced this mighty monarch to a piece of bread. For one hasty moment the enflamed king forgot God's law and lay with Bathsheba. The king could rule armies, but he could not resist the contours of a woman. The penitential Psalms are an everlasting monument to the power of the immediate over even those most devoted to eternal values.

> For I know my transgressions;
> And my sin is ever before me.
> Against thee, thee only, have I sinned,
> And done that which is evil in thy sight.[1]

The satisfactions of immediacy cannot be dismissed as an illusion, unworthy of freedom and rationality, therefore. It is true that the brute seeks the pleasures of eating, drinking, rising up, lying down, copulation, etc. But it is not possible to make an easy identification of the hedonic rites of man with any counterpart in the animal kingdom. The external act must never be identified with the inner experience. The spiritual height of man's freedom converts the simplest form of pleasure into an ecstasy which engages the whole person. Freedom raises intensity to the nth power. For this reason, freedom permits man to fall into the easy delusion of believing that the potential offerings of pleasure are far more elegant and gratifying than the facts themselves can support. The sexual impulse is never the result of a purely moral urge to propagate the race. Freedom converts its simplicity into a complexity. Through imagination man is tempted to presume a

---

1. Psalm 51:3-4.

finality and exhilaration in sex which the elements in the situation cannot sustain. Freedom encourages man to expect more than is actually there. If the sex act is consummated within the bonds of marital love, an atmosphere reigns in which spiritual vitalities and sympathies are exchanged. And if not, disappointment reaches back with its arm of regret. The spiritual heights of man make it impossible for him to remain tranquilly confined within the limits of natural form. Through the powers of imagination the child exchanges the wooden blocks in front of him for a towering skyscraper of pure gold. Through freedom the adult converts the simple sound of a motor into a noise of a torrential downpour.

C. *The Crux*

Solomon is extremely up-to-date in placing mirth first on the list of alternative options, for the gnawing urge within one to yield to immediate pleasures is powerful. Soul and body are so intimately related that spiritual satisfactions are carried along when the physical side of man is aroused. Modern man understands this no less than Solomon with his company of minstrels and dancers. Our contemporary culture is choked with machinery to make devotion to immediacy more efficient and satisfying. The tavern is arrayed with glittering plastic fixtures and drawn shades, while the cinema displays imaginary worlds for freedom to daydream in. And now, alas! through television the combined resources of many entertainment agencies march through the living room. Our castle has become a stage.

Regardless of how plausible the hedonic ideal may initially appear, however, the essential issue remains unchanged: *Is immediacy that value for which I should live and die?*[2] In gaining momentary pleasure have I struck rock-bottom values in life? Is the full height of my free potentialities exhausted?

---

2. *This is the only issue raised.* There is no question about the value of pleasure when it is subordinated beneath higher, and more spiritual ideals. The reader must not overlook this limitation, lest a needless misapprehension arise.

Mirth may be both easy and natural, but is man true to his own nature to reject the things which are unseen for the easy and the natural? Solomon concluded that mirth is vanity and emptiness. And the moment one examines immediacy in the light of his own nature, he will see the grounds for the Solomonic conclusion. There is an unmistakable incompatibility in the final union of the self with the immediate.

II. Boredom

A. *Fact*

Some deliberately *test* pleasure to learn whether it is the answer to our quest for security. Solomon illustrates this type. Others are casual and trivial in their devotion to immediacy. The masses illustrate this. And because the multitudes uncritically pursue the meaning of life, they are unable to detect the worthiness or unworthiness of the course they choose.

Let us return for a moment to the fact of freedom in man. Imagination not only creates our field of enjoyment, but it also causes the dilemma of existence itself. Contrast man and the cow! Observe that the freedom which gives man his glory is likewise the source of his uneasiness. Man does *not* enjoy the serenity of the bovine. The cow is quite content to remain within the confines of a stereotyped routine, lying down in the same barn with its head in the same stall and wandering to the same pasture to eat the grass. Stomach ulcers are indeed known to cows, but they are caused by the *interruption,* not the presence, of this routine. In contrast to this, man tears the walls out of his stomach worrying that his free progress is either not fast or skillful enough to deliver him from the hovering threat of routine. *Homo sapiens* chafes under the oppression of limitation. He resists capitulation to the contingencies and necessities of nature, blasting away one entrenchment after another, that his pent-up powers of freedom and progress might find new vents for expression. The nearest that man comes to the life of the cow is the routine of the felon. But the criminal grinds under the oppression; he longs for freedom, reaching out for an opportunity to express the potentialities of creativity (or destruction) boiling up within his breast.

When viewed as act, the difference between man and the brute may be summed up in one word: *self-transcendence*. Whereas the animal is at its best abiding by the forms of nature, man is man only when he soars beyond the limitations which define necessity. Man may *consider* the ant, but he cannot be an ant. Rousseau enjoyed an enormous influence through his colorful and lucid description of man's sad deviation from the natural conditions of existence, but the passing of time has hardly given concretion to the imaginative Utopia of the *New Heloise*. When man envies harmony of nature, believing he can return to natural bliss if he but abides within the natural forms, he further exhibits the pathos of his freedom. If man were not already beyond such an easy harmony he would never be dreaming of it in the first place — he would be engrossed in enjoying it by nature. A self-transcendent creature cannot play the role of a confined being without instinctively reaching out for fig leaves to cover himself with. When one enjoys the glorious power of self-transcendence, he cannot remain content in natural confinement. The cohesions which unite spirit with spirit must proceed from the bowels of creativity within the inner recesses of such spirits.

The powers of transcendence explain why man is not, and cannot be, a cow. By the glory of freedom man imagines new barns, more distant (and greener) pastures, higher hills to climb, fairer stock with which to cohabit. As long as the flow of expected satisfactions continue, alternatives do not trouble the cow. The social life of the bovine is simple. There are bullies and cliques among the animals, to be sure, but the complexities of courts, detention homes, and law enforcement agencies are unknown. Sermons are not preached to the wandering; morals are not codified for the transgressors.

But weep not, oh man, that you cannot be a cow, for natural contentedness destroys progress. Progress is different from sheer movement. Progress entails a passage from an envisioned to a realized goal. But this can be accomplished only through the assistance of freedom. The power of self-transcendence permits man to ascertain both the *terminus a quo* and the *terminus ad quem* in all movement. Freedom soars over history to learn whether movement is progressive, or simply random activity. If man lacked the faculty of freedom, therefore, he would extinguish the light of progress.

> Man's ability to transcend the flux of nature gives him the capacity to make history. Human history is rooted in the natural process but it is something more than either the determined sequences of natural causation or the capricious variations and occurrences of the natural world. It is com-pounded of natural necessity and human freedom. Man's freedom to transcend the natural flux gives him the possibility of grasping a span of time in his consciousness and there-by of knowing history. It also enables him to change, reorder and transmute the causal sequences of nature and there-by to *make* history.[3]

Because man can rise above the mutabilities of time and space (as Plato definitively showed), he is able to make contact with those eternal ideas which make culture possible. The animal leaves no cultural pattern behind it, for it moves through time without sensing a pressure of the eternal on it. By reaching out to eternity, man is able to tack between creativity and necessity, seeking always to overcome the latter through a more disciplined employment of the former. He never finally overcomes limitation, but the enjoyment of having tried is his portion. Culture is a token of man's uniqueness.

What results when this free individual tries to lose himself in immediacy? Self-transcendence rebels against such a premature finality, and *boredom* emerges. No combination of pleasures can ever exhaust the powers of freedom. The immediate is fixed, limited, and temporal, while freedom is soaring, unlimited, and at home in eternity.

3. Reinhold Niebuhr, *Human Destiny*, (New York: Charles Scribner's Sons, 1946), p. 1.

Man is a fickle, restless creature who moves impatiently from one momentary satisfaction to another. One pleasure collapses, only to be supplanted by another. Every satisfaction can be pursued but for a time, and then boredom sets in. The symphony is wonderful for the first three hours, but then it becomes vapid and we turn aside for relief. Football, like all sports, is seasonal. World traveling appears to be exhausting in pleasure — until one feels the gnawing pains of nostalgia within him for the hills of home. And hardly have the hills of home been revisited, but what we want to travel once more. Draw up the list. Make it as long as the sun's rays, but freedom will overtake it. As long as a satisfaction falls within the genus of immediacy, *i. e.*, as long as no eternal pleasures are generated within a commitment, the individual will inevitably suffer from boredom in its pursuit. Freedom makes this unconditional, money-back guarantee: Wine, women, and song will enchant, enrapture, and lure; but they will all fail when made a steady diet. Their nourishment will convert to a vomitive.

Experience bears out the fact that more than being just troublesome, boredom is actually a disease against which free men must fight. Boredom drains away interests and ambitions until in the end an individual careless about everything emerges. But in this disease, as in so many others, the toxin produces its own antitoxin. Freedom, which contains the cause of the ill, likewise extends to the user a cure. The boredom can be endured with patience when freedom breaks through the immediate and locates those time- and space-transcending satisfactions for which one may live and die without regret. Observe how the graduate student conquers the opposition of boredom by a determination to master the disciplines of his field. Under ordinary circumstances he could not bear the painful routine of retiring, rising, eating, examining, working. But spurred on by the resolute determination to gain wisdom, he willingly pommels his body into subjection. The athlete endures the grind of training that he may gain the crown. The author strives against years of boredom in writing and re-writing again, that he may win the goal of publication. The world of pleasure beckons these individuals, but its voice is spurned because a new love has been found, a love which out-runs the immediate. But since few will collide head-on with boredom to achieve the great in life, few there be who are great.

Even here the threat of new tragedy emerges, however, for men often conquer boredom guided by the inspiration of what, when gained, turns out to be but a further form of immediacy. In the freedom of spirit the university diploma rises as an ever-lasting token of joy; but soon it is lost in an attic trunk for want of satisfaction. The glory and fame of the football hero is never as sweet or lasting as the initial anticipation expected it to be. The prima donna senses that she hoped for far more than was ever made good. Thus, bordering perilously on boredom is the more serious problem, *frustration*. This will be discussed in short order.

B. *Significance*

What actually is boredom? It is that weariness of spirit which results when freedom is repetitiously related to an im-mediacy. Boredom is detected by the spirit's unwillingness to remain content with a presumed satisfaction.

And what is the apologetic significance of boredom? It is this: Since one is not able to remain content within forms of immediacy, one may validly conclude that there are poten-tialities within the vital man that the hedonic ideal cannot ac-count for. Whether or not there actually *is* anything beyond pleasure which can more effectively satisfy man, only careful investigation can answer. Our hope is that there is. For if man is capable of more than reality will ever allow him to ex-press, he is over-endowed — tragically over-endowed. Free-dom perceives that unless there is something beyond devotion to the immediately satisfying, lasting happiness will never be enjoyed.

III. Frustration

A. *Border Line*: *Vanity*

Vanity or emptiness, a favorite expression of Solomon, is
that feeling of stark hollowness which results when one has
trusted in things which vanish. It is that ineffable sense of
futility one experiences as he stands back helplessly and watches
his home and possessions being consumed by angry flames. It
is the emptiness in the pit of one's stomach when the enemy
pours into his city and confiscates in a day what has taken a
century to erect. It is any loneliness and disappointment which
causes one to ask, *What is the use?*

In his more skeptical moments, Solomon sensed a *cosmic*
vanity. He felt as if the weary routine of life paid no divi-
dends. There is a time to be born, and a time to die; a time to
kill, and a time to heal. Yet, in doing these things, how is one
edified? "What profit hath he that worketh in that wherein
he laboreth?" (Ecclesiastes 3:9) If *one* immediacy brings
boredom, will an endless series bring forth anything different?
There is a collective profitlessness to a this-worldly philosophy.
When the whole world is gained, the soul is lost; for there is
nothing in the material world that can finally satisfy freedom.
The free spirit simply holds the world it has gained, weeping,
like Alexander the Great, that there are no other worlds to conquer.

B. *The Valley of Defeat*

It was no mild feeling of emptiness that marked the low-
point in Solomon's grief. The registration of sorrow and recoil
was incisive. And the reason for this is that he gave himself
wholeheartedly to the experiment, deliberately throwing himself into the project. And the recoil was in direct proportion
to the investment-experiment. Frustration is that feeling of
defeat which comes at the end of a hopeful, but ill-fated,
venture. This was Solomon's portion.

It is an extremely skilled man who can so evaluate life that he is able to anticipate frustrations which lie ahead. The masses of the people tend to take their grief, like their happiness, a day at a time. The advantage of this latter method is that there is a certain bliss in ignorance. As long as old Scrooge (in Dickens' *A Christmas Carol*) did not examine the epitaph on the gravestone, he was quite able to sustain the illusion that the dead man on the couch was other than himself. But investigation of the fine details in the wind-swept cemetery exploded his optimism and sent him scurrying to the spirit for comfort and solace. Desiderius Erasmus delightfully eulogized folly in his classic, *Encomium Moriae,* pointing out (much to the consolation of the indolent masses) that the fool or the buffoon is the happiest of individuals; for such a one is protected from the poisoned arrows of frustration by the layers and layers of ignorance which encase his mind. The fool may burn to death in the same circus tent with the wise men who watch, but he is never troubled about the possibility of fires. He is too ignorant to worry about the future.

The way of the fool may seem to be pleasant, but who wants to be a fool? We are *men* and men let us be. And part of our endowment is the power of freedom by which we can understand, evaluate, and anticipate. Wisdom brings a steady peace. There is a risk in wisdom, to be sure, for one never knows when staking all but what the light of future knowledge will reveal a blind alley of despair ahead. But there is a greater risk in ignorance. If there *is* a way which leads unto life and satisfaction, one is pursuing a most unworthy course deliberately to remain in ignorance. Will a man know the doctrine before he wills to know it? Our predicament in this modern hour may be parallel to that of the individual whose body is host to a malignant cancer: If the disease is detected soon enough, there is hope for a cure. But if through willful ignorance and neglect no overtures are taken to learn one's condition, death may result. The praise of folly easily converts to the despair of folly.

Solomon himself clearly illustrates the risk which attends the individual who dares to know himself. He concluded (with Erasmian insight) that if one evaluates the meaning of life by a one-dimensional, this–worldly criterion, it is the wise man — the man who has made a concerted effort to come to himself — and not the fool, who is to be pitied. The reason is that, though both will come to grief through the frustrations of immediacy, the wise man comes sooner, for he *anticipates* that grief through his accelerated freedom. Like the condemned felon who dies a thousand times before he walks the last mile to the gas chamber, so the man who can find nothing to vindicate life dies before his time. He dies in spirit. The hungry child blithely runs into the house, ignorant that there is no food left; while the parent, knowing the situation, has despaired already. Solomon felt enraged when he compared the final end of the wise man with that of the fool who remained in ignorance. "Then said I in my heart, As it happeneth to the fool, so will it happen even to me; and why was I then more wise?" (Ecclesiastes 2:15) Solomon said he *hated* life when he learned that man was endowed with more longings and aspirations than the universe itself could ever placate. Sections of the book of Ecclesiastes read like Russell's *A Free Man's Worship* — minus the confident despair. If this world is all there is, Solomon felt certain that there was nothing to be confident of, not even of confident despair itself. If the end of living cannot justify the effort that one invests in living, just plain *despair* is all that one may justifiably entertain.

Is one better off in knowing, or being ignorant of, his end? This is a good, but irrelevant, question. One does not dare remain in ignorance. Whoever spurns the light of knowledge risks losing the meaning of life itself. *His* loss is serious. When once self-transcendence has been aroused, one cannot return to ignorance and again live with himself in peace. This is one plow which a man cannot turn back from without inviting a worse grief. We happen to be fearfully and wonderfully made. When freedom is aroused and man comes to himself, it is impossible (without self-destruction) to erase from the mind what has been gained. It is a case of trying to *diminish* one's stature a cubit by taking thought. Opened eyes will not be shut. We play little tricks on ourselves and quite against our own will. What we set ourselves deliberately to forget, that very thing we remember with greatest vividness. Knowledge is a dangerous thing, for it joins itself with our own souls. Socrates knew this well.

> Surely, I said, knowledge is the food of the soul; and we must take care, my friend, that the Sophist does not deceive us when he praises what he sells, like the dealers wholesale or retail who sell the food of the body; for they praise indiscriminately all their goods, without knowing what are really beneficial or hurtful: neither do their customers know, with the exception of any trainer or physician who may happen to buy of them. . . .For there is far greater peril in buying knowledge than in buying meat and drink: the one you purchase of the wholesale or retail dealer, and carry them away in other vessels, and before you receive them into the body as food, you may deposit them at home and call in any experienced friend who knows what is good to be eaten or drunken, and what is not. . . .But you cannot buy the wares of knowledge and carry them away in another vessel; when you have paid for them you must receive them into the soul and go your way, either greatly harmed or greatly benefited.[4]

The frustration which comes from persistence in immediacy is sometimes dodged by the deceiving option of overindulgence. There seems to be nothing objectionable to the lofty and exhilarating feeling of release which comes with taking dope into the blood stream — nothing, that is, save that we cannot do it with our whole person. The curse of the dope den is the after-experience, not the pleasure itself; for in the gaining of an intense pleasure we have left ourselves with a regret and insecurity which cancels out whatever value we may have passed through. If the pleasure of dope were *everlasting*, it might commend itself to the heart. This same terminal

---

4. Plato, *Protagoras*, 313c-314a.

frustration echoes through all efforts to convert a partial immediacy into a final satisfaction. The boredom may vanish, but a rotting sets in. An ambivalence results which leaves the individual suspended perilously between a fear to return to selfhood and fear to continue in self-indulgence.

Reinhold Niebuhr has penetrated rather deeply into this problem of ambivalence, especially as the issue relates to the place of the prides of life in human conduct. His analysis of the dread of drunkenness is typical:

> The drunkard sometimes seeks the abnormal stimulus of intoxicating drink in order to experience a sense of power and importance which normal life denies him. This type of intoxication represents a pathetic effort to make the self the centre of the world to a degree which normal reason with its consciousness of the ego's insignificance makes impossible. But drunkenness may have a quite different purpose. It may be desired not in order to enhance the ego but to escape from it. It would not be inaccurate to define the first purpose of intoxication as the sinful ego-assertion which is rooted in anxiety and unduly compensates for the sense of inferiority and insecurity; while the second purpose of intoxication springs from the sense of guilt, or a state of perplexity in which a sense of guilt has been compounded with the previous sense of insecurity.[5]

The speed with which men come to self-despair in life is directly proportioned to their own industry. Those who are simply bored with life, calmly taking their winnings and losings as part of the game itself, will continue in their inchoate optimism as long as the facts of their predicament remain hidden. But the blithe type of person can only postpone, not avoid, despair. He sustains his bold skepticism because he has

---

5. Reinhold Niebuhr, *Human Nature,* (New York: Charles Scribner's Sons, 1946, pp. 234-235. "Men drink to excess not so much because of the love of the drug as because of failures of personality. A man for whom life has lost its meaning turns to alcohol as a substitute, and as a temporary escape from an intolerable sense of futility. Thus alcoholism as a disease must be cured, if it cured at all, by the provision of adequate satisfactions and significance in the personal life of the ill person." D. Elton Trueblood, *Alternative to Futility,* (New York: Harper & Brothers, 1948), p. 16.

decided in advance that he will not rise to self-transcendence; he will not learn to know himself. This type of mind ought to capitulate to grief at once, for there is no element in his philosophy which can support optimism.

Others, however, confidently expecting that value gains will be forthcoming — people whose eyes have been opened, but opened to the wrong thing — take their losses very seriously. They do not cavalierly pretend that it does not matter whether life has any final meaning or not. They believe it has meaning; they trust their investments. And for this very reason they are more quickly catapulted into grief than those who praise folly. The crash of the stock market in 1929 illustrates this. Hopeful people by the score had put their trust in this form of immediacy. But after seeing their entire savings vanish in a few hours, they suddenly realized that in the game of life it is the *soul* which is up for auction. Devotion to money brings vanity and emptiness to the heart the moment the wealth is lost. The bored mind may wait for the next round of pleasure, hoping (though quite without foundation) that in the forthcoming experience there will emerge a satisfaction which will vindicate its course of action. But to whom shall the despairing turn? There is no next. All has been ventured. The ace has been thrown to the table, and all is lost.

Some recover from their grief, only to fall into the delusion of a new engagement. They approach the matter from a different angle and with greater caution, supposing that there is no essential cause for their previous despair. Whatever frustrations the accidental may previously have introduced, they resolve to eliminate them during the next engagement. But despair is only postponed, for the incompatibility of spiritual freedom and immediacy prevents flirtation from becoming a lasting romance.

Others fall, never to rise again. Learning the essential contradiction involved in trying to unite a free spirit with immediacy, yet perceiving no alternative devotion with which to be engaged, they turn to the despair of suicide. Suicide is preceded by a period in which a feeling of absolute emptiness floods the heart. But the violent destruction of the body is always a consequence of the soul's antecedent despair. When the spirit has nothing to draw it out (*i. e.*, no values for which it can live and die) it is already dead — dead, though living. Since there is nothing to live for, there is nothing left to exist for. When *consigned* to live, men seek death. Yet even in suicide man cries out that he is not a creature of a simple, one-dimensional world. As if in a final protest against such a suggestion, the free spirit reaches forth and asserts its vindictive authority against the involved self, unilaterally decreeing its destruction. The would-be suicide ransacks the libraries of the world to find the easiest passageway from life to death, thus screaming to the housetops, though quite unwittingly, that the nature of man contains a freedom able to reach to eternity.

Sandwiched in between the blithe and the despairing are countless millions who writhe in the twilight zone of hopelessness, yet clinging to the fond faith that through some yet unforeseen fortune the weary round of life may be broken. Lingering between life and death, though fearing both with a perfect ambivalence, they dare not face the essential meaning of life. Their hearts are storage depots of regret. The beggar envies the power and prestige of the president, while the president, weary of his office, envies the carefree way of the beggar. Rare indeed is the person who can conscientiously confess that he, like Paul, has learned to be content in what he has. Men would scramble for pen and paper if they were ever given an opportunity to draw up a list of the ways in which they think they could improve upon life. There would be changes in the self, the universe, the eternal. Many opportunities would be provided to rectify mistakes done in the past. But it would be interesting to see if a solution to *present* problems could be found, using ingredients *now* accessible.

Wish-thinking testifies to the power of self-transcendence in man, for if man were not free over necessity he would not understand the refreshment of new alternatives. The felon may employ freedom to dream of means of descending from his cell block to the distant streets below, but this protest against his incarceration will not break the lock on the cell or hoist up the much-wanted ladder. Solutions must be forged with the material at hand.

If humor is incongruity, then it is a cause for laughter to watch men walk obediently down the well-trodden path to the bordels of immediacy. Notice this: A spiritual being is trying to find heaven on earth! It is like watching a very large snapping turtle trying to crawl into a very small pipe. The head is in, and so is one leg — ah! the haven is plausible. But laughter mounts, for the pipe is already full when hardly a fraction of the creature is in. Yet, as we watch the effort of man to gain satisfaction through what by definition will bring grief and despair, our laughter subsides and the feeling of pathos enters. For the contest before our eyes is not a jest or a game of chance; it is a bloody, life-and-death skirmish where winner takes all. The souls of men are at stake in this clash of values. If we pity the turtle, we grieve for men. For we ourselves are men likewise, and we happen to know the meaning of this awful engagement.

Frustration, like the first sign of a disease, is a blessing if it stirs us up to find a cure; but it is a bane if it is identified with the disease. The despairing man may not be far from the kingdom — assuming that there *is* a kingdom to be found — for at least he has come to the end of the trail of immediacy and he is now open to other suggestions. But if his despairingness is confused with the disease, a hardening of interest may set in. Trust in riches, *e. g.,* often hardens the spiritual arteries. When the riches fail, hope vanishes. The deceitfulness of riches is exposed in one of the most ironic passages in the Bible.

> They that trust in their wealth, and boast themselves in the multitude of their riches none of them can by any means redeem his brother, nor give to God a ransom for him (For the redemption of their life is costly, and it faileth for ever) .... Their inward thought is, that their houses shall continue

for ever, and their dwelling-places to all generations; they
call their lands after their own names. . . . This their way
is their folly. . . . They are appointed as a flock for Sheol;
death shall be their shepherd: And the upright shall have
dominion over them in the morning; and their beauty
shall be for Sheol to consume.[6]

The more a man *trusts* in immediacy, the harder it is for him
to come to himself when despair sets in. Observe that it was the
wretched, the harlot, and the publican, and not the rich, who
repented when Christ offered an alternative to the pleasures of
the moment. The rich *had* their god.

IV. Guilt

The distance between animal and man, contrary to the zo-
ologist who worships the anatomical key, is measured by free
spirit. And as this distance becomes more apparent, there
emerges what is doubtless the most significant reason why man
has never been, nor ever will be, finally content within immediacy. This factor is *guilt*.

A. *Setting*

Man may suffer from a slow physical start in life (for the
kitten at a day seems more self-sufficient than man at three
months), but when the dormant potentialities within him are
nursed into expression, the industry of this upright creature is
abounding. Within a few short years this helpless creature
is ruling kingdoms with an iron rod. What accounts for this
industry? Why is man such an energetic, grasping, forward-
looking animal? Any answer to these questions must of necessity be complex, for man is no simple creature. But the most
convincing single reason to explain man's energy is that he
is responding to the inward lashings of the law of self-respect.

Man shares the law of self-preservation with the animals,
but he does not share self-respect. Respect is a combination

---

6. Psalm 49:6-14.

of self-preservation and self-transcendence. Freedom not only stands over all time; it stands over the ego itself. The self talks to the self, commanding, deploying, and condemning. Man may not always be able to see himself as others see him, but he can see himself as he knows he ought to be. When asked if he wants to grow up to be somebody important in the world, the child innocently (yet firmly) responds, Aye! Eyes grow wide as the little one has his indefinite possibilities of self-development spread before him. Is there meaning to ask the puppy if he is resolutely planning to be a real dog at maturity? Hardly. The real dog is made by natural pressures, together with a healthy stimulation from the hand of man. But the real man is a result of these external pressures, plus a generous quantity of *self*-determination.

Animal experiments may be applied to human behavior only with a threshold, therefore. While the animal instinctively seeks to preserve its own life, it is not guided by spiritual motives of self-respect. And the reason for this is that the animal never consciously interprets its own actions according to norms defining ideal animality. It is never consciously suspended within the tension of not being what it ought to be. Man, on the contrary, (if he is honest with himself) testifies to the impelling urge within him to be fully himself; an urge which emerges when freedom learns the rule of eternity standing over against time. The law of self-preservation, therefore, is no longer a simple force. It is compounded with the entire height and depth of a creature which is free in spirit and confined in body, yet retaining a dignity and self-respect which is natural to both freedom and necessity. Self-preservation is never a simple urge for biological survival in man. Being compounded with freedom it cannot be understood apart from the egotistic impulses for self-dignity.

The grief which comes out of disappointment in immediacy is thus very painful, for the free self reports back to the involved self that a course unworthy of the full potentialities of self-dignity has been pursued. Both the animal and man may writhe in pain over taking tainted food into the body, for example. But man's grief is higher and more intense than that of the animal, for in addition to the physical discomfiture there is the nettling, troublesome indictment of the free self. With a little foresight the accident could have been avoided. While the animal perhaps knew no better, man did. There was no logical necessity for the mistake. The mistake grew out of a careless use of freedom.

Freedom over the self makes living with the self a delicate assignment. Our individuality is corrupted the moment self-transcendence is destroyed, for our personality is sustained by the distinctiveness of freedom. But it is this very transcendence which places the self beside aspirations and ideals which the involved self may long for but which it seldom is able to seize. Friction sets in as the self is goaded on to make progress. Hence, the problem of life is not merely how to get along with others; it is also how to get along with the *self*. The self constantly elects greater horizons of venture than it ever can make good, yet realizing all the while that a full life is unpossessed without these ventures. A man may grit his teeth and bear up under the external criticisms heaped upon him in life, but he borders on complete frustration when he can no longer tolerate himself. When the free self charges down upon the involved self with condemnation and hatred, the very precondition of all recovery is jeopardized. Unless a man first believes in himself, he will hardly believe in anything else about him. An animal without restraint is vicious; but man without self-respect is despicable. Once the moral fibres in the spirit are cut and an I-don't-care attitude floods the heart, one quickly slides into outrageous depths of degradation and shame. "Skid row" is the clearing center for such worse-than-animal specimens of humanity. Natural forms are at the mercy of freedom. Therefore, when man lets self-respect go, he drops to a shame having no counterpart in the animal kingdom. There is a song which tells of a pig walking away in disgust when a drunkard came and sat down beside him. It is not far from the truth.

B. *Fruit*

Since survival is never simply an urge to remain an organism, human uneasiness can be understood profoundly only as *guilt*. The free self uncovers the ideal, while the involved self struggles to give it concretion. Failure to fulfill the ideal boomerangs back upon the health of the self, and the indictment of guilt is generated. If the self were not responsible for fulfilling the ideal, it would hardly interpret the ideal as normative and binding in the first place. It matters not what the content of the ideal happens to be — worthy or unworthy. As long as the free self rests in it as a definition of ideal selfhood, the self is responsibly related to it.   But at this point transcendent powers perceive that there is a discrepancy between the ideal assented to, and the fulfillment of that ideal through day-by-day living. This discrepancy issues in guilt. *Guilt is that feeling of inward culpability which arises when the self is juxtaposed beside the law of its nature.* The guilt may be mild or strong, depending on how high the ideal is and the strenuousness with which one seeks to fulfill it. But in either case there is an uneasiness within one which cries out against explaining man as simply a creature destined for immediacy. The *real* satisfactions of life lie in the area of suffering, not indulgence and pleasure. The suffering man rejects the partial in favor of the whole.

Guilt has its day of grace, indeed. A descent into gratification may so overpower the discerning faculties of the individual that he is left destitute of all sensitivity to the law of his life. But as long as a person's self-transcendence remains, as long as he is concerned to be a person, that long guilt remains. When indulgence finally narcotizes the voice of guilt, it likewise destroys the dignity of selfhood.

There is a progressive self-refutation in all attempts to satisfy the heart through gratifications indifferent to the ideal laws of our nature. This may be illustrated by the dialectic of sex. In *masturbation* the free self supplies the partner through

imagination. But (other things being equal) the result is always a feeling of incompleteness. Something within one cries,
saying, "You were destined for higher things." The *homo-
sexual* finds a partner, and so need only impute to the other
what is lacking through sexual likeness. But unless the day
of grace has been passed, there results a similar feeling of
having cheated the self through a whole commitment to only
partial conditions. In *fornication* the number and sex are complete; yet here each individual must supply a spiritual element
missing in the other partner. Each has used the other as a
means, whereas dignity cries out that others are to be treated
only as *ends.* Each fondly imagines that there is a loving yielding of the one to the other, but reality affirms that the union is
artificial and selfish. And as a consequence of such selfishness,
each member thinks less of the other. The boy loses respect for
the girl's femininity, and the girl thinks less of the manliness
and self-control of the boy. Each imagined that in the act he
was releasing vitalities which were noble and endearing in life,
but a feeling of having fallen short of this wells up within. Being capable of spiritual union in the act, while only uniting
themselves in body, there is a natural enraging of the soul within. Fornication cannot continue indefinitely between the same
two people. There will either be a break-through of love or a
break-through of hatred and bitterness. The dialectic of sex
points to the *marriage* relation as the only condition in which
the whole person is wholly satisfied. Since both body and soul
are yielded selflessly to the other, there is nothing to be re-
gretted in the end. The highest within the individual has been
accounted for. Divorce enters only when something remains
uncommitted. Love will deal patiently with every adjustment,
regardless of how unexpected the incompatibility may be.

Many claim that guilt is simply auto-suggestion. That is
partially correct. But accidental and peripheral guilt is to be
distinguished from that chronic, essential sorrow which attends
our nature as men. The dignity of our nature is learned only
when the transcendent self soars through imagination into the

world of the ideal. Essential guilt results when this dignity is
not sustained.

The literature of the world is replete with confessional lines.
It is the experience of great men that the more sensitive they
are to the law of their nature, the less satisfied they are with
themselves and the more they cry out in guilt. The quill in
many ages has been employed to express that feeling of uneasiness which comes when one realizes his lack of essential
dignity.

> O that I could repent,
>   With all my idols part;
> And to thy gracious eye present
>   An humble, contrite heart.

> A heart with grief oppress'd
>   For having grieved my God;
> A troubled heart that cannot rest
>   Till sprinkled with thy blood.

What can account for this universal phenomenon of confession? What, but the hypothesis that man cannot be explained within one dimension? What but man's qualitative
distinction from the animal kingdom?

Such questions elicit the easy objection that the masses of
the people show no postures of confession. They appear to
proceed night and day in their ordinary labor, all things continuing as they were from the beginning. There arises no
rumble of guilt as one walks down the street. In fact, not
infrequently it is as difficult to extract a confession from some
as it is to withdraw a deeply-rooted wisdom tooth from the
mouth. If the conditions of guilt are all present, why is there
not more admission? The condemned thief admits no guilt.
The white slave makes no confession. Where, then, is the
guilt?

Confession is a peculiarly difficult attitude to assume, for it
(apparently) runs cross-gained to the law of personal pride
within us. Egoistic security suffers when one lets others know
he is guilty. Social relations always make confession difficult.
Since we are in competition with other egos, one of the marks

of success is the want of admission that a goal has not been reached. Social life, let alone the Scriptures, teaches that when a contractor finishes half of a building, but cannot manage the rest for want of funds, he suffers the humiliation of eliciting public humor. He is charged with not having counted the cost before he started building. The same principle is true in guilt: Man must confess that he has taken on more than he has been able to make good. It is a defeat for the ego, and who wants to tell others about defeat? What rich man wishes to let others know of the nights of fear and uncertainty he passes through as senility sets in and hopes fail? What harlot wishes to herald the grief and shame which plague her heart? Each has set up an ideal, and though the free self willingly confesses to the involved self that the ideal has not been reached, it hesitates to confess it to others. The natural thing for the guilty child is to disavow the guilt, for the ego of the little one is at stake.

Thus, a distinction must be made between the inward presence of guilt and its outward confession. Even though not a man in the world admitted guilt, it still may be true that all are inwardly guilty. A self-discipline must precede confession, and not all rise to this exercise of spirit.

But actions — which speak louder than words — betray the universal presence of guilt. The bored individual tries to find security through a round of immediacy, flitting quickly from one engagement to another without pausing to inquire whether there may be an essential incompatibility between the ingredients. But this restlessness would not be present if there were no pressure within to be a self. The conscience of the bored person is nicely kept deceived through the expedience of overactivity. This may be illustrated in the case of the person who, obliged to offer an apology to a friend, runs away from his conscience; thus enjoying a type of peace by becoming so swallowed up in minor activities that he has no chance to think of guilt.

There is a vicious conniving between the free and involved selves in boredom (*though these selves are the same self*).

Man is so framed that the free self has the responsibility of guiding the involved self into commitments which leave the whole individual contented in the end. When freedom antici-pates a danger, for example, the whole self turns to the left to avoid it. In blithe boredom, however, the free self has an agreement with the empirical self not to look to the end to see if the course being pursued is either wise or faulty. The uneasiness of such a person is illustrated in the way he abuses those who show a prophet's respect for moral ideals. Herod committed murder when John broke up his easy conscience. There is an uneasiness among the careless when they are set next to the careful. "They are surprised that you do not join them in the same wild profligacy, and they abuse you; but they will give account to him who is ready to judge the living and the dead." (I Peter 4:4-5)

When freedom is aroused and the individual begins to sense that he is not yet fully a self, the perils of freedom and the degrees of guilt grow together. The frustrated individual differs from the bored person to the extent that conniving be-tween the selves has been ended. The frustrated self loses consolation in direct proportion to its perception of the vanity and futility of immediacy. The veil has been lifted.

The first symptom of weighty guilt emerges when one lingers in the twilight zone between the lightheartedness of boredom and the fear of frustration, a threshold in which the individual faces a decision whether to pursue a new immediacy or seek satisfaction elsewhere. The guilt here is not worn on the sleeve. While it is admitted that satisfaction cannot be found in hedonic offerings, yet the person cringes to rise to freedom and leave immediacy, lest on the way he encounter the very rule of his life which he fears most. Since such a rule out-runs the pleasureful, he knows he must repent. Thus, he tacks anxiously between a desire to continue gloriously as a free self and the fear of what attends this course. Happiness may be sought, but a love of darkness and indecision holds one back. A new bondage results.

The weight of guilt becomes more evident, and its manifestations more apparent in actions, however, when one tries to find happiness in an enthusiastic recommitment to immediacy rather than in pressing on to another option. At this moment the order is relayed to the free self to cease seeking other escapes; and a powerful prejudice results. Those who become uneasy in the accumulation of money, yet refusing to repent, usually turn their money into a god, *determining* that they shall be content within the devotion. From this point they are committed. And to sustain the illusion of the commitment they give strict orders to the free self not to listen to any other voices or see any other options. They dare not risk frustration's bitterness.

> But sometimes luxurious living is not so much an advertisement of the ego's pride or even a simple and soft acquiescence with the various impulses of the physical life, as it is a frantic effort to escape from self. It betrays an uneasy conscience. The self is seeking to escape from itself and throws itself into any pursuit which will allow it to forget for a moment the inner tension of an uneasy conscience. The self, finding itself to be inadequate as the centre of its existence, seeks for another god amidst the various forces, processes and impulses of nature over which it ostensibly presides.[7]

Men who thus look to their own activity to sustain them become touchy and irascible about their own way of life. The sprawling empire is so satisfying to the industrialist, that he tends to be impatient with anyone who challenges the worthiness of this commitment. The man who drinks does not want to analyze his act. He wants only to drink.

Time has a way of winnowing the grain of human choices, however, and those who debauch themselves through one devotion or another have a day of reckoning. Winston Churchill has sagaciously remarked that there is a stern, strange justice to the long swing of events. Since there is a progressive self-refutation in immediacy (for freedom and immediacy

---

7. Niebuhr, *Human Nature*, p. 234.

cannot mix), justice *will* be meted out to the heart. The
shackled, transcendent self will wriggle free as the sands of
time run out. Death is the specter which brings men all low
and equal. The daily diminishing of strength in man points
to the nearness of the termination of life. Groaning for a
security which cannot be located in the elements of immediacy,
the free self charges against the empirical self with vengeance;
until in the end either a coarse pessimism or actual suicide results. While suicides come from all strata of life, a common
denominator is shared by them all: There is no peace, save
through the destruction of the free self's urge to find peace.
Suicide is an act of shame, being prompted by guilt. Suicide
is a confession to the world that the individual has despaired
of finding a solution to life. It is a final, public admission that
one has bargained for more than he has been able to make
good in his own life.

The free self knows, while the empirical self cringes to
admit it, that a commitment is ideally satisfying only when
spiritual deposits of peace and comfort are laid on the heart
in the course of the act. But these deposits are absent from
immediacy, for the individual himself contributes everything.
He receives nothing save the meager pleasures gained during
the actual act. After the power to act vanishes, the satisfaction
vanishes with it. As a result, spirit is outraged at the very
thought that the hedonic ideal is really an ideal. It evaluates it
as a premature commitment, groaning for the higher securities
for which it knows it was created. Immediacy is a false finality,
bringing only regret and despair as its final fruit. The force
of recoil is directly proportioned to the energy employed in
initial commitment; even as the tone of guilt is proportioned
to the sensitivity of self-respect maintained. The higher one
rises in freedom, the more intense is his guilt in failing in
the goal.

There are two conditions under which men may pretend
exemption from guilt. *First,* they may assume that they have
actually succeeded in mediating the law of their nature, and

thus suffer from no want of perfection in their own person. *Second*, they may destroy the possibility of guilt by denying the existence of the ideals which elicit it. If the first course is attempted, sheepishness immediately results, for proud and selfish actions have a way of cancelling out the coherence of a pretension to perfection. The wise man (like Socrates) *disclaims* possession of perfection. But if the second alternative is elected, the result is the destruction of man's dignity; for only in relation to *rationes aeternae* over against him is the free individual grounded in dignifying relations. Furthermore, it is impossible *not* to be guided by ideals which outreach the possibility of fulfillment. Freedom dies when this role is snatched from it. One must be free to choose the ideal of not having ideals, and thus the contradiction continues.

V. Exhaustion

A. *The Feet of Clay*

When we relate the human venture to the problem of physical strength, we emerge with a final crushing case against immediacy. While strength remains, one may indeed continue in either boredom or frustration with consolation. The hope is always that the next venture will bring peace. But when the very antecedent condition for all engagement is destroyed and the individual is left without strength, there is an irremediable finality to the ensuing despair. As long as one can rise again to look decision in the face with power, hope remains. But when the very preconditions for choice fail, then the last vestige of optimism is shattered. This stage is *exhaustion*.

Man, as experience teaches, is a compound of both possibility and necessity. And the fundamental cause of the necessity is spirit's union with body. The fact of this union is indisputable, though the exact nature of it is extremely mysterious. A result of this joining together of freedom and necessity in the one vital man is sort of a Siamese twins effect where each side of the relation is limited in what it may perform by the strength of the other. This concomitance is experienced every day. When a common head cold upsets the normal harmony of the body, the keenness of the mind suffers as a consequence. And when physical suffering is chronic, morale in spirit is jeopardized. The greatest cause of suicide is desperation over chronic illness. The free spirit charges against its confined twin, lashing out against it for being so weak; until in the end the whole self is driven to the expedient of self-destruction as a way of escape. Spirit chafes under the limitations of body because it is endowed with an easy mobility unknown to flesh. Mind must deal with body as the nurse would with the child.

The question of physical strength is particularly relevant when the issue of immediacy is raised, for with but a few exceptions (such as memory) one can enter into the promises of pleasure only when the body is reasonably strong. Travel, adventure, and allurements in high and low places turn on the physical ability of the individual to rise to the occasion. The boy who believes his nature would be fully exhausted in a game of baseball may *wish* for fulfillment; but he cannot actualize the dream while his body is riddled with a besetting disease.

Although the body is under the sentence of death from the moment of conception, the free self can easily be prevented from reckoning with that fact. It is almost a psychological impossibility for a healthy person to put himself in the place of the corpse. One can sympathize with the death of all men — save himself. Yet, death is so certain that life insurance companies have reduced the mortality cycle to a very exact science. The time of death may be determined only within probability, but the fact is not. Like the egress and regress of the tides, death is a certainty.

Spirit is enraged at the very thought of a temporal limit to its venture. Since its native witness is that it was made to live forever, death enters as an unexpected intruder. And yet when the free man looks carefully at himself, he discovers that the elements in his nature are not in final harmony one with another. Whereas spirit soars toward eternity, the body is drawn down to the grave; and just at the very time when spirit is beginning to find itself quite at home in life, too. The wine satisfies one day, but then the body contracts an allergy which makes the fruit of the vine an emetic. Sex has satisfied decisively, but then hormones begin to fail as senility makes its home in the physical frame. The seaman is exhilarated by his life of prowess on the high seas, but the day comes when he must reluctantly turn in his uniform because of a weak heart. *Spirit* has not been exhausted. Hardly. It is only becoming used to its office, and enjoying it very much. The trouble stems from body; for it is the body which drags down the spirit. On learning that it is chained to a partner that cannot run as fast as it can, spirit chafes with bewilderment and and insecurity. How can its eternal plans be realized when it must remain handcuffed to a corpse?

Perhaps a more graphic way to express the union of soul and body is that of two mighty stallions — pulling, but in opposite directions. Spirit craves life in all of its everlasting fullness, but it is disappointed when it is introduced to death. Death is an unwelcome visitor, for spirit is filled with potentialities unbounding. Shall the ego stand idly by when the ravages of death try to move in upon it and swallow up its vitality? Body, weary from its continual fight against both diseases and elements of nature, holds out its arms to death in beckoning surrender, pleading that death overtake it and quench its miseries. The great controversy today over euthanasia testifies to the blessed hope which the body finds in death. And suspended between — or rather made up by — these antagonistic forces is the whole individual. As a spiritual being only a loss of interest can kill man; while as a physical being a misplaced injection of pure air can kill him. The greatness and misery of man remains as it did in the day when Pascal lamented the fact so picturesquely.

Because it is led to believe that life is found in immediacy, spirit goes along with a provisional commitment to the hedonic ideal. The vision of future, satisfying engagements keeps freedom champing at the reins to pull forward. But when the free self is quietly informed that the body cannot carry on, it feels enraged that it has sold out its potentialities so cheaply. How can spirit have happiness in pleasure when the framework needed for engaging in immediacy is missing? · Thus, man is again set against himself. The clown made others forget their sorrows through laughter, but who will assuage his sorrow when his own spirit goes to the grave? The ballerina enraptures the world with her flawless pirouetting, but who placates her spirit when another takes her place and she is forgotten? There is a *final* grief in impotency because the very conditions for making spirit happy are missing.

And yet the appetite of freedom remains. Men would continue forever if they had the strength. But tears will avail nothing when the great scythe of death clears away the world scene once a generation. The world traveler must lay down his compass; the successful surgeon must seek the healing fingers of another; the engineer must turn the throttle over to a younger hand. Yet, while death is active cleaning the world scene, spirit cries out in protest. Although it expected to stay on stage forever, it must pass through the wings in a moment, only to watch with jealousy as another takes its place.

Solomon realized that there is a finality in senility which consigns the spirit to a state of grief more bitter than that of either boredom or frustration. Therefore, he advised wise men to put their house in order while they enjoyed the control of their physical faculties. With the decay of the body there trails along a concomitant decay in spiritual discernment. The ravages of disease eat away at the clarity of our critical life.

> Remember also thy Creator in the days of thy youth, before the evil days come, and the years draw nigh, when thou shalt say, I have no pleasure in them; before the sun, and the light, and the moon, and the stars, are darkened, and the clouds return after the rain; in the day when the keepers of the house shall tremble, and the strong men shall bow themselves, and the grinders cease because they are few, and those that look out of the windows shall be darkened, and the doors

shall be shut in the street; when the sound of the grinding is low, and one shall rise up at the voice of a bird, and all the daughters of music shall be brought low; yea, they shall be afraid of that which is high, and terrors shall be in the way; and the almond-tree shall blossom, and the grasshopper shall be a burden, and desire shall fail; because man goeth to his everlasting home.[8]

Since spirit can be placated only when desires remain, there is no worse disease than the living death which results when one despairs of the very body which houses him. Youth can bound back with courage and hope, rising quickly when they fall; but the senile, weary of buffeting the fortunes of life, are anxious to enjoy the quieter securities. Upon discovering that there are no securities, therefore, a pitiful loss of interest results. Since there is no strength to create an engagement with a new immediacy, there is no desire.

But does it follow that when senility sets in, the heart *must* fail? No, for there are multitudes of aged people who are sweet and hopeful in their condition of pitiful physical wretchedness. They are exempt from despair because they gave their earlier strength to commitments which left deposits of spiritual strength on their own souls. This strength is now able to take over when power in the body fails. It is a sweet sight to see a happy spirit in a broken, disease-eaten body. It is sweet because the law of life has been found and met.

B. *Objection*

An initially plausible (but essentially pathetic) objection to Solomon's argument from exhaustion is the following: Why not take a day at a time? To fear the future is childlike. The plausibility is that it seems robust and chesty to live only for the day, taking what comes and smiling at it. It implies that those who allow future contingencies to alter their present state of mind are effeminate and uncourageous. But the pathos is that it asks a man to solve his problem by rendering null and

---

8. Ecclesiastes 12:1-5.

void the very powers which give him dignity. Selfhood *involves* the power of transcendence. If we insure our homes and our bodies against loss, is it foolish to insure the spirit against a similar loss?

It is the *duty* of the transcendent self so to guide the involved self that the whole person will have no cause for regret. And what activity ought the free self be engaged in more earnestly than that of learning whether there are conditions to be met for the acquisition of eternal life? Everlasting life is so dear to our interests that if we were informed tomorrow that we would live forever, we would receive the information as something we tacitly believed would be true all the while. There is hesitancy only when man faces *death*, not life. If a man despises himself for not having used foresight when the possibility of acquiring a huge fortune was suddenly thrown across his path, thus, how much more ought he to despise himself if a chance for immortal life is spurned?

Summary

Pleasure still lures men as the voice of the sirens near the Surrentine promontory lured Odysseus and his men. But the end of those who guide their ships toward it is yet destruction. The ship is the self and the destruction is the boredom of distaste and vapidness, the frustration of disappointment, the guilt of failure, and the exhaustion of weakness and despair.

Out of the involved dialogue between the self and the pretensions of immediacy there emerges a rather clear conclusion: "Final satisfaction is not here. Seek it elsewhere." The answer is negative, but unequivocal. Odysseus solved his problem by putting wax in the ears of his sailors and lashing himself to the ship. *Perhaps the free self can solve the matter by the expulsive power of a higher love.*

IV

Bread Alone?

WHEN asked recently what he thought was the most glorious year thus far in the history of man, a great educator and lecturer responded: *"Any* year during Christ's public ministry." Men find it easy to introduce Jesus Christ when they talk of the noble and the endearing. And yet the scale of values which Christ respected stands sharply over against standards which are understood and appreciated by modern man. This is especially true in matters of material possessions. Whereas Christ was very nonchalant about material gain, accepting each day's tasks as part of the discipline of discipleship, modern man is not at rest until he has mercilessly lashed his spirit on to find more efficient ways to accumulate. Jesus oriented his value perspective heavenwards, calmly beseeching men to pray to their heavenly Father to supply them their need. To do the will of God his Father was his food. This was hard for both the nervous multitudes and the uncertain disciples to understand, for it ran cross-grained to what they were certain was a primary human value.

Christ's nonchalance can be illustrated perfectly by the feeding of the five thousand. The very purpose in his apparent neglect of the problem of food was to teach his disciples the hard lesson of dependence upon the Father. Jesus appeared so engrossed in his labor of teaching that he gave no outward sign of interest in feeding the thronging multitude. Hence, Philip anxiously inquired, "How are we to buy bread, so that these people may eat?" (John 6:5) The question appeared to be perfectly in order. Good management required that foresight be employed. But Jesus exhibited a foresight of

83

his own. After witnessing to his complete dependence upon his Father, he multiplied the barley loaves and fish until all were satisfied. He then continued with his instruction.

When modern man takes time off in his quest for economic security to read about Christ's calmness, he is shocked. Would there be any progress in history if all men were that nonchalant? Does not Christ's attitude lead to indolence and laziness? Furthermore, while perhaps *Jesus* may have been able to multiply loaves and fish, *we* cannot. So, modern man closes the book and replaces it on the shelf. A true son of the Renaissance, he instinctively accepts the presupposition that the destiny of history lies in the hands of the most ambitious individual. Social and economic security is purely a scientific question, needing no supports from heaven. Faith and trust are as relevant in gaining security as flying lessons are to an earthworm. In competitive social relations one will get ahead only when he *works,* not prays.

I. The Two Jews

Someone has remarked that the destiny of our civilization turns on the triumph of one or the other of two Jewish philosophies of life. This is not far from the truth. Christianity stems from Jesus Christ and communism from Karl Marx — two Jews.

A. *Zeitgeist*

Modern man perhaps does not realize it, but he is an inchoate Marxist himself. The issue which separates Christ and Marx is one of basic values: *Is the material subordinate to, and explained by, the spiritual: or vice versa?* Jesus Christ preached the former, while Karl Marx taught the latter. And now mankind is blocked off into two great worlds to settle this question. And if the ordinary channels of diplomacy fail, armed conflict will be called in. When all the minor differences separating these two worlds are peeled away, the problem of the primacy of either the material or the spiritual remains. Christ taught that the problems of social conflict can be solved only when the deeper question of *sin* in the human heart is faced. Marx denies this, contending that *social security* is the problem; and that when this is met, the heart of man will be at peace. Christ replies that social insecurity is a by-product of spiritual insecurity, and that a final solution to man's inward predicament would not be found even if all social injustices and inequalities were leveled off.

"Oh, *no, no, no!*" cries modern man when he is asked if Marx is correct. We *cannot* be materialists. And yet the average man in Western culture happens to be a quasi-Marxist. While recoiling with perspiration from the thought of the communist ideology, he yet conducts his life according to the tacit presupposition that history is controlled by human initiative and that man's problems can be solved by the simple expedients of a new station wagon and a guaranteed annuity policy. Modern man wants his cake and penny, too. He wants the support of a Christian theory of values, while he himself is busily engaged in playing the role of a tacit materialist.

We are actually so involved in material commitments that we cannot clearly see the issues which separate the East from the West. Christ did not say either that material things are unimportant or that man must not work by the sweat of his brow to obtain them. He never encouraged people to believe that bread would be multiplied at simply the behest of their faith. The Son of Man retained prerogatives in his office which were not made the common property of his followers. Furthermore, Marx did not deny the real power and present value of ideological truth. He was well aware of the need of rallying vitalities if a nation is to be moved. Neither of these points begins to hit the central issue. Christ was a carpenter and Marx was a theorist; the philosophy of neither excludes such labor. Here is the crux: *Christ said that the material is a servant of the spiritual, while Marx said that the spiritual is a servant of the material.* On this question — this *toto caelo* question — the destiny of humanity rests.

Marxism is the logical conclusion to a long tendency within Western culture to displace the Platonic-Christian metaphysics with a this-worldly, materialistic value theory and a pragmatic method of verification. Plato believed that history is best understood through the world of Ideas. The Christian appeals to the mind of God. Marx esteems the spiritual an irrelevance in *explaining* history's pattern. The dialectic within historical movement is guided by the active collision of social contradictions. The tensions of struggle, not a fanciful world of Ideas, determines history.

Modern man will be able to cope with both the social situation and himself only after he clears his head and appreciates the dimensions of the issue at stake. The separation of East and West is not much ado over nothing. It is not just a logomachy. There is a basic value hierarchy in question: *Do the good, true, and beautiful have time- and space-transcending significance, so that the material is to be understood and evaluated by rationes aeternae; or are these so-called values simply arbitrary designations which we give to relative situations in time and space? Again, can man be explained on a one-dimensional view of reality? Is he just a complex animal? Or, is there a God to whom men are responsible? Is law changeless? These* are questions. Western man may think very highly of himself as a quiet, law-abiding materialist. But what he does not seem to understand is that all of the ingredients of communism are germinally present in his own world view. If all is relative, then it is relative that men lie under oath, that justice be ignored, and that we labor for world revolution.

B. *Basic Commodity*

The instant one turns from the immediacies of wine, women, and song to the lure of economic security, he senses that he has stepped into a new genus. Complexities instantly ensue.

One may resist the lure of the flesh, but he will soon faint on the way the instant he tries to oppose material provisions. Spirit is chained to body, and body presupposes the nourishment of food and the protection of shelter.

A glance at the classified ads in a metropolitan newspaper will quickly illustrate the place that economic security enjoys in daily life. Page upon page of small type herald the desperate pleas of those who, caught in the closing vise of economic insecurity, are desperately seeking a way back to normalcy and self-respect. There is no front more explosive than that of labor. When purchasing power is denied a man, he is so overwhelmed by a feeling of insecurity that personal shame reaches through his empty stomach to his own heart. And when hungry, disappointed men march together toward a seat of injustice, woe to those at ease in Zion! Artificial experiments in starvation prove that when gnawing hunger overtakes an individual, such a one begins to lose his sense of values. He becomes suspicious of others around him, imagining persecution and theft everywhere, until actual violence overtakes him.

Observe likewise that in the very places where one might expect a complete rejection of the things of matter, concern runs high. The minister of the gospel pretends devotion to the bread which comes from the mouth of God, and yet he is very solicitous to negotiate a fixed salary before he starts preaching. The monk renounces the world with great fanfare, but his renunciation is never so complete that he also renounces the fleshly security of soup and bread within the anchoritic colony. The lofty idealist somehow manages to continue eating juicy steaks — suspiciously nonideational realities. Christian Scientists boast of their unalloyed panspiritism, and yet not only is the plate eagerly passed to gather hard coins, but the dying are persuaded to leave all their worldly goods to the mother church. God is truth, life, spirit, love — yet, green dollars and silver coins are smuggled in somehow.

There is something humorous about an attempt to withdraw from dependence on bread. No matter how lofty an edifice we may erect within freedom, we must return at night to take up our abode in a world where we eat to live. It will never do to become so enamored of the eternal and changeless that we forget our involvement in the necessities of time and space, since man is body as well as spirit.

The most serious side of economic security is the fact that the happiness and security of others often depends on how successfully one maintains a livelihood. The relation between lover and beloved, father and child, is sweet for the very reason that the one relies upon the other in perfect trust. The child is free from worry because he knows that father and mother are busy providing the things needful for the body. He flings open the door *expecting* to find food on the table. And the parents feel their worth accented in a wonderful way when they can match the expectations of their children. Through weakness, the parents are made strong. The father experiences a warm satisfaction when he returns at the end of the week, his arms loaded with bundles for the family. He is the nonchalant sovereign in such a loving situation.

This is the exhilarating side of fatherhood — the other is less pleasant. When his resources are cut off and he is no longer able to meet the needs of his family, a reversal sets in; and the very responsibilities which initially brought joy are now the cause of inward grief and insecurity. It is not easy to explain the complexities of modern, economic machinery to staring, wondering eyes. They know nothing about the dialectic of competition and ruin.[1] The child only knows that his daddy, the food–getting–one, is all he has to look to. A man may overcome his own feeling of emptiness and hunger by resolution, but it is difficult to remain composed when other souls are implicated in the relation. For this reason either a

---

1. "By producing larger and larger quantities of commodities, and reducing their prices, capitalism intensifies competition, ruins the mass of small and medium private owners, converts them into proletarians and reduces their purchasing power, with the result that it becomes impossible to dispose of the commodities produced." Joseph Stalin, *Dialectical and Historical Materialism*, (New York: International Publishers, 1940), Marxist Library, Vol. XXVIII, p. 37.

lost job or unexpected social insecurity can so upset the balance of life that a normally pleasant individual becomes disturbed and bewildered. "We have not yet learned how to prevent business depressions, but we have at least come to see that the moral injury of prolonged unemployment for workmen and of closed opportunity for youth is a more serious and difficult problem than that of bodily hunger."[2]

Because men so easily lose their sense of balance when they suffer from social and economic insecurity, it is easy to see why communism is a plausibility — and especially to those fringe and minority groups within a culture which are exploited by the ruling classes. The health of a society fluctuates with the health of its material conditions. It seems true on the surface, therefore, that the "spiritual life of society is a reflection of the conditions of its material life."[3] And is not the dialectic plausible? Social contradictions are always pitted against each other.

> The dialectical method therefore holds that the process of development from the lower to the higher takes place not as a harmonious unfolding of phenomena, but as a disclosure of the contradictions inherent in things and phenomena, as a 'struggle' of opposite tendencies which operate on the basis of these contradictions.[4]

It is impossible to avoid the admission that Marxism is initially plausible. If man were an angel — or (for that matter) even half an angel — he might turn aside from the problems of economic security in favor of other interests. But he happens to be very much a man.

II. Marx States His Case

Complexity increases the instant we probe beneath the surface of communism, however.

---

2. Dagobert Runes (Ed.), *Twentieth Century Philosophy*, (New York: Philosophical Library, 1943), p. 36.
3. Stalin, *op. cit.*, p. 36.
4. *Ibid.*, p. 11.

A. *Rise*

It is very easy for an absolutistic system to crucify progress through a premature sanctification of the *status in quo.* The Republic of Plato illustrates such a threatened stagnation. Because the slave was deficient in *nous,* he was predestined to remain within his rank. Social stratification was settled on philosophical, not activistic, grounds. In the medieval feudal-agrarian society the infallibility of the church was used as a strait-jacket to hold the social order in line with the will of a religious and political hierarchy. Instead of offering the peasant an opportunity to use his free powers for progress, the wretched one was comforted with the pious word that through faith and obedience his lack of earthly blessings would be compensated many fold in heaven. "If we turn to the peasant and his aspirations, the darkest side of the Middle Ages is revealed. For him, strictly speaking, there could be no ideal; Christian resignation was his lot and human contempt."[5]

Modern man thumps his chest in pride, pleasantly assured that the system of capitalistic enterprise affords all men a plenary opportunity to express their creative freedom. But Marx responds by showing that within the capitalistic structure itself necessary contradictions lie. These contradictions in turn set class against class, until in the end a ruthless exploitation of the weak results.

> Among the most important contradictions of the capitalistic system, special mention may be made of the three following: First contradiction: The conflict between labour and capital. . . .
> Second contradiction: The conflict between the various financial groups and the different imperialist powers in their competition for control of the sources of raw material, for foreign territory. . . .
> Third contradiction: The conflict between the small group of dominant 'civilized' nations, on the one hand, and the

---

5. John Randall, Jr., *The Making of the Modern Mind,* (New York. Houghton Mifflin Company, 1926), p. 88.

hundreds of millions of persons who make up the colonial and dependent peoples of the world on the other.[6]

Marx and Engels appeared on the world scene at an hour when the newly emerging bourgeois class was in the process of refining a philosophy of life to defend its interests. Both the weakness of capitalism's internal structure and the need for an effective system of checks and balances began to protrude. Growing pains were in evidence everywhere. And in the process of such a growth no few mistakes in strategy were committed — the very errors communistic minds later exploited.

With a burst of enthusiasm the bourgeois individual declared himself free from the limitations which had shackled social life hitherto. With ingenuity and resolution the world could be conquered. Yet, out of this optimistic view of creative, historical possibilities there emerged a nest of new inequalities. Intoxicated with success as creators of a new destiny, the bourgeoisie soon ossified into a hardened class of self-sufficient overlords, converting their initial gains into an occasion for accumulating securities at the expense of their inferiors. Capital was hoarded and monopolies developed. The rallying vitalities of "free enterprise" and "capitalistic progress" were presumed to cover a multitude of sins. Workers clustered around the centers of industry, separating themselves from the soil which gave them birth. And before long the gap between the capitalistic employer and his workers was so wide that a new class of exploited, underprivileged people emerged: the *proletariat*. Marx and Engels took notes on all this.

The bourgeois fortress seemed impregnable. It defended its pretensions by a *laissez faire* optimism grounded in Hegelian philosophy. Hegel managed an easy sanctification of the *status in quo* by defining the real as the rational and the rational as the real, and by viewing history (from one perspective) as the autobiography of God. History is the endless

6. Joseph Stalin, *Leninism*, pp. 81ff. (Quoted in *The Strategy and Tactics of World Communism*, by Committee on Foreign Affairs, p. 9).

march of Spirit in search of freedom. Freedom is self-consciousness, and absolute self-consciousness is God. This meant "a sanctification of things that be, a philosophical benediction bestowed upon despotism, police-government, Star Chamber proceedings and censorship."[7] Hegel tried to close the gap between mind and matter by identifying movement in logic with movement in history. Beginning with the logical category of *being* (thesis) and proceeding to *becoming* (synthesis) through *non-being* (antithesis) he moved through the entire span of rationality, until all ended in the *Weltgeist*. Each logical triad led necessarily to the next, and that to the next, until the absolute was reached.

But Hegel failed to convince Marx. By coming to problems through the concrete situation, Marx sensed that the *result* of Hegelianism — however internally consistent its philosophical method might happen to be — was an intolerable sanctification of the privileges of this new middle class.

> Hegel is the interpreter of the tendencies of a semi-conservative bourgeoisie; what he sets himself to justify is not the future nor the past, but the present. Like all doctrinaire conservatives, he stops the evolution of the world at the present moment, to which he gives absolute value as the definitive and perfect result of rational evolution.[8]

Marx complained that Hegel failed to penetrate to the efficient causes which produced the actual changes in history. Hegel never understood that *concrete activity* (not the progression of logical categories) is the catalytic agent in change. This was serious, for it spelled the difference between progress or defeat for the proletariat. There unquestionably was a profundity in the theoretical structure of the dialectic, for progress *does* emerge out of the tension of contrarieties. But the cause of change is not so simple a matter as either Spirit seeking freedom or the relating of abstract, logical categories.

---

7. Frederick Engels, *Ludwig Feuerbach*, (New York: International Publishers, 1941), Marxist Library, Vol. XV, p. 10.
8. Roy Sellars, *et al.* (Ed.), *Philosophy for the Future,* (New York: The Macmillan Company, 1949), p. 45.

A study of actual history assured Marx that social contradictions are neither logical nor bloodless; they are real struggles between real people. To be practical and convincing, therefore, a philosophy of history had to be impregnated with a vital dynamic which man could control. An activism is called for.

> The purpose of his own social theories was to provide that knowledge of social tendencies which would most effectively liberate revolutionary *action*. Philosophy is not retrospective insight into the past; it is prospective anticipation of the future. It explains why the present is what it is in order to make it different. So often an expression of social quietism, or a means of individual escape, philosophy must now function as an instrument of social liberation. The social world is not inherently reasonable as Hegel claimed. It must be made reasonable. In the words of his well-known gloss on Feuerbach, 'Until now philosophers have only *interpreted* the world differently; the point is to change it.'[9]

Marx studied the socialistic movement in France in its immense effort to confer "on the mode of appropriation the same collective character as the mode of production."[10] But he felt that this experiment in socialism would not succeed because of the immature philosophical basis upon which it was reared. Being insufficiently class-conscious, the proletariat in France were premature in their attempted revolution. Since the contradictions in capitalism had not yet appeared, the proletariat grasp of the place of class struggle in emancipating men from the yoke of injustice was inchoate. Informed with an abiding rationalistic optimism, these doctrinaire socialists naively thought that convincing men of their *need* for social change was tantamount to effecting the change itself. Marx felt that a more realistic means must be resorted to if social changes are to pass from paper to act. The "reasonableness of the new order" is a very undialectical expedient.

Engels spent several profitable years in England, during which time a keen interest in the problems of the la-

9. Sidney Hook, *From Hegel to Marx,* (New York: Reynal & Hitchcock), pp. 25-26.
10. Sellars, *et al,* (Ed.), *op. cit.,* p. 54.

boring class developed. England had long been enjoying the fruits of the industrial revolution, so it was natural that she was the locus for the more obvious abuses of capitalism. Contrary to what philosophers might say, the actual struggles in history grew out of conflicts inherent in the social pattern. Classes warred on each other for social and economic security. Here lay the missing clue to the construction of a genuinely dialectical philosophy of history.

> In England, then economically the most highly developed country, any one could see that the true explanation of political struggles resided in the class struggle between the bourgeoisie and the proletariat. It was also unmistakably clear that this struggle between working class and bourgeoisie was based on the economic position of the two classes, on the fact that the bourgeoisie was in possession of all the means of production and piled up riches upon riches, while the working class, lacking means of production, was dependent solely on the sale of its labor power. Thus, here was the most obvious place to study the materialistic explanation of historical events.[11]

The new left-wing leaders received a cold reception from liberal bourgeoisie the instant their revolutionary doctrines leaked out. Intent on maintaining self-security through a sanctification of their own vested interests, the bourgeoisie resisted the intruders. This merely served as a barometric warning to the radicals of the impending storm ahead. In reply, they became even more radical.

B. *Crystallization*

Feuerbach supplied a radical, materialistic philosophy of the supersensible. He heaped barbed ridicule on the notion that there is a trans-temporal realm of normative truth. Such a stratum is nothing more than an unwarranted and fantastic conversion of sense knowledge. Since man extends his own petty virtues to infinity, and then with bent knee worships

---

11. August Thalheimer, *Introduction to Dialectical Materialism,* (New York: Covici-Friede, 1936), pp. 132-133.

them, theology is simply anthropology. Man worships himself. Feuerbach needed overhauling, to be sure, for he was informed with non-dialectical elements which impeded a thoroughgoing activism; yet his materialism enjoyed a convincing this-worldly emphasis. "Marx and Engels took from Feuerbach's materialism its 'inner kernel,' developed it into a scientific-philosophical theory of materialism and cast aside its idealistic and religious-ethical encumbrances."[12]

A synthesis resulted. From Hegel came the framework of dialectical tension, while from the materialistic heritage came a down-to-earth application. Thus, the name given to the finished philosophy: *dialectical materialism.* "It is called dialectical materialism because its approach to the phenomena of nature, its method of studying and apprehending them, is *dialectical,* while its interpretation of the phenomena of nature, its conception of these phenomena, its theory, is *materialistic.*"[13] Progress emerges out of tension, and the tension is created by a conflict between classes. The pattern of society, and thus the meaning of history, is fundamentally determined by the contradictions inherent in class ideology.

A comprehensive triad forms the basis of the social dialectic: the *thesis* is the exploiting class (bourgeoisie), the *antithesis* the exploited class (proletariat), and the *synthesis* the final fruit of class struggle (classless society). At the end of the short reign of the proletariat there emerges that utopian social order (described by Lenin in *The State and Revolution*) in which formal equality is converted into actual equality: "From each according to his ability and to each according to his need." The transition from inequality and injustice to equality and justice is no automatic, or even easy, passage. "On the contrary,

---

12. Stalin, *op. cit.,* p. 6.
13. Stalin, *op. cit.,* p. 5. "My dialectical method is not only different from the Hegelian, but it is direct opposite. To Hegel, the life-process of the human brain, *i. e.,* the process of thinking. . . is the demiurgos of the real world, and the real world is only the external, phenomenal form of 'the Idea.' With me, on the contrary, the ideal is nothing else than the material world reflected by the human mind, and translated into forms of thought." Karl Marx, *Das Kapital,* (Chicago: Charles Kerr & Company, 1912), Vol. I, p. 25.

such a transition usually takes place by means of the revolutionary overthrow of the old relations of production and the establishment of new relations of production."[14] Power must meet power if justice is to be established. Only realistic means can mediate the contradictions which arise in class struggle. There are always periods of violence as one system of organization gives way to another, for the abiding order is entrenched so deeply its roots must be dynamited. "Force is the midwife of every old society pregnant with a new one. It is itself an economic power."[15]

To recapitulate: Since freedom in economic struggle is compounded with both the pride of the heart and the inequalities of men, it follows that injustices will inevitably emerge within the social order. And when given a full opportunity to mature, these inequalities blossom into contradictions. The owners of the tools of labor gain greater and greater power over these tools, until finally so much machinery and capital is controlled that even the workers themselves become tools. The capitalists are the exploiting class, the proletariat the exploited class. This contradiction can only be resolved through the expedient of forceful pressures and (if necessary) violent revolution. The entrenchments of capitalism must be blown up, for only force can dislodge force. Communism labels this structure of emerging contradictions, plus the overcoming of them by directed force, the *dialectic of history*. And the dialectic is *materialistic* because the ideal is always a reflection of the concrete, never vice versa.

> This materialism is historical; it explains the movement of history essentially by the transformation of the conditions of material life, by the development of the forces of production and not by an alternation of philosophical, political, or religious conceptions which are but the ideological forms assumed in men's consciousness by the real motives of their actions. And this historical materialism is dialectic; it shows

14. Stalin, *op. cit.,* p. 43.
15. Marx, *op. cit.,* p. 824.

that the movement of history is linked to the development of the relations between the forces of production and the social forces.[16]

Marx claimed he turned Hegel "right side up again" by returning to a more realistic understanding of the relation between form and process.

The classless society is a goal commensurate with the freedom of man, for perfect brotherhood exhausts the height to which man may soar when progressively defining perfect social relations. Hence, both freedom and involvement cooperate in the unfolding of the dialectical tensions. Freedom finds means to release justice, while involvement profits from new-found security.

III. Competing Immediacy

Communism has made great strides since Marx quietly penned his *Das Kapital*. One is no longer privileged either to look at the movement calmly from a distance or to evaluate it simply as a sporadic, left-wing program to which Gamaliel's advice may be applied.[17] Communism has already infiltrated itself into the enemy's citadels. It is pushing its way across the globe so swiftly that decision cannot be delayed. Its collective might resembles that of the cloud of flying grasshoppers moving relentlessly toward a field of corn. Action must be decisive and swift, or all will be lost.

The first question which rises is whether or not Marxism is another form of immediacy. This issue must be settled with dispatch, for if it turns out that spirit cannot be fully exhausted in the ideal of the classless society, it may well be that our highest conceivable devotion has not been tapped.

There is an initial dilemma to be faced. And once this dilemma is understood, it will quickly appear that Marxism *is* an immediacy; for every weakness of the hedonic ideal applies *mutatis mutandis* to communism. The dilemma is as follows: If the classless society *is* attained, then the individual

16. Sellars, *et al.* (Ed.), *op. cit.*, p. 57.
17. "If this plan or this undertaking is of men, it will fail: but if it is of God you will not be able to overthrow them." (Acts 5:38-39).

becomes bored. And if it is *not* attained, then the individual is frustrated. There is no way out of this dilemma — granted the ingredients of communism. Let us enlarge upon this.

A. *Immediacy in Attainment*

The Marxist is extremely naive when he believes that through the simple expedient of a dialectical struggle, history will contain its own ideal. Marx and Engels suppose that when proper pressure is applied to the proper places, the classless society *will* emerge. But experience teaches that the best that can result from any shifting of centers of power is simply less *injustice*. Justice and injustice both remain. Only their locus and proportion have been altered.

There is a remarkable want of explanation by communists why it is that men refuse to remain content within the confines of the classless society once they have tasted its perfection. Since Marx's dialectic presupposes that historical tensions will continue endlessly, it follows that the perfect equality of the classless society will inevitably generate those inequalities which call for a renewed use of force once again. The contradiction is obvious. Spirit is inspired to wander by the intuition that when the highest *is* reached, the whole man will rest content. While it may infinitely create *within* that perfection, it will never seek to pass beyond it; for an overpassing of it would only result in a return to imperfection, and it was to avoid imperfections that it first wandered. Why, then, does the spirit refuse to remain content in the classless society? Why is the dialectic not completed when this state is reached? Should discontentment be a characteristic of *perfection's* appropriation? Is not discontentment symptomatic that the ideal has not yet been reached?

It is not hard to sympathize with the inevitability of greed and inequality in history, for any man who is honest with his own heart is too well aware of the non-rational vitalities of selfishness and personal interest surging up within him. Even the most altruistic compound their philanthropy with the sullying prides of self-assurance and conceit. Men grab what they want out of life — and they often grab with their left hand on the Bible while doing it.

But our problem is this: If the classless society *is* the *summum bonum,* why do men lust for other values after they have attained it? There will naturally be symptoms of discontentment until the moment perfection is reached, for it is the ideal of perfection which incites spirit on to act. But what is there *beyond* perfection that can attract? What "more" can be added to an "all"? Perfection should be as natural an environment for spirit as mellow clover is for the bovine.

There is only one satisfying conclusion to this problem: Since Marxism leaves man with an ultimate discontentment, it follows that it does *not* contain the outside ideal of freedom. We may yet not know *what* the perfect ideal is, but negatively we may conclude that it is not the classless society. Such a society is *an* ideal, but *ex hypothesi* it is not the *final* ideal. Men become bored when they give according to their ability and take according to their need. And wherever boredom is found, there the final potentialities of spirit are unaccented. This is an axiom. If boredom were not present, why should the dialectic commence all over again?

B. *Frustration in Non-Attainment*

Marxism induces its initiates to believe that the classless society *will* be attained. But let us suppose that it will never be reached — the more plausible alternative. Will pursuit of a constantly receding goal satisfy?

First, let us justify this alternative as a possibility. There is something exceedingly suspicious about the eschatological arrangement of things in communism. The confident promise is that right after the victory of World Revolution, Russia's Comintern will suddenly be converted into a democratic institution by the voluntary self-abdication of its power-grabbing rulers. This is a remarkable faith — remarkable indeed —

requiring a credulity which has no rival. How is it conceivable that the hardened criminals in Moscow will suddenly convert into harmless lambs, leading their flocks through vernal pastures in the classless society? Will men who have been taking far more than their need suddenly step down and by sheer resolution start taking only *according* to their need? Will the boiled cabbage of a classless society taste palatable to one so recently surfeited with caviar and vodka? Men since the dawn of history have been power grabbers, and only when the potency of God's grace overtakes the heart has there been a stepping down from this power — as when the Apostle Paul gave up his pursuit of the Christians at conversion. Is it *thinkable,* therefore, that subsequent to the revolution of the working classes and the dictatorship of the proletariat, that brutal, criminally-minded men will on their own steam suddenly convert into altruistic, docile spirits? What place can *materialism* give to the grace of God?

The incredibleness mounts.   Marx knows that power can be unsaddled only by the deliberate exertion of counter-pressures, and here he is realistic and persuasive. If cynical means are not employed, justice *is* advanced through the forceful shifting of centers of power. This is common knowledge in any society. But how can Marx persuade us that the power employed in world revolution will itself vanish away? Who will unseat the proletariat once they have enjoyed power? Minority groups have always become intolerable when in the saddle of power. Will it be necessary to murder the leaders? That may eliminate one batch, but who will then murder the murderer? *Ad infinitum.* Hegel's philosophy was informed by the immanent movement of the absolute. Marx exchanged this cosmic agency for the greedy, plotting competition of social units in conflict. Arthur Koestler, who found that the god of communism failed, is unequivocal in his description of the party's present ruthlessness.

> The only dialectically correct attitude was to remain inside, shut your mouth tight, swallow your bile and wait for

the day when, after the defeat of the enemy and the victory of World Revolution, Russia and the Comintern were ready to become democratic institutions. Then and only then would the leaders be called to account for their actions: the avoidable defeats, the wanton sacrifices, the mud-stream of slander and denunciation, in which the pick of our comrades had perished. Until that day you had to play the game — confirm and deny, denounce and recant, eat your words and lick your vomit; it was the price you had to pay for being allowed to continue feeling useful, and thus keep your perverted self-respect.[18]

If the communistic leaders are so intoxicated with their power today that criticism of the slightest kind "becomes deviationist sabotage,"[19] what shall make them lamb-like little guardians tomorrow? The answer is self-evident.

Surely the *possibility* (if not the actuality) of the non-attainment of the classless society is established. Let us proceed from there. The actuality of the classless society is always in the future, always just around the corner. No matter how near one comes to realizing it, it always recedes just enough to remain out of reach. Frustration and exhaustion are the only conceivable ends to such an arrangement. In greyhound races a small mechanical rabbit is kept moving just ahead of the dog, likewise just out of its reach. Through this expedient the energies of the dog are drawn out maximally. Always thinking that he is just about to warm his stomach with nice tender rabbit meat, the hound leaps and leaps. But it must be observed that this little trick works only by means of an illusion. The canine has to be tricked into action. The operators of the rabbit realize that since there is a limit to the dog's energies, a law of diminishing return sets in the moment they tax the dog beyond a fixed point. When the hound senses that the laps he must run are infinite in number, while the distance separating his chops from the rabbit remains the same, it takes no more than a canine's intelligence to conclude that

18. Richard Crossman (Ed.), *The God that Failed,* (New York: Harper & Brothers, 1949), p. 65-66.
19. *Ibid.,* p. 50.

further striving is futile. The same principle holds in the case of the classless society: Since truth *is* the material process, and since one has truth only as the process flows, one will remain forever frustrated within the communistic ideal. The classless-society rabbit can be sustained only through an illusion. But freedom will catch up to this deception, if given opportunity. And then woe to the involved self as the free self charges back with vengeance!

In an active club such as communism there is no place for senility. When a person is no longer able to make an active contribution to the party, he is eliminated. Party efficiency requires that. The beauty of this, however, is that the person is not given time to brood away in exhaustion. He is murdered before that fate sets in.

The conclusion is clear: Communism is an immediacy. Whether the ideal is or is not reached, the individual has happiness within the party only while he is able to take an active part. No deposits of satisfaction are laid on the spirit which will satisfy it when the energies of the flesh fail. What else could be expected from a *materialistic* philosophy? From a one-dimensional pot one cannot withdraw satisfactions for a creature whose freedom and involvement pitch him on two dimensions.

IV. The Problem of Confidence

Since communism denies that there is a world of truth by which history is interpreted and to which it is finally responsible, it follows that truth is made in the course of process itself. But because the process is controlled by the most active individuals, truth is made and destroyed as often as there is a shift in the centers of power in control. Whatever the ruler prefers, that becomes the truth.

A. *Why Trust Communism?*

Assuming for the sake of argument that communism has already gained control over historical process, it (presumably) follows that whatever it teaches *ipso facto* is the truth. Complications ensue! The promises of communism may sound soothing and alluring, especially to a member of a fringe or minority social class which suffers from injustice. But how can one be sure that these promises mean what they say? What test is there to learn whether or not communism is using words meaningfully? It is important that this be settled, for the promise of a classless society *may* actually mean the promise of a long vacation in the Siberian salt mines — without pay. And the place to settle this matter is on this side of the salt mines, for one becomes a bond servant after he renounces his rights in favor of party truth. From that point on he *cannot* ask the question.

We conventionally test internal consistency by an application of the laws of logic. The insane are distinguished from the normal, the wise from the average, by their degrees of consistency. But Marxism exempts itself from obedience to Aristotelian logic.

> For communist doctrine and communist practice, truth, as merely another weapon in the class struggle, becomes a political tool. The Party can (as it has) declare the theory of relativity or the Mendelian laws of heredity false, because 'counter-revolutionary,' as readily as it doctors statistics or rewrites history or invents a new childhood for Stalin. What communists call 'mechanical logic' — that is, the rules of objective inference and proof, the rules that permit us to test for truth and falsity — is replaced by 'dialectical logic.' The law of dialectical logic is simply that whatever serves the interests of communistic power is true.[20]

The communist is satisfied with the proposition that *his* might makes the right. Neither truth nor morality has any independent rights apart from what the party designs that it shall signify.

The law of contradiction asserts that a thing cannot mean A and non-A at the same time and in the same sense. This is such an ultimate law that there is no meaning to any term

20. James Burnham, *The Struggle for the World.* (New York: John Day Company, 1947), pp. 128-129.

which does not comply with it. If a term means both itself and not itself at the same time and in the same sense, it means nothing at all.

> The word *lamp* must signify a single thing both in the real world and in consciousness. If it signify a definite number of things, such as a piece of furniture, an ornament, and a paper weight, a special name may be given to each signification so that each name would signify one thing. But, if the significations be infinite, as those who deny this axiom must hold, then this lamp is also *not-lamp,* and, since it is not a lamp, it is both a calendar and not a calendar, as well as a book and not a book. That is to say, since the word *lamp* designates nothing . . . speech and philosophy have become impossible. The result is that all judgments become purely subjective and man is the measure of all things.[21]

Since the communist jettisons respect for the law of contradiction (for truth is *made* by historical conflict — it does not stand *over* history), he cannot expect one to pay attention to what he says. And the more he claims the truth, the more laughter should mount; since every word may signify not only A and non-A, but also an infinite number of other things. The communist cannot mean what he says until the law of contradiction first means what it says.

No proposition in communism may be trusted. The statement, "The classless society is being fought for," may mean, "The classless society is *not* being fought for." The assurance that communism is seeking universal justice may be but a cover for its seeking of universal *injustice.* In short, since the communist himself refuses to respect truth, and since his words may mean anything, one can not (and *ought* not) respect either the communist or his words.

Postwar negotiations with communism have broken down almost completely because the communist is able to assert nine or ten contradictions before lunch. Because the Western allies

---

21. Martin, *et al., A History of Philosophy,* (New York: Crofts, 1941), pp. 166-167.

thought that communism was subject to international codes of justice and morals, they tried to deal with it as with other collective egos. But negotiations have suffered violence by the refusal of communism either to say what it means or mean what it says. Moral integrity is the precondition for all successful arbitration. But communism disavows this.

The heart will not budge. There is too much at stake for blind commitment. If a wise man will not invest his money in a banking house which does not mean what it promises, how much less will he invest his soul in a system which heralds from the chimneys that it is exempt from telling the truth. Let communism preach! Let invitations follow invitations! One can only sit back and fold his arms and laugh — laugh loudly. Here are the elements of perfect humor: A system which announces in its invocation (the prayer is just a device to get heads to bow so that a monitor can count how many are present at the meeting) that it reserves the right to speak untruths without notice, and then proceeds with tearful overtures to persuade people of the system's *truthful* answers to the problems of life. It is a joke. Let laughter peal! And as communism vows a thousand oaths that it is telling the truth and nothing but the truth, let laughter increase! For the more communism continues to talk, the more sentences we have to write down which may not signify what they say. The oath is sworn — but the party may mean something else when taking it. Covenants are solemnly cut — but all fingers are crossed during the ceremony. Who has not heard of the story of the Briton who told the communist that not to say what you mean is lying? The communist responded by calling Moscow. As the incident was told to Uncle Joe, Stalin began to laugh. And before long all Russia was laughing. How perfectly humorous to believe that not meaning what you say is a lie! How can there be any lies, when what the party says is true because it says it? Truth has no independent existence. (Bridgman, take note: *Here* is operationalism par excellence!)

B. *Why Trust Communists?*

When the laughter subsides and one listens once again to the long sermon being preached by the party member, he now begins to wonder if those who rule the party are even human beings at all. If the system they are preaching is true, and if they themselves live by the system, Jekyll and Hyde have a lot to learn about robe-changing. Why, one part of the communist's life is spent in the role of pure demonism, while the next resembles that of an angelic being clad in haloed garments of radiant white. Cynical means are employed until the end of the proletariat's dictatorship. But in a flash all costumes are changed and out from the wings moves a slow procession of sweet, loving leaders who altruistically give their power up for the sake of their promises. History has had no parallel to this!

The existing individual has no difficulty sympathizing with the drift toward evil in communism, for he has a night-and-day struggle against demonic powers himself. The easiest course of resistance for one is to be proud, egoistic, and thoughtless of others. It is only the disciplined man who prefers the welfare of others to his own.

But what is difficult to believe is the easy, angelic side of the communist. The self cannot imagine *any* human being turning swiftly from a hardened life of violence to a peaceful life of charity and thoughtfulness. There is only one power which can convert a pretentious to a selfless ego, and that is a moral suasion which speaks to and against that ego in judgment. It is when eternity breaks into time to judge it. But *ex hypothesi* this condition can never be met in communism. The communist has no fear of ever having to repent; the dialectic protects him from that. Truth is made *through* his activity; it never exists above it to judge it. The central committee of the party *is* its own standard of truth. Committee members need give an account to none but themselves — and they are *always* well-pleasing unto themselves! Those who follow blindly can have their expectations postponed indefinitely through the very simple device of being told that conditions have not been reached for the end of world revolution and the beginning of world justice. Furthermore, the party leaders can easily persuade themselves (and all others by their power) that the relinquishing of their power would be bad for the party. Therefore, power must remain. Even in the classless society, there must be a ruling caste to enforce the Marxist rule — then watch for volunteers!

In short, there will *never* come a time in communism when the ego will be shattered through a moral conversion. Since truth is made through the materialistic process itself, and since power-intoxicated individuals control the direction in which this process flows, it is inevitable that both history's direction and the individual's pleasure will work together. It is always within the power of the Comintern to break some link in the dialectical chain, thus deliberately postponing the day when the party leaders must forfeit their power. They can piously repeat their *intentions* to abide by previously made promises, since they are not bound by their own word in the matter anyway. Their language is not responsible to any normative truth. In addition, they can continue to act in a manner unbecoming to men sincerely interested in the spread of justice— plundering the offices of comrades and abusing their privileges on every hand — and yet be responsible to none for their actions; for what they do is right because they do it.

And yet the sermon continues. The communist on the soapbox preaches passionately that all the forms of violence and sabotage which he sanctions are actually only a very temporary expedient; and that down deep inside him — behind the lying and beneath the cheating — is a very decent man who does not really lust after power at all. He assures his hearers that he is as sorry as anybody else that whole groups of people have been liquidated because they resisted some trivial whim of the party will. Hand-over-heart he pledges that all this is done purely for the sake of the proletariat, whose interests he deeply is committed to.

This whole arrangement is so peculiar, so incongruous, that one wonders what kind of a creature it is that speaks to him. How can vicious means bring non-vicious ends? "Dictatorship rests on a sea of blood, an ocean of tears, and a world of suffering — the results of its cruel means. How then can it bring joy or freedom or inner or outer peace? How can fear, force, lies, and misery make a better man?"[22] When people in ordinary social relations say and do peculiar things, we summon the proper authorities and have them committed to an institution. But what can be more suggestive of hereditary idiocy than the speech and deeds of the communist? If one were to take him seriously in what he says, one could only conclude that he is stark, raving mad. No human being could believe such contradictory things and be in his right mind. And if this communist is given to such unbalanced equations *before* I join the party (I should expect him to be on his best manners when he gives out the invitation), what might he do to me *after* I sign on the dotted line? *Let's run, rather than join!*

V. Beware of the Fine Print

In taking out any form of insurance, it is always prudential to examine the paragraphs of fine print. They are often minor only in size, not importance. The same principle applies on insurance for the soul — only more so, because more is at stake.

The confessional document, *The God that Failed,* is singularly significant. It is written by six men who believed they saw in communism a new hope for struggling humanity, but who in their enthusiasm to bring about this better world failed to read the fine print in the contract they signed. This book was written as a confession of this error. One and all learned through bitter experience what it is like to think that the soul is covered by insurance, when actually it is not. One commentator has called the volume "the dreadful *Canterbury Tales* of the twentieth century." In all six confessions there threads

---

22. Crossman (Ed.), *op. cit.,* p. 225.

the mutually shared disappointment: Since communism respects neither the individual nor the moral code upon which human decency is founded, none of the pledges or promises of the system can have any meaning. In short, the fine print in the minor paragraph is so exhaustive in the exceptions of coverage that are listed, that the policy itself is worse than useless.

A. The "Simple" Condition

It is perfectly apparent that one of the conditions one must meet in joining the party is that he sign away — now and forever — his own personal rights. Security is possible in a totalitarian framework only when party members give implicit obedience to every decree and order which filters down through official channels. Arthur Koestler describes the practical way this condition works out:

> To come back to life in the cell. The meetings, as I have said, started with one, sometimes two, political lectures which laid down the line. This was followed by discussion, but discussion of a peculiar kind. It is a basic rule of Communistic discipline that, once the Party has decided to adopt a certain line regarding a given problem, all criticism of that decision becomes deviationist sabotage. In theory, discussion is permissible prior to the decision. But as all decisions are imposed from above, out of the blue, without consulting any representative body of the rank and file, the latter is deprived of any influence on policy and even of the chance of expressing an opinion on it; while at the same time the leadership is deprived of the means of guaging the mood of the masses. One of the slogans of the German Party said: 'The front-line is no place for discussions.' Another said: 'Wherever a Communist happens to be, he is always in the front-line.'[23]

This *seems* like a fair bargain: In exchange for surrendering all your rights, you receive the sweet peace of knowing that you stand on the side of the only hope for humanity. You are certain you will lose your rights under capitalism anyway, so what is lost?

---

23. Crossman (Ed.), *op. cit.*, p. 50.

The print is small — very small — but it is there, nonetheless. The promises and pledges, the glories and the gains, are all printed in bold type; while in a type hardly to be noticed is the very insignificant condition that to gain these promises, one must play the role of Faust and sell his soul to the Mephistophelean communistic hierarchy. The ends to be achieved in communism are so high and exalted that one should blush even to think of placing such trivialities as truth, goodness, and beauty in competition with them. One should be ashamed for even thinking that the infinite worth of each individual may be balanced against the social triumph of the proletariat over greedy capitalists. Since the *party* defines the good, each individual must be prepared at a moment's notice to become a sacrifice hit for the good of the whole. The individual must learn to subordinate himself beneath party wishes. His consolation is that his warm blood will become the seed of communism.

All of this talk is superficially ennobling — but no more than superficially. Essentially, it is pathetic. There is nothing clearer to the existing individual than the foolishness of any arrangement, however promising it may sound, which lists the loss of the individual himself as one of the conditions to be met. It would be perfectly foolish to become a communist, and foolish in the strictest sense of the word. There may be injustices and corruption in non-communistic alternatives; but however bad off one may be under these circumstances, he will be worse off when he is officially made a means to an end. He thinks he is gaining security in the communist bargain, but the farce is that he will never be around to enjoy it. And when the self is gone, what possible difference does anything else make? *No* proposition is tempting if as part of its conditions the man himself is destroyed. Communism is fundamentally and basically a lie. It promises to bring the self into security, but in order to do so it must first wrench life out of the individual himself. This is poor barter. *Any* alternative is better than having the self destroyed. *No* end is valid if the cost in achieving it is the disregard of human values. What is anything worth if it lies outside the human reference?

"For what will it profit a man, if he gains the whole world and forfeits his life? Or what shall a man give in return for his life?" (Matthew 16:26) Let the communist rise and answer *these* questions.

Disgust and disappointment mingle quietly together when the individual is piously told that it is a system of *materialism* he is being sacrificed for. Upon understanding this, the self instinctively feels that something very worth-while is being sacrificed for something very, very cheap. The dying man resists the idea that he is only an animal, as if the only difference between himself and the pork he eats is sentimentality and convention. There is a dignity within him which cries out against identification with a one-dimensional view of reality. Man is made for eternity, and he can not be exhausted within the immediacies of time and space.

Men may be martyrs for a number of things in life. Some die in war, while others go to the cross for religious convictions. But here is a martyrdom which is perfectly foolish: That a spiritually endowed individual should sacrifice himself for a materialistic system. Shall the greater be destroyed to establish the lesser? The communist ideology is not exciting because it is axiologically repulsive. It does not respect the law of self-preservation within the individual. When one is called upon to render his own securities subordinate to those of the party, he is asked to betray himself. The "party" happens to be just a collection of greedy, self-seeking individuals. However high and noble the values of the party may be, and however loudly the central committee of the party may preach, therefore, the rational self remains unpersuaded and uncommitted. No option can increase our values which first destroys us as individuals. A rational man may be *forced* to act contrary to his own well-being, but he will not do so voluntarily.

The shock and depression experienced by those who penned *The God that Failed* illustrates the recoil of "Men without faces." They found through their own experience how perfectly meaningless it is to gain a world of promises and lose their own souls doing it. When Koestler came to himself, *e. g.*, he discovered that during the seven years he was serving the party he had actually been sleeping with the ugly Leah, when all the while he thought he was with the beautiful Rachel. Silone could hardly believe that men could sink to such depths. "I asked myself: Have we sunk to this? Those who are dead, those who are dying in prison, have sacrificed themselves for this? The vagabond, lonely, perilous lives that we ourselves are leading, strangers in our own countries · — is it all for this? My depression soon reached that extreme stage when the will is paralyzed and physical resistance suddenly gives way."[24] In his study of the social experiment in the Soviet Union, André Gide personally studied communism's fantastic leveling off of individuality, its shocking uniformity which destroyed all initiative, all art.

> What is demanded is approbation of everything done by the government. The slightest opposition and the merest criticism exposes its agent to the severest penalties and is, moreover, instantly suppressed. From top to bottom of the reformed social ladder, those with the best references are the most servile, and those who stand out independently are mown down or deported. Soon, in that heroic race which has deserved so well of our love and admiration, there will be left only the profiteers, the executioners and the victims. The small, independent worker has become a hunted animal, starved, broken and finally eliminated. I doubt whether in any country in the world — not even in Hitler's Germany — have the mind and spirit ever been less free, more bent, more terrorized over — and indeed vassalized — than in the Soviet Union.[25]

B. *Counting the Cost*

If regret is an inward proof that a man has acted foolishly, it behooves a rational person to exercise great care when he is

---

24. Crossman (Ed.), *op. cit.*, p. 111.
25. *Ibid.*, p. 188.

approached with overtures to become a communist; lest in his anxiety to foster what appears to be a new hope for humanity he actually casts his lot behind civilizaton's destruction.

It is not enough to be enraptured by the plausibilities of communism. Even if one is ensnared in injustices as part of a minority racial segment, let him retain his balance when acting. Let him not suppose that his initial infatuations in being recognized by a collective ego will support him when a conflict arises between this ego and his own. Let him read the testimony of Richard Wright to learn of his struggle to find shelter within the ranks of the party, *e. g.* Since he wanted to be a writer, the communist local threw its hands out to him in welcome, assuring him that it was just for such neglected and exploited people that the party existed. But step by step Wright descended into the throes of despair. The suspicions, bitterness, and even lunacy within the party meetings became intolerable. Finally, he was physically ejected from the line of march in the 1936 May Day parade.

> I headed toward home alone, really alone now, telling myself that in all the sprawling immensity of our mighty continent the least-known factor of living was the human heart, the least-sought goal of being was a way to live a human life. Perhaps, I thought, out of my tortured feelings I could fling a spark into this darkness. I would try, not because I wanted to, but because I felt that I had to if I were to live at all.[26]

Man *has* freedom. Let him use it! Let him learn *before* commitment what is involved in that commitment.

Let not the disappointed, seething masses which crowd around the labor temples in our great cities suppose that contentment will result the instant they cast their lot with a movement which pretends to espouse their cause. The cost *must* be counted, for man must continue to live with himself. Let the worker remember what Gide found when he studied com-

---

26. Crossman (Ed.), *op. cit.*, p. 162.

munist's finest flower within Russia itself, the very proving
ground for the ideology.

> The disappearance of capitalism has not brought freedom
> to the Soviet workers —– it is essential that the proletariat
> abroad should realize this fully. It is of course true that
> they are no longer exploited by shareholding capitalists,
> but nevertheless they are exploited, and in so devious, subtle
> and twisted a manner that they do not know any more whom
> to blame. The largest number of them live below the pov-
> erty line, and it is their starvation wages which permit
> the swollen pay-packets of the privileged workers — the
> pliant yes-men. . . . Granted that there are no longer any
> classes nor class distinctions in the Soviet Union; but the
> poor are still with them — and there are far too many of
> them. I had hoped to find none — or more exactly, it was
> precisely in order to find none that I went to the Soviet
> Union.[27]

It is no accident that the communist program always winds up
as a disappointment for thinking men. The free and involved
selves happen to be bound together by values which outrun
material conditions. The self knows that truth is *not* arbitrarily formed by an alteration of material processes. No material dialectic could ever generate the normative relation, "A
is not non-A." If the criteria of truth were not independent
of the program of communism, one could not meaningfully
ask about the truth of this or any other option. Likewise,
goodness is changeless. We know by nature the glory of the
courageous, the just, and the noble. By no dialectic can we
create the existence of normative goodness. As Plato long ago
asked, what is the worth of anything if we have not already
the good as our solid possession? Thus, what value is communism if it is not *good?* The system must be tested by a
standard it did not create.

If the fountain is corrupt, can the waters be sweet? Communism disavows the time-tested conviction of rational men
that there are *rationes aeternae* by which the free actions of
men are both guided and judged. Claiming exemption from

---

27. Crossman (Ed.), *op. cit.*, p. 183.

the normative standards of truth, goodness, and beauty, communism puts in their place criteria of its own. And the net result is that the party operates under one set of standards, while the heart functions by the light of another. What else could possibly result but conflict? "The false prophet preaches security to those who make their own inclinations the law of life and who thereby despise and defy God. *The prophecy is false because a life which defies the laws of life in order to gain security destroys what it is seeking to establish.*"[28]

The worker seeks both social justice and economic security; and he is justified in these pursuits. But it will hardly profit him to rush pell-mell to the first collective ego which vows its devotion to the preservation of these values. Philosophic roots must be examined to determine whether the system grows in soil which *ultimately* affirms or denies the primacy of such values. For example, the Declaration of Independence protects the rights of workers by its deep religious and metaphysical foundations. *"We hold these truths to be self-evident: That all men are created equal; that they are endowed by their Creator with certain inalienable rights; that among these are life, liberty, and the pursuit of happiness."* Here is a philosophy which affirms the equality of all men before law — the equality in rights and privileges of citizens of a common country; here we find a political statement grounded in the religious faith that the government shall protect all the citizens, showing favor to none because of birth or rank. This philosophy is based on an anthropology which assumes that man can be understood only in his reference to God. It is an anthropology grounded in a solid theology. It is Christianity. Being made in the image of God, man enjoys a natural dignity. The rights are "inalienable" because they may not be taken away from an individual without his consent; and to do so is to commit a criminal offense. Men are guaranteed freedom to dwell where they elect, to choose business relations freely, to worship God

---

28. Reinhold Niebuhr, *Beyond Tragedy*, (New York: Charles Scribner's Sons, 1937), p. 94. (Italics mine).

according to conscience, and to do whatever will increase their happiness — so long as the rights and equal liberties of others are not interfered with.

> Human relations are more than matters of expediency, sound psychology, or profitable business. They also are subject to moral and religious laws that are reflected in the conscience of mankind and which have been confirmed by the experience of men in all ages. If we accept the brotherhood of man under God, important conclusions follow. Each man has an inner dignity. with basic rights and duties. Life has an over-all purpose. Men must judge their conduct, not merely in terms of personal gain or convenience, but also as right or wrong. Service to society, and to personal interest, becomes important. Teamwork and cooperation follow. . . . The idea of man's basic worth is central to a free way of life for all.[29]

This matter must be carefully considered by the worker, for it is all involved in the wisdom of the initial choice. Marx must be watched in ultimate matters! He affirms that morality, religion, metaphysics, and all the rest of ideology and their corresponding forms of consciousness no longer retain the semblance of independence. It is easy to pretend that religion is but an opiate for the masses, but it becomes painful when an individual is caught in the outworking of such an irreligious philosophy of life. Without a philosophy which supports the value of individual worth, man is destroyed.

Like Esau, one trades his birthright for a mess of pottage when he forfeits his freedom for the illusory satisfaction of dialectical materialism. The pattern of communism is always a vicious orgy in the destruction of human souls. "At no time and in no country have more revolutionaries been killed and reduced to slavery than in Soviet Russia."[30] And this is not surprising. In fact, disposing of all who dare to think they are still individuals is really a good thing — provided that good-

---

29. *Human Relations in Modern Business,* (New York: Prentice-Hall, Inc., 1949), pp. 4-5.

30. Crossman (Ed.), *op. cit.,* p. 71.

ness be defined relatively as what the party wants, and not absolutely as in Christian philosophy and theology.

And so the bloody process continues! The communist has neither time nor interest to conciliate enemies, for he only knows one language: Crush all opposition.

> He must pretend that the opposition he is to crush is itself perverted, unnatural, and absurd, which in his heart he knows it is not; and he must persuade his own followers that the sacrifices they make are not made in order to increase his own power, but to bring about the goal which he, together with them, has in view. He must therefore create a state of continuous religious exaltation, for that is the only way in which one can persuade people to bear sacrifice cheerfully.[31]

An individual, who forfeits the dignities which make him a man, is guilty of self-destruction. He is a suicide. But sadly enough, in this venture of communism, he does not go to the gallows alone. He is involved in a program which by definition will leave the whole world in rubble.

> Communist ideology and communistic practice alike entail the destruction of these ideals of the supreme worth of the human person, of personal freedom and dignity. The subordination of the person to the collectivity, the state, the Party, the Revolution, the historic process becomes not merely an occasional necessity but a highest duty and a permanent norm; and not merely the subordination but the degradation of the individual. It is not carelessness but settled policy and integral ideal that toss away millions of lives to achieve quick agricultural collectivization, or rapid industrialization, that in a purge sweep ten million individuals into slave labor, that fight a war with oceans of blood substituted for machines and strategy, that uproot millions . . . from their homes and families, that pass laws holding families responsible for individual crimes, that in the interests of immediate political tactic turn the workers of Germany or Austria over to Nazism without a struggle. . . . The Moscow Show Trials revealed what has been true of the communist morality; that it is not merely the

31. Roger Lloyd, *Revolutionary Religion*, (London: Student Christian Movement Press, 1938), p. 124.

material possessions or the life of the individual which must be subordinated, but his reputation, his conscience, his honor, his dignity.   He must lie and grovel, cheat and inform, inform and betray, for communism, as well as die.   There is no restraint, no limit.   The slave must not merely obey but praise his master; and the master is himself crushed in his own chains.[32]

Marx and Engels are rather eloquent when they talk about chains. "Let the ruling classes tremble at a Communist revolution. The proletarians have nothing to lose but their chains. They have a world to win. Working men of all countries, unite!"[33]   But this eloquence is veiled in deception.   Its authors do not dare tell the working man that once he throws off the petty chain of social exploitation under capitalists, he will immediately be cuffed with the gross chains of disrespect, humiliation, and shame.   What weight have these iron links!

To one who himself for seven years found excuses for every stupidity and crime committed under the Marxist banner, the spectacle of these dialectical tightrope acts of self-deception, performed by men of good will and intelligence, is more disheartening than the barbarities committed by the simple in spirit.   Having experienced the almost unlimited possibilities of mental acrobatism on that tight-rope stretched across one's conscience, I know how much stretching it takes to make that elastic rope snap.[34]

There is no man quite as pitiable as the one who, having betrayed his own moral nature, tries to continue living as a man. The weight of the chain of social injustice is light compared to that back-bending load of ignominy and shame which results from having had faith in a *Weltanschauung* which destroys self-respect.

VI. But Why Such Power and Growth?

The case is not quite closed, however, for there are other factors which must be reckoned with if the *whole* man is to be

---

32. Burnham, *op. cit.*, pp. 127-128.
33. *Communist Manifesto,* (Chicago: Charles H. Kerr and Company, 1946), p. 60.
34. Crossman (Ed.), *op. cit.*, pp. 71-72.

satisfied. Coherence stands on the side of Christianity, but does *whole perspective* coherence? Sermons against communism are simply not stopping its growth. That is a recognized fact today. Furthermore, few within the party have apparently come to see the essential foolishness of their way of life. Communism may soon boast the attribute of catholicity, for it is found on almost every shore and in every clime. Why do men continue to flock to its fold for shelter? If the system is so unsatisfactory, why does it not disintegrate from internal weakness? Why do not communists immediately perceive that their god is doomed to failure? Arthur C. von Stein has deftly defined communism as "the opiate of the asses." But why do not more communists see asses when they look in the mirror?

The entire matter is wretchedly complex, for human motives are always compounded with personal interests. When a man wills something, he is already converted to the position; otherwise, why would he will it? It is not hard to state the *mechanics* of communism's stability. Every totalitarianism is constructed to eliminate internal combustion as far as possible. Being endowed with power beyond their rights, the flattered rulers enjoy holding their office, while those denied power are too deficient in rights to make complaint.

But this easy observation does not solve the cluster of remaining problems: Why does the heart feel a warm urge to join with communism, even after it has rehearsed the evils which necessarily attend that system? Why do men go against their reason and prefer a value which, though offensive to reason, commends itself to the will? What makes men with both financial means and friends of influence forfeit their own security to join the party? And once they are in the party, why are they so reluctant to leave? Is it simply communism's high moral end of universal justice? Or is there more? Analysis favors the latter.

A. *The Narcotic of Activism*

It is hard labor to think. This is especially true when the theoretical or abstract are in question. Hours of active thinking are hours of self-discipline. Few there be who think effectively, rising above the battle of the crowds. Our native preference is to act, not think. One has well said that if you make people *think* they think, they will love you; while if you make them think, they will not. Men persuade themselves of their worth by active pursuits. They serve on committees, pour tea, rush off to fires, hurry down to the club, review parades, and judge pies at the fair. Pride is accented very quickly through act, for the act is visible to all. The thinking man is often sent to drink his hemlock or bear his cross to Golgotha. The beauty of excessive activism is that the individual enjoys an inward peace without having to go through the hard labor of examining theory. By just keeping busy, men believe they are doing what is good.

Therefore, the heart flutters with joy when the day-and-night schedule of communism is cast before it; for communists are bidden to act, not think. Meditation is useful only as a catalytic agent to aggravate the tensions in history. The good communist, then, is the active communist. "The strength and vitality of Marxism-Leninism lie in the fact that it does base its practical activity on the needs of the development of the material life of society and never divorces itself from the real life of society."[35] This round-the-clock engagement in activity not only keeps men active, but it keeps them so active they have no chance to ask themselves whether *being* a communist is good or bad. It is against the Marxist stock company rules for an actor to inquire whether acting itself is worthy or unworthy. That was settled when one joined up for the show. The show must go on, for if the act stops, the tensions of history stop.

---

35. Stalin, *op. cit.*, p. 22.

B. *The Flood of Blessing*

Passion always magnifies evidences. The African witch doctor goes completely out of himself when the first random mist covers his face while he prays for rain — even though the mist may have been produced by non-prayer causes. His profound passion and inwardness atone for any deficiency in objective causal connections. In the same way, when the masses *expect* the Virgin to appear at an appointed hour, even the converging of evening shadows assumes this anticipated heavenly form. The combined science of the world cannot dislodge a faith which is based on will. Wanting to believe, verily men *will* believe.

Communism emerged at the close of World War II as a world power of great magnitude. Through a series of complex incidents — with an ineluctable fate as her ally — Russia came out of the conflict with a fist-full of aces for the game of postwar diplomacy. These successes have been interpreted by communists as an empirical proof of their world view. In addition, Marxist prophecies have started to come true. Socialistic movements have been instigated in even the major democracies; everywhere there is strife between worker and management; social revolution and unrest are world-wide in proportion; food and clothing are being distributed in an unjust and unbalanced way. These are not just tokens of blessings for communism — they are a veritable flood.

Enthusiastic in his faith that communism is the hope of humanity, the party member cannot but be enthralled over these fulfillments. The feeling in his heart must be comparable to Hitler's when he clicked his heels in joy as his *Wehrmacht* broke through to Paris. Success was guaranteed, for the evidences were too uniform to bear the weight of any other interpretation. Since the zealous communist magnifies the evidences far out of proportion, he cannot even entertain the thought that he *may* stand on the side of error and defeat. If all the logic in the world stood pitted against his commitment, his enthusiasm over the empirical successes would override it.

No one knows what tomorrow may bring. But if communist successes continue, one may presume in advance that it will become increasingly more difficult for blinded communists to see themselves in the true light. So thrilled will they be now that the party stands on the eve of world revolution, that it will be a practical impossibility for them to imagine the actual defeat and destruction of communism. Russia now controls an unbelievable percentage of the world's population.

This partially accounts for the reason why many find it easy to remain within the party. While disapproving of things perpetrated in the party's name, perhaps, they yet are wafted along by the belief that their cause will be vindicated by history. Men love to be in the company of those on the way to success. They want to be found in the inner circle of things, possessing the know-how. Note must be made of this.

C. *Egotistic Inflation*

Breathes there a man who has not dreamed of spending a weekend on a tropical island, free from all moral restraint and mores? Men fight a congenital urge toward the carefree and the irresponsible. Our struggle is to rise to high moral standards, for one need only release the hand brake and he flies down the grade.

One of the most powerful forces to help hold an individual within the bounds of decency is public opinion. Out of fear of what might happen to his social position, many a man has refrained from either fleshly indulgence or the wanton employment of power. Such restraint rests less on moral convictions than on a concern for what others would think if one yielded.

Communism dangles a most tasty bait before man's lust for freedom. It asks neither chastity, honesty, nor fair dealing from men as they carry on their social relations. The world belongs to the communist to use and to abuse. Communism asks one simple thing: Obedience to the party. When his pledge is made, one is free to employ whatever means are at his command to bring greater security to the party program. Who is not superficially tempted by this? Who cannot feel the tingle of drinking champagne out of fine-cut glasses? Who can miss the appeal to the ego that this abandonment of moral responsibility entails?

The first leap is easy. From then on, however, supporting forces come into play. *First,* there is an egotistic ecstasy in power-grabbing which overpowers moral resistance in the soul. The more power a man acquires, the more intoxicated he becomes to add further power. It is easy and natural to lord it over other people. And who will relinquish this prerogative once it falls into his lap? *Second,* there is a dear price which must be paid whenever a man *does* dare to inquire whether he is but an animal without ultimate responsibility. This price is *repentance.* To admit that one is sorry for an act is one of the most difficult postures for anyone to take.

When it is asked why more communists do not quit the party and own up to their foolishness, therefore, one answer is found in the question: Who wants to repent? Repentance has a strait and narrow way as its approach, and few there be who find it. There probably are multitudes of party members who would break if they had enough personal integrity and fortitude. They are weary of defending lying and cheating; they are weary of trying to persuade themselves they are only animals. But out of a fear of what it might mean to recant, they continue their half-hearted endorsement.

D. *Reprisal*

Withdrawing from any totalitarian organization is never easy. And it is especially difficult in communism, for the arms of its own Gestapo reach out into every port. A well-disciplined corps of spies keep constant vigil over every interest of the party. Party members are constantly watched, checked, and screened, for the least sign of vacillation is tantamount to party infidelity. A suspected individual must immediately be disposed of, lest his indecision become contagious. The individual party member is but a piece of goods: He can be ripped out of the garment at the will of his superior. One cannot withdraw from communistic commitments simply by passing in a slip of paper to the chairman, announcing his personal feelings, therefore. Faust cannot avoid the terms of his bargain that easily.

> The workers are cheated, muzzled and bound hand and foot, so that resistance has become well-nigh impossible. The game has been well played by Stalin, and Communists the world over applaud him, believing that in the Soviet Union at least they have gained a glorious victory, and they call all those who do not agree with them public enemies and traitors. But in Russia this has led to treachery of a new sort. An excellent way of earning promotion is to become an informer, that puts you on good terms with the dangerous police which protect you while using you. Once you have started on that easy, slippery slope, no question of friendship or loyalty can intervene to hold you back; on every occasion you are forced to advance, sliding further into the abyss of shame. The result is that everyone is suspicious of everyone else and the most innocent remarks — even of children — can bring destruction, so that everyone is on his guard and no one lets himself go.[36]

The problem of coming to oneself and leaving the party for greener pastures is never a simple situation which one can manage through self-resolution. The brandished sword of reprisal is kept dangling over one's head at all times, and only the slender thread of absolute party obedience can keep it from crushing its victim. If perchance one may be fortunate enough to escape with his own life, he then exposes his own friends and families to the ruthless reprisal machinery of the party. Blackmail is employed; hostages are taken and tortured; business affairs are dynamited and dissipated; boycotts are instituted. When one perceives what his own actions may bring upon others, he often prefers to drop out of sight and perish

---

36. Crossman (Ed.), *op. cit.*, p. 185.

quietly in Siberian exile. Thus, communism has built an iron curtain about the heart, a curtain of fear to break from initial pledges in favor of another option. Who can understand what it may mean to have the threat of death over his family if he fails in his party work — who save the man who now is passing through it? For the sake of the love of his family he goes against what his own moral nature decrees is best for himself.

When a person in the comfort of his own home asks the question why more communists do not recant, therefore, he ought not to phrase his query in too cavalier a way. Recantation may bring death both to the man himself and endless misery to those he leaves behind. The decision is easy only to those who are never called upon to make it.

E. *Involuntary Blindness*

We can believe only as we see. But since the communist is not allowed to see very much, how can he believe much? An iron curtain has so effectively hedged in the communist culture pattern that those who are caught in its valley have little or no idea of the true state of yonder mountain. Radio waves are jammed, the press is controlled, speech is restricted, and blockades of every type are set up. The party member is allowed to see and believe only what has been officially screened through the hierarchy. The result of this barrage of propaganda — a propaganda directed year in and year out with the express end of blunting critical judgment — is an incredible blinding of the mind. From the earliest days in school to the end of his conscious life the communist is regimented, told what to believe, warned of deviation. He lives as a prefabricated soul.

How simple it is to inquire about communists leaving the party. Yet, how difficult it is for them actually to do so!

F. *Lure of Novelty*

If one will analyze the science of advertising, he will discover that one of the most effective baits to induce purchasing is to arouse an individual's lust for *savoir faire*. We are bade to ac-

cept the newest, the latest, the most recent. It is chic and
learned to be found owning the fashionable, the thing-of-the-
month. Ladies will by-pass a whole counter of items, purchasing nothing; while they will claw each other on learning that
there are only "ten left — and when these are gone there will
be no more." University students resist devotion to tradition,
preferring membership in the newest campus movement and
carrying under each arm a volume on the latest form of infidelity. The recent is sanguine and challenging. There is
something self-validating about the latest. If it were not a
fresh solution to an old problem, why was it undertaken?

When judged in terms of the centuries, communism is a
novel world view. Its maiden voyage is now being enjoyed.
Therefore, it is understandable why the one who throws his
weight behind the party ideals enjoys a measure of thrill and
prestige. He believes he rides on the crest of the moving
front of history. The great German youth demonstrations
along Berlin's *Unter den Linden* in the communist-inspired
Whitsuntide rallies illustrate this. As the brigade cries
"friendship-friendship," its uniformed participants have their
egos inflated. Is it not thrilling to think one is on the side
of the reforming party?

In short, there *are* reasons why it is plausible to turn to
communism. Because it combines an appeal to our native
urges for pride and power with the noble ideals of economic
relief for the wretched and a classless society for all, communism is alluring. But for this very reason one must use
great caution before joining, for the caricature of life may be
an embodiment of death; *and in this case, it is.*

Summary

When one's economic equilibrium is upset, an anxiety
results; and if this anxiety is not checked by a higher good
it can drive a man to that desperation where he is tempted
to sell his own free rights. But what is overlooked is that
one cannot remain content within immediacy. The universal
testimony of people *not* socially or economically discontented

is that boredom goes right along with their station and place. Rancor and bitterness, if not suicide, plague the wealthy. Their disappointment in not finding contentment within economic security is a patent proof that the highest (and best) in man is yet unaccented. Most people who are surfeited with material things are miserable in their heart. They forget that "the eye is not satisfied with seeing, nor the ear filled with hearing." (Ecclesiastes 1:8) A person with eternal potentialities can never finally be satisfied with immediate material possessions.

Communism opens wide its arms to solve the problem of injustice, but it does it at the cost of rejecting the very spiritual and moral vitalities by which alone all decency is preserved. This makes a Judas Iscariot of a communist. He prefers the bag instead of honesty, righteousness, justice, and love. He demands economic and social security at such a cost that in the end he is willing to betray his own friends for the sake of a few shekels. But when he comes to himself, frustrated over trying to unite spiritual freedom with material coins, the free self charges on the involved self; and the hangman's noose is the only way out. Marx has betrayed the normative rules of morality and justice with the sweet kiss of dialectical materialism. Under one arm he carries the bag, while under the other he carries a hangman's noose.

Western culture is founded on the faith that there is an archetypical world of truth, goodness, and beauty which stands over history as its changeless norm. Plato called it the world of Ideas; Christianity calls it the mind of God. The just and the right are *exemplified*, not made, by the tensions of history. Antigone appealed to the laws written in the stars, and thus was a heroine for the Hellenes against the might of Creon. The issue remains unchanged since that time: Are the laws of our nature written in the stars, or do we make these laws within the relativities of history?

The lesson taught by this type of experience, when put into words, always appears under the dowdy guise of perennial common-places: that man is a reality, mankind an abstraction; that men cannot be treated as units in operations of political arithmetic because they behave like the symbols for zero and the infinite, which dislocate all mathematical operations; that the end justifies the means only within very narrow limits; that ethics is not a function of social utility, and charity not a petty-bourgeois sentiment but the gravitational force which keeps civilization in its orbit.[37]

---

37. Crossman (Ed.), *op. cit.*, p. 68. Let not the Christian mind weep and wail over its bloody conflict with communism, however, for the shame of having rejected the cause of the common man has long hung heavy over the Christian community. More often too interested in defending his own vested estates than in espousing the cause of the exploited, the Christian may yet be sent a plague of locusts to devour his fields of standing grain. When those who know not the true God assume the responsibility of defending the rights of the working man, they only heap judgment upon the Christian. Communism may have destroyed the foundations of our culture in an effort to release the latent powers of the common man; and for this it will reap the wild wind. But it cannot be forgotten that the detonation is really being set off by those who defy the stubbornness and pride of the children of light. When social justice must be defended by those outside of the covenant, what shall be the judgment of the covenant sons?

Part III

THE HIGHER IMMEDIACIES

V

Suffering For a Method

THE Christian Scriptures recognize that because man is both free and involved, while at the same time remaining an integral self, epistemology is no simple science. Epistemology answers the question: How do we know? It seeks to discover how access can be had to the data of reality, and what criteria must be met before an acceptable correlation of them can be enjoyed. And the reason why epistemology cannot be stated simply is that the free and involved selves have access to environments appropriate to their own natures. Through the five senses the empirical self measures those configurations which comprise the world of extension; while through an innumerable host of internal senses (*nous*, conscience, intuition, etc.) the free self is exposed to those non-sensory, non-extended essences which form the world of non-extension. Whoever would truly be an epistemologist, therefore, must reckon with the fact of this double environment. The self would not understand the meaning of extended reality if it were not already in possession of data gained through a contact with non-extended reality; even as non-extended reality itself would be incomplete if it did not terminate upon data and relations found in the material world. This is not to repeat the Kantian epistemology of form and content, for a carefully constructed Christian epistemology goes beyond such a structure. Biblical epistemology turns on the presupposition that the understanding genuinely has knowledge, even though the content of its assertions is gained through internal experience. It is *not* true that form remains contentless until it receives its material from sensory impressions of extended reality. It happens that many of the best-known things (love,

131

sacrifice, justice, honesty, etc.) are immediately perceived by the free self's contact with normative reality.

> Rise, my soul, and stretch thy wings,
> Thy better portion trace.
> Rise from transitory things,
> Towards heaven, thy native place.

In Biblical terms, a man has adequately correlated the manifold data of reality only when his heart is satisfied that every aspect of the whole person is accented. The *heart* is a term used to cover the complex man: body, spirit, and whatever else forms the totality of human nature. A "heart response" is a "concerned response" — a deliberate interest to integrate the entire person with reality.

The tendency of man is to satisfy but one part of his essence only, neglecting the importance of data which the inner man learns. And one reason for this neglect is the intangibility of the mysterious environment of spirit. Its data are obviously less easily manageable than those of the external environment of extension. And yet unless these hidden data are acknowledged, the inner spirit is left without those satisfactions which alone give man his glory. The height of man is measured by freedom, and freedom passes beyond the material world.

Jesus Christ often attacked the foolishness of man's attempt either to explain or to satisfy himself solely as a rational being who is able to correlate the quantitatively measurable. But on no occasion did he more sharply express the distinction between qualitative and the quantitative data than when he contested the scientists of his own day. *Times* knowledge is heart knowledge; *sky* knowledge is scientific knowledge.

> And the Pharisees and Sadducees came, and to test him they asked him to show them a sign from heaven. He answered them, 'When it is evening, you say, "It will be fair weather; for the sky is red," and in the morning, "It will be stormy today, for the sky is red and threatening." You know how to interpret the face of the heaven, but you cannot interpret the signs of the times. An evil and adulterous

generation seeks for a sign, but no sign shall be given to it except the sign of Jonah.'[1]

Caution must be exercised here, however, lest an easy misunderstanding result. Neither here nor elsewhere did Christ *disparage* scientific knowledge, for he recognized that an accurate measurement of the heavens is as much a satisfaction to the mind as it is a pragmatic guide in the practical affairs of life. One can understand more about the control of nature if he first knows something about the heavens. Who does not appreciate the fact that red sky in the morning is the sailor's warning, while red sky at night is the sailor's delight?

What Jesus indicted, however, is the conversion of *sky* knowledge into *times* knowledge. Once this happens, *i. e.,* once man so formulates his epistemology that he excludes *ex hypothesi* the possibility of knowing and verifying relations which pass beyond the quantitatively measurable, he not only destroys the partial truth of science but he also converts man into a farcical and inexplicable creature. Sky knowledge can tell us things about the *sky*, but it cannot tell us things about the *times*. And yet the things which really count the most — life, liberty, and the pursuit of happiness — depend on data which pass beyond the scientific laboratory.

I. The Triumph of Sky Knowledge

A. The Revolt

A warfare between the empirical and the mystical-rational schools of thought has continually raged since the first wise men of Greece began to wonder about the basic meaning of the universe. On the one hand, Heraclitus threw his hat with empiricism. Believing that knowledge (if any) comes through the five senses, he concluded that *all* things are in motion. *Panta rei.* On the other hand, Parmenides was impressed by the primacy of the internal senses, being convinced that the five physical senses are our least trustworthy avenues of knowl-

---

1. Matthew 16:1-4.

edge. The true is the conceivable, not the experiential. His conclusion was that *nothing* is in motion. Being is being. In this epistemological strife Heraclitus espoused the *a posteriori* cause and Parmenides the *a priori*.

While few have been as thoroughgoing and consistent as these early Greeks, the actual warfare between the empirical and rational minds has remained quite the same. The smoke of battle rises all about us today. Those who come through an empirical training tend to see virtue only in the *quantitative*. They bask in the relative, the tentative, the changing. While those who prefer the witness of the *qualitative*, having proceeded to reality through logic and inward intuition, love the warmth of the normative, the eternal, the changeless. Devotees of the *a posteriori* aver that they see only *claims* to truth, goodness, and beauty; while followers of the *a priori* retort that if it were not for antecedent absolutes there would be no meaning to the relative. We know the relative in the light of the absolute.

Mystical-rational methodology has been fighting a war of attrition for so long, that at the present hour the *a posteriori* reigns incontestably supreme in many high places of learning. For example, a recent edition of the works of John Locke simply left out his refutation of innate ideas. Why waste paper? It is an accepted presupposition that man is a creature of only one environment.

The success story of empiricism is both fascinating and complex: The Renaissance mind is characterized by an undaunted faith in man's infinite creativity. If sufficient opportunity is combined with a proper proportion of resolution, there is no practical end to what can be accomplished; for freedom dictates that nothing short of a complete subduing of all reality be its goal. Each day dawns clear with new creative possibilities.

But the Renaissance spirit has always been withstood by forms and traditions defended in the hallowed and hoary name of a premature *a priori*. Even if one reads only the bold type in history, he will quickly perceive the tendency of *a priorism* to kill off free progress. A feudal-agrarian economy in social relations so handcuffed the medieval man that he could scarcely move. A perfect pyramid was erected. God ruled the pope; the pope ruled the emperor and the church; the church and the emperor ruled the land vassals; and the land vassals ruled the peasants. A *natural law* was appealed to as the grounds for this arrangement. The "order of creation" presumably dictated that there is a final social, economic, and political-theological pattern for man to abide by. The "mind of God" stands on its side. As a result, those who exploited did so in the name of a natural law. They were exempt from all criticism on the ground that their words were continuous with the mind of God. The natural law, thus, was an iron curtain of its own type. It protected the privileged from threats of revolution and criticism by being a veil over the eyes of the exploited.

With one mighty heave, however, the Renaissance mind pulled away the props which supported this unbalanced social structure. And buried in the rubble was a faith in the *a priori*. Whether or not these Samsons destroyed more than a premature finality, only investigation can tell. In any case, the labyrinthine maze of medieval superstitions and inhibitions *was* razed. Man knows too much about his own free possibilities to be convinced that *any* form of social or political life is a finality. Only absolute justice defines the outside front of freedom. The relative, therefore, is always subject to improvement.

As the *a posteriori* began to triumph, its ideals congealed in what we know currently as the scientific method. The beginning of this method was crude and untested. Yet, even in its inception it was stubbornly bucked by an entrenched *a priori*. Scholastic philosophers paid lip service to the *a posteriori*, but they then swiftly looked away from nature to logically conceived, *a priori* forms. From a quick glance at a quivering leaf the scholastics *demonstrated* the nature and essential attributes of God — the most pretentious intellectual venture in all ages. The medievals checked texts more often than they did nature. Since Aristotle had showed that circularity and eternality were consanguineous, *e. g.*, it at once was deductively necessary that all the planets wander in circles. This was purely an *a priori* assumption. Its perfect expression was found in the world plan of Dante. Combining the mathematics of Ptolemy and the philosophy of Aristotle, Dante produced an astronomical almanac for the medieval mind.

> The outcome was a series of twelve heavens, one within the other, revolving at slightly varying rates about the earth fixed in the center . . . . The orbits had to be circular, inasmuch as they were made by a perfect God and the circle is the most perfect of all figures . . . . At the center of this orderly universe lay the earth. Its size was approximately known, and its shape . . . . In the center of this land lay Jerusalem. Somewhere in the East lay the Garden of Eden, the scene of man's transgression. Dante located it at the antipodes of Jerusalem, but some favored the island of Ceylon, or some other remote island or mountain. Wherever it was, it was surrounded by a wall of fire, and at present inhabited only by Enoch and Elijah . . . . Somewhere beneath the earth was Hell. Dante gave it definite shape, and order: it was a huge funnel, with the tormented sinners ranged around its sides in circles appropriate to their sin. At the very tip, in the center of the entire universe, farthest removed from God in the Empyrean, lay Satan himself.[2]

Dante deductively concluded that since the world was in its last stages, the end of the drama of salvation was about to be enjoyed. Egged on by an instinctive urge to be free (an imperative which guided, but was not discovered by, science) men of prowess observed for themselves the nature of the world. It was no longer necessary that the *a priori* be refuted by counterbalancing logical arguments. After traveling around the world, men saw with their own eyes how others lived and died. They found no Garden of Eden, no weird creatures, no end of the earth beyond the horizon. Hence, some of the fallacies in the medieval *a priori* were flushed out by actual scientific discovery. With the accumulation of wealth the bourgeoisie were sufficiently retired from subser-

---

2. Randall, *The Making of the Modern Mind*, *pp.* 32-33.

vience to others to become self-conscious of their own individual dignity and of the infinite creativity of spirit. As self-
assurance displaced blind obedience and faith, the *a posteriori*
displaced the *a priori*. Science discovered that the curse of
all knowledge is the penchant within men to anticipate, rather
than be obedient to, nature. The *a priori* cannot define the
conditions of nature.

B. Booty

The instant the *a priori* became the handmaid of the *a
posteriori*, science burst forth into full glory. It was as the
opening of the red rose to greet the morning sun — with all
its fragrance, too. The privilege of giving *formal* order to
the data of nature was farmed out to mathematics and logic.
But the *content* of these data could be gained only through
facts received by the five senses. Kant gave a rather definitive statement of the controlling epistemology undergirding
the scientific method.

> We apply the term *sensibility* to the receptivity of the mind
> for impressions . . . we call the faculty of spontaneously
> producing representations, or the spontaneity of cognition,
> *understanding* . . . . Neither of these faculties has a preference
> over the other. Without the sensuous faculty no object
> would be given to us, and without the understanding no
> object would be thought. Thoughts without content are
> void; intuitions without conception, blind. Hence it is as
> necessary for the mind to make its conceptions sensuous
> (that is, to join to them the object in intuition), as to make
> its intuitions intelligible (that is to bring them under con-
> ceptions) . . . . In no other way than from the united opera-
> tion of both, can knowledge arise.[3]

Post-Kantians discovered a veritable nest of non-empirical
assumptions in their master — such as the *Ding an sich* and
the transcendental unities. All these had to go, for only what
can be scientifically verified is true. While Kant left the
light of the internal environment of man still flickering dimly,
thus, later empiricists poked it out completely. And the most

---

3. Kant, *Critique of Pure Reason*, (tr. Meiklejohn), B75-B76.

tough-minded thinker to emerge from the skirmish was the positivist. More and more was lopped off the prerogatives of the *a priori* until in the end the only purpose of philosophy was logical and linguistic analysis. Only strict science can break through to reality's structure. Philosophy simply has the task of clarifying terms and sentences.

The most consistent *a posteriori* philosophy is logical positivism, or scientific empiricism. Its assignment is to inquire into the limits and structure of meaningful discourse. Just as the scientist sets up an operation that he may gain valid experimental ends, so the philosopher constructs a logic of language to attain assurance of significant communication. Hitherto it had been assumed that philosophy enjoyed the right to arrange words together to form *a priori* propositions about reality — rushing in as fools where the angels of science fear to tread. According to the scientific empiricist, this attempt to pass from proposition to reality is but a spread-out version of the ontological argument, sort of a "verbal magic." The questions which were not raised by the *a priorists* were the most important: What is meaning? What is knowledge? How is knowledge possible? With his best eye on science, the logical positivist sought to correct looseness in philosophy by importing a few scientific virtues into his method. To be scientifically worthy, philosophy must be precise, objective, unambiguous. It must arrange its own method so that the factors it deals with can be quantitatively measured. The puzzle of philosophy can be solved only after we know the limitations of sentences. The following chart serves as a typical classification of meaning.[4]

Cognitive meanings (Informational function)	Non-cognitive meanings (Emotive expression and appeal function)
Purely formal	*Pictorial* (*Imaginative*)
Logical-arithmetical	*Emotional* (*Affective*)
Factual (=*Empirical*)	*Volitional-motivational* (*Directive*)

---

4. Runes (Ed.), *Twentieth Century Philosophy*, p. 379.

A glance at this chart will show that positivism has carried Kant's epistemology to its logical conclusion. Only factual propositions — those which science can process in the laboratory by an operational experiment — terminate on reality. The rest may involve either a wish or just plain imagination. Non-cognitive meanings perhaps have the pragmatic value of getting people to do things in their practical life or of giving them solace in poetry and religion, but they have no informational function. They leave the formal and quantitative for the biological and qualitative. While they sometimes express how we feel or how we wish things were, only factually meaningful propositions can suggest experimental operations. John Dewey describes the steps in this epistemology as follows: A felt difficulty in our experience; careful clarification of what the difficulty is; careful preparation of hypotheses to account for a solution; mental elaboration through definite if / then, cause-sequence relations; *and a final testing through actual observation or experiment.*

Feigl nicely sums up the positivist-pragmatic classification of all sentences and expressions:

(1) Logically true sentences, also called analytic sentences. (2) Logically false sentences, also called contradictions. These sentences are true or false, respectively, by virtue of their form. . . . (3) Factually true and (4) factually false sentences whose validity depends upon their correspondence to observed fact. In the majority of instances this correspondence or non-correspondence is only incompletely and indirectly indicated by whatever is immediately observable. Therefore these sentences are usually not *known* to be true or false but are considered to be confirmed or disconfirmed to an extent which may vary considerably with the accumulation of favorable or unfavorable evidence. (5) Emotive expressions without cognitive meaning and the emotive components of otherwise cognitive expressions. Pictorial, figurative, and metaphorical expressions, exclamations, interjections, words of praise or blame, appeals, suggestions, requests, imperatives, commands, questions, and prayers belong to this category.[5]

---

5. *Op. cit.,* pp. 383-384.

Propositions have the power of suggesting operations, but truth emerges only in the measurable, here-and-now difference which the actual operation or experiment makes. At best, sentences have only anticipated knowledge. Knowledge is terminated when a proposition leads to measurable, operational differences. If there is no observable result in the experiment, one can conclude that the original sentence itself is non-cognitive.

The formal sciences (mathematics and logic) define the conditions under which operations are meaningful, but they become cognitive only when they terminate on an operation. They are tools for the experimenter. Logic is operational in that it leads the experimenter safely into a meaningful statement of anticipated knowledge. Systems of mathematics operationally suggest new serial relations, which in turn call up potential experiments. There are theoretically as many kinds of logic and mathematics as the freedom of man has energy to create. Each system is instrumentally true to the extent that it operationally gets one where he wants to go.

Because science cannot pass from the descriptive to the normative, one cannot formulate informational propositions about either ethics or metaphysics. There is no scientific operation which follows from either an ethical or a metaphysical assertion. Hence, neither has *cognitive* significance. Ethical sentences may be studied along with wishes or exclamations, but they cannot claim factual truth.

> Ethical norms or imperatives . . . may be reconstructed as sentences referring to a possible (usually not actualized) state of affairs and expressed with an emotional-motivational appeal. In the use of such terms as 'ought,' 'should,' 'right,' 'good,' 'duty,' etc., lies the irreducibly directive component of moral value-judgments. An ethical imperative like the Golden Rule simply means: 'Would that everybody behaved toward his fellowmen as he expects them to behave toward him.' This sentence, having its accent in the emotive appeal, could not possibly be deduced from a knowledge of facts only; it is neither true nor false. It is rather an

invitation (suggestion, request, exhortation, or command) to *make* the contained factual sentence true.[6]

Hitherto it was supposed that one *could* proceed from logical or *a priori* premises to the necessary existence of absolute values; for man participates in a double environment. But the logical positivist denies cognitive sentences about absolutes. The "quest after certainty" is a search for the will-o'-the-wisp. "Absolute values as well as categorical imperatives can be expressed only in emotive language."[7] There is no test by which an absolute can operationally be managed. A domesticated value is a relative value — a value which can be manipulated in an actual experiment.

How then is the meaning of an ethical sentence measured? By the actual operational difference the sentence makes when tested by its effect on the needs and interests of man in concrete situations. A sentence which does make an operational difference is cognitive to the extent of that difference. Pragmatic truth is present only when perceptible differences can be measured. Truth does not exist *in vacuo*. If an hypothesis does not work, it is not true. As for metaphysical sentences — well, they are too hopelessly non-operational even to be discussed. One world at a time!

C. *New Bondage*

And so the swing of the pendulum has been completed. In classical philosophy the only sentence worth-while *was* the normative, while in modern scientific empiricism the normative is altogether disclaimed. Men once believed they could reach reality through data intuited by the inner light; positivism knows only the light of science. It was previously supposed that propositions were objectively true whether or not they could ever be carried out into concrete experience; positivism

---

6. *Op. cit.*, p. 402.
7. *Ibid.*, p. 403.

now scorns the notion as prescientific. No statement is factual which cannot terminate on an operation.[8]

A new species of slavery has emerged out of this revolt from the medieval *a priori*. It is a bondage to the *a posteriori*. While our diplomats are frantically searching for solid moral ground in the cold war with Russia, *e. g.* — knowing that unless it be normatively true (*independent of a scientific operation*) that destruction of the world by aggressive warfare is wrong, civilization is doomed — the positivist optimistically repeats the simple formula that there is nothing wrong with the world but a poor application of science. Simply by maturing to the meaning of the operation, men will destroy bigotry, hatred, and injustice. Such a blind optimism can be accounted for only by positing a new bondage.

The gap between the man on the street — the one who still feels the compulsion of imperatives as part of his own nature — and the scientific empiricist is immense. Logical positivism declares out-of-bounds the very absolutes which give life meaning. The vitalities which we hold dearest, values for which men at war are asked to die, are quietly removed from the category of factual propositions and shifted to the emotive. The absolutes which guide our daily life are scientifically worthless.

> There are two rival systems that must have their respective claims adjusted. The crisis in contemporary culture, the confusions and conflicts in it, arise from a division of authority. Scientific inquiry seems to tell one thing, and traditional beliefs about ends and ideals that have authority over conduct tell us something quite different. The problem of reconciliation arises and persists for one reason only. As long as the notions persist that knowledge is a disclosure of reality, of reality prior to and independent of knowing, and that knowing is independent of a purpose to control the quality of experienced objects, the failure of natural science to disclose significant values in its objects will come as a shock.[9]

---

8. This type of epistemology has elicited the well-known joke: Two positivists meet on the street. "You're fine," said the one. "How am I?"

9. John Dewey, *The Quest for Certainty*, (New York: Minton, Balch & Company, 1929), pp. 43-44.

But the bondage is somewhat plausible, for it is the valid conviction of the positivist that truth is only as secure as the method which establishes it. We may have inner moral convictions, witnesses of conscience, hunches, intuitions, and inexpungible feelings of the heart; we may have logical and metaphysical persuasions in abundance; *but if the propositions which describe them cannot meaningfully be classified, of what value are they?* What claim may they boast to truth?

Thus, the scientific empiricist suffers for a method. Since truth is only as valid as the method which establishes it, suffering for a method is higher than suffering for the truth. The resulting taxation on the positivist's spirit is immense. He must go against inner convictions and feelings; he must stand against the crowd, waving the securities of metaphysical and theological havens in favor of scything out a path through the forest of uncertainty. He is not only *willing* to hate father, mother, sister, brother, and children for the sake of a method; he has already done it. He *has* left tradition, the comfort of easy *a priori* correlations, and the prestige of selling packaged absolutes to a needy world. He is as hard-headed as James could ever wish a thinker to be. Could spirit find a more exhausting assignment than to stand vigil over the treasure chest of meaning itself? Does *anything* have meaning if we are unsure of the meaning of meaning?

D. *Degrees of Servitude*

Men are going to remain under bondage no matter what proportion of their convictions are drawn from *a priori* or *a posteriori* options, for we are the bond servants of whatever devotion we happen to serve. Therefore the issue is *which* bondage we shall elect. Is man at his best in the role of a scientific empiricist? Has positivism struck rock bottom in defining the outside potentialities of freedom? Is there anything wanting when the whole man commits himself wholly to the scientific method?

The decision can only rest on the calculus of probability, since the factors in the problem are immensely complex. But perhaps major clues can be found which will suggest with a measure of clarity which direction wisdom should take. In any case, one cannot postpone decision, for want of decision may put him outside of personal salvation.

II. Setting the Wedge

Since one is not a positivist already, but is rather being approached about becoming one, he must decide the issue by non-positivistic criteria. In this decision he cannot be expected to use the criteria which are at stake in the first place. All he can do is to employ his best judgment to see what is involved if he accepts or rejects positivism. In becoming a positivist — like building a tower or engaging an enemy in battle — one must first count the cost.

A. *Biography of a Positivist*

It is interesting to notice that those who themselves are now positivists did not employ the chart of positivism when turning to logical empiricism in the first place. They worked through the history of philosophy, weighed the problems involved in one type of verification as over against another, and then *decided* to be positivists. It was not written in the stars that they so decide, nor were they under the compulsion of an irresistible power. They chose because the values which the postivistic ideal offered appealed to them.

If this observation is valid, *prima facie* evidence has been established for the existence of a method of verification more primitive than that of the scientific ideal itself.

It is a plain fact of history that conversions to positivism (like conversions to everything else) are accomplished quite independently of the chart of meaning which scientific empiricism rests on. A mysterious point was reached when the potential positivist became inwardly satisfied with the form of epistemology detailed in the chart. And at that instant potentiality passed into actuality and the mystery of motion was again exemplified. The person craved a security in verification, and in scientific empiricism he found it. Therefore, he *chose* to become a positivist. The only compulsion for the choice was this urge for solid epistemological footing. There was neither metaphysical nor pathological force applied, for the potential positivist remained free and unrestrained while deliberating what position he should finally choose. He had the power to choose other than scientific empiricism. *Positivism* did not force the issue, for freedom has sovereignty over the method itself. The proof of this is the way one investigates other epistemologies before he throws his weight behind scientific empiricism.

People come to positivism in very different ways. Some enter its fold for quite worthy reasons; others for less worthy. Personal pride may decide the issue, or aesthetic considerations may control the decision. But the point is that, worthy or not, one *did* respect a non-positivistic epistemology when coming to positivism. How could one possibly employ the very criteria which were in question? If he employed them, he did not *become* a positivist: he always was one.

B. *And Thus —*

The question now arises: When accepting positivism, was the potential positivist justified in using a standard of meaning other than that detailed in the chart of scientific empiricism? If the answer is that he was *not* justified, then one may be so forward as to ask what business he has being a positivist at all? And what business does he now have trying to convince non-positivists of the superiority of his system? Is the non-positivist responsible for employing positivistic criteria? If so, it is just like asking a man how refreshed he felt from water he has yet to drink.

And if the answer is that one *is* justified in using other than positivistic criteria when seeking to ascertain whether or not to become a positivist, *then the scientific empiricist admits there are other ways to make contact with reality than via the chart of meaning he defends.* This is important, for if one has the right to use non-operational sentences in deciding for or against positivism, why is he not likewise justified in employing that same method in deciding for metaphysical and ethical truths? This is the issue which must be faced.

Should the positivist retort that the use of non-positivistic criteria in becoming a scientific empiricist is but a temporary concession to the weakness of the flesh, and that subsequent to the initial decision one may use only positivism to evaluate other alternatives, one can only pause to demand that credentials for this conclusion be presented. Is not *this* decision likewise made on non-operational grounds? What scientific experiment can establish its ontic references? One must not forget that the only authority one has for remaining a positivist is the continued assurance (established by whole coherence) that the method remains the best. No super, super experiment can settle this question.

The upshot of the matter is that the virtues of positivism *may* be weighed by non-positivistic criteria. Just as the would-be positivist himself decided for or against the method under the suasion of values which appealed to him, so the contemporary mind must do the same thing. He must not be frightened by the structure of operationalism, for he is yet in possession of a freedom which is sovereign over such an epistemology.

But what standards should we follow? The answer to this is easy. What did the potential positivist follow when he came to positivism? He made his decision in the light of what he believed would bring integration and happiness to his own person. He chose because he felt he would be left with greater difficulties if he refrained from choosing. In short, he set up a pair of balances. In the one side he placed the values he longed for; in the other he placed the chart of positivism. Seeing that the latter balanced with the former, he chose in its favor. This is what each man must do for himself, for the decision cannot be made vicariously.

Therefore, our only problem is to learn whether positivism increases or decreases the sum total of our values. One should commit himself wholeheartedly to that which gets him where he wants to go; and the goal toward which he moves is a total integration of his person with the total universe over against him. If devotion to positivism can account for this end satisfactorily, one would be axiologically foolish to spurn it. But if it happens that through marriage to the system one is brought to grief and unhappiness, it would be even more foolish to accept it.

Science is our servant, not our master. Whenever a strict application of the scientific method forces one to deny in theory what experience avers to be true, freedom must cut cables with the method. Was man made for the method or the method made for man? That is the issue. If in becoming a positivist the individual is immediately enslaved by an epistemology which denies things which the heart affirms, in plain Faustian language the free individual is selling his own soul. What value is left, if after reducing all meaning to semantics I find that I have reduced my own dignity to insignificance? Who will be on hand to enjoy things?

If one is to preserve his dignity, he must retain his right to veto the scientific method whenever it is not found useful. And if this right is blocked by positivism, one cannot be blamed for rejecting that epistemology. It would be quite unworthy for one to scuttle his freedom in favor of a burdensome bondage to scientific empiricism.[10]

10. "Let it be clearly understood that nothing whatever has been said here against science and scientific method properly understood. The argument is simply that science has its limits in the very nature of what it is, and that while it is always right to begin with the empirical facts and to operate with the experimental method, you cannot stop there. By all means measure all that is measurable, and analyse all that is analysable, but when that is done you must go on from the facts to the significance and purpose and value of the facts; from the mechanical to the teleological; from the natural to the transcendental; from all that is measurable by our standards . . . to the more universal view of philosophy and theology." Henry Bett, *The Reality of the Religious Life,* (New York: The Macmillan Company, 1949), p. 100.

III. The Loss of Metaphysics

The seriousness of the matter is sharpened up somewhat when the implications of the positivistic division between cognitive and non-cognitive sentences are studied in detail. At first blush it seems but a trifle that all propositions which do not fall within the pale of science are non-cognitive in meaning, and hence have only an emotive or appeal function. What possible difference does this distinction make?

A. *Legerdemain*

The first difference is that one must found his epistemology upon an offensive contradiction. The positivist is unequivocal in his announcement that only propositions which terminate in an operation are cognitive. So, well and good. But what operation shows the measurable consequences of the sentence, "Only propositions which terminate in an operation are cognitive"? The answer is obvious. That which states a condition of all meaning cannot be tested by anything more primitive. In the case of the general statement of positivist epistemology, therefore, we have a sentence which, though it has cognitive meaning, cannot terminate in an experiment. For this reason the chart of positivism is based on a contradiction. The positivist does not *wish* that the proposition stating the conditions of all cognitive sentences be cognitive; he declares in fact that it is. Hence, whoever would choose positivism must be prepared to swallow a major contradiction at the outset. One must use the weapon of metaphysics to slay the specter of metaphysics. Such is the strategy of scientific empiricism.

Everett W. Hall has nicely laid his finger on this contradiction. He shows by a rather convincing argument from the protocol sentence that positivism is either metaphysical or it is meaningless. One may take his choice; in either case the consistency of scientific empiricism is lost. Positivism asserts as a *statement of fact* that reality can be verified one way as over another. But such a statement itself is at least one proposition which the method of positivism cannot process.

By a 'protocol sentence' he means a sentence reporting a direct observation. But this leads to a dilemma. Either he must turn over all determination of what sentences are protocol sentences to the special sciences, or he must admit that he, as philosopher, can in some cases decide that certain sentences are protocol sentences. On the first alternative, he (the philosopher as logical analyst) can *never* decide what sentences are meaningful and what meaningless; and so he can never assert, 'all metaphysical sentences are meaningless,' in fact, he cannot even assert, 'some metaphysical sentences are meaningless.' He must leave it to the sciences to determine, *seriatim*, which metaphysical sentences are meaningful and which meaningless.[11]

But trouble emerges at once on this alternative, however, for it is next to impossible to determine what is the result of direct observation and what the observer has imparted through his own presuppositions. Scientists are never more unclear than when they try to define the exact relation which subsists between reality and the observable.

If the logical positivist should choose the second alternative above, he could then retain his assertion that all metaphysical sentences are meaningless but he would have to admit into logical analysis, and thus into philosophy, non-formal sentences, sentences in the material mode that are true or false. For, clearly, to assert that a sentence is a protocol sentence is to assert that it stands in a certain relation not to other sentences but to a direct observation. But now the very basis for claiming that all metaphysical sentences are meaningless has collapsed.[12]

One may squirm and twist, but he cannot *meaningfully* make statements about reality which deny the possibility of such statements in the first place. Repeating the assurance that only what science can verify is true will not rescue the case. "The statement, 'all verifiable sentences occur in the sciences,' is itself not a sentence to be found in the language of any science, yet it is obviously factual, not formal."[13] Can a meta-

---

11. Runes (Ed.), *Twentieth Century Philosophy*, p. 162.
12. *Op. cit.*, p. 163.
13. *Loc. cit.*

physical statement disqualify metaphysics? "The same can be said concerning, 'all metaphysical sentences can be wholly translated into formal sentences.' I conclude that logical positivism must either be wholly tolerant toward metaphysics or else become metaphysical itself."[14]

The great constants in language — being, number, true, good, etc. — can be asserted of anything that can be known or valued. These constants (or transcendentals, in scholastic terms) state the minimal conditions of being in all meaningful predication. They cannot be tampered with, altered, or supplanted without altering the possibility of meaning itself. They form the framework within which the scientist may alter other conditions to bring about controlled change; but they themselves cannot be varied by a more primitive test to see if they are veracious existence referents. They form the only thinkable conditions under which anything may have meaning predicated of it. Discussion of the constants of language, therefore, is purely metaphysical. And yet it is a discussion which breaks through to reality. It probes into actual conditions which must obtain in all possible existents. There is no meaning to *positing* the meaning of the constants, for the very act of positing draws its significance from the antecedent constants. There is no experiment by which the scientist introduces "existence" as a factor, *e. g.* If the object lay outside the category of existence, what would he be experimenting with? Can the nonexistent be measured? *Conditions* of existence may vary, but not existence. Even non-being is a type of existence. It exists under the conditions of non-being.

It is thus not possible to give a significant positive verification of a metaphysical hypothesis, *i.e.*, to observe whether existence varies in an asserted fashion with some variation in the conditions of existence. In fact, 'the conditions of existence' is itself a misleading phrase. *Any* conditions, if they actually obtain, are existent. We cannot put various conditions together and *then* get something existent, as though we could have conditions before we had anything existent.

14. *Ibid.*, pp. 163-164.

So Berkeley's *'esse est percipi,'* Hobbes' 'the universe is the aggregate of all bodies,' Schelling's 'the world is subject-object,' Whitehead's 'events are prehensions,' are all assertions of universal constants; any *actual* instance of any general term, these propositions assert, is an instance of the constants involved.[15]

There is something humorous in the effort of the positivist to disclaim the right of the metaphysician to make cognitive sentences, since a whole cache of metaphysical ultimates must be presupposed before that denial itself has significant meaning.

An intellectual stalemate results. To become a positivist one must deny the possibility of cognitive assertions about the very conditions of all existents. One must either wink at this contradiction, and so lead the free self to betray the involved self by breaking from the normative laws of honesty and truth; or one can respect the contradiction and fold up his pursuit, turning to another interest. This is not an indictment of the personal honesty of positivists -- each man must stand or fall before his own master. But it is at least a formidable barrier standing in the way of one's becoming a positivist himself. "Whoever knows what is right to do and fails to do it, for him it is sin." (James 4:17)

The most satisfying way out of the dilemma is frankly to admit that there is a natural limit to the scientific method and that metaphysical propositions must be dealt with by a method convenient to their subject matter. Or better, the scientific procedure enjoys an application of coherence which is more perfect than can be pursued in metaphysics — *though both employ coherence.* The one is able to control conditions in an actual experiment, while the other must alter them by hypothesis, postulation, and dialectical interchange. The weakness of positivism stems out of its unsuccessful attempt to take a method which is useful in one area of our experience and make it sovereign in all other areas. It exhibits the reductionism inherent in the ideal of science itself. Science is indis-

15. *Op. cit,* p. 173.

pensable in dealing with the type of data for which the method was created. But it becomes pretentious when it moves out of this sphere and tries to pronounce about the conditions which make all experiments antecedently meaningful. Can a method designed for processing only the quantitative, be employed to evaluate those qualitative relations which are foundational for all meaning?

> Scientific method (if we may speak of anything so manifold as *a* method) is the best method there is, in the sense that it gives us the most reliable evidence *for the sort of beliefs it properly examines.* But it does not follow that it is the best in the sense of the most appropriate to *every* belief. Even within science it is important to distinguish between the problems, 'What method is most reliable absolutely,' and 'What method is most reliable for a given subject-matter?' Many biologists and social scientists argue: 'Physics has developed the most reliable procedures, therefore we should adopt its methods in our field.' They fail to see that, *when applied to biological or sociological phenomena,* the physicist's methods may be less reliable, since less relevant, than distinctively biological or sociological methods. So, although it is true that scientific methods are more reliable in science than metaphysical methods are in metaphysics, still, I contend, metaphysics should develop its own relevant procedures and not try to force scientific methods to function in its field.[16]

B. *Social Confusion*

Human behavior always snarls up the nice correlations of science. People are so unpredictable and whimsical that pure science would fare much better if all of its correlations could be made by electronic machines. A perforated tape is automatically fed into one end of the machine; while flawlessly accurate quantitative relations flow out of its inner electronic bowels. For this reason the free spirit feels like a bungling, unwanted intruder when it wanders into the physics laboratory to observe what is going on. The electronic machines flash and grunt with anger as freedom enters to disrupt the per-

---

16. *Op. cit.,* pp. 169-170.

fection of mathematical precision. This is very hard for the ego of the individual to take, especially since *he* is the one who made the machines in the first place.

One may easily swallow his *own* pride, resting assured that his individuality is but a sacrifice hit for the advancement of science; but what happens when he chances to meet another person? Before we ever heard of science (as illustrated in the case of all children) we believed it possible for spirit directly to meet spirit through the soarings of freedom. The heart of the child is knit to the heart of the parent with such a presentational richness and immediateness that all question and doubt vanish. However mysterious the transaction may be, it happens to be a fact of experience that spirit leaps into spirit and each knows the other with a satisfying directness. If *anything* is real, it is the factualness of those whom we love, those whom we daily sacrifice for. If this be not true, why do we see the high and low pass through the throes of despair when a loved one is suddenly taken by death? Why does not the distance between two stars affect us in the same way? The answer is that we never know quantitative relations with the intimacy that we do qualitative. Qualities of love, joy, hope, friendship, peace and faith have a way of blending with spirit that quantitative relations do not. They are the very stuff of spirit. They make up its fiber. Just as the constants of language are *sine qua non* for all rational meaning, so the constants of spirit are *sine qua non* for all inner satisfactions. Remove the satisfactions and you remove the antecedent conditions of life.

And yet the scientific empiricist (who himself is sustained by vitalities which satisfy his free spirit) dares to pretend that sentences describing the values of spirit are non-cognitive. Who can hear this hard doctrine? Positivism rules out cognitive speech about spiritual values on the ground that they cannot be subjected to scientific analysis. In what way can the data of love or joy be reduced to a measurable quantity? How long is hope? How much does peace weigh? Yet these values are the most real things we know. Would not the individual be axiologically foolish to forfeit faith in the things which really count that he might have the paltry privilege of analyzing sentences which count for little?

Fellowship is a cordial meeting of spirit with spirit. But how can propositions about fellowship be reduced to a scientific experiment so that one may refer to relations of love as cognitive? Try approaching another person armed with a conventional if-then formula! The very moment one objectively calculates or deliberates before another person, refusing to release the vitalities of his own free spirit until he is satisfied that there *is* another person before him, that instant the communion of spirit is shattered and the counterattacking powers of suspicion array themselves for battle. Experience testifies again and again that it is only when we forfeit interest in objective validation and give ourselves in trust to the heart of another that we enjoy fellowship. The surest, most reliable way to shatter fellowship is to approach another and say in a deep, scientific monotone: "Hold still for a while. I want to see if you are a person." The introduction of the very question crucifies the possibility of one's ever knowing the other as a person. Science measures arms and legs, cranial capacities and frontal lobes, but it never measures spirit. How can it, when it blocks the way to spirit by objective analysis?

It is sometimes asserted that science is able to advance good reasons to establish the probable existence of other persons. But the free spirit is incensed, not consoled, at this profound announcement; for if anything is indubitably known it is the existence of other hearts. The experiences of love and joy are so vivid to spirit that their sharp impressions on the heart make quantitatively measurable data appear illusory. For example, lovers often become so satisfied with the union of hearts that they have no memory of rain having fallen on them during the evening stroll. If fellowship does not make up the stuff of reality, where can reality be found?

Laughter peals as the scientist announces with a straight face that there probably *are* other spirits, as if the evidences are now converging on a strong hypothesis. The statement is factual, perhaps, but it is perfectly foolish. It is as foolish as that of the man in the lifeboat who piously announces at the end of the twenty-sixth day at sea that there *is* a mass of water about them. Some things are so well known in life that the announcement of their reality only provokes humor. (Or pathos?)

The positivist may be positively overjoyed on the day science announces that sentences about other individuals are at last factual; but it is questionable whether his wife will be glad to have the news broken to her. Once she suspects that the factuality of her spirit is at the mercy of a scientific operation — as if her husband can love her only when a ticker-tape report from the laboratory gives him the go-ahead sign — she will assert her own factualness by seeking out a person who, though he may know little about science, knows a lot about life. Love is not subject to the verdict of anything. Love is the only condition under which everything else thrives.[17]

The folly of using only the scientific method to learn what sentences are and are not cognitive is becoming more and more clear. Science first drains off all the spiritual vitalities for which men live and die, and then it seeks to console them by offering a safe and sound method by which inconsequential relations can be tested. But why gain the insignificant at the cost of everything that is precious? We are absolutely certain about the factualness of love, peace, joy, hope, faith. What is advanced if these are lost and in their place are put a few mathematically accurate (but experientially worthless) correlations? The question is not simply a sentimental one. It is the duty of philosophy to *explain*, not deny, life as we know it.

C. *Cosmic Confusion*

Freedom not only enjoys transcendence over both the self and other spirits. Its potentialities likewise include a flying visit around the universe, and it will not rest until it has completed such a journey. Freedom anxiously wonders what the

---

17. This assertion will be established in the next chapter.

whole of things is like, that it may determine in advance whether or not there are lasting values in reality. Does it make any *cosmic* difference how we conduct ourselves here?

As we focus our thought again on our initial inquiry concerning the universe—this mysterious Other-than-ourselves —and ask, What is it? we inevitably face the question of its relation to the things we value most. Does the universe have friendly regard for our ideals of beauty, virtue, justice, truth? Are these 'written into the scheme of things' or are they the evanescent ideas of a creature soon to be snuffed out into oblivion? As one contemporary writer has put it: Are the things we value most at the mercy of the things we value least?[18]

Positivism makes short work of these questions. Because they rest on metaphysical assertions, they lie quite outside of the pale of the scientific method. It is not possible to make cognitive sentences about ultimate value, so that is that.

But the end is not quite yet. Since science cannot show the *existence* of cosmic values, positivists conclude (quite without justification) that the *nonexistence* of cosmic values is proved. This easy passage from agnosticism to confident negative assertion establishes the possibility -- if not the actuality — that science's objections to absolute value rest more on moral than evidential grounds. If this be not true, why the positivist's

---

18. Alfred G. Fisk, *The Search for Life's Meaning,* (New York: Fleming H. Revell Company, 1949), p. 67. "From our human point of view, this alternative must necessarily take some form as this: 'Is the spirit of the universe or the ultimate nature of things akin to what we recognize as greatest and best, or are such standards and distinctions but human parochialisms, sheerly irrelevant in a wider reference?' . . . Is our self-conscious life with its ideal ends but the casual outcome of mechanical forces, indifferent to the results which by their combinations they have unwittingly created, and by their further changes will as unwittingly destroy, or is it the expression, in its own measure, of the Power that works through all change and makes it evolution? Is the ultimate essence and cause of all things 'only dust that rises up and is lightly laid again,' or is it the Eternal love with which Dante closes his vision, 'the Love that moves the sun and the other stars'?" A. Seth Pringle-Pattison, *The Idea of God in the Light of Recent Philosophy,* (New York: Oxford, 1920), pp. 40-41.

eagerness to deny all absolutes in the name of a truth which itself is an inchoate absolute?[19]

In any case, scientific empiricists continue to leap from an absence of scientific evidence for cosmic values to a full-orbed description of what a value-wanting universe is like. The most famous tirade against teleology has been given by Bertrand Russell. Who has been able to read his essay, *A Free Man's Worship,* without sensing uneasiness? Combining literary eloquence with a fecund imagination, Russell has spelled out words which are some of the most quoted in our century.[20]

But an equally frank (though less extensive) account is the recent article by W. T. Stace, "Man Against Darkness."[21] While Russell is quite happy to wash his hands of religious things altogether, perfectly convinced that matters of faith are nothing but a block to progress anyway, Stace freely admits that man lost a great deal when faith vanished. Modern man lives in a greatly impoverished universe. When men were able to believe both in God and a world to come, they had a support for values which now is wanting. "With the disappearance of God from the sky all this has changed. Since the world is not ruled by a spiritual being, but rather by blind forces, there cannot be any ideals, moral or otherwise, in the universe outside us. Our ideals, therefore, must proceed only from our own minds; they are our own inventions." (p. 53) Man inhabits a dark, dead universe. "We do not live in a universe

---

19. As the Ph. D. candidate who responded when asked by his positivist professor whether he still believed in absolute truth: *"Absolutely not!"*

20. "That man is the product of causes which had no prevision of the end which they were achieving; that his origin, his growth, his hopes and his fears, his loves and his beliefs, are but the outcome of accidental collocations of atoms; that no fire, no heroism, no intensity of thought and feeling can preserve an individual life beyond the grave; that all the labours of the ages, all the devotion, all the inspiration, all the noonday brightness of human genius, are destined to extinction in the vast death of the solar system, and that the whole temple of man's achievement must inevitably be buried beneath the debris of a universe in ruins—all these things, if not quite beyond dispute, are yet so nearly certain that no philosophy which rejects them can hope to stand."

21. *The Atlantic Monthly,* Vol. 182, Number 3, (September, 1948).

which is on the side of our values. It is completely indifferent to them." (*ibid.*)

It was neither the rise of higher criticism nor the fact of organic evolution which killed hope. Religion, Stace is certain. can rise above these peripheral issues. The real executioner is the scientific presupposition that there are no final causes. "The final cause of a thing or event meant the purpose which it was supposed to serve in the universe, its cosmic purpose." (p. 54) Since men of science learned that the impersonal laws which control motion on the earth likewise govern the heavens above, what could commend itself more easily than the presupposition that the whole universe is a purposeless machine? "The world, according to this new picture, is purposeless, senseless, meaningless. Nature is nothing but matter in motion. The motions of matter are governed, not by any purpose, but by blind forces and laws" (*ibid.*)

> It is this which has killed religion. Religion could survive the discoveries that the sun, not the earth, is the center; that men are descended from simian ancestors; that the earth is hundreds of millions of years old. These discoveries may render out of date some of the details of older theological dogmas, may force their restatement in new intellectual frameworks. But they do not touch the essence of the religious vision itself, which is the faith that there is a plan and purpose in the world, that the world is a moral order, that in the end all things are for the best. . . .Religion can get on with any sort of astronomy, geology, biology, physics. But it cannot get on with a purposeless and meaningless universe. (*ibid.*)

With commendable candidness Stace discounts the possibility that either philosophy or science will eventually rise to save men from the fate of cosmic pessimism. The *cause* of the disease cannot become the cure. Nor can one return to the fleshpots of pre-Newtonian cosmology, for one never advances by retreating. But suppose another prophet or Messiah came? Would not such be able to restore lost hopes to men? Alas, no! "No one for long would believe in them, for modern men have lost the vision, basic to all religion, of an ordered plan and purpose of the world. They have before their minds the picture of a purposeless universe, and such a world-picture must be fatal to any religion at all, not merely to Christianity. (p. 56)

The self gasps: Is *this* my portion for devotion to the scientific method? Have I nothing left to which I may devote myself with whole satisfaction?

Stace continues: "No civilization can live without ideals, or to put it in another way, without a firm faith in moral ideas. Our ideals and moral ideas have in the past been rooted in religion. But the religious basis of our ideals has been undermined, and the superstructure of ideals is plainly tottering." (p. 57) Nothing is accomplished in leaping from the *need* of an ideal to an untrue view of the cosmos as its support. "I am sure that the first thing we have to do is to face the truth, however bleak it may be, and then next we have to learn to live with it." (*ibid.*) It happens to be too late to change things. Since we *do* know of the valuelessness of the universe, let us seek to live by that knowledge. Opiates and dreams are but a form of dishonesty. A solution to our problem must move realistically within the facts as they are available. While we may tolerate the "minor illusions" of love, fame, glory, power, and money as means by which men surreptitiously bring about human happiness, we cannot look upon the "great illusion" so casually.

> There is plenty of evidence that human happiness is almost wholly based upon illusions of one kind or another. . . .There is no reason why we should have to give up the host of minor illusions which render life supportable. There is no reason why the lover should be scientific about the loved one. Even the illusions of fame and glory may persist. But without the Great Illusion, the illusion of a good, kindly, and purposeful universe, we shall *have* to learn to live. And to ask this is really no more than to ask that we become genuinely civilized beings and not merely sham civilized beings. (p. 58)

Our salvation is a confident comprehension of the real world as it actually is. Man must become intellectually mature. "If he cannot he will probably sink back into the savagery and brutality from which he came, taking a humble place once more among the lower animals." (p. 58)

There is something very, very mysterious about Stace's article. While disclaiming all absolutes, Stace yet recommends an absolute devotion to the facts as they are in preference to the facts as we wish they were. Is not this a finality? Is it not a value claim which science cannot process? What operation can test the cognitive meaning of the sentence, "True science consists in a devotion to the real facts." The proof that Stace is already under an absolute compulsion is the easy way he passes a universal negative judgment against the possibility of religion and science's ever coming to terms.

> I am surprised to see that Professor Stace assumes the mantle of the prophet. He might have said soberly that religion *ought not* to exist alongside of science; but wishful thinking prompts him to predict that it *cannot* last much longer and is now on the point of disappearing. This is far from being an empirical observation.[22]

But waiving the question of internal consistency, the heart feels there is yet something exceedingly suspicious about the situation. For example, Stace generously allows that a person continue with the "minor illusion" of love. Since there is no quantification of love which the laboratory may process, propositions about love are not factual. "Love is satisfying" is not a protocol sentence. No mathematical machine, no litmus test, can process this proposition. But the immediate comeback of the heart is that it is the scientist, not the lover, who is under illusions. Dare we say that the satisfactions the father enjoys with his son, and the mother with the infant, are but *minor illusions?* If these are illusions then *a fortiori* the

---

22. Walter Lowrie, "Calling Attention to God," in *Theology Today*, Vol. VI, Number 3, (October, 1949), p. 365. Lowrie is far too generous in defining the things which Stace can and cannot do. It is not correct that Stace may meaningfully say that religion *ought not* to exist along with science. Oh, he might *say* it, but as a positivist he can mean no more than this is what he happens personally to like. The sentence can have no cognitive meaning. Stace can only mean: "I would like it if religion did not exist along with science." This would be like our being told that Stace does not like spinach. *But what do we care about this?*

scientific method is more of an illusion; for the reality of love is far more apparent than either the method of science itself or the purposeless universe which it purports to find. When the positivist continues to pretend that the love which spirit finds in spirit is a minor illusion, he only adds pathos to pathos.

We are piously bidden by Stace to be devoted to the facts as they are. But the heart wonders why it should be devoted to *anything* — since nothing ultimately matters anyway. Suppose, *e. g.,* it is known that the universe will end in a big puff of smoke. Nothing could kill initiative sooner. "Let a man say of his highest endeavor after truth, or beauty, or social righteousness, 'It is a lost cause: the universe is against it,' and it makes a profound difference to his endeavor. Why struggle for that which is already lost?"[23] It is a psychological impossibility for a man to devote himself enthusiastically to something which he plainly knows will make no difference. It may be pleasure to dig holes in the sand by the edge of the water, for example, since the spirit of man is temporarily challenged in its race to hold the walls from collapsing. But once a saturation point is reached and it is known that the fight is futile, enthusiasm wanes. One cannot willingly live and die for a hopeless cause. If hope is to be nourished, there must be some chance of winning. But if the world is so constructed that there is no final meaning to things, then enthusiastic devotion collapses. We may live and let live while the curse of existence is upon us — but goodness knows why. No cosmic difference is made if we kill off everybody else or commit suicide ourselves. It is just a matter of personal choice how we live. Science cannot help us in the least.

But possibly our fretting is needlessly aroused. Perhaps Stace is just reciting homemade poetry or telling a pointless joke. We might take him seriously if he were guided by the absolute, "That philosophy professors always and without exception tell the truth when they are writing articles for

23. Fisk, *op. cit.,* p. 68.

The Atlantic Monthly"; for then we would know for sure he actually meant what he said. But Stace deliberately disavows devotion to truth as an absolute.

> I do not urge this course out of any special regard for the sanctity of truth in the abstract. It is not self-evident to me that truth is the supreme value to which all else must be sacrificed. Might not the discoverer of a truth which would be fatal to mankind be justified in suppressing it, even in teaching men a falsehood? Is truth more valuable than goodness and beauty and happiness? To think so is to invent yet another absolute, another religious delusion in which Truth with a capital T is substituted for God.[24]

A sigh of relief may be taken. There is no longer any need to refute Stace's arguments, for he seems quite willing to place other values above telling the truth. Perhaps this very article may be one case in which he has suppressed the truth because it might be fatal to mankind. Stace may mean just the opposite of what he says. Who knows? Certainly the reader does not. Therefore, why should he be responsible for examining the arguments?

It turns out that communism and positivism have something negative in common. Each places a private value above devotion to truth. And watch out when that happens! The fairest promise may be but a disguised untruth, advanced to promote the well-being of a cause, but not of mankind.

IV. The Loss of Ethics

Let us turn from the problem of metaphysics for the time being. When evaluated in isolation of ethics, metaphysics generally appears dry and dusty. But what the contemporary man must be reminded of is that ethical propositions have cognitive meaning only when they rest in metaphysical ulti-

---

24. "Man Against Darkness," *op. cit.*, p. 57. Stace assures us that there may be times when men should not be told the truth about reality: yet he closes his article by asserting that the only hope of mankind is for men to be told the truth about reality and to live according to it. *Which is it?*

mates. The positivist knows this; so, he jettisons both meta-physics and ethics. When once one realizes what life would be like without cognitive ethical sentences, however, he will quickly rush back to his old friend metaphysics for comfort and solace.

It is easy to appreciate the *academic* reason why positivism unloads ethics. Since the scientific method must reduce all quality to quantity, it is impossible to affirm *meaningful* ethical relations. How long is an ought? How many parts are there in an imperative? The questions are obviously mean-ingless. Ethics, thus, can express only an emotive meaning. The ought must bow to the god of measurement. "If the idols of scientists were piled on top of one another in the manner of a totem pole the topmost one would be a grinning fetish called Measurement. Both chemists and physicists fall down and worship before Measurement."[25]

A. *The Uneasy Conscience*

The initiators of the scientific method were (as a whole) God-fearing in their cosmology. They would hardly have had courage to embark on their venture if they were not al-ready firmly persuaded that the true, good, and beautiful were time- and space-transcending values. The scientific ideal is *judged* by these criteria; it does not presume to find them. Science is worthy only when it advances truth, promotes the good, and displays the beautiful. The history of science, therefore, is gloriously replete with the accounts of men who reckoned not themselves dear that they might advance truth. No body of men — not even the clergy themselves — could be cited for greater scrupulosity in honesty. Scientists would resign their profession rather than announce to the world a conclusion which they knew did not follow from the evidences. They sense with a perfect intuition that unless the value of telling the whole truth is absolute, science itself is foundation-

---

25. Anthony Standen, *Science is a Sacred Cow*, (New York: E. P. Dutton and Company, 1950), p. 82.

less. Truth-declaring is the tie that binds free men in a common enterprise.

> Value judgments are undoubtedly inescapable, but the value judgment on which science in the Western world is based is the sacredness of truth. It is incompatible with a system that breeds a disregard for objective truth or undermines the standard of personal honesty that requires a man to submit unfavorable as well as favorable evidence when he is testing a hypothesis. Science is possible because there are men engaged in it who *will not* sell out to the political boss, who *will not* falsify reports to support a preconceived notion, who *will* stay on the job even when the ordinary rewards are denied. Science, then, depends on ethical foundations, the chief of which is the unmercenary love of truth.[26]

The difference between the scientist who has faith in things which transcend time and space and the one who does not is that the former *includes* the witness of the heart in his philosophy of life, while the latter forces the testimony of the heart to pass through the cylinders of a preconceived scientific methodology. The latter claims to be more consistent, more hardheaded. But is this correct? Degrees of consistency are measured by success in arranging *all* the known facts, not just some of them. And if there is any datum which is sure, it is that we are morally responsible beings. We are under a categorical imperative which cries out against immoral actions. In short, man has conscience. "One of the surest facts of human life is the fact that moral demands are made upon us which we cannot refuse without the sense of having somehow fallen."[27] Whenever we defy the laws of honesty and justice, we feel sheepish and small. A power within us indicts us for having acted in a role unbecoming to a free, moral creature.

Freedom compounded with morality gives man his essence. The dog may think, but, alas! only man is free to think about thinking. In short, he is free. He can communicate an honest

---

26. D. Elton Trueblood, *The Predicament of Modern Man*, (New York: Harper & Brothers, 1944), p. 41.

27. John C. Bennett, *Christianity—And Our World*, (New York: Association Press, 1936), p. 5.

report of his findings, or he can contrive a dishonest answer. In the area of moral freedom the glory of man lies.

It is only in his epistemology, not in his active life, that the positivist dares to introduce the doctrine of ethical relativism.

> I know that Professor Stace has taken care to have his children baptized and now sends them to Sunday School. Recently he assumed the solemn obligations of a sponsor at the baptism of the child of a friend, promising to 'take heed that this child learn the Creed, the Lord's Prayer, and the Ten Commandments, and all other things which a Christian ought to know and believe to his soul's health.'[28]

One can hardly alter the fact that he is a man, simply by taking thought.   When the positivist finds that his automobile is stolen, *e. g.*, he swiftly rushes to the nearest police station to report the dastardly matter.   He solemnly protests that the culprit *ought* not to have done this.   He is not just expressing an emotion or a personal wish.   He speaks to the officer in charge of the station with sentences that both understand as cognitive.   The positivist is likewise very positive that other men must not molest his wife and family.   The proposition, "My home must not be entered by force," is as cognitive as any sentence science ever reduced to an operation — *i. e.*, judging from the *actions* of the scientific empiricist.

Is it humor or pathos to watch a positivist proctor an examination on ethics, lest any student be found cheating? While both professor and student supposedly agree that in actual life one *ought* not to cheat, each professes to believe the peculiar doctrine that the ought is but an emotive expression.   But why does the good professor *wish* that they do not cheat?   Is it just a habit which the university has fallen into? There may be rhyme or reason to forbid cheating now and then, just as one would forbid having classroom windows opened on cold days; but why the exceptionless pattern?

---

28. Walter Lowrie, "Calling Attention to God," *op. cit.*, p. 367.

Why not permit cheating on *alternate* exams? Why, except that both professor and student know that ethical sentences *are* protocol propositions? The professor may teach in his class that ethics are relative to each situation, but when the university regents pass an unjust rule, he and the whole department with him suddenly hand in resignations. The observer may be naive here, but such action looks suspiciously like what he would expect if ethics were absolute.

It is interesting to observe how heroic and noble both Russell and Stace are in the final paragraphs of their monographs of gloom. With a burst of religious enthusiasm the reader is pepped up for an altar service. He is courageously to throw his head back, resolving once and for all (*absolutely*, in other words) that he will give his devotion to the facts as they are. This is the best policy for free, rational men: *Face the darkness of the future with confident despair!* Alas, no Christian evangelist ever pleaded with men to hit the sawdust trail with a more heartfelt passion. *All* is lost if men do not awaken to their illusions (such as love) and remain honest before the facts.

But a major problem remains. *Ought* one be devoted to all the facts? Or, is the option simply a matter of personal preference, such as wanting to boil cabbage? If words mean anything, Russell and Stace seem to be saying, "I *ought* to accept science wherever it leads me." I do not read "I like science; but of course your tastes may be different." Neither could rise to the eloquence of enjoining men to give up all their satisfying illusions in favor of the repelling, dismal facts if they were not persuaded that the issue involves an imperative. But if this be true, then the humorous situation emerges once again of seeing men live according to the very principles they disavow in their epistemology. Is not inconsistency a mark of untruth?

The uneasy conscience of scientists and positivists is illustrated perfectly by the April, 1949 forum at the Massachusetts Institute of Technology, when men of the laboratory gathered with philosophers and educators to discuss the great issues of human destiny at the mid-century crisis. The forum was called "The Social Implications of Scientific Progress — an Appraisal at Mid-Century." The glory of the twentieth century has protruded no more conspicuously than in the staggering advances made by science. Scientists are literally seeking for new worlds to conquer. But through all of these triumphs there may be traced the new and more awful specters of poverty, immorality, wantonness, hunger, and social insecurity. Yet the full optimism of the scientific method was right there in the front row. In the opening address Dean John Burchard suggested that the twentieth century might even see a scientific control of man's thoughts. Winston Churchill, shuddering to think of free spirits being reduced to the ignominy of robots, commented that he would be very content if his task in this world were done before that happened. Nobody was blinded to the issues of the hour. Scientific progress had come to the point where the harnessing of man's heart was far less successful than the harnessing and predicting of nature. Jacques Maritain defended a two-dimensional view of reality, pleading for a return to the wisdom of Christianity and the Greeks. Percy Bridgman and Walter Stace opposed him. Bridgman declared that problems which could not be brought within the scope of the scientific method (such as ethics) should be passed by as "inconsequential." Stace spoke about "a new morality founded on the psychological laws of human behavior."

And so at a forum in one of our great institutions of science the battle between the *a priori* and the *a posteriori* was taken up again. In reviewing the terrible twentieth century, Winston Churchill ominously warned that the flame of Christian ethics is still our highest guide. The issues were clear as the forum came to a close: *Is man a creature continuous with eternal values, or is he a one-dimensional being who must face the mysteries of his destiny alone?* In short, does he participate in *one* environment or *two?*

B. *Uneasy Civilization*

During World War II a great deal was said about the fifth column. Its method was to infiltrate itself into the inner machinery of a social structure and then at the appointed moment initiate internal collapse through sabotage and violence. As one stands at the crossroads in this contemporary period, however, he wonders whether those who convert perfectly good science into perfectly bad metaphysics do not constitute one of the most dangerous fifth column organizations in our present culture. By infecting the minds of students with the opinion that morals are relative and that a man has no more final destiny than an animal, they are training a generation of leaders to understand much about technology but little about a moral power which can control it. We suffer today from an internal decay which threatens to rot away the very beams and crossbeams of our own civilization. And the difficulty is not the science, but the individuals into whose hands the tools of science have fallen.

> The fact that our life is so gravely threatened in the brightest day of technical achievement is not a criticism of the engineers *qua* engineers, but it is a criticism of all of us as *men*. The paradox of failure at the moment of success is by no means a condemnation of technical progress, for such progress is morally neutral. It gives the surgeon's knife, and it gives the gangster's weapon. Our predicament is a commentary, not on instruments and instrument makers, but on the human inability to employ both scientific knowledge and technical achievement to bring about the good life and the good society. Man is an animal who is peculiarly in need of something to buttress and to guide his spiritual life. Without this, the very capacities that make him a little lower than the angels lead to his destruction. The beasts do not need a philosophy or a religion, but man does.[29]

There is little doubt but what scientific empiricists are (in general) most amiable and pleasant individuals, ones who would be first in their own actions to disclaim violence and

---

29. Trueblood, *op. cit.*, pp. 16-17.

destruction. But that is not the point. The point is that in his teaching, the positivist is undermining the very moral and spiritual vitalities upon which our culture was founded and which alone can dignify man. *His* personal piety may stem from his Christian heritage, but where shall the piety of his pagan students come from? Certainly it cannot come from positivism. It must come from a structure of values which disavows the pretension that all cognitive sentences are resolved by operations. Respect for human dignity, respect for justice, the preference of truth to error, goodness to wickedness, beauty to ugliness are *normative* values which have *a priori* justification. Who will be around to check the results if the following sentence is carried out into an experiment: "Destroying civilization through hydrogen bombs is a bad thing." In this instance truth crushed to earth *will not* rise again, for no scientists will remain to construct new operations.

> In our day science and the machine are feared as the Frankenstein Monster which turns on its creator and destroys him. Civilization may be hurtled back into worse than barbarism by the forces which man has evoked. As geology has disclosed great groups of animal life which, once dominant, disappeared . . . so man, if unable to fit himself to the environment of science which he has brought into being, may become extinct.[30]

The positivist may disconcernedly shrug his shoulders, dismissing the fear of the world's destruction as an unscientific emotionalism; but as he consigns the world to easy chaos, he ought to make a careful check to see that his blithe ways are not the result of an inadequate method rather than truth itself. May it not be that the imperative within him to remain true to science — *come what may* — is a clue to the limitations of the scientific method itself?

Our civilization has hardly recovered from the shock of seeing a powerful nation like Germany descend to the filth of

---

30. Kenneth Scott Latourette, *The Christian Outlook*, (New York: Harper & Brothers, 1948), p. 187.

bestiality, a nation endowed with a technological genius the envy of the world. Who can account for the easy fall of this great power? Hitler schemed up the philosophy, yes; but where did he receive his power? Part of the answer is that the scientists themselves were delinquent. Being without moral foundations, they easily fell prey to the paper hanger's madness. Stephen Spender describes this pleasant little co-operation between Hitler and "morally neutral" scientists as follows:

> In Hitler's Germany, the scientists lent themselves to schemes for sterilizing and destroying the mentally unfit, for exterminating whole populations, for using human beings as the subjects for experiments. A friend of mine, himself a scientist who went to Germany after the War to study the activities of German scientists, told me that what shocked him most was to discover that when human beings were made available to German scientists for experimental purposes, they were used with ruthless extravagance, often to make experiments which were completely unnecessary. I am not suggesting that scientists everywhere would do the same thing. But it is necessary to point out that scientists can derive from science *qua* science no objections to such experiments as exterminating the mentally unfit. If they do object, they are acting upon non-scientific values. Modern science has produced no reason to prevent science from being directed by governments toward purposes of enormous destruction in every country. Science is simply an instrument, for good or for bad. For it to be directed toward good, whoever directs it must have some conception of humanity wider than that of a planned scientific society.[31]

Chemist Anthony Standen sagaciously warns that "We must watch scientists carefully, to see that they do not put anything over on us — to see that we do not learn, by personal experience, what science can *do to men*."[32] Germany exhibited what scientists can do to men. Russia is following in this pattern. Who will be next? No laboratory operation can answer this question.

---

31. Crossman (Ed.), *The God that Failed*, pp. 259-260.
32. *Science is a Sacred Cow*, p. 221.

A warning comes to America with the appearance of the significant volume, *The Abuse of Learning,* by Frederic Lilge. The observation is made on the jacket of the work that what happened to Germany *may* happen at home. "The author refrains from pointing out parallels. But anyone who knows the problems confronting education in America will find in *The Abuse of Learning* a warning of what *may* happen here." It is well that we review what happened in Germany, lest we ourselves become narcotized by similar forces.

So complete was Germany's break from the *a priori* and so enthusiastic its acceptance of scientific empiricism that a new idolatry grew up about the laboratory. The old school criticized the deficiencies of education under the new leaders of science, protesting that specialization robbed the student of both perspective and maturity. But the old school had not long to live. Helmholtz, whose ideas on science remained representative in the nineteenth and part of twentieth centuries, dodged the obvious indictment with typical scientific blindness. "Scientific research, he said, was beginning to yield tremendous benefits to society. It made possible industrial progress and greater material welfare for the mass of the people. Could it not be argued and urged, therefore, as a moral duty?"[33] And so the muddle began. An ambiguous, woolly-minded humanitarianism supplanted a rigorous moral theory. But the deficiencies of the new educational theory remained. In one hand Helmholtz extended the alabaster dreams of scientific progress, while in the other he held a philosophy of life which completely disqualified interest in human values as a part of the core curriculum in the university.

> Yet they fell in with the popularizers when they mistook progress in science for universal progress, or when they assumed that an ampler supply and a greater perfection of technical means would automatically bring about the realization of human ends. Like so many others, Helmholtz seemed

---

33. Frederic Lilge, *The Abuse of Learning,* (New York: The Macmillan Company, 1948), p. 75.

not to regard human ideals and values as individual achievements and, in consequence, of no importance in education.
He rather inclined to regard them as natural endowments,
or things to be taken for granted. This misconception explains why, when speaking on behalf of the work of the
university as a whole, he could think only of the advancement of knowledge and gave no thought whatever to the
problem of so integrating and realizing knowledge in individual human beings that it might contribute to their achieving
moral and intellectual maturity.[34]

Hidden away in the laboratory, the scientist took no active
part in the shaping of the moral life of the German nation.
He was too busy creating physical comforts for man, to worry
about such a triviality as spiritual morality.[35] A radical nationalism was being incubated in Germany, and the scientists
were busily creating the vacuum into which it would rush.
Helmholtz led the way.

For by leaving the moral life uncultivated and its purposes
undefined, he invited that heedless preoccupation with technology which has helped to precipitate the catastrophe of
German culture. One need only remind himself of the growth
of German nationalism which paralleled that of modern German science, to realize the ominousness of the situation. As
the sense of individual responsibility diminished and with-

---

34. *Op. cit.,* p. 76.
35. "Here is a little story about a scientist, to illustrate what they don't
see. In the world-renowned aquarium of Naples, a friend of mine met a
scientist who was engaged in experiments on fish. He had them attached
by string to a device which made a record of their tail movements. Some
of them were entire fish, others had had portions of their brains removed.
The brainless fish made smooth regular curves on the recording instrument, but the tails of the untreated fish made distressingly irregular movements. The scientist was delighted with this discovery. 'See,' he said, 'it
is the higher brain centers that *disturb* the basic movement pattern of the
muscles. The brainless fish make beautifully regular movements.' This
scientist was unable to see any sort of connection between what he was
doing in the aquarium and what was going on around him in Italy, where
Mussolini made the trains run regularly, but did not allow anyone to think
a single thought that was contrary to the ideas of his regime." Standen,
op. cit., pp. 202-203.

ered away, nationalism—that 'heroic infirmity,' as a great
German of the eighteenth century had called it—was ready
to fill the void.[36]

Once it was taken for granted that "universities were research centers and that teaching was incidental,"[37] reductionism set in with vengeance. Büchner, Vogt, and Moleschott
revived French materialism. Emil Du Bois-Reymond falsely
glorified the age of scientific optimism. "He proclaimed that
there had never been a greater period in the history of civilization than the nineteenth century, when for the first time
science furnished culture with a stable and lasting foundation."[38] Ernst Haeckel reduced reality to a blunt monism.
"The so-called higher faculties of the human mind were only
the sum total of the psychic functions of the cells of the brain.
Man had developed like other mammals from lower forms of
life, from which he differed only in degree and not in kind."[39]
His enthusiastic pupil, Wilhelm Ostwald, reduced everything
to energy. "From the basic law of the preservation of energy
he derived an ethics, the categorical imperative of which was
summed up in the simple formula, 'Don't waste energy!' This
was his solution of the problem of values."[40]

The outcome was the worship of the almighty atom.[41] The
great *Wissenschaft,* which was supposed to *liberate* man,
actually reduced him to ignoble globules of protoplasm and
mechanical patterns of conditioned reflexes.

> Having denied responsibility and freedom to human life,
> they invested the atom with a singular dignity and restored
> the soul to the cell. Their complete disrespect for tradition,

---

36. Lilge, *Op. cit.,* p. 76.
37. *Ibid.,* p. 77.
38. *Ibid.,* p. 79.
39. *Ibid.,* p. 80.
40. *Ibid.,* p. 81.
41. Standen properly sees the humor in this worship. "But while we are
watching them, we can get a great deal of amusement. We can, and should,
laugh out loud at scientists, and this will be the very best way to prevent
them from regulating us, or averaging us, or conditioning us to synthetic
happiness. For what are they doing? The most laughable thing in the
world. They are all crowding round and bowing low before a Sacred Cow."
Op. cit., p. 221.

their incapacity to distinguish between the world of fact and
the world of value, and their reduction of the human person
to a thoroughly determined mechanism constitute an emphatic denial that education is a moral problem at all.[42]

When reductionism passed over to nihilism and irrationalism, and the emptiness of science could no longer be hid, a
wave of reactionaries vied with each other to gain the hegemony of the national mind. Since science had no answer to
man's most important questions, a change was in order. "It
was this doctrine of the meaninglessness of science, and the
confusion of what is with what ought to be, which appealed to
certain Germans and which more and more characterized the
irrationalist revolt."[43]

Irrationalism soon became a weapon in the hands of the
dictators. It was a perfect cover for their vicious doctrine
of power. "Even a casual survey of the Nazi literature shows
that irrationalism with all its ramifications is an integral and
essential part of the National Socialist philosophy."[44] Hitler
made good use of the positivist's arguments that morals are
relative and that there are no eternally objective standards of
right and wrong.

> If Nazi irrationalism is right . . . then it follows that the
> nation-state has the right to determine what the content of
> its own national science shall be and also how the science
> can best be cultivated. . . .If Nazi irrationalism is right and
> there is no eternal objective standard of what is morally
> right or wrong but only a series of racial or national codes,
> then it is obviously the duty of the German nation-state to
> determine what the German code of morality shall be, and
> . . . to see that the German citizens follow the precepts of
> this code . . . . If Nazi irrationalism is true, it is obvious
> that there can be no such thing as natural law or a law of
> reason applicable to all peoples and all nations. To say that

---

42. Lilge, *op. cit.*, pp. 82-83.

43. *Ibid.*, p. 129.

44. William M. McGovern, *From Luther to Hitler*, (Boston: Houghton Mifflin Company, 1941), p. 630.

the civil law or statutes of any one state must conform with the dictates of the universal rational law is ridiculous.[45]

One can only work and hope that America will never run the disastrous course which Nazi Germany has taken. But in stemming the drift toward moral irresponsibility in our modern impasse, there is nothing clearer than that the scientific method is impotent to deliver us. By definition it cannot pass from the descriptive to the normative; while it is only the normative which can direct and inspire the hearts of free men. How, then, can we continue to look to the scientists as the leaders in our present world situation?

> They can't ask the right questions, they don't know how to get the answers, and they can't tell what to do with the answers when they have got them. And since it is *these* people who have a position of extraordinary prestige among us, although they know so little that is worth knowing, we must watch them very carefully, for they are not to be trusted to do anything either for or to men.[46]

A firm place must be given to the moral witness of the heart as a source of data from which hypotheses are formed. Man lives in a *double* environment. Conscience cries out against the possibility of man's being explained on a one-dimensional view of reality. His freedom is compounded with moral responsibility, and moral responsibility proceeds from an eternal ought. A great deposit of moral insight has been laid by sensitive men in all generations, a deposit which was appealed to when the Constitution of the United States was drawn up. Our country was not founded, nor could ever have been founded, by men guided by the positivist chart of meaning. The scientific method could never rally the moral foundations needed to give fiber to a free society.

Illustrative of the moral bewilderedness of modern scientists is the case of Dr. Klaus Fuchs. Early in the spring of 1950 he was sentenced by a British chief justice to serve fourteen

45. McGovern, *op. cit.*, pp. 647-648.
46. Standen, *op. cit.*, p. 202.

years in prison for engineering a deliberate betrayal of the Allied nations by delivering atomic secrets to Soviet Russia. The testimony of Fuchs was pathetic and heart-rending. He confessed that he had been so steeped in laboratory technique, that it just never occurred to him that moral principles might be involved in the act of selling atomic information. Sentences about morality are but a petty series of emotive expressions. Since nothing in the physics manual (or the chart of positivism) offered any guidance on questions of morality or ethics, Fuchs reduced the question to an operation — being promptly led off to jail as a reward for his attempt.

Fuchs did not long continue in his blindness, however. During the trial his eyes were opened to the fact that man lives in a double environment and that such values as honesty, decency, trustworthiness, and character are no less veracious and objective than the values of chemistry and physics. Before marching off to prison, a broken and beaten man — but at least a man — he thanked the court for a fair trial. Shaken and bewildered, he found it quite a shock to make the transition from the life of a scientific robot to that of a human being. He learned by grief that the world of extension is subject to the prior witness of the world of spirit.

Two observations may be made about the Fuchs trial. *First,* society did not apply the epistemology of positivism when it instinctively rose up and condemned dishonesty and cowardness. As part of his created endowment man possesses a sense of right and wrong, virtue and shame, truth and falsity. These *rationes aeternae* are as much a part of his nature as an instinct to protect its young is part of the animal. Such spiritual values define man's dignity. When they are corrupted, man is corrupted. Disintegration sets in the instant we try to live contrary to their clarion cry. In the real assignment of living, therefore, nobody applies the chart of positivism.

Second, Fuchs was obediently following the moral code taught him in the university. Why, then, did he stand alone in trial? Why did not his professors come to his rescue and propose a scientific operation to show the court that society had no right (*ought* not?) to condemn a man by such minor illusions as changeless standards of right and wrong? Alas! when all the evidence was called in, not a positivist stood at Fuch's side. But was full justice done? Is not the accomplice as guilty as the criminal?

As we bring the matter to a conclusion, we at last have a perspective with which to evaluate the loss of metaphysics. Without ethics we have bestiality in the most vicious form; but without metaphysics as a foundation for ethics, bestiality remains. Ethical insights are grounded in metaphysical values. Unless sentences about morality are rooted in time- and space-transcending values which form part of the structure of reality itself, it is impossible to have normative truth.

Since we have to live with both ethics and metaphysics, however, why not learn to get along with them? The sentence, "The hero is more praiseworthy than the coward" *is* cognitive. Justice *is* to be preferred to injustice. It *is* the duty of men to treat others as ends and never as means. Since the basic intuitions of truth and goodness surpass all relative expressions of them, there *is* cognitive meaning to metaphysical sentences. Science is tested by truth and goodness; it cannot operationally test whether there is a meaningful difference between truth and error, good and bad.

No doubt it is extremely difficult to establish a perfect balance between *a priori* and *a posteriori* elements in a consistent epistemology, for it is very easy for the *a priori* to get out of hand and snuff out progress and freedom. But in an effort to clean the house, it is perfectly foolish to burn it down. The solution to the contemporary predicament does not consist in an exceptionless denial that *a priori* sentences can contact reality. The moment we kill off the power of *a priori*, that instant we crucify the reality of the second environment. In our daily life we somehow manage to reach ultimate reality through inward suasions and convictions which belong to us by nature. We live and move and have our being in a transcendental realm of values. When an epistemology forces us to deny in theory what we must live by in fact, it is as inadequate as it is inconsequential.

Summary

The scientific method was conceived as an effective way to weed the tares of *a priori* error from the fields of natural knowledge. Its relevance to *quantitative* data is so incontestable that the degrees of a man's natural knowledge can be measured by the degrees of his faithfulness to the method. If nature is to be understood, she must first be patiently studied and obeyed.

What has happened, however, is that philosophers, lusting after the precision of the scientific method, have used science to measure the *qualitative and normative*. The final result has been a costly reductionism, until now it is not even possible for one to make cognitive statements about his own soul. A new cult has arisen — the cult of positivism. A new religion has started — worship of the scientific method. And the faith which binds the members of this cult together is the blinding creed that man was made for the scientific method and not the method for man. Science revolted from a poor expression of a good *a priori*, only to end up with a good expression of a poor substitute.

The heart refuses to be troubled any further by an offer to live and die for the scientific method. It is a pretty poor bargain when one trades everything in life that counts for the anemic gain of being able to classify sentences.

Whoever continues to repeat the stupid claim that sentences about justice, honor, chastity, self-control, piety, holiness and love are non-cognitive, should be laughed at — laughed at good and hard. He shows not only a want of education, but also a want of common sense. There are standards so ultimate to all meaning that all else is judged by them. How then can they be judged a subordinate method? If science is not *good,* what is it good for? If science is not *true,* why should one believe it?

VI

Philosophical Ataraxia

ONE of the unique ways in which Scripture pays tribute to the primacy of spirit in man is the distinction uniformly made between types of wisdom or knowledge. According to Christian revelation, one has not yet reached perfection in wisdom until he enjoys *fellowship*. Through its rich quality of absolute immediateness, fellowship exhausts the knowledge situation. When spirit clasps spirit in the intimacy and mutuality of fellowship, the heart is able to perceive conclusions so directly that the need for minor premises is ruled out.

It is the scholastic, not the Biblical writer, who is responsible for the definition that man is a rational animal. Scripturally, *man is a sentient creature qualified to worship God.* Man releases his best powers when he enjoys communion and fellowship, not when he perceives rational connections in a formal syllogism.

But an explanation must immediately be proffered, lest a profundity be mistaken for an artless commonplace. First, a clarifying distinction must be made between *knowledge by inference* and *knowledge by acquaintance.*

There is a well-known ambiguity in the word "knowledge." It is reflected in many languages. On the one hand we may know something by inference (*savoir, wissen,* etc.), while on the other we may know it by direct experience (*connaitre, kennen,* etc.). The former is knowledge by inference and the latter knowledge by acquaintance. I *infer* the existence of the electron; I am *acquainted* with the physicist.[1] Biblical writers consistently place acquaintance knowledge above that of inference, believing that the former is more akin to the immediateness which God enjoys. Creatures must learn by discursiveness, while God knows by an eternal intuition. God has perfect acquaintance knowledge of all things: man gains glimpses of this perfection by analogy only.

But further distinctions are called for, if a full appreciation of the Biblical epistemology is to be enjoyed. Conventional philosophy draws no significant distinction between *acquaintance knowledge of things* and *acquaintance knowledge of persons,* while the Biblical writers do. According to Scripture there is a measurable difference between direct acquaintance with a city and direct acquaintance with a friend. Both are *direct,* to be sure, and thus pass beyond knowledge by inference in richness; for no amount of indirect knowledge of a city can match the satisfaction of a personal visit. Yet, since like meets like only in the transcendental realm of fellowship where spirit enters spirit in direct acquaintance, acquaintance knowledge of things is less satisfying than acquaintance knowledge of persons. *Perfect* perception is found only in love, for in the experience of love the conclusion is so immediate and satisfying it is almost ineffable. The lover needs no sermons to be told that all relations outside that of love fall short of perfection. A world of encyclopedias and an eternity of university courses could not surpass the excellency of knowledge which the mother enjoys as she holds her babe in arms and unites her heart to that of the little one.

---

1. In the broadest connotation of the term, of course, *all* knowledge is inferential; for we can know nothing until the data presented to the heart are first processed. Data do not wear little identification tags with their names nicely printed on. And even if they did, the mind would still have to infer the meaning of the names. The difference between knowledge by inference and knowledge by acquaintance is that the one reaches its conclusions by means of middle premises, while the other does not. Through inference knowledge we infer conclusions indirectly; through acquaintance knowledge we infer them directly.

A body of knowledge values must be respected, therefore. And in this structure the foot cannot say to the hand, I have no need of you; or the ear to the eye, I have no need of you. All of the types of knowledge are appropriate for the office and object to which they are assigned. Epistemologically, God has tempered the faculties of knowledge together, giving abundant honor to that which seemingly lacks. Knowledge by inference, while *sine qua non* for the perception of valid connections, is yet a handmaid to knowledge by acquaintance; for by inference we can only anticipate the perfection which we enjoy immediately through experience. And acquaintance knowledge of things is a handmaid of acquaintance knowledge of persons, since the former contains only in type what the latter enjoys as fulfillment. To be acquainted with the hills of home is fine; to be acquainted with mother or father is more excellent.

But the end is not yet. The apex in the pyramid of knowledge is personal acquaintance with God. When the creature finds his way to fellowship with God, the image and likeness returns to the center and source of its being, there to enjoy that perfection of love which human relations can approach only by finite degrees. Human love opens the way to divine love; but once the divine love has been tasted, human love is then evaluated in the light of its perfection. There is no greater height of free potentiality, and thus no more conceivably perfect form of knowledge, than that enjoyed when the dust returns to the potter to experience fellowship and love. God's love is compounded with both omnipotence and immutability; hence, it can never fail to satisfy either through want of power to save or through resolution to meet spirit in fellowship.

The Biblical indictment of purely rational knowledge must be understood within its context, therefore. When men reach the finest their spirit is capable of, they will be found fellowshiping with God. Perfection of knowledge is reached not by perceiving rational connections, but by enjoying intimate, personal acquaintance. When knowledge by inference is made an end in itself, idolatry results.

The perfection of knowledge by acquaintance can be illustrated by the strategy of the little boy in the school yard. Seeing his friend with a bag of jelly beans in his hand, he walks over beside him. And to make perfectly sure he receives his portion of the sweets, he appeals to the highest knowledge relationship. *You know me!* he cries, holding out his hand. And he does not mean that the other has simply a cognitive awareness of his existence in time and space or an acquaintance knowledge of his physical characteristics. He means that they are so intimately tied together in fellowship that he has a right to stir up the other's responsibility to share the jelly beans.

In like manner, a man enjoys wisdom in the final degree only when he can turn his eyes toward the Author of heaven and earth and reverently declare through the medium of prayer, *Thou knowest me!* There is no thinkable progression beyond fellowship. In fellowship spirit clasps spirit in glorious mutuality.

Solomon clearly illustrates this ambiguity of knowledge. In the book of Ecclesiastes[2] he describes the emotion of frustration which is encountered when a free man tries to make knowledge by inference his highest goal. "For in much wisdom is much grief; and he that increaseth knowledge increaseth sorrow." (1:18) Yet, the book of Proverbs teaches that through the possession of knowledge felicity is enjoyed. "Happy is the man that findeth wisdom, and the man that getteth understanding. For the gaining of it is better than the gaining of silver, and the profit thereof than fine gold." (Proverbs 3:13-14) The contrast between these two moods is conspicuous indeed. Their reconciliation is as follows: In the one case Solomon looks upon knowledge as a purely rational relationship, unoriented in fellowship, while in the

---

2. Let not the reader stumble over our choice of Solomon as the author of Ecclesiastes. If he prefers another author, well and good. The argument in the chapter remains quite the same even if "X" be the writer of the work.

other he views it as terminating upon fellowship with Jehovah God. That spells the difference.

In like manner the Apostle Paul decries wisdom as a foolishness of this world. (I Corinthians 1:20) Then, again, wisdom is so exalted and satisfying that it is said to proceed from God himself. (1:24) Jesus Christ disputed with all who boasted of their comprehension of formal, rational relations; but he was jealous to defend the perfection of his own wisdom which proceeded from the Father.

The same elements are found in all these instances. Knowledge by inference is a handmaid to knowledge by acquaintance. Man *must* employ his mind with astuteness; he *must* use the laws of logic to guide him into paths that are rationally coherent, for contradictions he cannot assent to. We should only commit ourselves to that which is rationally consistent. Foolishness we must not believe. But the highest knowledge terminates in fellowship. Less than this draws out less than the whole man. The Bible defends the primacy of reason as the faculty through which all options must clear. But it likewise teaches that formal rationality performs its job only when it remains a humble voice in the wilderness, preparing the way for fellowship.

I. Satisfaction Through Reason

The history of philosophy proves that only the initiated are able to appreciate this fine, Biblical distinction, however. It is a remarkably uniform presupposition of all classical philosophy that the real man is the thinking man and that rationality best expresses freedom. Man is made free through a rational perception of the meaning of reality. In Platonic language, man accentuates the finest portions of his nature only when he soars dialectically to the world of Ideas and enjoys an immediate perception of the pure rational essences which he once knew in his preëxistent state.

A. *The Universality and Necessity of Rationality*

When spirit passes from the limited option of suffering for a method to the broad commitment of suffering for rational knowledge wherever and whenever it may be found, it instinctively realizes that a new genus has been entered. Since the lover of wisdom prejudices neither ethics nor metaphysics, accepting rational connections from every source, the easy objections against the positivist do not apply to him.

No man can meaningfully deny the primacy of the laws of logic. Their universality and necessity are secured by the simple fact that nothing has significance apart from them. Men do not invent the fundamental laws of logic, for nothing would mean anything if logic did not first mean what it says. In the words of McTaggart, no man ever tried to break logic but what logic broke him. Even the man who tries to argue against the priority of logic must in his argument employ the very canons which he is seeking to destroy. Using logic to disprove logic is as foolish as catching rapid breaths while preaching that it is not necessary to breathe.

Why, then, did the Biblical writers fail to include a section on formal logic in Scripture? The answer is that they *presupposed* man's rationality. They were so absorbed in revealing the richness of fellowship with God that the labor of listing the laws of formal logic was left to others. And it was upon Greeks in particular that the responsibility of defining (but not inventing) the canons of rationality fell. The definitiveness of their labor remains a monument to man's powers of acumen. Successive thinkers have conceived of other *types* of logical relations, but the basic core of formal logic remains the same today as when the Greeks first set it down.

The foundation of all meaning is the law of contradiction. Plato formulated it as follows:

> The same thing clearly cannot act or be acted upon in the same part or in relation to the same thing at the same time, in contrary ways; and therefore whenever this contradiction

occurs in things apparently the same, we know that they are really not the same, but different.[3]

Meaning is possible only when a term signifies one thing at a time. A *meaningful* thing is always other than its contradiction, for a term which means both itself and its opposite has no significance. "To affirm a proposition is to deny its contradiction; to predicate A of something is to deny non-A of it. An all-inclusive affirmation would include its opposite, and would be no affirmation at all."[4] The presence of contradiction is the surest negative test for truth. The lie is but a contradiction compounded with forethought and intention. The liar pretends to be sincerely reading off reality, while yet conniving with the self to misrepresent reality. He breaks the law of contradiction.

Aristotle reduced Plato's insights to manageable, formal argument, thus bequeathing a sharpness and clarity in logical expression conspicuously wanting in the dialogues of his teacher. In the Fourth Book of the Metaphysics he irrefutably proves that the law of contradiction is non-hypothetical. He accomplishes this by showing that *nothing* has meaning unless the canon of non-contradiction possesses antecedent truth.

> The most certain principle of all is that regarding which it is impossible to be mistaken; for such a principle must be both the best known . . . and non-hypothetical . . . which principle this is, let us proceed to say. It is, that the same attribute cannot at the same time belong and not belong to the same subject and in the same respect . . . . And if an opinion which contradicts another is contrary to it, obviously it is impossible for the same man at the same time to believe the same thing to be and not to be.[5]

If an individual says he does not care to obey the law of contradiction, pretending that he will make out as best he can without it, one can only check him off his calling list; for he has denied the very condition without which it is impossible

3. *Republic,* 436b.
4. Raphael Demos, *The Philosophy of Plato,* p. 160.
5. *Metaphysics,* IV, 1005b.

meaningfully to persuade him either of his own error or of anything else.

When men call for a *proof* of the law of contradiction, Aristotle reminds them that there are relations so ultimate to all meaning that there is no meaning to calling them into court for examination.

> Some indeed demand that even this shall be demonstrated, but this they do through want of education, for not to know of what things one should demand demonstration, and of what one should not, argues want of education. For it is impossible that there should be demonstration of absolutely everything (there would be an infinite regress, so that there would still be no demonstration).[6]

If we prove A by B, B by C, and C by A, we reason in a circle. And if we prove A by B, B by C, C by D *ad infinitum* we are quagmired in an infinite regress, and we still want demonstration. The only demonstration of any absolute is this: Without the presupposition of its existence nothing else has meaning — not even the denial of that absolute.

And it is to this negative type of demonstration that Aristotle resorts. He is content with showing that the denial of the universality and necessity of the law of contradiction reduces man to the absurdity of being a common vegetable.

> We can, however, demonstrate negatively even that this view is impossible, if our opponent will only say something; and if he says nothing, it is absurd to seek to give an account of our views to one who cannot give an account of anything. . . .For such a man, as such, is from the start no better than a vegetable. . . .The starting-point for all such arguments is not the demand that our opponent shall say that something either is or is not (for this one might perhaps take to be a begging of the question), but that he shall say something which is *significant* both for himself and for another; for this is necessary, if he really is to say anything. For, if he means nothing, such a man will not be capable of reasoning.[7]

6. *Metaphysics*, IV, 1006a.
7. *Loc. cit.*

By this cleverly worded argument Aristotle shows that once something significant has been said, the individual has already admitted the otherness of the thing's contradiction. And this, in fact, constitutes an application of the law of contradiction. Words must have a finite number of meanings; for if they mean *everything*, they mean nothing in particular, and hence mean nothing at all. There is no possible way to avoid this conclusion and still retain rationality. To *mean* anything, a term must exclude its own contradiction. If "horse" means both itself and "non-horse" at the same time, together with meaning "cat," "bottle," "upstream," etc. *ad infinitum*, it has no meaning at all and is plain foolishness.

Since it is impossible *meaningfully* to affirm and deny the same thing at the same time, therefore, consistency is genuinely a rock-bottom condition for all significant predication. If it is affirmed that God is one and that the world is round, for example, one cannot at the same time and in the same sense significantly affirm that God is many and that the world is non-round.

Consistency is the universal test for validity. The insane break the law of contradiction too frequently to remain socially tolerable; the ignorant cannot manage the law with commendation; the wise man has control of his thoughts, construing his propositions consistently; and capping the pyramid is the sagacity of God: "The Father of lights with whom there is no variation or shadow due to change." (James 1:17) Since he is completely consistent, God is absolutely trustworthy.

While one might meaningfully deny hedonism, communism, and positivism, therefore, he cannot significantly gainsay the primacy of reason as a test for validity. If a protest is to *mean* anything it must draw its significance from the very canons of rationality being questioned. For this reason it takes comparatively little imagination to appreciate why philosophers have been prone to convert knowledge by inference into an end in itself, defining the real man the rational man and the real act the act of thinking. That which is a condition of all meaning must itself lie close to the essential nature of ultimate reality.

B. *Suffering for Rationality*

It was an accepted presupposition in classical philosophy that the essential man is the thinking man.

> The classical view of man, comprised primarily of Platonic, Aristotelian and Stoic conceptions of human nature, contains, of course, varying emphases but it may be regarded as one in its common conviction that man is to be understood primarily from the standpoint of the uniqueness of his rational faculties. What is unique in man is his *nous*.[8]

When Plato divided the four faculties of the soul, reason answering "to the highest,"[9] he was in effect laying the groundwork for his entire axiology.   In the Republic social strata are measured by a man's ability to manage rational arguments. The philosopher-king was lodged securely at the apex of the pyramid, while the slave, "a troublesome piece of goods,"[10] formed the broad foundation.   The former nurtured the power of dialectic within his soul, while the latter was devoid of such a gift.   Through dialectic one makes firm contact with the absolute nature of things; and by means of this venture one comes to acquire the highest satisfactions of life.

> Then dialectic, and dialectic alone, goes directly to the first principle and is the only science which does away with hypotheses in order to make her ground secure; the eye of the soul, which is literally buried in an outlandish slough, is by her gentle aid lifted upwards.[11]

When one has perceived truth through dialectic, he must indeed return to the cave to assist those who are still groping in the world of shadows.   But this return is always by way of concession.   It is not a humanitarian effort grounded in the

---

8. Reinhold Niebuhr, *Human Nature*, p. 6.
9. *Republic*, VI, 511d.
10. *Laws*, VI, 777b. Aristotle classified the slave as "a living possession." *Politics*, I, 3, 1253b.
11. *Republic*, VII, 533c.

presupposition that each individual possesses an infinite dignity. Plato simply advised the philosopher-king realistically to adjust himself to the fact that the world is a mixture. Ideally, men ought to be free from their bodies, and hence be released from the cave. It is a concession for the philosopher to teach the ignorant. But he realizes that the slaves, merchants, and soldiers which comprise the social foundation make the leisure of his own meditation possible. Without the support of this social and economic framework the philosophic ideal would be jeopardized. Even as the philosopher must pamper his own body to keep his soul well, therefore, so he must pamper the body of the citizens to keep society well.

The sin of man is ignorance, even as his virtue is knowledge. When a man has found rationality, he has exhausted the full heights of his own nature.

> For the Greek mind, though sensuous, was always clear and rational, always lucid, always appreciative of form; and the rational life had therefore always a peculiar charm for it. This appreciation of the rational life finds expression in the Socratic ideal of human life as a life worthy of a rational being, founded in rational insight and self-knowledge—a life that leaves the soul not demeaned and impoverished, but enriched and satisfied, adorned with her own proper jewels of righteousness and truth. Plato and Aristotle follow out this Socratic clue of the identity of the good with the rational life. For both, the life of virtue is a life 'according to right reason,' and the vicious life is the irrational life.[12]

Thus, the history of Greek philosophy strikingly illustrates the ease with which men pass from the true premise — the universality and necessity of rational forms — to the false conclusion — that man expresses the best within him when he follows the contemplative life. Socrates standing in the fields, gazing up into the heavens, is a dramatic exemplification of the philosophic ideal.

---

12. James Seth, *A Study of Ethical Principles*, (New York: Charles Scribner's Sons, 1910), p. 153.

However, philosophy actually waited until the seventeenth century for the rational ideal to receive its most incisive expression. Benedict Spinoza, a Dutch philosopher, cast rationalism in a bold and consistent form. And one of the interesting features of the Spinozistic excursion into axiology is the deliberate way rationality is examined as a power to meet human satisfactions. Systematically questing after personal happiness, Spinoza finally found peace, not in fellowship with a personal God, but in the intellectual perception of clear and distinct ideas.

On the Improvement of the Understanding, e. g., was written expressly as a confessional document. Comprising Spinoza's attempt to trace the steps involved in his turning from the frustrating options in life, the volume forms a remarkable counterpart to the book of Ecclesiastes. It is significant not only that it tells of a Jew seeking the meaning of life, but also that it comes to a conclusion diametrically opposite that of Solomon. This makes the examination of this document exciting.

> After experience had taught me that all the usual surroundings of social life are vain and futile; seeing that none of the objects of my fears contained in themselves anything either good or bad, except in so far as the mind is affected by them, I finally resolved to inquire whether there might be some real good having power to communicate itself, which would affect the mind singly, to the exclusion of all else; whether, in fact, there might be anything of which the discovery and attainment would enable me to enjoy continuous, supreme, and unending happiness.[13]

With Solomonic perspicacity Spinoza perceived the legion of disappointments which necessarily attend the lower immediacies. "When such pleasure has been gratified it is followed by extreme melancholy, whereby the mind, though not enthralled, is disturbed and dulled."[14] Spinoza, likewise, glanced dis-

---

13. *Philosophy of Benedict de Spinoza,* (Elwes tr.), (New York: Tudor Publishing Company), p. 1.
14. *Ibid.,* p. 2.

approvingly at the ideal of the classless society. "The more we acquire, the greater is our delight, and, consequently, the more we are incited to increase both the one and the other; on the other hand if our hopes happen to be frustrated we are plunged into the deepest sadness."[15] The pursuit of fame destroys man's quietness and individuality. "It compels its votaries to order their lives according to the opinions of their fellow-men, shunning what they usually shun, and seeking what they usually seek."[16] The lower immediacies are *perishables*. Whenever man seeks to find something changeless in them, therefore, he recoils from their mutability in disappointment.

Only the immutable can give immutable satisfaction. "But love toward a thing eternal and infinite feeds the mind wholly with joy, and is itself unmingled with any sadness, wherefore it is greatly to be desired and sought for with all our strength."[17] This is the chief good: Knowing the nature "of the union existing between the mind and the whole of nature."[18]

But how can one find these immutable connections? Hearsay is unreliable, and sense perception informs man of only the accidental characteristics of being. The missing clue was found in Cartesian epistemology. Clear and distinct ideas, such as the propositions and axioms of Euclid, contain immutably necessary relations. We perceive these immutables by what Descartes called "the rational intuition." The first principles of knowledge are perceived intuitively, while all other principles are deduced from them by clear and distinct ideas. Intuition is the undoubting conception of an unclouded and attentive mind, and springs from the light of reason alone. Deduction is a passage of the mind from a true premise to a valid conclusion.

------

15. *Loc. cit.*
16. *Loc. cit.*
17. *Ibid.*, p. 3.
18. *Ibid.*, p. 4.

Spinoza understood intuition as perceiving things through their essences. Presupposing that "the idea in the world of thought is in the same case as its correlate in the world of reality,"[19] he constructed a complete system of dialectically necessary relations. There is no possibility of error as long as one acquires his knowledge in the proper order; and there is no possibility of unhappiness while immutable relations are retained. Perfect happiness comes from perfect knowledge; and perfect knowledge comes from the intuition of clear and distinct ideas.

The definition opens the way. "A definition, if it is to be called perfect, must explain the inmost essence of a thing, and must take care not to substitute for this any of its properties."[20] Clear and distinct ideas are a fruit of valid definitions.

> Ideas which are clear and distinct can never be false: for ideas of things clearly and distinctly conceived are either very simple themselves, or are compounded from very simple ideas —that is, are deduced therefrom. The impossibility of a very simple idea being false is evident to every one who understands the nature of truth or understanding and of falsehood.[21]

The results of Spinoza's magnificent effort to identify the totality of reality with rational necessity are set down in his *Ethics*. Geometry is the perfect pattern. By the expedient of a series of propositions, demonstrations, corollaries, and Q. E. D.'s — one implying the next like Chinese boxes inside one another — Spinoza believed he reached a perfection in happiness beyond which it is not thinkably possible to pass. Man is at his best when he basks in the light of rational essences.

II. The Contest of Destinies

Few have had the courage to turn to the rational ideal with quite the determination that the Dutch Jew did, for Spinoza

---

19. *Ibid.*, p. 13.
20. *Ibid.*, p. 32.
21. *Ibid.*, pp. 22-23.

yet remains in a class by himself. But his belief that man can find happiness through the perception of rational connections is still espoused by many. Almost every graduate student in philosophy toys with that ideal now and then — if not accepting it altogether. If man is a rational animal, what could more effectively draw out his final potentialities than thinking?

But if reasoning is such an obvious pleasure, why did Solomon come to a conclusion opposite that of Spinoza? Was it want of acumen that drove him to the conclusion that the increase of knowledge brings the increase of sorrow? This is a shaky solution, for the wisdom of Solomon was immensely great. It may be that in resolving this problem one will find clues to solve the broader issue of philosophical ataraxia itself. Can the contemporary mind find final happiness perceiving rational connections, or is there yet a more richly satisfying commitment beyond?

A. *The Solomonic Lamentation*

Solomon was a realist in his theory of values. Since it was his conviction that the meaning of nature can be learned only after the facts of nature have told their own tale, he followed a scientific method of his own type. Anxious to learn what the structure of nature was, therefore, he turned to read off its broad outlines. His purpose was not simply inquisitive. Caught in the torrential stream of historical events, Solomon was exceedingly anxious to know how he stood in the broad nature of things. He *wanted* to believe that there was meaning to life, but this faith could be entertained only after nature had spoken. Nothing would be gained by anticipating nature with a convenient *a priori*; for what is, is.

The expectation of Solomon was that he would know the truth and the truth would make him free; but when he did come to know the truth, the truth left him in shattering disappointment. His personal aspirations were so incompatibly related to the data of history that the job of living, rather than being made lighter through knowledge, was rendered intolerably burdensome. In describing the disappointments in his own investigation of history, Solomon has left behind passages which ring with contemporary significance.

Solomon provisionally conceded that the wise man excels the foolish man as light excels darkness. A rationally blinded man is a pitiable creature in his own way. But a question soon arose about the ultimate profit of wisdom's possession. And the conclusion he came to was that there *is* no final profit to wisdom.

> Then said I in my heart, that this also is vanity. For of the wise man, even as of the fool, there is no remembrance for ever; seeing that in the days to come all will have been long forgotten. And how doth the wise man die even as the fool! So I hated life, because the work that is wrought under the sun was grievous unto me; for all is vanity and a striving after wind.[22]

How would an employee feel if, after putting in a full week's work at the company, he received exactly the same wages as the man who had been out fishing all week? The inequity is self-evident. Solomon evaluated life by the same criterion. What profit is there if no *ultimate* difference is made between the wise man and the fool?

But the inequity reached down even to the beasts of the field. Solomon tried to discover where man's superiority over animals lay, but all he learned was that while both man and the beast were doomed to the same end, man alone knew it. Consequently, man died before his time. He died by anticipation.

> For that which befalleth the sons of men befalleth beasts; even one thing befalleth them: as the one dieth, so dieth the other: yea, they have all one breath; and man hath no preeminence above the beasts: for all is vanity. All go unto one place; all are of the dust, and all turn to dust again.[23]

Even if a man artificially stirs up an enthusiasm to make his life count, he ultimately must leave everything behind to an

22. Ecclesiastes 2:15-17.
23. Ecclesiastes 3:19-21.

unknown heir. "And who knoweth whether he will be a wise man or a fool? yet will he have rule over all my labor wherein I have labored, and wherein I have showed myself wise under the sun." (2:19) Can a man conscientiously work for years on a delicate instrument, knowing all the while that the instant he turns his back another will come and smash it with a hammer? Hardly. We must believe somehow that what we do with all our might will make a difference in the long run. And it was such a difference that Solomon was unable to locate.

There likewise was a vexatious, weary round of life which troubled the peace-loving spirit of this king.

> For everything there is a season, and a time for every purpose under heaven: a time to be born, and a time to die; a time to plant, and a time to pluck up that which is planted; a time to kill, and a time to heal; a time to break down, and a time to build up. . . .[24]

Lay all of these exercises end to end, and what is left? "What profit hath he that worketh in that wherein he laboreth?" (3:9) The same routine which satisfies the animal is maddening to man.

The oppression, injustice, mismanagement and sorrow in the world suggested the conclusion that history was a farce, quite without meaning. Why then live? "Wherefore I praised the dead that have been long dead more than the living that are yet alive; yea, better than them both did I esteem him that hath not yet been, who hath not seen the evil work that is done under the sun." (4:2-3)

The final picture is that of a free man, confident that only through the suasions of eternal verities will his spirit be satisfied, coming to the realization that the elements which form the very stuff of life itself are inherently contradictory. Rational knowledge of what must be did *not* give Solomon peace. It upset him as much as a knowledge of impending electrocution does the incarcerated felon.

---

24. Ecclesiastes 3:1-3ff.

Why struggle at all if nothing has any final meaning? When nature is contrary to a value, it is better to give in immediately and be done with it. Only the fool will try to drain the oceans dry, for example; for nature is against the project. With each bucket of water removed, another quickly flows in its place. In like manner, what sense is there in striving for truth, goodness, and beauty if the universe is against these values?

B. *The Spinozistic Rebuttal*

Quite aware of the same general problem, Spinoza was fully prepared to defend his conclusion that happiness *does* come through a rational knowledge of nature. His impatience with the conclusions of the book of Ecclesiastes was manifest. He felt that Solomon labored under an erroneous understanding of the place man maintains in the universe. This initial error brought the problem of evil upon him needlessly.

In his celebrated appendix to part one of the *Ethics* Spinoza turned from his geometrical pattern to pause for an important explanation. His words were directed to those who, like Solomon, were bothered with the problem of evil. He asked: Is there any meaning to use the attributes, justice and injustice, goodness and evil, worthiness and unworthiness, when discussing *necessary* relations? Shall one fret over the moral implications of the Pythagorean theorem? Is it good or bad that mathematical relations are necessary? Since such questions are obviously meaningless, Spinoza wonders why one presumes it is meaningful to apply the epithets good and bad, just and unjust, worthy and unworthy to the structure of nature. The fallacy is that men think nature works for their end; therefore, they are frustrated when it fails to follow this pattern.

All such opinions spring from the notion commonly entertained, that all things in nature act as men themselves act, namely, with an end in view. It is accepted as certain, that God himself directs all things to a definite goal (for it is said

that God made all things for man, and man that he might
worship him).[25]

Men believe that nature is ordered the same way that they
order their own lives — namely, according to ends congenial
with human wishes. But they forget that if nature is ordered
according to *reason*, then what must be must be. The rational
is the necessary. Each effect in nature may be traced to the cause
which preceded it, and that to the cause which preceded it, etc.
Thus, throughout the whole of natural process only rational
necessity, *never* a concern for human ends, is the vital force.
And when one does not understand this, he is guilty of looking
for teleological purposes within rational necessity. An appeal
to the "will of God" is but an asylum of ignorance.

> Thus it comes to pass that they only look for a knowledge of
> the final causes of events, and when these are learned, they
> are content, as having no cause for further doubt. If they
> cannot learn such causes for external sources, they are com-
> pelled to turn to considering themselves, and reflecting what
> end would have induced them personally to bring about the
> given event and thus they necessarily judge other natures by
> their own.[26]

The final result of looking for purpose in nature is a super-
stitious cult in which feelings and prejudice supplant the use of
reason. Nature is confidently expected to support human ends;
the gods are interested in the welfare of men. This initial
error is the cause of the frustration which Solomon so poeti-
cally laments. If men employed their *minds* to learn the real
essence of nature, they would understand that there is no
ground for the belief that nature is concerned with human
ends.

In his *Ethics* Spinoza outlined the basic reasons why he
believed it valid to identify nature and necessity. "There is
no need to show at length, that nature has no particular goal

25. *Philosophy of Benedict de Spinoza*, pp. 70-71.
26. *Ibid.*, p. 71.

in view, and that final causes are mere human figments."[27]
Through an elaborate form of the ontological argument he
established the existence of God. As indicated, he proceeded
from self-evident definitions through clear and distinct ideas,
to necessary conclusions. The foundational definition is that
of substance. "By substance I mean that which is in itself, and is conceived through itself; in other words, that of
which a conception can be formed independently of any other
conception."[28] The mind chooses substance (or God) as its
beginning because it is the clearest of all ideas. "The existence
of substance follows also solely from its nature, inasmuch as its
nature involves existence."[29] Since everything else must be
conceived through substance, it would be foolish for one to
attempt a denial of God; for the denial to be meaningful must
itself be conceived through substance. Or, another way of
putting the matter is that God must be because there is nothing
which could prevent existence.

> If, then, no cause or reason can be given, which prevents
> the existence of God, or which destroys his existence, we
> must certainly conclude that he necessarily does exist. If
> such a reason or cause should be given, it must either be
> drawn from the very nature of God, or be external to him —
> that is, drawn from another substance or another nature.
> For if it were of the same nature, God, by that very fact,
> would be admitted to exist. But substance of another nature
> could have nothing in common with God (by Prop. ii), and
> therefore would be unable either to cause or to destroy his
> existence. As, then, a reason or cause which would annul
> the divine existence cannot be drawn from anything external
> to the divine nature, such cause must, perforce, if God does
> not exist, be drawn from God's own nature, which would
> involve a contradiction. To make such an affirmation about
> a being absolutely infinite and supremely perfect, is absurd;
> therefore, neither in the nature of God, nor externally to his
> nature, can a cause or reason be assigned which would annul
> his existence. Therefore, God necessarily exists.[30]

---

27. *Op. cit.*, p. 73.
28. *Ethics*, I, Def. 3.
29. *Ibid.*, Prop. 11, proof.
30. *Loc. cit.*

God did not create the world, for to create is to act out of purpose and not necessity. "This doctrine does away with the perfection of God: for, if God acts for an object, he necessarily desires something which he lacks."[31] If God created for a purpose, he is wanting in a perfection which he desires to have gratified. But this is impossible, for God by definition is all perfection. His being is ordained by rational necessity, not choice.

This step links nature with God in eternal necessity. In fact, God and nature mean the same thing, for their difference is simply terminological. God is the whole of reality, and the whole of reality is nature. It is foolish, therefore, for man to suppose that nature is ordained to bring about the gratification of human ends. The whole of nature is as necessary as the axioms of geometry. History flows from the nature of God with the same inexorability as the triangle flows from its definition. Therefore what *meaning* is there to assign attributes of good, bad, well-ordered, or ill-ordered to nature? Is a *triangle* good or bad, proper or improper? A triangle is a triangle, an order of necessary relations. Solomon ought no more to complain of injustice in nature than he ought to criticize the morals of a demonstration in geometry.

> Many argue in this way. If all things follow from a necessity of the absolutely perfect nature of God, why are there so many imperfections in nature? such, for instance, as things corrupt to the point of putridity, loathsome deformity, confusion, evil, sin, etc. But these reasoners are, as I have said, easily confuted, for the perfection of things is to be reckoned only from their own nature and power; things are not more or less perfect, according as they delight or offend human senses, or according as they are serviceable or repugnant to mankind. To those who ask why God did not so create all men, that they should be governed only by reason, I give no answer but this: because matter was not lacking to him for the creation of every degree of perfection from highest to

---

31. *Philosophy of Benedict de Spinoza*, p. 73.

lowest; or, more strictly, because the laws of his nature are so vast, as to suffice for the production of everything conceivable by an infinite intelligence, as I have shown in Prop. xvi.[32]

The resulting peace of mind is hailed by Spinoza as incontestably satisfying, for it rests on the intuitive truth that everything in nature proceeds from the infinite attributes of God with the same necessity that a triangle flows from its definition. When the presumed fortuities of injustice and maladjustment in the world are evaluated *sub specie aeterni*, therefore, their moral attributes vanish and in their place rests pure rational necessity. The peace is "the intellectual love of God." It is the thrill which a mind has when it sees reality *sub specie aeterni*. It is illustrated in a minor way by the delight the student has when he perceives the necessary steps in a geometric proof. It is complete, wanting nothing. "From the third kind of knowledge necessarily arises the intellectual love of God. From this kind of knowledge arises pleasure accompanied by the idea of God as cause, that is. . .the love of God; not in so far as we imagine him as present. . .but in so far as we understand him to be eternal; this is what I call the intellectual love of God."[33] This way of finding peace of mind may seem hard to the uninitiated. "But all things excellent are as difficult as they are rare."[34]

C. *Resolution*

The issue which separates Solomon and Spinoza is clearly before us. The former says through knowledge man is brought into disappointment, whereas the latter claims that through knowledge comes peace. Which lies nearer the truth?

The first observation of the heart is that Solomon at least makes us *sympathize* with his problem. Who has not faced the throes of sickness or sorrow without sharing that well-

---

32. *Op. cit.*, p. 77.
33. *Ethics*, V, Prop. 32, Cor.
34. *Ibid.*, Prop. 42, Note.

known empty feeling in his soul that perhaps life is deficient in final meaning? Who has not lamented the evils and injustices in history, wondering if there is any meaning to individuality in the long run? It is simply a fact of our own daily experience that often the increase of knowledge *does* bring the increase of sorrow. Is the mangy leper consoled to know that what must be, must be?

In contrast to this, Spinoza makes us smile a bit. A certain amount of intellectual curiosity is indeed aroused as the mind pores over the propositions in the *Ethics,* for the work is a monument to pure rationality; but when one places the book down at the end of his reading, he cannot but burst out into laughter as he juxtaposes himself — part of nature — with what Spinoza has finished proving about nature. The joke is that the *free* individual is asked to assent to a view of nature which excludes the possibility of freedom itself. It is like asking a man to raise his right hand in token of his allegiance to a philosophy which has just finished proving the nonexistence of all hands.

What persuasion can the Spinozistic arguments enjoy when the power of freedom in man is the clearest datum in the whole world? It just so happens that man has *not* proceeded from God by rational necessity. Man is *not* part of an immense triangle. Man is a choosing, weeping, laughing creature. One's free choices are sufficient to demolish Spinoza's immense pantheistic edifice forever. There can be no free choices in rationally necessary relations.

But the humor increases when one remembers that Spinoza himself *chose* the system defended. Did geometric necessity force him to forsake the lower immediacies in favor of the consolations of reason? Hardly. He was led by free choice. And Spinoza likewise freely wrote his books to persuade other people freely to choose his position. There would be no meaning to his literary labor if choosing and rejecting were not contingencies which depended upon the inner will of man himself. Yet, contingency is the one element which can not be incorporated into a *sub specie aeterni* structure. *Sub specie,* what must be, must be. Is there any meaning to pleading with men freely to accept a system which makes such a free decision itself *a priori* impossible?

No writer in modern times has more impatiently recoiled from a rationally necessary world view than the Copenhagen gadfly, Sören Kierkegaard. Fresh from his studies in the German universities, Kierkegaard experienced in his own person the shock of seeing Hegelianism convert free men into impersonal centers of rational necessity. He saw students everywhere bowing low in the dust before the master dialectician. Yet, for all its wonder, Hegel's tortured, logical dialectic was unable to accommodate the free individual himself. Hegel conceived of history as the search of the *absolute* for freedom — not a search by individual spirits. So, the more Kierkegaard considered the incompatibility of free personality and rationally necessary categories, the more he seethed within.

Kierkegaard resorted to barbed irony when attacking Hegelianism. Rather than laboriously proceeding through each Hegelian presupposition, exposing internal deficiencies one by one, he preferred simply to laugh. He could think of nothing funnier than to meditate upon this strange and weird being who lives *sub specie aeterni*. Kierkegaard caricatures Herr Professor as one sitting up night after night laboring over his system, anxious to get it into the hands of the publisher by the time the university officials gather to discuss professorial elevations. Now and then the professor becomes upset as he makes typographical errors — such as in the paragraph which is to prove that all reality flows from God with logical perfection! Alas, one fair day he snatches up his bulky manuscript and announces to his university class in philosophy that he has finally completed the system which identifies the flow of history with the same necessity that binds logical categories. The students, gaping with amazement, are swept into discipleship by the sheer erudition and profundity of his labors. They quickly decide in favor of the system which happens to leave out the free individual himself. Then the professor, taking on a new lease in life, stands in line to receive his monthly check. *This* time he has earned his money well, for he has bequeathed to humanity a rational system which accounts for everything but humanity.

When Kierkegaard checked with Hegelians to inquire how they got started in their system, they replied monotonously that they simply began with the immediate. But this vagary could not disguise the real facts. Kierkegaard was perfectly aware that men became Hegelians by *choosing* so to be. He also knew that the bad infinite forced Hegel himself to choose a point within the history of the absolute to start his philosophy of history. And the cause of his preferring one point over against another was *not* rational necessity. Hegel chose because it suited his preference, not because of an eternal procession of logical categories.

At this point Kierkegaard wondered if he ought to run from such strange creatures. People that live and move and have their being *sub specie aeterni* are more peculiar than any men from Mars might possibly be. What could their appearance signify? Kierkegaard is worthy of being quoted *in extenso* here.

> One must therefore be very careful in dealing with a philosopher of the Hegelian school, and, above all, to make certain of the identity of the being with whom one has the honor to discourse. Is he a human being, an existing human being? Is he himself *sub specie aeterni,* even when he sleeps, eats, blows his nose, or whatever else a human being does? Is he himself the pure 'I am I'? . . . Does he in fact exist? And if he does, is he then not in process of becoming? And if he is in process of becoming, does he not face the future? And does he ever face the future by way of action? And if he never does, will he not forgive an ethical individual for saying in passion and with dramatic truth, that he is an ass? But if he ever acts *sensu eminenti,* does he not in that case face the future with infinite passion? Is there not then for him an either-or? Is it not the case that eternity is for an existing individual not eternity, but the future, and that eternity is eternity only for the Eternal, who is not in process of becoming? Let him state whether he can answer the following question, *i.e.,* if such a question can be addressed to him:

'Is ceasing to exist so far as possible, in order to be *sub specie aeterni*, something that happens to him, or is it subject to a decision of the will, perhaps even something one ought to do?' For if I ought to do it, an *aut-aut* is established even with respect to being *sub specie aeterni*. Was he born *sub specie aeterni*, and has he lived *sub specie aeterni* ever since, so that he cannot even understand what I am asking about, never having had anything to do with the future, and never having experienced any decision? In that case I readily understand that it is not a human being I have the honor to address. But this does not quite end the matter; for it seems to me a very strange circumstance that such mysterious beings begin to make their appearance. An epidemic of cholera is usually signalized by the appearance of a certain kind of fly not otherwise observable; may it not be the case that the appearance of these fabulous pure thinkers is a sign that some misfortune threatens humanity, as for instance the loss of the ethical and the religious?[35]

Some may find reasons to question the details of Solomon's lamentations, but they cannot meaningfully find fault with his conviction that man happens to be a free creature who happens to make choices. And these choices are influenced by what reason learns is the nature of reality. If reality is a relentless flow of rational necessity, man is not part of it; and his plight is all the worse. What consolation is there to learn that one is not even part of nature?

Part of reality *must* be volitional, for if all of nature is deductively necessary, time has no meaning. The time element is quite irrelevant in geometrical relations. Spinozistically, reality is a tremendous figure in geometry where all is motionless and silent. Nature is an eternal, silent blob of necessity. Not even hot steam rises from this pile of angles, for that itself would involve another contingency, and contingency takes time. Whenever God is about to speak, there is no "about"; so, there is no speech. Reality is an infinite-sized, squatting Buddha having an eternally changeless grin on its

---

35. Sören Kierkegaard, *Concluding Unscientific Postscript*, (Princeton University Press, 1941), pp. 271-272.

face.   This is the plenitude; this is the rationally necessary *I am*.

> Our principle of plentitude—in what may be called its static form—is thus inherent in the very substance of Spinoza's doctrine. From the timeless immutability of the World-Ground he argues directly to the necessary 'fulness' and also the necessary invariability of the temporal world's contents. But the paradox of that principle is more apparent in his philosophy than in others. . . .From the eternal logical necessity belonging to an essence there is, in truth, *no* valid argument to any conclusion about existence in time. For time itself is alien to that necessity; it is an alogical character of nature. Whatever is true of an essence is true of it all at once; but what is true of the temporal world is not true of it all at once. Becoming and change, as such, simply do not fit into an eternal rational order. The attempt to pass over from that order to one in which some things have their being at one time, and quite other things at a later time, is a *non sequitur,* and worse; but this was required by the principle of plenitude—was most clearly of all so required when that principle was regarded as an implicate of the principle of sufficient reason. If a literal realization of all genuine possibles is essential to a reasonable world, everything and everybody should have existed, and every event should have occurred, from all eternity, in a *totum simul;* but nature is not a *totum simul.*[36]

Before one can extract comfort from rational necessity, therefore, he must first deny his own decision life. Perfect, rational connections subsist only in a deductive system. But a free spirit cannot be forced into such a system, regardless how hard one grunts and shoves to make it fit. It may (or may not) be plausible that *God* spends eternity doing nothing but basking in abstractions, but it is ridiculous to think that *man* either does or can. Man is a contingent, choosing creature, free to roam eternity in spirit but very much bound in time and space as a finite being. If the philosophical ideal of ataraxia is to be defended, therefore, it will have to be pitched on a level which admits that there are nonrational aspects in

---

36. Arthur O. Lovejoy, *The Great Chain of Being,* (Harvard University Press, 1936), pp. 154-155.

life. Where there is freedom, non-necessity is found. We have not yet inquired if God is free; but we are quite assured that man is.

III. Want of Vocation

If the first problem of ataraxia is the metaphysical swallowing up of the individual into an all-embracing, rational whole, the second is the destruction of the real man in history (the only man a sensible philosopher should concern himself with) by supplying him no vocation. If life consists in the uncommitted posture of meditation on rationally necessary connections, man will suffer atrophy in his spirit. He will shrivel up and die. Spirit is destroyed, not by being engulfed in the absolute, but simply by having nothing to do. If plenitude slams an iron gate between nature and the possibility of contingency, thus blocking the possibility of a union of the two, other philosophic ideals simply snip the vine of spirit where it joins the root, leaving the fruit to wilt.

A. *Suspended Animation*

The history of philosophy has had some very weird twists to it. This is especially true when one examines the mutually excluding ways philosophers try to establish the same point. An illustration of this peculiarity is the way the *skeptics* have gone about establishing philosophical ataraxia. While they may have joined with Spinoza on the common premise that man is best when he thinks, they got at the matter in a way which would have greatly irritated the Dutch lens grinder. Spinoza could not move because he knew too much; the skeptics could not move because they did not know enough. There was no need to read Zeno's paradoxes, for neither could move anyway. Spinoza had no time, and the skeptics had no reason.

The skeptics found their own brand of peace by remaining suspended within a decisionless state of uncertainty. Not knowing anything for certain, it is unwise to be committed to anything. Inner equilibrium is shattered whenever men start to risk things. So, the best thing to do is to sit tight and do nothing.

A typical paradigm is Pyrrho. "His philosophy, in common with all post-Aristotelian systems, is purely practical in its outlook. Scepticism, the denial of knowledge, is not posited on account of its speculative interest, but only because Pyrrho sees in it the road to happiness, and the escape from the calamities of life."[37] How can men act intelligently when they are ignorant of the real nature of things? At best we can only perceive things as they *appear* to us, not as they are in their absolute nature. "We can be certain of nothing, not even of the most trivial assertions. Therefore we ought never to make any positive statements on any subject."[38] The only worthy course for a wise man is to refrain from decision on everything, insisting that things only seem so or that a course is chosen just because it appears better.

This may seem to destroy, not establish, happiness; but the skeptics did not see the matter in quite that light. A quiescent imperturbability resulted. What can trouble a man when he possesses the rational assurance that he will never have to decide anything? Unhappiness cannot make inroads, for a soul which refrains from commitment is relieved of the deceitfulness of illusions. "Unhappiness is the result of not attaining what one desires, or of losing it when attained. The wise man, being free from desires, is free from unhappiness. He knows that, though men struggle and fight for what they desire... such activity is but a futile struggle about nothing, for all things are equally indifferent, and nothing matters."[39]

> To the Pyrrhonist nothing was in itself either an evil or a good, and so he thought that life for him was especially easy. For instance, he who considers riches a good in themselves is unhappy in the loss of them, and in possessing them is in

---

37. W. T. Stace. *A Critical History of Greek Philosophy*, (London: Macmillan and Co., 1946), p. 362.

38. *Ibid.*, p. 363.

39. *Ibid.*, p. 364.

fear of losing them; while the Pyrrhonist, remembering the
maxim, 'No more,' was untroubled in whatever condition
he might be found. The loss of riches was no more an evil
than the possession of them was a good. He who considers
anything good or bad by nature is always troubled.[40]

Little time need be spent (nor *was* spent by subsequent
philosophers) examining the skeptic's case for ataraxia. The
trouble is that man is committed to exist whether he elects it
or not; life is made up of the stuff of decision. We grow by
decision. Decision comprises the very moral fiber of spirit.
To be committed to nothing is but a negative way of committing suicide. The heart of man is a veritable reservoir of
potentialites. Free possibilities within the individual, like an
impatient, mighty stallion, champ to move into action. And
when they are crushed or restrained, spirit suffers atrophy.
Decision life is to the spirit as physical exercise is to the
muscles of the body: When either stops, a shrinking of the
member results; until in the end death itself sets in. The price
one is obliged to pay for the joy of skeptical ataraxia, therefore, is the destruction of the inner man himself.

It was humorous to follow Pyrrho around for a day watching him — a man — playing the role of non-man. Not fearful of "wagons, precipices and dogs," he pretended complete
disconcern with life. Often a friend saved him from danger
— but this made no difference. "On another occasion, he was
frightened by a dog and climbed a tree, and, when accused
of inconsistency, he remarked that it is a difficult thing to lay
aside humanity altogether."[41] Indeed it is — and funny too!
If the worm who tries to lay aside wormness should be laughed
at, man appears just as funny when he tries to deny manhood.
We *must* act; there is no other option. Loyalty to friends,
contracts, and laws all call for decision. The destiny of history
lies in the hands of individuals who can act quickest and with

---

40. Mary Mills Patrick. *The Greek Sceptics,* (New York: Columbia
University Press, 1929), p. 276.
41. *Ibid.,* p. 40.

greatest persuasion. Therefore, it *does* make a difference what choices we make.

Angels may (or may not) be uncommitted; that is beside the point. Man *must* be committed. Our contemporary predicament requires that we launch out, regardless of how wanting in perfect demonstration the bases of our loyalties may be. Pyrrhonism collapsed because the conditions of a changing society called for swift and decisive commitment. As the Romans threatened to swallow up the Greek world, a desperate urge for survival displaced the easy principle of skeptical quietism. The sound of marching soldiers in the distance made it unambiguously clear that it was far from inconsequential how one acted. Those who did not act risked their chances again of ever having the opportunity. And in our own atomic hour the clarion cry of commitment resounds in the breast of every concerned man. The difference between the happiness and the despair of the whole race may turn on how quickly our collective mind rallies to those eternal loyalties which define the true, the good, and the beautiful. The mind may *discover* these connections, but man is man only when he is committed to them in his person.

B. *The Surprise Reversal*

Lying between the skeptics and Spinoza is a formidable bloc of mild rationalists who, while continuing very much to act, nevertheless still believe that the thinking man is the essential man. A straight line can be drawn from Socrates to the modern positivists, for in practically every type of philosophy it is axiomatically assumed that when man thinks correctly he accents his essence most effectively. But the very fact that knowledge-devotees continue to act, rather than just think, suggests that the whole matter may be more complex than a surface reading can show.

A false view of man underlies all philosophies which place a premium on inferential thinking as an end in itself. It is a simple thing to equate man with mind, pretending that the

real man is the thinking man; but it is not so simple to do
so with hand over heart. Is the I which walks around the room
essentially *nous*? *It is not.* The I is the whole person — intellect, emotions, will, etc. The I is the totality of all that is
meant to be spirit and body compounded in personality. The
individual is an organic whole, and thinking is one phase of his
activities. Thinking is never achieved in isolation of the rest
of our faculties. One must experience *joy* in thinking — that
accounts for the emotions. And he must *will* to think — that
accounts for the volitional life. Thinking is a tolerable pastime because of the delights in the whole man which it calls
up. It would be perfectly repulsive to imagine oneself as pure
nous. Nothing could be more boring than sitting still medi-
tating on rational relations all life through. There is no life
at all until all of what it means to be a man is committed.

When one closely examines the anatomy of enjoyment in
thinking, therefore, he discovers an extremely surprising fact.
The joy which is experienced is not the satisfaction of the act
at all; the joy is the satisfaction of *love*. Love is the inward
emotion of satisfaction which is aroused whenever a person is
committed to something pleasureful. It is not the doing which
is the satisfaction, but the love; for once the same act fails to
sustain interest, it elicits the disgusting feelings of boredom or
disappointment. The act is but the occasion for the rise of
pleasure. Socrates wandered into the market places, stirring
up conversation about virtue, because he found satisfaction
(love) in doing it. The Greeks around him took pleasure in
selling pots or stealing from friends. Aristotle found satisfaction in the clarification of metaphysics. If he had not
enjoyed doing it, he would have turned to pursuits more pleasing. But observe that love is the only satisfaction which men
have ever had pleasure in. We eat ice cream rather than hammer our finger because the one act calls up satisfaction while
the other does not.

For example: The positivist may pretend that his devotion
to epistemology is a purely objective concern, but he cannot
convince others that this is the case. He scurries to the uni-

versity library to examine the latest publications on epistemology because in so doing he elicits the satisfaction of love within him. He *loves* his work! It is an activity which interests him. The positivist's labor in drawing up a chart of meaning is only furniture for eliciting the satisfaction of love. To identify the act with the satisfaction itself is error. We pursue the hobby which we enjoy, and it matters not what the form happens to be — baseball, making airplanes, or spearing fish. As long as the emotion of love is called up within us, we pursue it. The man in cloth pretends that he preaches solely for the glory of God and the moral good of the people, but his motives are never that unalloyed. Compounded with his work is the fact that he enjoys preaching. He *loves* to shepherd the flock.

The proof that it is the love, not the act, which is the thing sought, is that the same act can be entered into with wholeheartedness one minute, while the next we hate even the thought of such a pursuit. Some people love to drive an automobile *e. g.,* for driving calls up a feeling of satisfaction within them; but after seeing a horrible highway accident, they then loathe the sight of an automobile. The activity remains exactly the same in both cases; but not being able to elicit love any longer, it is turned from and berated. The hobby which bores is abandoned.

This is a sure conclusion: When love vanishes, the value of all else vanishes, too. Love is the precondition of everything. We freely do only what interests us.

It is admittedly a profound mystery why the same act does not call up the emotion of love in all men. Some love tennis, and others despise it. Personal interests are complexly compounded with a jungle of contributing factors of heredity and environment, plus an infinite quantity and variety of fortuitous factors bounding in from every side. Slight matters of physical strength, allergies, etc. can spell the difference between one's finding satisfaction or bitter disappointment in a job. Though we are all "cut out" for different places in life, we are never perfectly sure who did the cutting or what pattern was used; we only know we are what we are.

But the actual mechanics involved in eliciting the satisfaction of love are quite irrelevant, anyway, for the point remains the same whether we can lay our finger on the nature of this process or not. We walk in the park because we find interest in it. We would turn the other way if opposite emotions were called up through the effort. We would stand on our head and kick our feet in the air by the hour if such were a tested means of enjoying life. We refrain from such irregular calisthenics, not because there are logical or moral arguments against it, but because no love is generated within us when we do it.

The point is so crucial that it must be labored. We often hear it said, "Do you enjoy your work?" If the question were put accurately, it would read as follows: *"Is this particular work the type which elicits the experience of enjoyment?"* The labor itself is but an accidental means of finding an abiding experience, for the task which grieves a man one day is able to give him pleasure the next.

The application of this principle is as follows: The reason why men so easily conclude that thinking is living, is that rational connections *do* initiate a stable flow of satisfactions in the heart. Men in all ages have enjoyed solving puzzles and dilemmas. There is an unmistakable satisfaction in working out the solution to a problem in geology or in understanding the reasons why gas goes up rather than down. Our penchant for curiosity is deeply engrained in human nature itself. The sciences have progressed under the steady hands of those who could not comfortably live with themselves until they began to find out the meaning of the universe. Wisdom *has* a proud glory to it. As Spinoza so lucidly saw, the reference point of true wisdom is stable.

The reason why both Solomon and Spinoza disqualified pleasures, riches, and fame as candidates for the office of final commitment in life, is not that the emotion of satisfaction was not called up during the act. Hardly, for it is the very *pres-*

ence of intense joy which makes wine, women, and song so alluring. The inadequacy is in the *duration* of the satisfaction. Being changeable in themselves, the lower immediacies cannot generate a changeless love in man. Wisdom, however, is not deficient in this way. Rationally necessary connections will abide yesterday, today, and forever. Validity is immutable.

But the problem abides: Is it possible to enjoy complete happiness in the act of thinking? If our daily experiences mean anything, the answer is an unequivocal negation. Love is complete only when like meets like. The love which one experiences as he rationally traces the route of the blood stream is never as perfect as the love which wells up within him when he is near his own family. Learning chemistry may call up satisfaction, but such a satisfaction is colorless compared to the joy of marrying a girl whose spirit has entered that of the chemist. The proof of this is that we label a man demented who rescues his scientific apparatus during a raging fire while deliberately leaving his wife and children to perish in the flames. Love is so intense in fellowship because there is a two-way flow of vitalities. Each member of the love relationship complements the other. The language of spirit can only be understood by another spirit. We weep with each other because spirit within us is able to enter into the inner urges of spirit over against us.

Why does a father breathe a sigh of relief to know that his children are safe, even though a windstorm has destroyed all his other possessions? The answer is that the children elicit from him a more abiding love than do physical properties. So deeply have the children gotten their hooks into his heart that he feels that life itself is empty when their love is taken away from him. Fellowship engages the whole spirit. This is the secret of its glory.

Thought can engage only part of the whole man — or, more accurately, it can engage the whole man only partly. Though men can understand rational relations, rational relations cannot understand men. People are complete only when they are understood, noticed, and appreciated. They are hurt when their ego is passed by without being appreciated. Yet, only persons can know persons; only heart can sympathize with heart. Rational relations have never entertained an ounce of concern for the whole race of men put together. The rational devotion is completely unilateral.

Graduate students often speak of "the fellowship of learning." What is actually meant is not that man can have fellowship with a triangle, but rather that learned men share loyalties in a common pursuit of truth. This is the only conceivable way learning can be a fellowship. The human heart and abstract rational relations cannot mix to form fellowship, for two incompatible qualities are being juxtaposed. The triangle is an *it*; man is a *person*.

The more deeply spirit enters spirit, the more exhilarating and intense is the resulting experience of love. Observe man's power of empathy: Early in April, 1949, for example, the world's heart was sent beating as the news was flashed that a small girl, Kathy Fiscus, had fallen into an open well shaft. The little girl was jammed inside the rusty pipe ninety feet below the surface of the ground. In a frantic effort to save the child, radios in greater Los Angeles beamed out a call for rescue workers. Men from all over Southern California rushed to San Marino, offering their help. And when the men arrived, they dug with *fanatical* fury. They had enjoyed studying the rational theories of engineering in school. The fascination of observing rational connections had indeed given them pleasure. And they had often dug into the ground before, receiving real joy in their work. But when they put the shovel to the soil mindful that the life of a small girl depended upon how skilled and swift they were in their work, a love spurted up within them, the satisfaction of which they had never experienced before. They worked around the clock, begrudgingly taking time off for even food and rest.

What could account for this sudden burst of vitality? Plain digging would not have done it. *They dug as they had never dug before because the satisfaction of love within them was more intense than it had ever before been.* Their heart was empathically joined with that of the dying girl. That was the answer.

In the empathic office one person reaches out and takes the sorrows and griefs of another, bearing them in his own person. The mother takes the weakness of the child and makes it her own. She knows of no satisfaction in life greater than this, for through the weakness of the little one she is made strong. Every longing within her for satisfaction is met when she holds the little one near and senses its helplessness.

A final clarification must be made, however, lest a new misconception arise. *The primacy of fellowship as a value does not in the least cancel out the primacy of reason as a test for truth.* It is the office of reason to examine alternative options, carefully determining what constitute the optimum conditions which call up fellowship. Since the intellect is the guide of the heart, it will hardly pay for one to run helter-skelter in his pursuit of love. There *is* a rationally perceptible difference between a baby and a tree, and it is the job of intellect to point this out. Reason has the power of analyzing alternative commitments, classifying the potentialities of each to call forth satisfaction.

Nevertheless, man fails to accent his best if theoretic perception does not convert into the thrill of personal fellowship. It is enjoyable to understand the theory of medicine or of bridge building, but these excitements are paltry when laid beside the warmth of heart which comes when the medicine is injected into the sick and dying and the bridge is erected for the increase of human pleasure. There is no conceivable labor which is not made lighter, no devotion not made more enjoyable, when it is compounded with an increase of human happiness. The prize won is fully enjoyable only when others are there to share, commend, and enjoy it.

When philosophers persist in believing that the thinking man is the best man, therefore, they unwittingly encourage the development of a generation of misers. Some misers dry up their souls collecting pieces of gold; others do it by collecting rational connections. The type of decay in each may differ, but the principle involved is quite the same. A personal spirit is juxtaposed with an impersonal thing. The mellowing vitalities which are the real stuff of life come only when spirit finds satisfaction in commitments which terminate upon the security and interests of others.

IV. Want of Consolation

However one may try to smooth it over with flowery treatises on the glory of rationality, the fact remains that devotion to the philosophic ideal is but another form of immediacy. There is satisfaction in thinking only when one actually *thinks*. When he ceases to think, the pleasure likewise ceases. The rational ideal is simply another person-thing affair in which a gradual wearing down of the potentialities of spirit sets in. In the end, the ego is deficient in strength to continue the terms of the relationship and satisfaction fails. Impersonal, rational relations are no more able to support and console the weak than impersonal sex, money, or science. The ineradicable flaw in all forms of immediacy is their failure to compensate by depositing accumulations of satisfaction which spirit may repose in when strength is wanting. The *it* is impotent to take any initiative in supporting the longings of the heart.

A. *Admonition to Youth*

Since freedom enjoys the power of anticipation, it is well that a person pursue in his youth what will sustain his happiness when strength diminishes. Freedom should remember the correlation which subsists between strength and interests. As our strength is, so is our power to appreciate.

It is well to observe how Solomon terminated his argument: "Remember also thy Creator in the days of thy youth, before the evil days come, and the years draw nigh, when thou shalt say, I have no pleasure in them." (Ecclesiastes 12:1) The striking thing about this species of argument is that it turns on the rather self-evident observation that there is a difference between the interests of the aged and those of sanguine youth.

Because of its power to engage budding rational faculties, the philosophic ideal appeals strongly to youth. The whole structure of general education revolves around the training of eager, supple minds. As the mind passes through the first stages in learning, however, it is subject to the easy fallacy of concluding that there is no theoretical limit to wisdom's power to satisfy. The fleeting days in college and graduate school just whet our appetite for learning. Life lies ahead with its infinite opportunities for gaining knowledge

What is overlooked in this blithe optimism, however, is the dependence of interest in rational matters upon personal strength. While men have the power of youth to lean on, they are determined, swift, and sure, never bowing to final defeat, stumbling for the moment but quickly rising again. But when senility sets in and even the least physical effort is exhausting, men are cautious, slow, and weary, fearing what is high and insecure, reaching out for the lasting and the peaceful. Freedom must assess the phase changes which inevitably overtake the individual, lest in an initial enthusiasm youth choose a value which will not stand up under the abrasions of time.

Satisfaction from meditation on rational connections is one of the values which may easily promise more than it ever can make good. If one has ever roamed through the endless halls of a home for the aged, for example, he has observed a rather universal want of interest in solving geometry problems among those who are weak and suffering. In college days a new edition of the works of Aristotle would have sent the heart spinning for joy, but when it is a burden even to keep one's eyes open, a world of new editions is of no interest. It is a full-time job sustaining the body, let alone the spirit.

It is exceedingly easy for ruddy youth to smile at Solomon's warning, crying out in the full flower of sanguine optimism that bridges will be crossed when they are reached. Such an attitude is characteristic of foolishness, however, for it marks a betrayal of freedom's power (and responsibility) to anticipate the future. It so happens — whether youth elects it or not — that one remains the same person on the bed of despair that he was as he marched to the front to receive his graduate degree in philosophy. The body may have changed several times, but the spirit is quite the same. The person remains an integral unity from the cradle to the grave. Marriage vows, for example, overpass the accidents of time and space, requiring that the bond of fidelity be pledged until death parts spirit from spirit. Social and economic relations are rooted in the presupposition that an abiding personality persists integrally through all physical alterations. A man is still a debtor, though he may have contracted his obligations a hundred years previously.

One tampers with *himself*, therefore, when he is cavalier about freedom. He is consigning his own person to despair. The aged are very much human beings. They do not lack a participation in the essence of humanity. They think, weep, hope, pray, laugh. But the burden of senility attends every thought, every tear, every hope and smile. And the only power which can enter into one's burdened heart and give it peace is the non-rational vitality of spirit meeting spirit. The senile crave love, but a love which does not require an expenditure of physical or mental strength on their part. The aged are weary.

The person remains very much a pleasure-seeking creature, but the pleasure must now come from a source which shares the responsibility of sustaining the love relation. But is it not self-evident that only other *persons* can perform this assignment? And is not God the only person with enough power to enter the heart when the physical faculties become a burden? There is no lovelier sight than to see a helpless old person bask in the sweetness of the Holy Spirit's comfort. As our strength to sustain the love relation fails, God assumes command.

Because the mind of man sometimes fails only after the body reaches a desperate stage in decay, the philosophic ideal is more deceiving than the lower immediacies. Some are able to think clearly at great age. Others take up the study of new languages, even traveling abroad for their research — while all the while pushing hard their threescore years and ten. The sex passions may fail, but the power of the mind remains.

What may be overlooked, however, is the rather significant datum that the body *will* fail. Time will take care of that. It is still true, therefore, that one ought to seek in times of strength what will sustain him most in times of weakness. It is a simple practice of storing up nuts for the winter. Every aged philosopher is fighting a war of attrition. Bit by bit his strength will fail, until finally all of his energies are absorbed in sustaining physical existence. In this ignoble conflict, physical exhaustion always wins.

Spinoza is persuasive only to the person who plugs his ears and will not hear the whole story. One's attention must be called to the fact that the happiness which comes through the perception of clear and distinct ideas is really not as abiding as a first examination may seem to show. The student in geometry only needs to catch a severe head cold to feel his interest in the Euclidean connections wane. And who is consoled at the funeral of his friend to be informed of the precise rational connections which define the chemical decomposition of his body? What soldier leaping from the trench to attack the enemy in distant darkness finds solace in the rational theory of war? In the real task of living we do *not* follow the philosophic ideal.

What Spinoza should have said is that, though the clear and distinct ideas are changeless, man's power and interest to apprehend them is not. The instant one stops thinking about rational connections — either through inattentiveness or want of power — that moment pleasure is cut off. Wisdom is *potentially* able to satisfy rational men throughout eternity; but the appropriation of that potentiality happens to be at the mercy of the response powers of the individual himself. Sex will satisfy a man as long as he can keep up the satisfaction. So will *any* immediacy. But the trouble with immediacy is that one cannot keep up the satisfaction, for energies always fail us.

Spinoza is correct in saying that necessary connections do not fail man because of any inherent deficiency in themselves. *They fail by default.* It is the human being that causes the failure. Men lack either the resolution or the strength to continue thinking about rational connections. Therefore, Spinoza is sadly mistaken in concluding that the intuitive perception of clear and distinct ideas defines the highest thinkable satisfaction for man. Freedom can perceive with a flawless intuition that a *perfect* commitment should leave deposits of satisfactions on the spirit which are able to sustain love even after physical vitalities have failed. What fear would the aged have if perfect satisfaction were their possession? When love is near, all else is accidental. But rational relations take no initiative to generate love in the heart. Therefore, they are *not* the highest conceivable option for man to pursue.

B. *Rebuttal*

One of the more plausible objections to this conclusion is the pretension that when physical strength to *pursue* further knowledge fails, one can retreat to the inner chambers of his own mind and bask in the storehouses of knowledge already won. As power to gain more fails, memory compensates.

It is true that memory is a remarkable faculty in man. By its power one is able to glance backward, calling in the past for re-examination and study. Plato has properly named memory and anticipation as two of our surest ways to find happiness.

But this assurance is itself conditioned by the ability of man to control his thought life. Memory is not an automatic source of satisfaction. Unless it is controlled, it can just as easily call up degenerating and disgusting thoughts as it can pleasureful ones. Memory must be directed and pampered. If it is to be serviceable to man, it must be harnessed by the discipline of direction. Memory of sad things can lead to grief, not satisfaction.

The problem, therefore, is still the want of strength and interest. The power to recall clear and distinct ideas will some day retire from us. How then can memory always be depended upon to trip the satisfaction of love within us? Memory is a consolation only to those able to control it. When strength fails, an unbridled memory may charge back on the spirit, bringing it into grief by reminding it of things it were better to forget.

Others contend that the time span of senility is far too brief for us to be concerned about it. Death will speedily come to claim us. As long as we have had a full life of satisfaction in wisdom's possession, that is plenty. To ask for more is selfishness.

Freedom laughs out loud at the charge of selfishness. It is no less worthy to want happiness at the *end* of our earthly life than it is at the beginning. And would it not be foolish to choose a life of partial satisfaction when whole happiness was within reach?

But the issue is far more serious than merely that of a short time span. The point is that there is an *essential* defect in ataraxia. From the very terms of the problem freedom knows in advance that spiritual frustration is inevitable.[42] This means that the philosophic ideal cannot stand the test of time. It suffers from a progressive self-refutation. When pursued long enough, it fails. And is this not proof it was not really man's highest ideal in the first place? Would there be an *inevitable* impotency in abstract connections if they represented that which is most able to exhaust spirit?

Furthermore, one will have completely missed the point if he thinks that the case against ataraxia rests on what men

---

42. As in the case of the enterprising farmer who entertained the exciting hypothesis of saving money by mixing sawdust in the oats he fed his horse. As he increased the quantity of sawdust each day, he diminished the quantity of oats. Just as he reached the point where the horse was being fed all sawdust, however, the animal died. The hypothesis was a good one—except that it did not work. And the reason why the hypothesis failed is that the basic elements in the experiment were incompatible to begin with. It took time for the fallacy to be flushed out, but the contradiction was present from the start.

actually do. The indictment would remain true even if a senile philosopher died with a broad smile on his face and a fresh edition of Xenophanes clutched lovingly in his arms. What people do, and what they ought to do, are two different things. Suppose that a person's philosophy is the thesis, "There is no water." When he immerses his right foot in the lake, he cries, "I feel no water whatever." When he drinks, he says, "I know of an illusion of water only." And suppose that his last days are spent on a sinking ship. When he goes into the sea and submerges beneath the waves, his dying cry is, "There is no water!" This man *ought* to have seen the folly of his philosophy, whether he ever did in actual practice or not. And the same is true with ataraxia: A spiritual man may cry in his last hours, "The finest satisfaction in life is contemplating rational connections!" But he *ought* to cry, "I am a spiritual being, and fellowship defines my nature."

Grief at the end of the process may well be a token that one has wrongly determined the meaning of life at its beginning. There ought to be no essential defects in an absolute commitment. Instead, a progressive self-validation should result. The more often spirit enters into engagement, the more sure the resulting satisfaction should be. As in marriage, each time of searching brings deeper pleasure. And if divorce marks the end of the romance, it is a patent proof that spirit made a mistake in choosing a partner at the start of the romance.

In any case, devotion to rationality is not the highest *thinkable* value in life. It may perchance be the best we have — the question must be investigated. At least it would be hypothetically more satisfying to pursue that which not only gives pleasure during the hours of *strength*, but which likewise affords that same pleasure in hours of weakness and despair. A two-way commitment is thinkably better than a one-way. This is a safe conclusion.

Summary

One of the distinguishing ways man is sovereign over the animals is his power of rationality. Whereas animals can think, man has the power to think about thinking. In short, he is free. The lure of perceiving connections in life can be illustrated perfectly by the instance of the young chemist who, whenever he commenced work in the laboratory, testified to the power that the subject had over him. The thrill of being absorbed in such an activity was so great that he lost all conciousness of time, esteeming even the consuming of food a burden, since it temporarily took him away from the source of this all-consuming enjoyment. The greying geologist poring over a new specimen of rock stratum, the botanist engrossed in the examination of a fresh shipment of exotic plants, the patient physicist constructing a complicated apparatus for testing a new by-product of atomic power — all are convincing instances of the dynamic of the rational ideal. One can safely conclude that when something wields such a power that man becomes *lost* in it — and not just now and then, but continually and repeatedly — it indeed is an exciting option.

Because of this pleasure attending rational and natural connections, however, men have been tempted to conclude that the real man is the rational man, and that the individual is at his best when he is in the laboratory puttering around with chemistry or erecting pieces of physics equipment. The truth is that thinking is inferior to the act of promoting fellowship, since the latter engagement trips more abiding satisfactions in us than the former. The act is only the occasion to call up within us satisfactions; it is not an end in itself. The proof of this is the way activities become vapid and insipid the moment they fail to elicit satisfaction. When we become bored, we turn to something else for pleasure. Satisfaction in fellowship is a more intense pleasure than that found in chemistry or botany because like meets like in mutual sympathy. There is no boredom in love.

The rational ideal is but another form of immediacy. By defining satisfaction as the union of a person with a thing, it underrates the power of man for fellowship. It overlooks the fact that an immediacy is but a one-sided satisfaction. The pleasure is there only when either strength or resolution to engage in rational pursuit remains. When either interest or ability wanes, the satisfaction diminishes in direct proportion. Being a chemist is excellent — as long as there is interest in chemistry; as long as one has the physical and mental power to rise to the interest; as long as the conditions prevail for chemistry to be possible. But if these factors are wanting, what then?

Devotion to other persons shows the first sign of a break in immediacy, for an act of self-sacrifice toward others leaves deposits of peace and satisfaction on the soul which linger sweetly after all else has vanished. When the lover is weak and bewildered, the beloved is made strong; for through weakness love is perfected. After the laboratory burns, after the university library is sacked by the enemy horde, the husband can remind his wife that since they still have each other, they have the thing which really counts. Love is a two-way satisfaction, for each has an interest in the other. Therefore, it lies in a new genus.

Paul said that wisdom cannot satisfy. "As for knowledge, it will pass away." (I Corinthians 13:8) And he did not mean that there will come a time when the geometry of Euclid will be invalid. If understood that way, knowledge does not fail. When man forgets rational connections, God will remember. Rationality is an everlasting relation — just as Spinoza defined it. But Paul did mean that, when evaluated as a power to meet and satisfy the inner longings of the human heart, knowledge would pass away. Wisdom fails through default, and the cause of default is man, not the wisdom. There will come a time when either power, resolution, or the presence of optimum conditions will fail. It is at that point that knowledge fails.

What else could be expected from an immediacy?

Part IV

THRESHOLD OPTIONS

VII

Devotion to Man

WHILE spirit may be happy over having escaped from the immediacies of Egypt, it has no reason to rejoice that Canaan has yet been reached. The Jordan is not even in sight, let alone being crossed. In its transition from devotion to impersonal values to the vitalities of personality, spirit has brought new complexities down upon itself. Shall we define human or divine personality as our ultimate? Or, is there a sharing of ultimacy? And if so, what is the exact relation between them? In what order should our devotion appear?

The Christian answer to these questions is unambiguous. Ultimacy belongs to God alone, for it is only through the antecedent sovereignty of the divine person that created personalities are worthy of devotion. Love for God is expressed in worship, and love toward man in self-sacrifice. Man possesses a lovable dignity because he is made in the image of the Father God.

The ethic of Christianity, therefore, is based on what is conventionally known as the two tables of the law. The first four of the Ten Commandments summarize man's duty to God, while the last six detail the relations which should subsist between men. This order is everywhere respected in the corpus of revelation. Man is dignified by his vertical relation to God. He enjoys no autonomous rights. The Biblical revelation nowhere details a complex philosophic anthropology to establish this point. It simply declares it, assuming that when a man knows the meaning of his own free heights, he will perceive for himself the impasse spirit reaches whenever an attempt is made to dignify man independently of the divine

227

essence. The relative is known only in and through the absolute.

When Christ completed the law in his word and person, he did not depart from the essentiality of this two-table structure. He simply filled the law full, stepping up the Ten Commandments by defining the law as love. Whoever loves both God and man *has* fulfilled the commandments.

> And one of the scribes came up and . . . asked him, 'Which commandment is the first of all?' Jesus answered, 'The first is, "Hear, O Israel: The Lord our God, the Lord is one; and you shall love the Lord your God with all your heart, and with all your soul, and with all your mind, and with all your strength." The second is this, "You shall love your neighbor as yourself." There is no other commandment greater than these.'[1]

In plainest tongue, Christ presumed to declare the very law of our own dignity, the very law of life. To live is to love; and perfect love is found only when we know and enjoy God on the one hand, and when we live self-sacrificially for one another on the other. This is the final definition of our powers of spirit. When our free height is exhausted, worship for God and self-sacrifice toward our brother will define our conduct.

When there is a choice between the will of God and the will of an earthly loved one, therefore, one is to choose God every time. "If any one comes to me and does not hate his own father and mother and wife and children and brothers and sisters, yes, and even his own life, he cannot be my disciple." (Luke 14:26) The reason for this priority of order is that apart from the God who both dignifies and sustains him, man is without essential value.

I. Humanism: Contender for Man

This Christian structure is by no means a cut-and-dried proposition for the contemporary mind, however. In fact to

---

1. Mark 12:28-31. *cf.* Deuteronomy 6:5 and Leviticus 19:18.

the majority of people it is extremely unclear that an analysis of the meaning of life necessitates the priority of devotion to God. And the color guard for this vast mind is humanism. To use Biblical terms in describing it, humanism is that philosophy of life which contends that our highest known value is man and that the second table of the law is able to rest on its own foundation. Devotion to man is a satisfaction which is completely independent of the question of God. Some people *choose* to love God, but they must not pretend that any compulsion for that act flows out of our knowledge of values. Anthropology does not rest on theology.

> 'Religious humanism,' or simply 'humanism,' indicates, if not a theoretical denial, at least a neglect or a practical denial, of theism, for the sake of substituting as a religion a would-be scientific and ethical absorption in human affairs without reference to God. So well established has this use of the word now become that it appears in the unabridged second edition of *Webster's New International Dictionary*, where it is defined as 'A contemporary cult or belief calling itself religious but substituting faith in man for faith in God.'[2]

The reason why spirit immediately senses that a choice between humanism and Christianity will be difficult is that both defend values which terminate on persons. Each is agreed that less than devotion to living personalities is an affront to the dignity of man. Humanism comes as far as, but refuses to go beyond, the second table of the law. Or, more accurately, it says that this is the only table there is. It is first *and* second. In deciding between these two options, the heart has no other recourse than carefully to evaluate what it is left with if it chooses one over against the other. Which leaves the whole individual with the least cause for regret?

A. *Devotion to Science*

Because of its unswerving faith in man's infinite self-perfectibility, it is natural that humanism joins with positivism in

---

2. Arthur Hazard Dakin, *Man the Measure*, (Princeton: Princeton University Press, 1939), xi.

the conviction that society's ills grow out of man's refusal to employ his own natural endowments. Man *has* a glory about him; let him therefore utilize it. Let him prove his perfectibility by a sober commitment to those forms and methods which allow him to release his potentialities maximally. And king of all methodology is the scientific method.

> The development, over the past four centuries, of a universally reliable method for attaining knowledge is a far more important achievement on the part of science than its discovery of any single truth. For once men acquire a thoroughly dependable *method* of truth-seeking, a method that can be applied to every sphere of human life and by anyone who faithfully conforms to certain directives, then they have as a permanent possession an instrument of infinite power that will serve them as long as mankind endures. Scientific method is such an instrument.[3]

There is no need for man to permit a premature *a priori* to shackle him; there is no need for dreams, revelations, or tea-leaf speculations. If our head is clear and our method good, there is no practical limit to the ends which may be accomplished. "Humanism believes that man has the power and potentiality of solving his own problems successfully, relying primarily on reason and scientific method to do so and to enlarge continually his knowledge of the truth."[4]

And when we *do* employ good reason and good science effectively, what is discovered about the nature of the universe? Negatively, nothing is learned which can support the theistic postulate that nature is ordered by God.

The universe is a big, mathematically regulated, natural, purposeless mass. This is all that science finds. There is nothing to be gained by speculating on either the origin or end of the natural world, for these questions lie outside of the pale of science. They are simply superstitions. Beyond man there are only pointer readings.

---

3. Corliss Lamont, *Humanism as a Philosophy*, (New York: Philosophical Library, 1949), pp. 236-237.
4. *Ibid.*, p. 20.

Humanism believes in a naturalistic cosmology or metaphysics or attitude toward the universe that rules out all forms of the supernatural and that regards Nature as the totality of being and as a constantly changing system of events which exists independently of any mind or consciousness.[5]

The penchant in man to prefer the spectacular and the mysterious must be overcome by disciplined insight. Xenophanes long ago called man's hand at anthropomorphism. By deifying one's own virtures, one supposes that supernatural beings exist which have the same virtues. If oxen and horses and lions had hands with which to mold, they likewise would shape their gods after their own images. Do not the Ethiopians make their gods black and snub-nosed? Do not the Thracians say theirs have blue eyes and red hair? In the same way Feuerbach suspected that theology is simply anthropology. Man abstracts one of his own virtues, raises it to the nth power, and then bows down and worships it. But he only worships himself.

Let's be honest with ourselves! the humanist insists. If science exhibits the want of any higher value than man, let us as rational beings remain content with that conclusion. Nothing will be gained by wishing for relations that do not exist. It might be *nice* to believe that God exists or that the universe has final causes in it, but personal wishing will not make things so.

Would it not be better, if that is the case—more honest and less open to the charge of insincerity—frankly to give up the term 'God' and to work out our religious philosophy entirely in other concepts, at least until enough people have learned this important lesson so that the term might be redefined without danger of bewilderment?[6]

---

5. *Op. cit.*, p. 19. "The new science of religion begins with the known phenomena, namely, the religious experience of man, and works toward the unknown. It admits that God is as yet unknown. In fact, if we are to have any science of religion at all, it must be agnostic about God. We may discover God some day, and we may not." Charles Francis Potter, *Humanism a New Religion*, (New York: Simon and Schuster, 1930), p. 1.

6. Edwin A. Burtt, *Types of Religious Philosophy*, (New York: Harper and Brothers, 1939), p. 354.

Humanism and positivism share a common rejection of everything which is not subject to the scrutiny of carefully defined science. Thus, humanism *suffers for a method*. Hardheaded and rigorous, the humanist courageously disaffiliates himself from the whole body of theistic tradition which has gone before him. This calls for real suffering.

B. *The Primacy of Human Values*

The distinctiveness of the humanist is not exhausted in his relentless obedience to empirical science, however, since his methodological suffering is shared with positivism. His *unique* contribution to spirit lies in the field of understanding and conserving human values. His argument is simply this: While we may not have evidence that God exists, we *do* know of the existence of human beings. In lieu of the one, therefore, let us devote ourselves with wholehearted absorption to the preservation of the other. Whatever the ultimate nature of reality may be, science does not presume to know. But one thing is sure: There *are* loves and friendships, physical and mental wants to be met and satisfied. It is the undeviating conviction of the humanist that the responsibility of increasing justice and happiness in the world is so taxing in its requirements, that the committed spirit will lack no satisfaction. Since there is no actual limit to the perfectibility of brotherhood in history, each generation has an infinite assignment before it.

> Humanism is the conviction that personality is the explanation of the universe, that man himself is the highest manifestation of this personality, and that the powers resident in the individual and society are sufficient to insure progress toward an ideal society of ideal persons.[7]

Science (presumably) can assimilate a religious ideal which is built around the primacy of human values. Humanism is this religion. In place of idle speculation about questions of providence and creation the humanist is content to investigate

---

7. Potter, *op. cit.,* p. 14.

problems of individual and social integration. Man is very much here, and it is the duty of both religion and science to find the causal connections which will prevent individuals from being frustrated either by the universe or by their relations to each other. For example, labor problems must be studied and solved. Satisfactory means must be discovered for the equitable processing and distributing of food and clothing. Instead of belittling himself as a chronic sinner, therefore, man must begin to realize his potentialities for self-perfectibility. The funeral dirge of man's impotency has been played long enough. "Humanism believes, in opposition to all theories of universal predestination, determinism or fatalism, that human beings possess true freedom of creative action and are, within reasonable limits, the masters of their own destiny."[8]

But what about the first table of the law? Has not Christianity declared that man derives his dignity from *God*? Humanism counters by asking whence a gorgeous rose derives its dignity. Does the rose spill out its fragrance only when we first postulate God as its author? The answers are self-evident. Beauty is its own testimony. Why then is it needful that *human* values — the most evident of all — require the support of a transtemporal mind? If a man will simply open his eyes to the meaning of life, he will perceive that values are real whether God exists or not.

Whatever it be called, Humanism is the viewpoint that men have but one life to lead and should make the most of it in terms of creative work and happiness; that human happiness is its own justification and requires no sanction or support from supernatural sources; that in any case the supernatural, usually conceived of in the form of heavenly gods or immortal heavens, does not exist; and that human beings, using their own intelligence and cooperating liberally with one another, can build an enduring citadel of peace and beauty upon this earth.[9]

8. Lamont, *op. cit.*, p. 20.
9. *Ibid.*, p. 21.

By reversing the field, thus, the humanist emerges with the plausibility that he defends the rights of spirit even more than the theist. More is demanded of man if he has no everlasting arms to lean on. According to the humanist, only man is on hand to preserve worth-while values; and if he does not attend to their preservation, no one will. That is how serious he views the situation. But the assignment is zestful and challenging because man is capable of performing it. Man's problem is want of *resolution,* not want of possession.

Humanism is deeply impressed by the obvious fact that the most powerful opposition to the progress of man has stemmed from theistic religion. Science has had to fight for every inch of ground it has gained. The history of theism has hardly been a success story. The divine will is often appealed to as an *a priori* justification of the most flagrant evils: social injustice, political intolerance and pride, racial bigotry, inquisitorial persecution, arrogance in high places, and religious fanaticism or quietism. Faith in the infinite perfectibility of man encouraged Renaissance minds to break with those religious forms which stifled social progress. Humanism joins in their train.

Humanism is assured that any *prayer* of man — if prayer there must be — should be one of forgiveness for not using the potentialities which are already his. Under no circumstances ought one dare to pray for an increase of grace. Man is already capable of infinite self-betterment. He must learn to distinguish between pious modesty and sheer laziness. He must turn from his "moral holidays" and roll up his own sleeves for work. Quietly resting in the everlasting arms of the absolute as a solution to social and political problems will only enervate, not promote, man's fight for the right. Let us educate ourselves to appreciate the role of right reason in a free democracy, not catechize our minds into a passive submission to a god. Humanism "is a philosophy of joyous service for the greater good of all humanity in this natural world and according to the methods of reason and democracy"[10] We must cease praying for a *deus ex machina* solution to our own woes. Our responsibility is to make a little heaven out of this world, not postpone present action on the grounds that there are "better things to come." Anticipation of heaven and fear of hell are baits for those who have not yet arrived at selfhood. Tell men what they *can* do, not what they cannot.

> Much of the emphasis in supernaturalistic ethics has been negative, calling on men continually to deny many of their most wholesome impulses in order to keep their souls pure and undefiled for that life after death which is so very much more important than life before death. In this ethics the prospect of supernatural rewards and punishments in the future overshadows present conduct; the values decreed by supernatural authority override those of the natural and temporal order in which man actually lives. The emphasis of Humanist and naturalistic ethics is *positive*, recommending the greater and more frequent enjoyment of earthly goods on the part of all men everywhere and unendingly. It is an ethics that repudiates ascetic other-worldliness in favor of buoyant this-worldliness. It is against all defeatist systems which either postpone happiness to an afterexistence or recommend acquiescence to social injustice in this existence. [11]

Theism has betrayed freedom by prematurely clamping a cap on present perfectibility.

Humanists likewise turn against professing scientists who force a limit to our creative potentialities. The cult of doom which has so recently arisen in positivism is disgusting to consistent humanism. Just as the medieval peasant despaired of finding a cure for tuberculosis, so Bertrand Russell and others despair of finding a way to counteract the second law of thermodynamics. What is the essential difference between the two attitudes? Is it scientific to decree limits to a creativity man has not yet tried?

---

10. Lamont, *op. cit.*, p. 18.
11. *Ibid.*, pp. 274-275.

What I want to deny emphatically is the necessity of any ultimate doom for man, a fate often predicted today by pessimistic scientists rather than by theologians longing for the Day of Judgment. I deny the *inevitability* of this earth becoming uninhabitable at some distant date and of all the living creatures upon it being extinguished. I acknowledge that this *may* happen; but there is at least a chance that developments in science, and in social and international cooperation, over the next five or ten or hundred million years will be able to prevent the final disaster. [12]

By tracing its history back through science and art to the golden age of Pericles, humanism refutes the groundless charge that it is an ephemeral novelty. Men are humanists whenever they believe in man. "Humanism means simply human-being-ism, that is, devotion to the interests of human beings, wherever they live and whatever their status."[13] Humanism is a proportioned blending of the insights of naturalism, materialism, the Reformation, the Renaissance, poetry, fine art, literature, science, and industry. It draws its heritage from any and all religious, philosophic, and scientific sources which defend the intrinsic goodness and inexhaustive perfectibility of man.

C. *The Balanced Menu*

Two essential elements characterize modern humanism, therefore. *First,* by adhering to the scientific method as its means of verification, it is a type of methodological suffering. *Second,* it boasts a depth perception which claims to be commensurate with the height of our free possibilities. Each element is significant in its own right. Let us say a word about each.

What comment need be added concerning the value of the scientific method? Science's story has already been written by the glorious history of technological progress. Were it not for the reaching out of man's Renaissance possibilities we

12. *Op. cit.,* p. 138.
13. *Ibid.,* p. 23.

might well remain bound by the superstitions and obscurant-
isms of the medieval synthesis. And who wishes to return to
stifling, feudal-agrarian society? Likewise, is not spirit ex-
hilerated by the ideal of devotion to man? When compared
with other goods and ideals, personality emerges as the highest and finest good.

Love was quickly recognized by the Greeks as a plausible
explanation for the link between potentiality and actuality.
Eros is the dynamic urge in the lower to be the higher and in
the higher to mirror itself fully in the lower. Plato taught
that God's love for infinite self-expression is the clue to creation. Aristotle moved love into the hierarchy of the rational
forms, the lower admiring the higher, and all moving in love
for the unmoved mover.

Science may (or may not) have ruled out the need for
postulating a conative element in nature, but it cannot deny
the obvious fact that the only way potentiality passes into
actuality in *social* relations is love. If personal interest is not
called up when problems of justice are discussed, *e. g.*, no act
will follow. If he is to fight with all his heart, the soldier
must love the cause. If he is to make progress in the control of
nature, the scientist must love the laboratory.

Humanism is convincing and penetrating when it subordinates love-for-a-thing to love-for-the-individual, and it is here
that it severs ties with immediacy. The difference between
love for an impersonal thing and love for man is that whereas
the former brings satisfactions only during the actual engagement, the latter leaves deposits of satisfaction on the heart
which are accessible long after the act. Whoever sacrifices
something of himself to increase the security of another keeps
a satisfaction on tap which never leaves him. No pleasure
lingers like that of sacrificial love, for it has a quality about it
which no extension of love for a thing can ever provide. As
he lives for others, one feels so good inside, so clean, he perceives at once that he is dealing with the very law of his life.

Love called up by a cordial relation of man to man never
bores or frustrates. The mother never receives her children's

love in such a concentrated dose that she must beg for a change in diet. Human love is fresh and satisfying each moment. Everything else in the world may fail and disappoint, but it is characteristic of fellowship never to fail. It contains its own dynamic of satisfaction. Pure love leads to nothing else, being itself the perfect end. Love is simply spirit entering spirit in fellowship. Intensity of satisfaction in love wears well because the more it is juxtaposed beside spirit, the more like meets like. The result is a flaming peace.

Charles Dickens has captured the mood of humanism in his classic work, *A Christmas Carol.* The tight-fisted curmudgeon, Scrooge, chafed because he had to live in a world of insane people, a place where men turned to such foolish interests as charity and good will. The groveling old man (trying very hard to be a thing when he remained very much a person) felt that the world would be far better off if each man minded his own business. But when the Christmas spirits vividly displayed before him the inevitable end of such a life, and what joys he was missing by trying to find his love by hoarding money instead of helping Tiny Tim to live, he came to the realization that mankind was his business and that without fellowship and charity there is no life at all. He leaped with joy when he came to himself and discovered afresh what it meant to be a person.

One of the first responses of the child is that of love. No formal training is needed for one to recognize the value of love, even as no discipline is required to sustain it. A child perceives love's meaning by intuition. The little one nurtures no personal prejudice against others because of their race or creed. He knows only people, and all people are good people. When we study the cycle of life, therefore, let our prayer be that we may remain as little children. As one passes through adolescence into adult life, he foolishly prefers his own security to that of others, just as he foolishly seeks satisfactions within the deceptions of immediacy. But time has a way of exposing one's folly, for when senility overtakes the heart and strength is wanting to pursue the lower pleasures, one again seeks out the plain values so intuitively followed in childhood. Only when the warmth of love remains do the aged know peace and satisfaction. Life is a challenging labyrinth of conflicting alternatives. Men wander through one maze of passages into another in an effort to find the meaning of life, only to turn at last to the starting point and discover that the love which is natural to the child is the only value in life that counts.

All love becomes part of the soul, be it a love gained through immediacy or one which has come through self-sacrifice. But the difference between these types of love is that whereas one progressively disintegrates the person (as with Scrooge) the other progressively integrates him (as with all who have learned to sacrifice for others). The only satisfaction which the heart can continue to absorb without reaching a point of saturation is the love which terminates in personality.

Therefore, the heart is *glad* when it turns from a devotion to immediacy to the pursuit of human securities. One feels good when he labors for an ideal cause; but he feels better when he labors for real men. Whenever one dares to bring himself to the point where he places his own security in a subordinate position to that of his neighbor, he feels his best. This hierarchy of values in love is quickly recognized by the concerned heart. The instant an individual sacrifices something to make the unfortunate more secure, that moment there wells up within him a feeling of dignity which can be explained only on the hypothesis that the law of life has been fulfilled. There is an ought written on our heart which commands men to learn the meaning of their own life through fellowship and sacrifice. Being *capable* of loving others, man will not finally learn satisfaction until he actually does. There is an unmistakable loss of dignity in the heart of one who is presented an opportunity to do good to another, but passes it by. The searching eyes of the starving, the groping hands of the blind, the pitiful crying of the orphaned children all have a way of staying with a person. They are invisible hands of judgment pointing toward the heart and shaming it before the free self. If the meaning of life is not closely connected with this spurned opportunity, why do we feel so sheepish and little when we turn aside from an opportunity to do good? If such a life does not run cross-grained to a healthy spirit, why the inner disintegration which comes from selfishness? The humanist, therefore, is on solid ground when he refuses to define the normative life in lower terms than a selfless devotion to all individuals. The moment we attempt to turn from this ideal to an alternative which leaves personality out, that moment we betray our self-dignity.

Therefore, *should we not devote ourselves to humanism?* Need the contemporary mind pass beyond this option for its final security? These questions can be answered only when, granting the premises of humanism, we see where we are led.

II. Two Masters

Humanism has sought to sustain a delicate balance between devotion to science and devotion to man. Science supplies the method of knowing, and man supplies the values for which we strive. Attractive as the structure may first seem, however, it immediately opens problems which are serious and searching.

A. *Circumstantial Evidence*

When the humanist speaks in the roll of a scientist, he is very humble and tentative in his assertions. He denies that there is any code which has final authority, any moral law which is not subject to the verdict of tomorrow's scientific investigation. Every hypothesis is threatened by the facts. But when as a philosopher he advocates ideals which define human welfare — such as universal justice through a fair distribution of goods — he speaks in an absolute tone of self-assurance and finality. One is not asked if he personally *thinks* it would be worthy if the devotion to man were included among his interests. The humanist comes, rather, declaring that one *ought* to seek the preservation of human values.

The introduction of moral obligation immediately relieves humanism of a right to claim that its ideal rests on consistent scientific conclusions. By an enlargement of man's control over nature, science may tease out new methods to increase human security; but it cannot in all eternity form a laboratory experiment which can tell a man what he ought to do. *Ex hypothesi* science is limited to a description of reality. Its outside possibilities are exhausted in the enumeration of things as they actually are in nature. When science leaves description, advocating either what cannot be or what ought to be, it has left good science to become poor philosophy. Science describes, but never prescribes.

How, then, can the humanist presume to announce as *finalities* both that man's values are the highest in the universe and also that they ought to be preserved? The obvious answer is that the announcement is based on convictions gained independently of an application of the scientific method. Because he asserts that it is not meaningful to refer to ethical or moral propositions as cognitive, the positivist is scientifically more persuasive than the humanist. Positivism clearly perceives that there is no if-then operation which can produce one ounce of normative truth.

Humanism really turns out to be another form of *a priori* religion, therefore. The humanistic ideal of devotion to man rests more on an intuitive grasp of intrinsic values than on conclusions supplied by science. It happens to be experientially — though not scientifically — true that one cannot deny the objectivity of human values without defying his own dignity. This type of experience is not the kind that science can process in the laboratory, for it is an immediate intuition. It stems out of spirit's awareness of its own peculiar environment.

B. *Implication*

This is not the full end of the matter, however. Once the non-scientific hypothesis of *human* ideals is granted, the wedge

is set for the entertainment of other non-scientific ideals likewise — as, for instance, the duty of man to worship God.
The humanist is not a positivist. He realizes there *is* factual
significance to ethical propositions. There *is* cognitive meaning to the proposition, "One ought to preserve justice and
equality among men." In short, he tacitly admits that the
scientific method is strictly valid only in those areas where a
quantification of the data is possible. And such a quantification cannot be enjoyed when the normative characteristics of
truth, goodness, and beauty are in question. Therefore, one
does not learn the ideal of humanism through laboratory
methods. He first decides the ideal on other grounds; he then
uses the infinite potentialities of both reason and science to
foster it.

How, then, can the humanist rule out the knowability of
God on the authority of the scientific method? Where in the
range of science is the laboratory method less in order than
when the existence of an absolute sovereign God is probed?
Is it possible to prove that God does or does not exist by collecting footprints or by measuring the distance between a
number of planets? What science has actually done is this: It
has presupposed *a priori* that the universe is a purposeless
machine. And from this *a priori* assumption it concludes the
nonexistence of God. But may it not still be possible that for
reasons sufficient to his own will God created the machine?
Is *this* a cognitive sentence: "The universe is a not-made-by-
God machine"? If it is, then one need search no further for
patent proof that cognitive meanings are *not* limited to scientific
experiments, for there can be no experiment of this matter.
And if it is not, then the nonexistence of God does not follow
from the scientific method. Yet, it is in the *name of science*
that humanism dismisses the existence of God. The case for
theism is not seriously discussed.

Is this not an unsatisfactory arrangement? When defending
the validity of human values, humanism is quick to break
with science; while in the instance of the finality of divine
values, science is followed with adulation. There is only one

satisfactory conclusion that can be reached: Either one must break with science on the finality of human values, and so destroy the ideal of humanism; or he must at least leave open the possibility of God's existence. Whether we will ever *want* to discuss God's existence is a matter which has not been settled. But it is well to keep the door ajar. It is far from clear yet that a non-God option is to be preferred to a faith grounded in the existence of the Almighty. Haste in axiological matters may bring axiological waste.

III. The Issue of Motive

A. *The Problem of Self-Love*

The clearest thing about human motives is that in and through every decision or act there threads the ubiquitous power of self-love, "For we are born self-centered. What affects ourselves seems to us more important than what affects others, unless those others are members of our own circle."[14] Nothing can appeal to man, therefore, unless it really *appeals*. Values which increase self-security draw us on with a magnetic power, while those which threaten our security are shunned. "For no man ever hates his own flesh, but nourishes and cherishes it." (Ephesians 5:29) No man needs to be taught to love himself, since we are all born with an inward thirst for self-security. For this reason it is a psychological impossibility for one to prefer what he knows will diminish his happiness. Even in foolish choices people *think* they are augmenting personal security.

There is nothing unworthy about loving the self. Even Christ recognizes this when he bases our love for neighbors on the strength of our love for self. We are to love our neighbor *as ourselves*. If self-love is ever destroyed, initiative will be destroyed; for we progress only as we are drawn into commitments which concern us. The interesting is that which pleases our ego. When offering the gospel, therefore, Christ

14. William Temple, *Christianity in Thought and Practice*, (New York: Morehouse Publishing Company, 1936), p. 86.

appeals to the ego. He promises men that by giving up one type of selfishness (before men) they will gain a new and higher selfishness (before God). If we follow him, we receive peace in heart and treasures in heaven. All of this appeals to self-love.

The first test of humanism, thus, is to determine whether one increases or decreases his own security by following the program. Not even the most nobly worded cause can make inroads into the heart of man if it does not first direct its overtures to self-love. Man happens to be just a man.

A *prima facie* interpretation of humanism seems to suggest that the ego has nothing to fear. Is it not true that when all of mankind is made secure, each individual will participate in his share of security, too? By devoting myself to others, therefore, I appear to reap an inevitable gain myself. If the whole family is happy, each member will benefit in turn.

When the ego takes a closer look at the implications which flow from a devotion to all men, however, a feeling of uncertainty displaces the provisionally gained satisfaction. Since there are no few times when a conflict rages between social and individual good, self-love does not have the easy time in humanism that it expected. Why should the individual *ever* prefer the well-being of the collective ego to his own? It is easy to understand why it is wise to be devoted to those who are in a position to reciprocate with securities of one sort or another, but what sense is there in sacrificing the self for those who lie outside of this area of influence? Let us suppose that during a time of famine an individual has stores of food in his cellar which none outside of his own family know of. And suppose that people around him begin to die for want of food, while he continues to enjoy plenty himself. If their death does not affect his security in any way, why should he open up his food stores and share with them? Why should he risk his own physical well-being for the sake of those who will never be able to repay him after he does sacrifice? The problem is serious in humanism, since it admits of no divine sanctions to encourage the individual to respect the needs of others.

The only urge is a horizontally oriented self-love. We are not responsible to God.

The upshot is that humanism satisfies the ego only up to a given point. As long as the well-being of those to whom we are devoted affects our own well-being, self-love stumbles over no problems. For example, it is wise for a wealthy man to contribute to near-by social agencies on the selfish ground that discontented masses may band together and rise up against him in force, taking all he has left. It is far better to dole out enough charity to keep social forces in subjection than to risk complete insecurity. But why should one dole out *anything* if his own security is not jeopardized? The demands of the world are so great that if one exposed his treasure chests to the grabbing hands of the needy everywhere, he himself would be poor before the afternoon was over. And the ego recoils from the thought of reduction to poverty!

But the problem becomes even worse when one realizes that devotion to men is not something which can be requited by the clean little gesture of sending food packages to the needy. Albert Schweitzer did not find contentment until, after packing his bags and journeying to the edge of the forest primeval, he requited his indebtedness to the colored man through the sacrifice of his own person. If one were really devoted to all men, he would postpone seeking his own security, selflessly sacrificing himself for others. But this is a hard doctrine to hear. Who can bear it? Self-love wonders if it should get so serious about this business of serving men that the cost is one's own life. Why not just do a *little* for others and then call it quits? Suppose a building is on fire, for example. Will we not retain our own dignity if we make a sincere effort to extinguish the flame by holding one of the hoses? Why rush into the burning building, endangering our own lives to save those whose life or death will make no difference to us anyway?

The humanist may respond that we experience a real good feeling inside when we sacrifice ourselves for others. But what is overlooked is that this feeling proves nothing, unless man is made in the image of God. If we were ultimately responsible to God for our actions, we might see some meaning in loving our enemies and praying for those who mindfully despise us. God would give us rewards for our service — thus saving self-love. But since we are responsible to ourselves only, and not to God, it seems far wiser to control our feelings by mind rather than have our mind be controlled by feelings. Perhaps this supposed good feeling is simply the result of a glandular secretion. It may even represent a distortion. Perhaps we ought to see a doctor about the whole situation, for it does seem very peculiar that we should feel good as a result of destroying our own social and economic security. Logically, we should feel bad. Self-love cannot solve such a riddle.*

B. *The Uneasy Conscience of the Humanist*

Since the collision between individual and group security presents a problem too obvious to be by-passed, humanists have been open to admit the difficulty.

> As I have already pointed out, an individual's loyalty to the larger social good may under certain circumstances cost him his very existence or at least considerable suffering. *We must frankly admit that a man's uncompromising dedication to the happiness of others may lead to unhappiness on his part.* A pure conscience is not in itself sufficient to offset the persecution of governments or the cruelty of tyrants. As Aristotle sensibly observed in his notable book, *The Nicomachean Ethics*: 'To assert that a person on the rack, or a person plunged in the depth of calamities, is happy is either intentionally or unintentionally to talk nonsense.'[15]

This admission is as curious as it is commendable. It is commendable because it involves the frank confession of a touchy matter. But it is curious because it seems to say that an in-

---

*[*Note*: This argument is actually unworthy, of course; but its invalidity cannot be exposed by a one-dimensional *Weltanschauung*. An argument based on self-sacrifice really leads to the postulation of *God*. But such an implication would immediately destroy the humanistic ideal, for man would no longer be the highest ideal we can verify.]

15. Lamont, *Humanism as a Philosophy*, p. 297. (Italics mine.)

dividual can deliberately choose that which he knows in advance will diminish his own happiness. In all candidness one wonders if the humanist himself is not likewise intentionally or unintentionally talking nonsense. Why follow humanism if it leads to unhappiness? We repeat: It is a psychological impossibility for an individual deliberately to choose unhappiness. There is no meaning to any choice unless the choosing individual at least *thinks* he will gain well-being as a result.

Pathos mounts when the humanist applies the salve of consolation to the self-sacrificing individual. As the individual suffers unhappiness, he is supposed to be consoled knowing that the *collective* ego increases in security through his own loss. Noble thought! "On the whole. . .a society in which most individuals, regardless of the personal sacrifices that may be entailed, are devoted to the collective well-being, will attain greater happiness and make more progress than one in which private self-interest and advancement are the prime motivation."[16] Whether this is meant to elicit a feeling of pathos or humor, one must judge for himself. In any case the existing individual believes it rather stupid to place the good of the social ego before his own. What is so worthy about society? If the *individual* is not infinitely worthy, then a society (which is composed of other unworthy people) is not any more valuable. And if the individual *is* infinitely worthy, it is all the more ridiculous for one to sacrifice himself; for the collective ego cannot be any more worthy. Does infinity augment when added to?

In an effort to impregnate the ideal of self-sacrifice with a this-worldly, moral appeal (for humanism has no eternal sanctions to support it), the humanist spreads before the ego some choice morsels. Three reasons are drawn up to assure the individual that through devotion to others he will increase his own well-being. *First,* "a society of truly cooperative and socially conscious individuals will be able to achieve and maintain those higher material and cultural levels that provide the

16. *Op. cit.,* p. 298.

broadest foundation for human happiness and progress."[17] *Second,* "a cooperative society fits in with and fulfils some of the fundamental aspects of human nature. Man . . . is a gregarious creature. . . . Generally speaking, men experience their deepest and most enduring joys, not as solitary hermits on some mountain top or desert isle, but in association with their fellow-citizens."[18] *Third,* "loyalty to a worth-while social aim can bring stability and harmony into men's lives. . . .Allegiance to the social good serves as a beacon that illuminates to some degree most of life's problems."[19]

This list is partially convincing because it is partially true. We *are* gregarious creatures who through cooperation find a greater fullness of selfhood. But what must not be overlooked is that social cooperation is always at the mercy of egotistic security. When once the individual discovers that cooperation with others diminishes his own well-being (as the man who fights a city ordinance because, if passed, it will force him to spend money fireproofing his own hotel), he is left without a convincing reason why he should seek the harmony of the whole. More personal gains are enjoyed if, at times, a man rejects the well-being of the social group in favor of his own. And at this point the ideal of humanism breaks down.

The difficulty is that the collective ego is an abstract, impersonal entity, lacking the organs of response needed to appreciate the meaning and worth of a delicate act of self-sacrifice. Other individuals can appreciate sacrifice, but the social group cannot. It is too unwieldy and too abstract to respond to deeds of generosity and courage done over and above the call of duty. And yet, sacrificial love is perfect only when responses of appreciation are manifest. The husband looks to the wife for evidences that she appreciates the price he is paying to make her happy. The mother looks to the sick child for glances of appreciation as the months and months of sacrifice are made. Society cannot give these glances, since it

---

17. *Loc. cit.*
18. *Ibid.*
19. *Ibid.*

understands only what increases its broad security.   It knows nothing of the hidden meaning of delicate values.

What emerges out of this side of humanism is another immediacy.   Sacrifice for *individual persons* passes beyond immediacy, indeed, for spirit enjoys love in fellowship.   But sacrifice for *impersonal society* lies in precisely the same category as sacrifice for pleasure, economic security, or the scientific method.   Once again an attempt is made to unite a person with a thing.   But lasting pleasure in a marriage relation is found only when both members perform all the marriage dues. In immediacy, however, the impersonal party has no interest in reciprocation.

Since abstract "mankind" is but a thing, therefore, let it be treated as a thing.   As in the devotion to any immediacy, wisdom dictates that one proportion his service to the value he receives in return.   For instance, one should put no more into the afternoon of fishing than will balance the total quantity and quality of values he expects to come from such a sport. If one sacrificed his life for a single afternoon of fishing, men would call him demented.   Why?   Well, simply that he failed to proportion his devotion to the values received.   In like manner, wisdom dictates that sacrifice for society be pursued only to that point where the values received balance the values invested.   To sacrifice one's very life for society would be as foolish as dying for a game of tennis or a bag of gold.

All hail to a devotion to those who are in a position to reciprocate security for security!   The man in New York City *should* cooperate with those social agencies which keep fringe groups contentedly in their place.   It is to his advantage.   But why should he trouble himself about the distant Hottentots? A man should use care in the way he distributes his goods, lest he end up without any.

There is no valid argument which can clinch the humanistic ideal. Good science and good reason were supposed to lead us to humanism, but neither has done it.   *Science* cannot show us that we ought to be devoted to all men, for moral imperatives cannot be processed by the scientific method.   And *ra-*

tionality does not help, for a this-worldly self-love says that it is irrational to sacrifice for those who are unlovely. If the ego justifiably prefers golf to horseback riding, what is wrong with preferring devotion to some, rather than all, men? Is it "contrary to reason" to do what one prefers? As far as the ego can tell, it is an irrational work of supererogation to live and die for the abstractions of a collective ego.

But are we not living in "one world"? Has not technology brought men so close together that unless we seek the good of all we shall perish? Possibly so. But the motive is still self-love, not the elevating moral principle of seeking the happiness of others independently of our own. Through a fear of annihilation we may be forced to band together; but we do not move toward world government and mutual concern out of nice moral considerations. America is sharing food with the world, perhaps, but she was begrudgingly forced into it. As a result of lend-lease and the Marshall Plan, the citizenry have been converted into a complaining, grumbling ego; for with every billion sent abroad our taxes at home have grown higher. We look back on the "good old days" of isolation when we were not forced by world conditions to think of world neighbors as ourselves. And self-love prophesies that if ever conditions revert to peace again, selfishness will again express itself in isolation. And why not? What does the individual gain if he sacrifices himself for those who are in no position to reciprocate? In plain language, he gains *nothing*.

IV. The Problem of Power

But there is more to the problem of humanism than simply the dilemma of self-love. On two separate counts human love suffers from a deficiency in power. On the one hand love is at the mercy of both the fickleness of human personality and the contingencies and fortuities of time and space, while on the other it requires more obligations in its imperative than the heart has power to match. Let us examine these in this order.

A. *The Failure of the Arm of Flesh*

Since human love is subject to the frailties of the personality equation, it is frequently the cause of a grief as intense in its pain as love is intense in its pleasure. Not infrequently a boy thrills to surrender his heart to the fair maiden, only to receive a note from her in the next mail telling him that she has found a new, and more satisfying, love. The ring so recently purchased is then returned. The result is a lonely heart; and — as Tschaikovsky knew — none but the lonely heart can know its sorrow. The instant love is taken from the heart, one is left with a pain and emptiness the awfulness of which is almost indescribable. The trouble lies not with the *nature* of love, for its glory is inimitable; the trouble is that love is subject to the vacillating and capricious conditions of personality.

In addition to capriciousness, human love remains at the mercy of the vicissitudes and fortunes of time and space. Inasmuch as the lover gives away his heart to the beloved, it is a dangerous venture to love. The one knits himself to the other with a weave so fine that the points of union and separation are invisible. In the most accurate sense of the term, the two have become one. This means that when conditions of love prevail, absolute satisfaction and exhileration prevail. The mother who holds the infant in her arms, feeling the weakness of its beating heart next to hers, experiences a peacefulness in love, the constituents of which are perfect in themselves. She could wish for nothing more than an eternity of the same love.

But the trouble with all devotions to man — mild or strong — is that the conditions which make love possible do not always obtain. And when the conditions fail, the resulting loss is more tragic than a mere want of love; the loss is a ripping of the heart out of its socket and a pouring in of the acid of chronic concern, fretting, and worry. When the mother must lay her little one to rest in yonder cemetery, tossing a stray rose over the sod which rests so heavily on the form of that tiny body, her own heart is laid to rest with that of the infant. A father may know of no greater joy than when the family gathers in fellowship at the table. He would gladly continue forever in this satisfaction. But what agony pierces his heart when enemy troops overrun the land and he stands helplessly by at gun point watching his wife and daughters being herded into a boxcar to be shipped away to the officers' brothel.

Human love promises far more than it can ever make good. It offers to the heart an endless satisfaction, but what it often gives is a token of peace, then a lifetime of agony. After one joins his heart to another, only to watch that one sink into the throes of disease and death, he dies with that one. Euthanasia is a live social question because pity in the heart of the lover sometimes expresses itself in the destruction of the beloved's consignment to physical existence. Human devotion promises satisfaction, but it often brings sleepless nights, years of fretting and concern, unmanageable financial commitments, and moral despair. Many who live in loneliness and gloom are in that pitiful state because of a love which, through one fortuity or another, was shattered.

It is significant to observe that human love is often the cause of suicide. Nor do we have reference to the uncalculating rashness of those who, in an emotional fit over being jilted in love, dash themselves to destruction. Such a motive is completely unworthy. But there are suicides who prepare a carefully calculated note to wife and family, expressing love to each and trusting that despite this action they will carry on in happiness. In such a case the love for others is the *cause* of the discontentment. Perhaps a father has lost his employment, and so is unable to provide the things which are needful for his family. His own self-respect charges in upon him, condemning him to worthlessness. The eyes of his hungry children follow him as he is declined by one employment office after another. Rather than face his wife and family again, he prefers the destruction of his own body.

The problems of human love are not occasional and incidental. They are deeply etched in the scroll of existence itself. Sorrow and disappointment are essential, not peripheral, to the human drama. Friends are hardly made, but what the auld lang synes are toasted and heart parts from heart. History is on the march; and with the dropping of each grain of white sand in the clock of time, new shifts in human relations are defined and new hearts joined and separated. Human love, thus, is an exceedingly precarious venture. We cannot do without it, but the instant we make it our trust we risk being cast into the throes of sorrow. Love is perfect only when conditions for its satisfaction are obtained.

Regardless how mildly one defines the condition of love — be it a mercy work or the advancement of justice among coal miners — the resulting satisfactions are always subject to the frailties of the human equation. The League of Nations illustrates this. There came a day when its founders stepped down and watched both the cause and their satisfaction fail. When the conditions collapsed, everything they had striven for collapsed. And even when conditions for social work prevail, those for whom the sacrifices are made tend to be ungrateful and complacent, taking these generosities quite in stride and offering nothing in return. And once love is a one-way proposition, we are back on the level of the immediacies.

Whether or not God exists is a matter that each person must settle in his own heart. But as a problem of thought one cannot deny that the love which an omnipotent being offers is theoretically preferable to the love man offers; for it is united with a personality freed from all whimsicality on the one hand, and a will which enjoys complete power over the prevailing conditions on the other. If there is a God, and if this God is able to love us, a satisfaction will be gained which defies the frailty of flesh as well as the shifting of the conditions of time and space.

But is there no bridge which can lead us to God? Must we only yield the superiority of God's love as a problem of thought? The answer to these questions depends upon how seriously one enters into the obligation to treat others as ends and never as means; for in direct proportion to his moral earnestness he will develop the conviction that without God as his sure support nothing is finally meaningful — not even the ideal of humanism itself. Let us turn to an investigation of this next step in the journey of suffering.

B. *The Failure of the Heart*

It is questionable if any thinker in the history of philosophy was more qualified to speak of the ideal of humanism than Immanuel Kant. When he finished his prodigious labors in ethics, he concluded that devotion to all mankind was nothing less than a rational obligation. The duty to treat others as ends only and never as means is as binding on the individual as the most conclusive formula of mathematics or physics. It is a purely rational relation. The moral man is the rational man, the one who acts out of motives governed solely by a respect for law.[20] It is our rational duty to act only on that maxim whereby we can at the same time will that it should become a law universal. This is categorical; this is imperative.

Since the rational is the universal and the necessary, it follows that law is rational only when it likewise is universal and and necessary in its obligations. There can be no exceptions to a law, or rationality is jeopardized. Translated into humanistic terms, the Kantian ideal requires that we put aside all egotistic motives in favor of a response to law as a rational duty. The categorical (as opposed to the hypothetical) conceives of the good in itself, not a good which is the means to something else.

The underlying principle here is the familiar optimism that the real man is the rational man and that freedom is most unqualifiedly pure when it acts solely out of respect to law. Man is less than a man if he allows his decisions in life to be controlled by self-love. He should act purely out of a respect for the right.

With the introduction of the Kantian argument, thus, the heart instinctively feels that a new approach to the humanistic

---

20. "Nothing can possibly be conceived in the world, or even out of it, which can be called good without qualification, except a *good will."* Kant, *Metaphysic of Morals*, (Abbott tr.), p. 11.

option has been defined. Whereas humanism has hitherto been defended by the scientific method (and found to be faulty as a result), Kant appealed to *a priori,* rational arguments. The philosophic case for humanism is, as a matter of fact, far more convincing than the scientific. Even though the individual may be unable to understand all the connections which Kant appealed to in defending the rationality of the categorical imperative, he yet instinctively assents to the veraciousness of the imperative itself. Whatever lacunae there may be in the Kantian system,[21] the inner heart gladly submits to the truth of the conclusion. In fact, one experiences a relief in submitting, for he feels as if he had actually been arguing against humanism because of the way it was defended, rather than the ideal which it stands for. The categorical imperative expresses something so noble that one cannot reject it without endangering his own dignity. *Can one argue for the privilege of being selfish without having a red face?* No man can deliberately exclude others from the unity of spirit and still be sensitive to the meaning of self-respect. Since the sobbing of the undernourished black baby and the pitiful face of the white are both of deep interest to those who know what it means to be a human being, it follows that there is a power written on our nature which cries out against the exclusion of others from our concern. However difficult it may be to express such a unity, it happens to be part of our experience that we all participate in a transcendental community of spirit. Our best is corrupted the instant we permit ourselves to hate another person.

Being capable of treating others as ends, therefore, the inner man gladly throws his hat in the ring on the truth of the categorical imperative and his obligation to fulfill it. We may *act* as if we reject others from our concern — and indeed we do — but no sensitive man can articulate the deliberate exclusion

---

21. For example: How did Kant establish the fact that *all* men are rational, and thus worthy of our devotion? In his epistemology he leaves no place even for the *knowledge* of other spirits, let alone that all men are to be treated as ends and never as means. The Christian appeals to the image of God in man. But to what could Kant appeal?

of others without suffering a sheepish feeling inside. There is a community of respect in which we all share.

Hardly has the admission of our duty been made, however, but what the problem of performance emerges. It is easy to say that we should act only out of a rational respect for law, but who is capable of doing it? If we take Kant's philosophy seriously, *no man can be moral.* It is impossible for an individual so to divorce himself from the suasions of self-love, that he may act solely out of rational duty. Acts are never purely moral, even as thinking is never purely rational. Man is a complex person, and perched high on the kingly throne of the heart is the power of self-love. Every act must first appear before this throne to receive its clearance papers, for men are initiated to act only when they are egotistically pleased with a proposition. The ideal of rationality appealed to Kant's ego, *e. g.;* for if such a pursuit had not pleased him he would hardly have pursued it.

There is little question but what a soulless machine can deliver acts which are free from egotistic corruptions, but did Kant address his theory of morals to machines? Hardly. He directed his labors to free men. And men are aroused to action, not by a spark of electricity or the moving of a master gear, but by the flame of personal interest. A free man will sacrifice nothing unless he is assured beforehand that his own happiness is augmented in the act.

How, then, can a man be moral? Since it is psychologically impossible to free the self from egotistic motives, no action is moral. If a man is not personally interested in being rational, a whole world of books will not help him. Men corrupt logical consistency as often as the expedient suits them. If the conclusion to a rational argument runs against values that they wish to preserve, they deny the conclusion and so save the values. Such a program of egotism passes under the noble name of *rationalization.* We see the right, but we prefer the wrong. We deliberately fabricate arguments in order that our actions might appear plausible; even though the heart cannot clear the morality of such a procedure. Observe how children caught taking cookies will deny their guilt by contriving reasons which justify their act. What they are really seeking to preserve is egoistic security, not the morality of the act. If the outer man ever admits what the inner man does, the ego will be humbled before men. There is a turpitude in the heart which induces men to prefer personal security to an easy submission to rationality. Rationality can be prostituted at the whim of the ego. Defendants on trial will often plead not-guilty throughout an extended court trial, only to shift their plea to guilty in the last minute because the ego fears the consequences of conviction.

Therefore, experience cries out against any easy moral theory which teaches that the will is on the side of the mind and that man's radical evil springs out of his emotional life only. The fact of the case is that our will is more often on the side of pride, for it clears only what will serve the interests of the individual. There is a power of pride in the heart of men which constantly reaches out for ascendancy, a power not always in harmony with mind.

It is quite true that men receive a certain amount of counteracting power as a consequence of *seeing* the right. It is a remarkable thing (and very difficult to explain) how a fearful person will be converted into a man of prowess simply by seeing his duty. The football player breaks out into a cold sweat as he thinks of walking out on the field for the deciding game; but when the time for action comes and he sees what is to be done, a sympathetic vitality in him rushes to his side. Courage takes over, and he plays the game with determination. But the power of mind over the heart reaches an optimum point, especially when *moral* questions are at issue. The more one tries to pursue a life of perfect morality, the less he feels that mind can supply the requisite power to fulfill that duty. And in no instance is the conflict more conspicuous than when one tries to fulfill the Kantian theory of goodness. While the heart entertains no rational objection to the categorical imperative, a difficulty arises when one tries to *be* good. It is sad (but true) that one can think of *no* act of will which was directed purely by a respect for law, for in each and every decision the ego was on hand to engineer things. In honest Kantian truth, therefore, man is *never* good. We may rationally see the right, but we non-rationally prefer egoistic security. Even the initial decision to accept Kant's definition of the unconditioned good is itself an act which is subject to the mercy of the ego. One will give assent to this or any other rule only after it has been screened through personal interest.

One way to avoid this problem is to identify *thinking* about the right with the *doing* of the right. But this is spiritual suicide, not a genuine moral escape. There is a peculiar quality about the values of fellowship and love which distinguishes them from thinking. *Fellowship and love exist only when one actively treats his neighbor as an end and not as a means.* Antecedent to the act these vitalities have only potential existence. They are and are not as the individual acts or refrains from acting. Love comes into existence only when spirit is loving and kind. One may rationally *assent* to the categorical imperative, but he cheats and deceives himself (being perhaps the worst sort of a fellow) if he denies the need of *being* loving and kind.

Sören Kierkegaard defined as his life's work the calling of men back to the art of being ethical. With extraordinary insight he perceived that the ethical exists only when the in· dividual mediates the terms of ethical decision in his own volitional life.   Apart from the act, the ethical is nonexistent. Freedom may perceive rational ethical connections as an if-then problem of thought, but thus far one has only understood the conditions which prepare the way for being an individual. "The real subject is not the cognitive subject, since in knowing he moves in the sphere of the possible; the real subject is the ethically existing subject."[22] One *ethically exists* only when another person can follow behind, and by noting the things he does, arrive at the meaning of the law of our life.   The genuinely unconditioned good is not just a good will, there-

---

22. Kierkegaard, *Concluding Unscientific Postscript*, p. 281.

fore, *but also a good act.* If a man *wills* to do the good, but
never gets around to doing it, that man is hardly good. "If a
brother or sister is ill-clad and in lack of daily food, and one
of you says to them, 'Go in peace, be warmed and filled,' without giving them the things needed for the body, what does
it profit?" (James 2:15-16)

When the ethical life is understood as *act* — so that a person
ethically exists only when he mediates the rule of eternity
in a temporal decision — it is easy to perceive (in language used
to describe greedy children) that one's eyes are larger than
his stomach. It is extremely simple to recite the ideal of humanism, for example, but who can live according to it? Has not the
transcendent self ascended to more than it can ever make good
in the empirical self?

> The plight of the self is that it cannot do the good that it
> intends. The self in action seems impotent to conform its
> actions to the requirements of its essential being, as seen by
> the self in contemplation. The self is so created in freedom
> that it cannot realize itself within itself. It can only realize
> itself in loving relation to its fellows. Love is the law of
> its being. But in practice it is always betrayed into self-love.
> It comprehends the world and human relations from itself
> as the centre. It cannot, by willing to do so, strengthen the
> will to do good. [23]

The more deliberately one engages the Kantian ideal, therefore, the more uneasy his conscience becomes. Not only is the
initial acceptance of the ideal compounded with selfish interests, but every subsequent rededication is likewise attended
by a renewal of the very pride and selfishness which the program was originally introduced to control. The upshot is that
we are worse off knowing the right than we were in our former
estate of ignorance. What value is a knowledge of the right
if we lack the power to perform it?

The matter is extremely serious. If the data in our own experience have been interpreted accurately, one is forced to
the unsavory conclusion that our nature has a moral defect

---

23. Reinhold Niebuhr, *Human Destiny*, p. 108.

in it. It may be contrary to modern parlance to speak of "original sin," but no mood of sophistication can disqualify the fact of an evil suasion within us. The more one tries to live selflessly for others, the more conscious he becomes of a power of self-love within him. The great confessional literature in history has been penned by those who have become sensitive to this conflict in their own experience. They assent with their affections to what they cannot perform in their actions. A typical example of this is the Apostle Paul. The more perfectly he gained insight into the law of his nature, the less he seemed able to perform that right. "I do not understand my own actions. For I do not do what I want, but I do the very thing I hate. . . . For I do not do the good I want, but the evil I do not want is what I do." (Romans 7:15-19) Paul found that there were two laws or powers at work in his heart. The one was the law unto righteousness and the other the law unto sin. While Paul's affections stood on the side of the right, his power to do the right did not. In short, he suffered from a moral defect in his nature.

It is at this point where the first piles are driven for the bridge which leads us to God. If man is to conquer the defect in his nature and fulfill the obligations of the categorical imperative, he must be given a power which is not his own, a power which comes from a source of morality beyond himself. We dare not retreat from the law of life, for the farther we move from the ideal of devotion to others, the more we withdraw from our own self-dignity. But the more sensitive the heart becomes to the responsibility of morality, the more perspicaciously it realizes that an absolute moral impasse is reached. How can we live according to an ideal which requires us to employ powers of which we are deprived? One is not an individual if he *dissents* from the law; yet he becomes an immoral individual the instant he does assent. Which is better?

The more earnestly one embraces the ideal of humanism, therefore, the less he is persuaded that the second table of the law can remain without anchorage in the first. The fact that the humanistic ideal contains a duty which man's nature cannot assimilate is a patent proof that the ideal points beyond itself. While correctly perceiving the rule of our obligation, humanism yet fails to solve the problem of how a man can overcome the prides of his own ego and live according to that rule. It is impossible for mind to overpower the sinful tendencies of the heart, since such tendencies are nonrational vitalities which are not subject to mind. They must be made subject to another power. In Christian language, man needs *grace.*

This moral dilemma does not *prove* the existence of God, for it may be that God does not exist. But what is clear at this point is that — axiologically evaluated — an option in which the second table of the law draws meaning from the first is theoretically better than one which does not. *If there is no power beyond man to assist him in doing the right, he is betrayed into a state of moral desperation. The individual will hate himself if he denies the right, and he will be uneasy with himself if he confesses it. The one destroys the dignity of man, while the other shatters self-confidence.*

The wedge has now been set for a transition from humanism to theism. An analysis of the meaning of guilt in moral action will complete the shift. Let us turn to this final problem at once.

V. The Problem of Guilt

A. *The Anatomy of Uneasiness*

Since a sensitive man cannot fall short of a moral ideal without feeling a diminution in his own reservoir of self-respect, it follows that personal uneasiness and guilt are elements which must be accounted for in a theory of morals. Self-respect lashes the individual to close the gap between what man *is* and what he *ought* to be. When a man sets a goal for himself and then fails to make it, he feels far less secure than when he can look back upon the commitment knowing that all he undertook has been completed. If a building is left half-finished because the builder failed to use foresight, scorn and ridicule are heaped upon him.

Devotion to the ideal of humanism is one sure instance where the free self bargains for an obligation greater than the involved self can ever make good. The result (other things being equal) is guilt. Now the question arises: What *kind* of guilt does one feel when he fails to treat all men as ends and never as means? This is the final problem to be faced.

There is nothing more universal in experience than the qualitative difference between the guilt one suffers when he transgresses an impersonal law and that which arises upon the occasion of offending a person. In the one instance guilt is met simply by the payment of an impersonal offering, such as a fine for fishing in spawning waters or a jail term for stealing money; whereas in the other there is no payment acceptable outside of personal contrition itself. Since person has offended person, spirit will reunite itself to spirit only after the posture of confession has been assumed. Offense to a person steps up the intensity of the guilt by moving it into new genus. Let us study these types of guilt in more detail.

When a man is caught driving through a traffic light and is brought into court for trial, *e.g.,* guilt is present; but it hardly passes beyond the minor disgruntlement of having been careless in the first place, or being caught at all in the second. After the fine is paid, one is only sorry that he was put to this inconvenience and expense. The court does not exact from him a confession of *personal* sorrow for guilt, being satisfied when the obligations of law are met. This is one type of guilt.

The other species of guilt is no more intimately compounded with the witness of conscience and self-respect, to be sure, for *all* guilt is a testimony that man has performed less than what freedom assents as the rule of his life; but it possesses a unique quality which is wanting in the other. When one treats another human being as a means to his own end, preferring to defraud the other than suffer loss oneself, the sensitive heart experiences a guilt which cannot be assuaged by a simple payment of money or a service of time in jail. The law which defines the very dignity of one's being has been slighted, and hearts can be united in fellowship only after personal confession has been made. It is far more taxing on the soul to walk up to a friend and offer a personal apology for having offended him than it is to slip a five dollar bill from the wallet and pay the court for having exceeded the county speed laws.

This intense form of guilt is experienced in all instances where the offender must face the offended. If a watermelon is stolen, *e.g.*, it is easy to make restitution as long as the offense is kept within an impersonal framework. The melon is paid for and things continue as they were from the foundation of the world. But when the boy must face the farmer and pay for his melon by telling him how sorry he is that he went beyond his own rights, heart stands before heart and there is a mutual recognition that each participates in an over-ought which runs far beyond this particular situation. A mystical bond of fellowship has broken. Neither has created it, both passively participate in it. Each is tense and uneasy when the moment arrives for the two hearts to meet, even as each is blithe and satisfied subsequent to the confession.

Study how the young son feels when he talks back to his mother. As he storms out of the house, leaving his sobbing parent behind in the kitchen, the dagger of guilt is plunged so deeply in his heart that he would gladly pluck an eye out for peace. And the more he writhes under the guilt of knowing he has broken the heart of his mother, the more clear it becomes that both he and she participate in a transcendental, mystical, matrix of fellowship; and that when this is broken the full power of an eternal ought launches out against the offending heart. The boy can roam the world, seeking release in one divergent activity or another, but he will find that the sword of guilt follows him wherever he goes. It is white with heat and piercing sharp. A placenta of fellowship protects the entire range of spirit's freedom. There is haven neither under the earth nor high in yonder blue. Wherever spirit soars, there is the indicting voice of guilt, reminding man that the law of love has been broken.[24]

The wandering boy needs no *instruction* on how to find peace. It is far clearer to him than he wishes that he must personally return to the farm and, throwing his arms around his mother, make restitution through confession. What he needs is courage to do it, for there is a law in his heart which wars against the law of life. This law is pride. It compels the boy to continue on his way, confidently assuring him that there will come a time when an easier solution to the problem will be found. Whether or not the boy ever finds peace of conscience will depend on how he resolves the warfare of these two laws within him. If he persists in following the council of pride, he will go to his grave with guilt; whereas, if he overcomes this drag in his nature and arouses himself to do the right, he will experience an instant and complete release from his burden.

When heart breaks heart by destroying fellowship, therefore, spirit is left with an uneasiness which is far less manageable than the guilt which rises out of cheating on an examination or plagiarizing a paragraph from an ancient author. The father who loses his temper before his wife and children suffers a grinding deep inside of his heart which cannot be explained simply as the consequence of acting in defiance of rational consistency. There is a gnawing away at the very roots of character itself. We sense a betrayal of our own persons whenever we venture to wander from the obligations of charity. A guilt within us for not doing good to others bursts out of its own accord. We do not *elect* to call forth the lump in our throat when we see a poor dying person and yet turn aside

---

24. "Whither shall I go from thy Spirit? Or whither shall I flee from thy presence? If I ascend up into heaven, thou art there. If I make my bed in Sheol, behold, thou art there. If I take the wings of the morning, and dwell in the uttermost parts of the sea; even there shall thy hand lead me, and thy right hand shall hold me. If I say, Surely the darkness shall overwhelm me, and the light about me shall be night; even the darkness hideth not from thee, but the night shineth as the day: the darkness and the light are both alike to thee. For thou didst form my inward parts: thou didst cover me in my mother's womb." (Psalm 139:7-13.)

from helping him. It is just there, that is all. And the more
we try to crucify it, the more it is resuscitated.

Our original question, however, was to learn the species of
guilt which is involved when freedom falls short of treating
all men as ends rather than as means. Is it the simple guilt
of being rationally inconsistent? Or is it the soul-rending
sorrow of having ruptured fellowship by damaging the transcendental unity of spirit?

*The answer to these questions depends upon what one thinks
of the ethical assignment.* Is it enough just to have a good
will? Or is ethical perfection expressed only when a good
will issues in good works? To put it another way, shall one
merely *intend* to do the right; or shall he actually *witness* to
the right in his own person by being upright? Is a man ethical who *wills* the right but never *does* the right? Or does
the ethical come into existence only when one actually mediates
through righteous living the law which defines the right?

The sensitive spirit makes quick work of these alternatives.
The law of life deals with a unique relationship. Fellowship
exists only in the *act* of being a fellow one to the other. It
comes into being only when hearts are kind, thoughtful, loving,
and gentle, even as it departs under conditions of rancor and
jealousy. There is no love except where there is a lover. The
act is the thing itself. Therefore, the law of our being defines
a condition which may be met only when one *is* the truth in
his own person; not when he satisfies duty through so paltry
an obligation as giving rational assent to its terms. The proof
of any assent is the performance.

Kierkegaard was quick to expose the uneasy conscience of
the ethicist who confuses simple assent to duty with an ethical performance of that duty. He caricatured the ethicist as
one who offers a full semester's course on the moral imperative, but who would not *dare* face the question whether he or
anybody within his hearing is ethical in his person. *That*
would be unethical! Or, if the question is not unethical, it at
least is irrelevant; for the job of the ethicist is simply that of
defining the rational conditions of morality, not investigating

into his own life to see if he lives according to these conditions. And what is the smoke screen which the ethicist throws up as a cover of protection about him? It is *irony,* that device of barbed inquiry and reply by which the ethicist escapes personal implications of the ethical contradiction. "Irony arises from the constant placing of the particularities of the finite together with the infinite ethical requirement, thus permitting the contradiction to come into being."[25] The contradiction is that the ethicist saddles himself with an obligation which he makes no profession to fulfill. And yet, he is calm and unshattered in his ego throughout the whole transaction. But, why does the ethicist employ irony as his incognito? "Because he grasps the contradiction there is between the manner in which he exists inwardly, and the fact he does not outwardly express it."[26]

To revert to our illustration, nothing is clearer to the heart of the offending boy but what his duty consists in the *act* of treating his mother as an end and never as a means, not merely the *intention of his will to do so.* The will may be good, but the act may be bad. *The really unconditioned good is the good act which flows from the good will.*

B. *The Over-ought*

Let us draw out further implications from this same illustration. How is the *mother* able to occasion such an overwhelming flood of uneasiness in the heart of the boy? What power does she command, that she is able to travel around the world and indict him with sorrow and guilt, until he returns to make his confession? The gnawing in his heart continues even while she sleeps. It is aroused while she either does the family laundry or is occupied with other things. Is *she* hexing him, or is there a transcendental order of moral responsibility which they both participate in and which is controlled by a will superior to finite will? The latter alternative seems mys-

25. Kierkegaard, *Concluding Unscientific Postscript,* p. 448.
26. *Ibid.,* p. 450.

tical and unscientific when first entertained, but the more one
reckons with the factors involved in his own experience, the
less satisfied he becomes that any alternative can explain the
data.

Is not the offended person merely the *occasion* for the rise
of the feeling of guilt, not the cause? The feeling of uneasiness is too powerful and too confronting to be aroused by the
timid mother. And the offending party does not cause it, for
he is the one fighting against its rise. His act occasions guilt's
emergence, but it is not the causal agent. If it were possible,
the offending party would take a scalpel and cut out the fear
and shame. Would one deliberately cause the very thing he
hates most? Men respect, rather than disavow, the law of self-
love within them. The boy who talks back to his mother would
like nothing more than to control his inner spirit. He would
be pleased if he could so alter his person that he would be satisfied with the act of being disrespectful to parents. But he lacks
this control, for guilt smashes every hastily fabricated defense.
There is no pill he can take to cure this disease!

If neither the boy nor his mother exercises causal control
over the act-guilt relationship, who then does? Do other men?
Hardly. One need only stop other people on the street and
they will disclaim any part in the matter. They are too occupied with their own difficulties to pretend a power over the
moral condition of others. Men may boast of a lot of powers,
but this is one which they universally disclaim. No individual
is conscious of enjoying a moral control over the lives of others,
as if through his own ability he can give and withdraw peace.
Each man is a passive participant in a stratum of over-ought
which neither he nor his neighbor has created. If there were
merely two people in the world and the one severed fellowship
with the other, the resulting guilt would be no milder than if
the world were overpopulated. The proof of this is that in
any guilt situation involving two people neither is conscious
of any relation subsisting between the severity of their own
uneasiness and the existence of other people outside. The
son senses that his problem takes in none beside himself and

his mother. If in imagination he conceived only the two of them existing, he would find no consolation for his aching heart. If anything, he would feel worse. If she were the only other existing person, he could not even release his gregarious instincts without being threatened with a simultaneous responsibility to repent.

The conclusion is that upon the occasion of injuring another person, one is mysteriously catapulted into a realm of personality which wields powers of both condemnation and forgiveness that outrun anything either a single man or all men collectively considered could have arranged. Through offense one is thrust into this transcendental, mystical stratum of guilt, even as through apology and forgiveness he is mystically restored to happiness and peace. The human factors of both offense and apology are simply the finite occasions for a power beyond man to release both guilt unto condemnation and peace unto forgiveness.

Is there a more thinkably satisfying explanation than that the power behind this transcendental bond of fellowship is the person of God? The guilt is toward a person, indeed. But human personalities at best are only occasions for the stirring up of a guilt which commands time- and space-transcending rights over the human heart. Is not conscience compounded with the word and will of God, instructing and condemning the heart? When the wayward son feels the full weight of shame, he senses that it is a guilt which proceeds from eternity into time. And when the mother forgives the son, she realizes that her words are but the occasion for another power to release the tension of sorrow in the boy's heart and once again to restore fellowship. The mother does not profess (nor does she actually hold) any power to change the heart of the boy. If she forgave the son, and yet the boy continued to feel guilty, she would be at her wit's end. The power of forgiveness is as mysterious as the power of guilt which originally drove the boy back to his mother's side. Since this power to forgive outruns the accumulated moral strength of all men in time and space, who but God could wield it?

Now it begins to grow clear why the second table of the law *must* derive its authority from the first, for duty toward man raises problems which it has no resources to solve. Men may *realize* that they are accenting the best within them only when they love their neighbors as themselves, but what have they gained through this knowledge? They have only had a shower of guilt brought down upon them as a consequence of their want of complying with this kingdom of ends. By no conceivable manipulation of the self, either through a more rational resolution of the will or by a wider application of the canons of ordinary science, can one eliminate the power of self-love in the heart; and yet this power is the very vitiating acid in the ethical life. Born self-centered, we remain in the same condition throughout our life. Every option must first clear with personal interest and concern. If ever we are to be delivered from this vicious circle, help must come from the author of our nature. Resources of power must be gained from the very source of the moral over-ought itself. Every human effort to withdraw from self-love is itself corrupted by the gangrene of self-love. And thus the drama continues!

> The universal and undiscriminating love of God which is set before us as the norm of our own perfection is something for which our natural endowment provides no equipment. We cannot lift ourselves, so to speak, off the center of self and reconstruct ourselves about God as center. All we can do in this direction is to submit ourselves to the influences which have this transforming power, if any such there be.[27]

It will hardly do for the humanist to reply that he is not responsible for the normal moral limitations of life, contending that science has discounted the existence of God as a valid proposition; for it is the responsibility of good science to explain, not deny, the facts as they are found. And what part of our experience is more incontrovertible than the voice of eternity pressing in upon us in conscience? Conscience screams out that reality is more than one-dimensional. It "is the sense of being seen, commanded, judged and known from beyond

27. William Temple, *Christian Thought and Practice*, p. 86.

ourselves."[28]   Neither a thing, nor an impersonal relation, nor
a combination of conditioned reflexes could shatter the spirit
with the thoroughness and the persistence of conscience.   Person meets person when conscience speaks.   "This word spoken
from beyond us and to us is both a verification of our belief that
we are dealing with a different dimension than animal existence; and also a revelation of the actual and precise character
of the person with whom we are dealing."[29]

If it happens to be good science that men should be treated
as ends and never as means (the ideal which the humanist is
responsible for), then it is likewise good science to declare for
faith in the existence of God. The mark of an acceptable hypothesis is its ability to explain the facts as we experience them.
And nowhere in the total sweep of our experience are the facts
more plain than in the realm of morals. There are *rationes
aeternae* which press in upon spirit from every side: The duty
to be honest, to seek justice, to hold other men in the bond of
fellowship.   The moment we turn aside from that law which
we admit defines the happy, normal life, we at once feel a guilt
and shame well up in our hearts.

Observe how scientific hypotheses are made: One of the
most remarkable of astronomical discoveries was that of the
planet Neptune.   When it was noticed that Uranus was de-
viating from the orbit assigned to it in the light of gravitational
forces bearing on it, the conclusion was quickly drawn that
there must be another, and hitherto unknown, residual force
in the vicinity which was causing the deviation.   The existence of a new heavenly body was postulated, therefore.   When
mathematical calculation combined with observation, lo, it was
found that a new planet *was* the cause of the deviation. This
planet was called Neptune.

If it is good science to postulate the existence of Neptune
to account for known astronomical data, is it not good science
to postulate the existence of God to account for known data

---

28. Reinhold Niebuhr, *Human Nature*, p. 128.
29. *Ibid.*, p. 130.

in human experience? The data which one experiences as he passes through the cycle of guilt and forgiveness form the real stuff of freedom itself. The man who tries to deny their reality is espousing a philosophy which neither he nor anyone else can live by. Our life is steered by the presupposition that the values which define the true, good, and beautiful have a commanding authority about them which cannot be exhausted. There is a progressive self-refutation in the philosophy which denies it, a progressive self-disintegration in the heart which defies it. No one can long continue being a man if he runs contrary to the *rationes aeternae* which give meaning to propositions, confidence in social relations, and pleasure in perception.

Since values can exist only in a mind (for their nature is such that they have no relevance to non-spirit), and since the values with which we are confronted in the cycle of guilt and forgiveness are time- and space-transcending, it follows that the mind which supports them must likewise be time- and space-transcending. What mind can this be but God?

If a man tries to live without principles, he is a creature of no account, worse than the animals; for wielding the power of freedom, his efforts at destruction, distortion, and corruption have no equal among the brutes. But the moment a man strives to be a man, he at once perceives (if he is sensitive to the facts as they are and is not blinded by an *a priori*) that his dignity is drawn from the existence of principles which stand authoritatively over him and which outrun the entire history of the human race. He can conceive of neither the first nor the last man living according to any other obligations than those which define the minimal dignities of his own life. The first man on earth would have suffered from a progressive self-disintegration if he had defied the law of life. Thus, what else than the mind of God can satisfactorily account for the ubiquity of values?

Summary

Impressed with the fact that devotion to man lies close to the very law of our life, humanists have set down a theory which purports to satisfy the whole man. By combining the skill of the scientific method with the satisfactions found in serving humanity, both head and heart are accounted for. What can be lacking? A good method is united with good values.

A careful study of the implications of humanism reveals, however, that the program implicates the heart in more commitments than either good science or good thinking can assimilate. Not only is there no solution to the collision between the individual and collective ego, but also the fear is that since the power of both guilt and forgiveness outruns anything which men could either initially originate or ultimately call to a halt, there is a power beyond human power which must be included if the whole heart is to be satisfied. *This power is God.* It will do no good to become sophisticated or fashionable at this point, protesting that such a suggestion is either anti-scientific or contrary to the canons of rationality, for good science and good rationality should account for the facts as they are. The heart refuses to be deluded. If only God's existence can account for the transcendental realm of fellowship in which we all participate, one would run contrary to both science and mind (let alone his own self-dignity) if out of motives of pride or fashion he refused to assent to the conclusion.

Humanism has tried to float the second table of the law without the dignifying foundation of the first, but the experiment has failed. Man has no dignity, and thus he is *not* worthy of our devotion, if he does not participate in a transtemporal, trans-spatial realm of values which give normative expression of the ideal law of life. The inscription on Harvard's Langdell Hall sums up the relation between act and value: NON SUB HOMINE SED SUB DEO ET LEGE.*

------

* "Not under man but under God and law." [Attributed to Bracton by Sir Edward Coke in the conference of James the First and the Judges of England at which it was settled that cases were to be decided by the courts and not by the King in person. 12 Coke's Reports, 63 (1612).]

If one balks at the idea of postulating a transcendental realm
of spirit to provide a normative basis for law and order in
shifting social relations, he should be briefed on the implications of his position. Since from flux only flux can come, it
follows that it is neither scientific nor rational to define the
categorical imperative as unconditional. Kant, let us remember, was *constrained* to reintroduce the existence of God into
his philosophy. He knew that without such a postulation the
over-all unity of rationality would be jeopardized. If nothing
is timelessly obligatory, then it is meaningless to say that it is
an obligation that we treat all men as ends and never as means.

Since we happen to know by nature that the man who defies
the ideal of humanism suffers a disintegration of his own person, our solution is not a denial of the ideal that humanism
stands for. We must press on beyond humanism to theism,
for the obligations of the one force us to postulate principles
underlying the other. As we enter into the cycle of guilt and
forgiveness, we are catapulted into a realm of over-ought in
which transcendental powers of both condemnation and forgiveness are met. The fact of these data makes the postulation of God's existence both scientifically and rationally satisfying.

When faith in God is enjoyed, man's dignities have a stable
point of reference; but if God does not exist, then each cultural pattern is subject to the accidents of time and space. If
God remains, the categorical imperative remains; if God is
taken away, the Brazen Rule of Bernard Shaw remains: "Do
not do unto others as you would that they would do unto you;
their tastes may be different." Let each man decide for himself which he shall choose.

VIII

Devotion to God

THE Christian Scriptures are denunciatory of idolatry in every manner or shape it may appear. Since the idol is set up as a competitor to Jehovah God (if it be true that Jehovah God *is* the sovereign one), it is guilty of usurping glory that belongs to another. The idol may be but a piece of wood from a tree, or it may be a god of fertility or weather. The one is denounced by Isaiah (44:15ff) and the other by Hosea (2:5ff). The Biblical writers never extend a hand of congratulations to a person who has found his way to the existence of *a* god; for such a one may yet be a long distance from *the* God. When bowing down to ultimates, it is greatly to one's advantage to accept no substitute for the true absolute. An error at this point may result in an ultimate loss to spirit itself.

Christianity has been content to defend the existence of but one God. And this God is the Trinity — three eternal persons in one divine essence, just and powerful, holy and merciful. God is personal, sovereign, and simultaneously transcendent and immanent. Through his power the world is explained; through his justice the moral ought is explained; and through his mercy reconciliation is explained.

In establishing the *existence* of God, however, the Scriptures proceed in inverse order to general philosophy. *Whereas philosophy seeks to explain the heart by a God gained through an examination of nature, Christianity seeks to explain nature by a God gained through an examination of the heart.* The presupposition which guides the latter is that solving the dilemma of sin and guilt is far more important than resolving the origin and nature of the time-space universe. If God is able to satisfy the *heart, a fortiori* he can satisfy the mind.

Furthermore, what does one gain if he explains the physical world, but has no solution to the shame and guilt of his inner person?

The Bible arranges no formal, dialectical proof of God.[1] And one reason for this omission is that nothing significant is known of God until a person directly experiences him through fellowship. In all personal relations knowledge by acquaintance must accompany knowledge by inference. The boy *knows* the girl (in the sense that his whole person is satisfied) only when he loves her. A person's knowledge of another person remains truncated and incomplete until it terminates in fellowship and love. If this is true, how can one know *God* until his spirit has united itself with the Spirit of God in rich, presentational fellowship? Scripture teaches that men are brought into this fellowship through the redemptive, atoning work which God himself wrought on man's behalf. In Christ, hearts are born anew. This at least is the claim of the writers; only careful investigation can establish its worthiness.

Philosophy has never been able to formulate an approach to God which appeals to the man on the street, for the God of the philosophers is postulated to account for just about everything except unrest and guilt in the heart. A purely formal approach to nature is shallow and colorless to a man whose heart is full of longings and aspirations. The common man has not been so corrupted in his ways that he supposes himself at his best basking in the light of rational connections. The warm, intimate love which is experienced in family and societal relations possesses an excellency to satisfy the inner man which has no counterpart.

---

1. "For not only is it now plain to us that the Hebrews did not reach monotheism by a metaphysical approach, but it is doubtful whether they can be held ever to have reached the kind of monotheism which would be interesting to a metaphysician at all. What they were anxious to affirm was not that the gods of other nations did not exist, but that they were not worthy of worship; and, as we have seen, it is possible that the nearest approach they ever made to denying their existence was to say that they were no gods but only demons." John Baillie, *The Interpretation of Religion,* (New York: Charles Scribner's Sons, 1941), p. 429.

The average man gladly follows Christ, therefore, while turning aside from the classical philosophers, because Jesus alone patterned God's relation to the penitent spirit after the order of fellowship which subsists between the lover and the beloved in human relations.

> The secret of our Lord's insight is the universal secret of all religious insight: it is simply that His thought of God kept pace with His thought of human life. It was because He had a great new thing to say about how men should live with one another here below that He had this great new thing to say about what God above was like.[2]

Christ understood that the best in human nature is released only when men selflessly seek each other out in love, not when they legalistically pursue justice.   While justice defines the minimal terms of tolerable social relations, love will not rest until every obstacle blocking the way of complete happiness has been removed.   Christ made no attempt either to alter or to improve upon our native faith that love constitutes the finest expression of freedom.   He simply proceeded from this intuition and gave cosmic significance to the relation of love. While rejecting the humanistic ideal as incomplete, therefore, he nevertheless *built* upon its insights rather than derogating it as untruth.   Christ expressed the profundities of eternity and heaven in humble concepts borrowed from the experiences of the children sitting with their parents before the family hearth.   "The life of the family, He would say, provides us not only with the pattern by which our own actions should be guided, but also with our surest clue to the nature of the Most High God."[3] The relation which man has to God is analogously the same as the relation the son has to his father: The father will receive the son back into fellowship the moment the boy gives signs of confession and apology.   The heart of the father reaches out in longing for the return of the son, ample provision having been made for his reception back into

---

2. *Op. cit.*, p. 440.
3. *Ibid.*, p. 441.

the home. The only condition to be met is the son's expression of apology.

Christ exposed the inadequacies of all other approaches to reality through a most artistic and inoffensive technique. Without even mentioning competing philosophies and religions by name, he cancelled them out one by one through the irresistible force of his own approach. He so stated the relation between time and eternity that one who argued with him experienced a sheepish feeling inside of having betrayed his own self-dignity. Christ knew (while classical philosophers apparently do not) that the values which touch the inner cravings of one's own heart are the most interesting things to a person. Once the heart has found satisfaction, all else quickly takes its rightful place. And since classical philosophers refuse to talk about those things which are dear to the heart, the heart refuses to relate itself congenially to classical philosophy.

Christ made fellowship with God the Father the primary value in life. Since he was sent to perform nothing but the will of the Father, doing the Father's will was his delight. In contrast to this, philosophers tend to make man's need of God a last-minute affair. God is called in as an expedient to give philosophic completeness to a system. Take Kant, for example. After speedily dismissing the relevance of God in the first critique, he reluctantly called God back when the primacy of the pure practical reason was defended. Though God was completely useless for epistemology, he was very useful as a limiting concept to give completeness to the system. Had it not been for his need of a unifying idea, however, Kant would have had no call for God at all. What Christ made central, Kant pushed to the periphery.

The question of God's existence will not stay down. In the great *Syntopicon,* for example — the two-volume concordance of the Great Ideas in the Great Books [edited by Mortimer J. Adler] — the topic "God" has the greatest number of entries: 7,065. If the existence of God were ancillary to the human quest, it would hardly have received this ovation of interest by great minds in all ages. History has a relentless way of beating matters out to their true issues.

The Christian heart is completely satisfied that Christ exhausted our perfection when he defined God's relation to men after the analogy of a father's love for his own family; for the best and sweetest we know on earth are the loves which are expressed in home relations. What perfection can surpass that of parent loving the child? Is the highest in heaven lower than what we know to be the highest on earth? This would be the case if we believed in a God who is discontinuous with the values we already hold dear in the family ties of love. If God is not at least our sovereign heavenly Father, the heart is dissatisfied. We *have* the Leah of human love; the divine Rachel must be fairer.

Since no man can generate love by an act of his own will, the love of God is a free gift. Man can only will to meet the conditions within which God gives his gift of love to men. Whoever wills to know the doctrine will *know* whether it is from God or from men. To assist the heart in making the first overtures toward willing God's gift of love, therefore, let us examine several typical alternatives to the Christian doctrine of a sovereign heavenly Father. If dissatisfaction with other God concepts is reached, a hunger for God as Father may be created.

I. The God of Physics

The Bible refuses to rest its proof for God on formal arguments from nature. Its order of inquiry is as follows: When men recognize and confess their own sinfulness, God gives them the gifts of forgiveness and love. Then, with the eyes of their hearts opened they commence to see God reflected in the works of his creation. The moment the heart enjoys fellowship with God, that instant vision is restored.

This approach to God through fellowship seems too fuzzy and mystical to philosophers, however. (Though how else *could* a person be known?) In lieu of a full appreciation of knowledge by acquaintance, philosophers energetically set out to find God by a formal inquiry into the objective data of nature. God is postulated to account for the facts we observe through our senses. But the result is, that though we gain a cognitive understanding of a first cause, we do not *know* God — in the sense of being intimately acquainted with him.

Since Aristotle has bequeathed the most elaborate expression of the cosmological argument, what could better serve as a test case than to analyze the success of his venture? If the master's labor is disappointing, where shall the disciple appear?

A. *The Unmoved Mover*

The basis of Aristotle's argument for God is his view of nature. Since all motion has an element of *potency* in it, and since the potential cannot be the cause of itself — otherwise it would be *necessary* and not potential — it follows that motion is not accounted for until one postulates a principle which, though free from all motion itself, is nevertheless the cause of all motion. The potential is that which may or may not be. But if all being were characterized by potentiality, there must have been a time when all being was not: for in eternity all realizable combinations would have been realized. But if there were a time when all was not, then it follows that nothing presently is, since from nothing nothing can come. But experience proves that there is being; therefore, something must be noncontingent. As Kant would put it, if anything is, something necessarily must be.

Aristotle solved the problem of motion by conceiving nature[4] after the order of a metaphysical hierarchy of forms. Each species of being is individuated by the particular way that matter is informed. On the lowest end of the scale of metaphysics is pure matter (a limiting concept), while on the upper end is pure form (God). Between these outside reaches of being lie an infinite number of types of informed matter.

---

4. A natural object is "that sort of substance which has the principle of its motion and rest present in itself." *Metaphysics,* 1025b.

Form is that in a thing which determines its kind or species, while matter is the indeterminate subject of reality, the potential, the stuff which is informed. The perfection of each thing is its form, while the imperfection is the resistance of matter. Since the material sets a limit upon the purity of form, nature is mixed. Nature consists in the uninterrupted succession of being from the lowest formations of matter to the purest forms. Each form is matter for the higher; as even the matter of the higher is the form for the lower.

The resistance of matter is illustrated by the artist who has a perfect form in his mind, but who cannot express it because of the coarseness of his brush, paint, and canvas. Matter is a drag in nature which blocks perfection's expression. Matter accounts for the purposeless in nature; it is a force of recalcitrance.

If matter is the principle of retardation in nature, of what service is the principle of pure form? This is a problem for first science to solve. "First science deals with things which both exist separately and are immovable."[5] It is first because it examines that genus under which all other genera are subsumed, the genus which is at once first and universal. The existence of pure form (God) must be postulated for the reason that matter, being but the possible or the potential, possesses in itself neither power of motion nor principle of generation. *Motion* may be (and is) eternal, but that does not cancel out the need for some being which is the *cause* of eternal motion. However, since each form is regarded as the matter of a higher form, and thus suffers from potency, there is no relief from the potency-act relation until a pure form is presupposed which, free from all matter, eternally enjoys the full actuality of pure essence. Relieved of the drag of matter, God is *actus purus*. It (since God is impersonal) is the cause of all else, while itself is caused by nothing.

But how can God *move* things, if it refrains from all movement? Aristotle draws a distinction between the impulse of a

---

5. *Op. cit.,* 1026a.

form to realize itself in matter and the motion of purpose which proceeds from the form itself. The unmoved mover moves nature by inciting lower forms with the urge to be like the higher. God is the *final,* not the mechanical cause of nature. God moves nature to act as the picture in the art gallery moves visitors to express admiration: While changing others, it itself remains changeless. Nor has it any knowledge of being the cause of the change.

> There is, then, something which is always moved with an unceasing motion, which is motion in a circle; and this is plain not in theory only but in fact. Therefore the first heaven must be eternal. There is therefore also something which moves it. And since that which is moved and moves is intermediate, there is something which moves without being moved, being eternal, substance, and actuality. And the object of desire and the object of thought move in this way; they move without being moved. The primary objects of desire and of thought are the same.[6]

God touches the natural world through its influence, not through contact of pressure. "Hence if anything imparts motion without itself being moved, it may touch the 'moved' and yet itself be touched by nothing — for we say sometimes that the man who grieves us 'touches' us, but not that we 'touch' him."[7] God is pure form, having neither magnitude, parts, division, or passions, producing motion through infinite time and exercising everlasting power. "We say therefore that God is a living being, eternal, most good, so that life and duration continuous and eternal belong to God; for this *is* God."[8]

When one inquires what God does with itself, the answer is that it thinks about its own self-perfection. This is not a selfish pursuit, for God is not a person. Even the slightest introduction of such personal characteristics as will, pleasure in creation, or love would spoil the symmetry of the picture.

---

6. *Op. cit.,* 1072a.
7. *On Generation and Corruption,* 323a.
8. *Metaphysics,* 1072b.

God is postulated to solve the problem of potency-act, not to assuage the longings of a sinful heart. Being pure form, the only possible thing God can do is to remain everlastingly absorbed in self-thinking.

> This divine spirituality is conceived of in a purely intellectualistic manner; its essential nature is solely thought directed upon itself. All doing, all willing, is directed toward an object, distinct from the doer or the willer. The divine mind, as pure form, needs no object; he is sufficient for himself, and his knowledge of himself (*theōria*), which has no other goal than itself, is his eternal blessedness. He acts upon the world, not through his motion or activity, but through the longing for him which the world has. The world, and what takes place in it, arises from the *longing of matter after God.* [9]

If the attention of God were fixed upon the universe, God would then know the nature of change and corruption; but this would entail growth in knowledge (for nature contains accidents), and any change in perfection would jeopardize divinity. "Evidently, then, it thinks of that which is most divine and precious, and it does not change; for change would be change for the worse, and this would be already a movement."[10] God is always active — for act is better than potency — but the only act which is commensurate with pure form is everlasting self-reflection. God makes no decisions; there are no gains or losses in the display of its glory. Since man is best when he *thinks* (not loves), on what other analogy could God be conceived, save as the eternally thinking one?

> On such a principle, then, depend the heavens and the world of nature. And it is a life such as the best which we enjoy, and enjoy for but a short time (for it is ever in this state, which we cannot be), since its actuality is also pleasure. . . . And thinking in itself deals with that which is best in itself, and that which is thinking in the fullest sense with that

---

9. W. Windelband, *A History of Philosophy,* (New York: The Macmillan Company, 1931), p. 146.
10. *Metaphysics,* 1074b.

which is best in the fullest sense. And thought thinks on itself because it shares the nature of the object of thought: for it becomes an object of thought in coming into contact with and thinking its objects, so that thought and object of thought are the same. [11]

B. *What about Man?*

If ever an attempt were made to wed like with unlike, it is in Aristotelianism. Man is no more able to remain satisfied with a God that is pure, self-concerned intelligence than is the young lover with a mechanical robot. What fellowship can a living heart have with a thinking thing? A small satisfaction results from being able to explain the cause of motion, to be sure. But this is a paltry offering, since it is simply one further form of immediacy. Philosophical ataraxia has already been disqualified on the grounds of inadequacy.

Philosophers often speak of the "intellectual love" that one may have for God. But when the phrase is analyzed by one who happens to remember that he is still a human being, it becomes either a case of ambiguity or sheer stupidity. If it means that I experience satisfactions by intellectually perceiving God, then it is but a way of saying that upon the occasion of thinking I have pleasures called up within me. And we have already proved that perfect satisfaction comes only in the act of fellowship. But if it means that I love an impersonal God with my heart, so that I enter into the unmoved mover with fellowship, then it is silly talk. Can a man have fellowship with a problem in geometry? Can he yield compassionately to the cork on a wine bottle? It would be a queer (but hardly a human) being who would thus act. Fellowship is a union of hearts in mutual interest.

When pressing beyond the ideal of humanism, the heart has no intentions to abandon the essential gains already made. Since the person-person relation best expresses the powers of spirit, a cosmically directed act of freedom will fully satisfy only when it bears similar characteristics. Who can have

---

11. *Op. cit.*, 1072b.

fellowship with an impersonal, self-concerned center of rationality? Aristotle adjudged love to God both absurd and irrational. If this be life, let humanism reign!

There is little wonder that the Schoolmen swarmed over the unmoved mover in a Herculean philosophic effort to blast away its less religiously suitable parts.[12] What could ring with a more leaded thud than the announcement of an impersonal God? It may be a pleasant pastime to think about this God and wonder what it is doing. One could sip a cup of coffee and include such a topic along with the implications in physics if the world were square or how many pints of water there are in the Indian Ocean. But for the real business of living, for the uncertain G. I. in the foxhole who greatly wants to disbelieve that he is only an animal, the idea of an impersonal God is perfectly useless. Such a God is so busy thinking about itself that it would not recognize a world even if it saw one. But do not blame God for this, for an impersonal center of rationality is no more accountable for its actions than are falling stones.

Why try to force man through cylinders made for nonpersonal things? If man cannot rest satisfied with the immediacies of pleasure, riches, and fame, what value is there in arranging a wedding with the unmoved mover? Better well hung than ill wed! Let us remain men and perish in Bertrand Russell's purposeless universe rather than convert our spirits into centers of impersonal rationality, playing the roll of frustrated little creatures who *wish* they were pure intelligence but are not. Ten minutes filled with the vibrant satisfactions of faith, hope, and love would mean far more to spirit than an eternity of sitting still, staring milky-eyed into the endless abyss of pure rationality. Life is not exhausted in thinking. Life is

---

12. The deficiency in Aristotle is (at least) "threefold, namely, a failure to understand first, exemplarism, then Divine providence and lastly the disposition of this world with a view to the other." Etienne Gilson, *The Philosophy of St. Thomas Aquinas*, (St. Louis: B. Herder Book Co., 1939), pp. 14-15.

rich only in fellowship — loving, sacrificing, hoping, forgiving, enduring.

The practical outcome of the Greek attempt to unite a person to a thing is reflected in the tragic lines of the dramatist. Life ends in an essential contradiction. The forces which bring great men down to the dust are left unsolved at the end of the drama. All men share their defects. Man has no right to call on God for help, for God would be soiled in its purity to be concerned with so corruptible a thing as man. Man is informed *matter,* and that is awful! So, Socrates wanders in Hades yet, questioning all, but learning nothing.

Christ defined God through concepts analogous to loving family relations. "Pray then like this: '*Our Father* who art in heaven, hallowed by thy name . . . .' " "And thus, for a metaphysic which has emancipated itself from physical categories, the ultimate conception of God is not that of a pre-existent Creator but, as it is for religion, that of the eternal Redeemer of the world."[13] Aristotle defined God through purely rational concepts. He formulated no prayers to God, for God could not hear them; and it would pay no attention even if it did. Man's dignity is sullied by its being compounded with matter. Man must remain in nether gloom.[14]

II. The Problem of Locus

The question of the nature of God can never be discussed independently of the problem of God's locus. What if God *were* a person, but either withdrew too far away or remained

---

13. A. Seth Pringle-Pattison, *The Idea of God in the Light of Recent Philosophy,* p. 412.

14. "The God of the physicists turns out to be curious and unreal. But this, as Eddington points out, is only to be expected for if we proceed to analyse religious experiences by scientific methods then we get the only kind of God that science can think of — a personification of abstract principles. And so the God which results is unreal in the sense that one is compelled to think of Him as having affinity to the nature and organization of an atom—that is, of pure mathematics—rather than to the nature and organization of a man." Leslie Paul, *The Meaning of Human Experience,* (New York: J. B. Lippincott, 1950), p. 36.

too close to us to be of succor; what would be gained that
we do not already enjoy in humanism?

A. *Transcendence without Immanence*

The pride of man externalizes itself in some very strange
ways. But one of the most questionable is the habit of sending
up periodic ultimatums to heaven, outlining for God exactly
what hand in the pie of nature he may have. For instance,
man arbitrarily decides now and then that if God interferes
with nature too much, science's powers to predict will be
ruined.

> For, obviously, the real existence of miracles, which are
> contraventions of the normal course of things, would turn the
> world from a system into a chaos, would wrench it from
> human control, and would place it at the whim of some
> supernatural being, whether deity or devil. Such a world
> would respond to witchcraft but not to science. The sorcerer
> would triumph over the physicist. [15]

And so to oblige those who are thirsting for a monotonous,
nonmiraculous view of nature, a padlock is clamped on the
doors of heaven and God is quietly told to busy himself with
something else until called for. And as a result of such an
arrangement, man unwittingly declares his independence from
the very source of his own dignity. A god without immanence
is a god without relevance.

The deistic controversy which raged in England during the
first half of the eighteenth century remains to this day a classic
illustration of one of the persisting problems in theology:
How close should God get to his creation? Great thinkers,
such as Toland, Collins, Tindal, Woolston, and Chubb, defended the thesis (with varying degrees of stress) that God
need only have started the process of nature. From then on
resident laws within the universe itself are able to carry the
process on. What need is there for further divine intrusions

---

15. B. Dunham, *Man Against Myth*, (New York: Little, Brown, 1947),
p. 28.

when God has impregnated nature with the powers of natural law, and mind with the light of rationality? In his *Reasonableness of Christianity*, John Locke defended the proposition that one ought to accept only those parts of a religious system which commend themselves to the faculty of reason — a perfectly wholesome demand, for who would want to be found believing the *unreasonable?* Toland caught up the mood in his *Christianity not Mysterious*, and (unconscious of the fact that he had decided on unworthy grounds what constitutes the conditions of rationality) spoke out for free thinking in Christian doctrine — finally ending up a pantheist! In 1730 Tindal handed the deistic divines their sharpest weapon: *Christianity as Old as the Creation: or the Gospel, a Republication of the Religion of Nature.*

> All Divines, I think, now agree in owning, that there's a Law of Reason, antecedent to any external Revelation, that God can't dispense, either with his Creature or himself, for not observing; and that no external Revelation can be true, that in the least Circumstance, or minutest Point, is inconsistent with it. If so, how can we affirm any one Thing in Revelation to be true, till we perceive, by that Understanding, which God has given us to discern the Truth of things; whether it agrees with this immutable Law, or not?[16]

What need is there to postulate the immanence of God? Through his revelation in nature, God has adequately equipped men with the full light of his will. God will not arbitrarily interfere with the laws of nature, for that would be to act in a manner unbecoming to rationality. Since the natural world constitutes a sufficient expression of God's mind, what can be added to that which is already complete? Revelation can add nothing, for revelations are partial and preferential. A universal God owns no such quality of character, for he gives to all everywhere an equal opportunity to know the mind of his eternal will.

---

16. Matthew Tindal, *Christianity as Old as the Creation,* (London, 1730), p. 189.

When the deists finished pushing God to the perimeter of history, they left behind what was supposed to be a rationally satisfying view of life. God impregnated reality with laws and then flew off to busy himself with other things. In short, God is transcendent but not immanent.

Deism's epistemology was soon challenged, however, and the movement began to crumble from internal inconsistency. In his *Candide,* Voltaire questioned the rationality and purposiveness of the laws of nature, showing from the Lisbon earthquake of 1755 that the data of nature were hardly sweet and consistent enough to support supernatural religion. Pierre Bayle asserted that *all* dogma was contrary to reason, even the dogma of transcendence. David Hume, pursuing Locke's empirical (*tabula rasa*) presuppositions with dogmatic consistency, disclaimed even the possibility of metaphysical assertions. When the cycle was finished, thus, skepticism was in the saddle.

B. *Immanence without Transcendence*

Lying at the opposite extreme, and consequently subject to a quite different expression, is the penchant in other thinkers to curb the freedom of God by tying him so closely to the course of nature that the two become indistinguishable. Pantheism denies God's transcendence altogether.

The nearness of God is required on both religious and epistemological grounds. There is a mystical satisfaction in the thought of God as the Great All. Instead of having to go far off to find God, man need only expand his chest and look about him; for the universe is alive with divinity. Christian Science illustrates the religious prosperity that attends a theology of absolute immanence. "Christian Science reveals incontrovertibly that Mind is All-in-all, that the only realities are the divine Mind and idea."[17] Since God is all, all is God.

17. Mary Baker Eddy, *Science and Health with Key to the Scriptures,* (Boston: Joseph Armstrong, 1906), p. 109.

Whatever is not truth, light, goodness, and love is but an "illusion of material sense." Christian Science teaches that mind is all and matter is naught.[18]

> Nothing is real and eternal, nothing is Spirit, but God and His idea. Evil has no reality. It is neither person, place, nor thing, but is simply a belief, an illusion of material sense. . . . God, good, being ever present, it follows in divine logic that evil, the suppositional opposite of good, is never present.[19]

What need is there for human unrest when one is sheltered by so grand a theme? The dew on the flower is fragrance from the lips of God.

The epistemological grounds for pantheism have already been explored in examining Spinoza. When man shingles out into reality long enough, he inevitably comes to a pure immanence: God is the totality of nature. Spinoza identified nature and God — *deus sive natura, natura sive deus*. One cannot gainsay the initial lure of a consistent monism. Plotinus felt it; Hegel felt it. If one truth is contained within another, and that within another, until the Absolute is reached, then the entire universe is manageable. But once a qualitative difference between the categories of human reason and the person of God is introduced, the disturbing unbalance of seeking a perfection through imperfect means results. Transcendence introduces a discontinuous relation between God and man. So that a ladder will not be needed to get up to God, therefore, pantheism brings God down to man.

Time would fail us to examine the myriad types of pantheism. Nor is the labor necessary, for one common denominator is shared by all: The solution to the problem of the one within the many is the identification of the one with the many. Man experiences no difficulty relating the universe and God if he makes no separation between the two to start with.

---

18. *Loc. cit.*
19. *Ibid.*, pp. 71-72.

C. *Too Little or Too Much*

When the heart is asked to choose between complete transcendence and complete immanence, however, it feels like the thirsty man who, after begging for water, is told that he must either drink twenty-five gallons in one breath or go without drinking altogether. He will die if he does not drink, and he will burst out his organs if he does. Pray tell, then! how can a sensible decision between the options be made?

All species of deism partake of one questionable glory: The God they defend is irrelevant to the human venture. Is it not a trifle to say that God wound up the universe and then let it go? Why not just say the universe wound itself up? Since the question is one which passes beyond laboratory experiment, the scientific evidence for both is about equal. And revelation cannot help, since deism has disqualified the need for its voice. Axiologically, what is the difference between an impersonal unmoved mover and a personal, deistic God? Aristotle "conceives of God as so wrapped up within his own beatitude that he remains unaware even of the existence of the world of time and change and imperfection."[20] But is there any new consolation gained in learning that though God really knows about the world, he is too occupied about other things to have fellowship with men? Hardly. Much, in fact, can be said to show that a disconcerned *person* is less satisfying than a disconcerned *thing*. Love seeks out to save the lost. And if God does not even care that men have a feeling of guilt and uneasiness in their heart as a result of falling short of the rule of their life, it is difficult to see how he can claim even the moral requisites of his office. When a man has both the resources and the power to bring comfort to others, and yet refrains from doing it because he is too occupied with self-consuming activities, we label him a monster. Where shall God stand, when he has perfect resources and power, and yet passes by the hearts of men reaching out for fellowship?

---

20. Alan Richardson, *The Gospel and Modern Thought*, (London: Oxford University Press, 1950), p. 19.

Love is not something which can be postponed. If fellowship does not bind two hearts together now, discord reigns. There is no alternative ground. Translated cosmically, man becomes bitter on learning that his urge to worship is blocked by an infinite distance brought on by God's own choosing. Inasmuch as God is too distant to meet the needs of men, deism on the one hand corrupts the very possibility of solving our dilemma. *The feeling of guilt*, not simply the urge for a consistent epistemology, has driven the heart from trust in man to trust in God. And the search for God can be completed only when the heart of man unites with the heart of God in perfect fellowship. But our guilt stands in the way of this fellowship, for God is holy and man is sinful. How can holiness and sinfulness have concord? Therefore, God must break through into history and announce the exact terms which must be met for our reconciliation. We can know how to be saved only after God graciously condescends to tell us. Being men and not God, we cannot know what terms define the meeting out of justice to sinful men until we are instructed with heavenly wisdom.

Prayer and worship are on the divine-human relation as fellowship and devotion are on the human. Each series expresses tender, inner emotions which crave satisfaction. But deism rules out the very framework needed for the consummation of this peace, for God is too far to hear us.

Pantheism, on the other hand, ends up with such a crowded universe that the space between God and man is filled in. The *nearness* of God is indeed needed for fellowship, for there is a comfort in learning that God is nearer than breathing, closer than hands and feet. But when God *is* both the breathing and the hands and feet, then it is unclear what the ontological difference between God and man is. A clumsy, overcrowded world results. Fellowship arises out of a relation *between* numerically distinct spirits. Someone has defined fellowship as two fellows in a ship. And if nothing else is adequate about the definition, at least the word *two* is. The spirit of one fellow can leap into that of the other in warm satisfaction only when the two fellows are not the same fellow. Fellowship may *unite* spirits, but it does not confuse them. The father empathically enters into the heart of his dying child, but it is still the child, not the father, that is on the bed dying. But if I am part of God, the numerical difference is obliterated and fellowship is sullied. Love looks away from itself to another. It is outreaching. But what is there to reach if the universe is already filled up with God? This is one side to the difficulty.

And an equally serious problem is the soiled hands God is left with as a result of this friendly little identification of his nature with the flow of history itself. *Man* may be extremely flattered to think he is part of God, but how does God feel to learn that he is exemplified by man? If I am part of God, then God is as stained as I am. My greed, voraciousness, mendacity, and lust are all attributes of God. It is no "illusion of the material sense" that our hearts are proud and lustful; nor is it an illusion that the world is infested with many wicked men and women who respect neither the changelessness of truth nor the inherent dignity of the individual. One can only pity the practitioner of the Christian Scientist Church as she pleads that our evils are but illusions, for the reality of our evils is much more clear to us than the arguments of Christian Science against them.[21] Does not the Christian Scientist appeal to the ego? And is not the ego the center of self-love? If the precondition for accepting a system is selfish interest, that condition cannot be cancelled out after one is safely inside the system. God becomes selfish, too.

Pantheism leads to an insoluble contradiction. When the free individual says "God does not exist," one of two conclusions must follow, since the statement is either true or false. If it is true, then pantheism is untrue, for it is true that there is no God. And if it is false, then God is mendacious, not ex-

---

21. Has the Christian Scientist ever paused to answer the following problem: If I cannot trust my senses when they report death and pain, how can I trust them when I read the works of Mary Baker Eddy? The latter data are far less compelling than the former.

hibiting the first moral condition requisite for fellowship. In either case a cul-de-sac is reached.

When two men are drowning together, the one might be able to save the other if he had a solid place to hold on to. He may swim well, but if the sea is too wide and the shore too distant, they both drown. In like manner, a double drowning is the inevitable consequence whenever history is identified with God. God might save history if he were not so much a part of the process itself.

The collapse of the liberal theology of immanence illustrates the point perfectly. Liberalism made the regrettable mistake of identifying the vital force in history with God himself. Liberalism interpreted social progress as but another designation for the kingdom of God. All was well as long as the progress of social evolution pointed in the direction of this kingdom goal. But when the moral front of history exploded from the horror of two World Wars, it became evident that both God and man were drowning. The result has been a complete disintegration of liberal optimism and the rushing into being of its sanguine successor, neo-orthodoxy.[22] Neo-orthodoxy has come to appreciate the following rather important observation: If God is to be of service to man in the interpretation and salvation of history, he must stand sovereignly over history as its creator and judge.

One may not personally care to accept the Christian view of God and man, but at least he cannot deny the axiological advantage of a theology which, in addition to understanding God as Father, establishes *both* his immanence and his transcendence. God is the sovereign creator. While the world depends on him, therefore, he does not depend on the world. Yet, God

---

22. "Disintegration is not too strong a word. The defeat of the liberals is becoming a rout. Harried by the fundamentalists on the right flank and the humanists on the left, their position has long been a difficult one; but it could be maintained as long as their own morale remained unimpaired. Now their morale has cracked, rebellion and desertion are rife within their ranks, and the greater part of their forces are ready to 'flee when no man pursueth.'" Walter Marshall Horton, *Theology in Transition*, (New York: Harper and Brothers, 1943), Part II, p. 2.

is providentially in control of nature as its immanent pre-
server, guiding and ordering it according to the pleasure of his
own will. Transcendence insures the heart that God is far
enough away from the world to save significance for history,
while immanence insures it that he is near enough to hear
prayer and receive worship. Whenever this delicate relation
is misunderstood, the time-eternity balance is upset from one
side or the other.

III. The Problem of Power

But even if one brings himself to the place where he is willing to consider the case of a transcendent-immanent God as a
live option, the coast in not yet clear for open-water sailing.
One of the most baffling issues ever to engage the mind of
man lies yet ahead. *This is the problem of evil.* So disturbing
are the implications of this problem, in fact, that mature philosophers of religion have been forced to go scurrying back to
redefine God's nature again. And out of this industry has
emerged another challenging conception of deity which Scripture scores as untrue: *The finite God.*

If there is any aspect of God which the Biblical writers are
unambiguous about, it is the attribute of absolute sovereignty.
God created the world *ex nihilo* by the pleasure of his own
will. There was no necessity either inside or outside the divine
being which made creation obligatory. The act of displaying
glory *pleased* the Almighty. The plans were elected and the
work done. In like manner, God presently sustains the world
by the word of his sovereign power, for at the slightest beck
and call of his own will all things would immediately revert
back to nothingness. "O Jehovah, the God of our fathers, art
not thou God in heaven? and art not thou ruler over all the
kingdoms of the nations? and in thy hand is power and might,
so that none is able to withstand thee." (II Chronicles 20:6)

It has not taken free men long to perceive the difficulty that
sovereignty raises, however. Whereas pantheism is harassed
defining the relation of evil to the *being* of God, theism is

troubled defining its relation to the *will* of God. Axiologically, what is the difference if God *is* the evil in the world, or if he *deliberately chooses* a world out of which evil should grow? Is not the difference between these two expressions simply terminological? At first blush it might seem so — although the Biblical writers, let us remember, would strongly deny it.

The problem of evil has been classically stated by Epicurus: Either God wants to prevent evil, and cannot do it; or he can do it and does not want to; or he neither wishes to nor can do it, or he wishes to and can do it. If he has the desire without the power, he is impotent; if he can and has not the desire, he has a malice which we cannot attribute to him; if he has neither the power nor the desire, he is both impotent and evil, and consequently is not God. If he has the desire and the power, whence then comes evil, or why does he not prevent it? All of the ingredients of the problem are here.

At this point one catches himself glancing back at the unmoved mover with a feeling of nostalgia. If there is one argument in favor of an impersonal deity it is this: The unmoved mover cannot meaningfully be called in to account for the evil in the universe. Aristotle had no problem of evil to face. The mismanagement in the natural world comes from a fortuitous collision of competing forms. Evil in nature is simply an accident, for God has no concern for the world. While one may not be able to *worship* Aristotle's God, at least such a being has no moral questions written over it.

Thus, one can hear the voice of Aristotle calling across the centuries, pleading that only when God *is* disinterested in the world is he philosophically worthy; for once God is assigned the role of sovereign creator, then he is responsible for sanctioning things which men are obliged to call evil. And if God deliberately elects what is evil, then there seems to be no other conclusion but that his nature is discontinuous with the good. How then is he God?

A. *Tertium Quid*: *The Finite God*

The finitist says that a being who deliberately creates things which decrease human happiness (and thus are evil) is not God. Sheer tyrannical power cannot command the respect of moral men. Power has value only when it is compounded with goodness. Therefore, we must solve our problem as follows: While retaining the absolute goodness of God, we must sheer off enough power to relieve him of any responsibility for creating evil. In short, God must be conceived as finite.

Plato felt the full sting in this type of argument. If God is the author of mud, hair, and filth — not to mention the grosser evils in nature — then it is difficult to see how his will is cordially related to the good. If the harp is worthless (*qua* harp) when it does not conform to the pattern of goodness, what is God worth when he likewise falls short of perfection?

When faced with ethical problems in creation, therefore, Plato relieved pressure on God's responsibility by parceling out the creative labors to subordinate deities and powers. God personally created the things which cleared with his goodness (such as the souls of men), but the demiurge — and its subordinates — handled the less pleasant creative activities.

> Gods, children of gods, who are my works, and of whom I am the artificer and father, my creations are indissoluble, if so I will. All that is bound may be undone, but only an evil being would wish to undo that which is harmonious and happy. . . .And now listen to my instructions: — Three tribes of mortal beings remain to be created — without them the universe will be incomplete, for it will not contain every kind of animal which it ought to contain, if it is to be perfect. On the other hand, if they were created by me and receive life at my hands, they would be on an equality with the gods. In order then that they may be mortal, and that this universe may be truly universal, do ye, according to your natures, betake yourselves to the formation of animals . . . . I will hand the work over to you. [23]

23. *Timaeus*, 41b.

God initiated creation because of his perfect goodness. Desiring the fecundity which comes through self-reproduction, God — exempt from all jealously — ordered being to fan out into a plenitude. "And being free from jealously, he desired that all things should be as like himself as they could be. This is in the truest sense the origin of creation and of the world . . . . God desired that all things should be good and nothing bad, so far as this was attainable."[24]

The most interesting part of this quotation is the last phrase, *as far as this was attainable,* for it teaches that God was frustrated in accomplishing the full measure of his creative plans. Something blocked his efforts. A force stood in the way of the complete realization of his will, and the answer is that God struggled with the passive and recalcitrant nature of matter. A time-space environment comprises the "receptacle" for the creative overtures. The receptacle was not created *ex nihilo;* it is a datum which God had to deal with gently, being the only stuff at hand which could be informed with the fecundity of being. "The receptacle is the factor of perishing; it hinders things from achieving genuine reality."[25] The analogy is again that of the artist who has an ideal of perfection in his own mind, but who, because of the imperfection of the matter with which he deals, can never communicate that perfection to the canvas.

> God's activity, according to Plato, is not *ex nihilo;* it is like the productive activity of an artist or a sculptor, working over their materials respectively. In creating the world, God is operating upon something which he has not created, namely, the timeless receptacle; creation is transformation . . . . Thus, God is not omnipotent. God is the author only of the good in the world, not of the evil . . . . The evil is the result of the passive cause. God is limited, even frustrated, by the resistance of the receptacle. [26]

---

24. *Op. cit.,* **30a.**
25. Raphael Demos, *The Philosophy of Plato,* p. 69.
26. *Ibid.,* p. 106.

God is finite, for he wills more perfection than the creative receptacle can ever assimilate.

Plato properly sensed that in whatever sense God may be deficient, the deficiency *cannot* lie in his goodness; for the moment we lose respect for God, that instant he is serviceless as a solution to the problems of philosophy. If God is not good, what is he good for? For this reason Plato went out of his way to show that God is not causally related to evil in the world.

> God, if he be good, is not the author of all things, as the many assert, but he is the cause of a few things only, and not of most things that occur to men. For few are the goods of human life, and many are the evils, and the good is to be attributed to God alone; of the evils the causes are to be sought elsewhere, and not in him. . . .Let this then be one of our rules and principles concerning the gods, to which our poets and reciters will be expected to conform — that God is not the author of all things, but of good only. [27]

The finite-God hypothesis has a long and glorious history, therefore, reaching back through the story of philosophy to the venerable Plato. The contemporary mind is faced with a doctrine of no recent vintage.

Typical of modern finitists is William James. He found the hypothesis of a finite God a challenging alternative to the tyranny of absolute monism — chiefly Hegelianism. Measuring religious doctrines by their cash value, *i. e.*, by the here-and-now differences they make in the lives of men, James scored the value of absolutism a near zero. The absolutist (James taught) is a lazy sort of a fellow, quite uninterested in finding a working solution to the problem of evil in the universe. When viewed *sub specie aeterni*, evil conveniently becomes a good. Thus, why struggle for things which make a measurable difference in history, for the absolute has already

---

27. *Republic*, 379c-380b.

overcome evil from eternity.[28] James was greatly concerned
with what a succeeding lecturer (Lovejoy) has called "the
great chain of being." If the relation between time and eternity is not kept lubricated and loose-jointed, the result will be
a frozen concept of process. We need gaps in the nature of
reality, lacunae; in short, we need a *pluralistic* view of life.
There is no meaning to our ideals unless such goals are both
possible and unfinished. If God sovereignly does it all, there
is nothing left for man to do.

The only way to escape the auto-intoxication of monism
"is to be frankly pluralistic and assume that the superhuman
consciousness, however vast it may be, has itself an external
environment, and consequently is finite."[29] Man will be shoved
right out of the universe if the monistic view of reality succeeds. More will be gotten done, more accomplished prag-
matically, if we accept as our view of God "the notion that it
is not all-embracing, the notion, in other words, that there is
a God, but that he is finite either in power or in knowledge, or
in both at once."[30]

One of the most convincing writers on the finite God is the
contemporary personalist, Edgar Sheffield Brightman. Returning to a more Platonic approach, Brightman bases his
case for the limited deity on axiological consistency. His starting point is a coherent conception of values. *"Value means
whatever is actually liked, prized, esteemed, desired, approved
or enjoyed by anyone at any time. It is the actual experience
of enjoying a desired object or activity. Hence. value is an

---

28. "What do believers in the Absolute mean by saying that their belief affords them comfort? They mean that since, in the Absolute finite
evil is 'overruled' already, we may, therefore, whenever we wish, treat the
temporal as if it were potentially the eternal, be sure that we can trust its
outcome, and, without sin, dismiss our fear and drop the worry of our finite
responsibility. In short, they mean that we have a right ever and anon to
take a moral holiday, to let the world wag in its own way, feeling that its
issues are in better hands than ours and are none of our business." William
James, *Pragmatism*, (New York: Longmans, Green and Co., 1943), pp.
73-74.
29. James, *A Pluralistic Universe*, (New York: Longmans, Green and
Co., 1943), pp. 310-311.
30. *Ibid.*, p. 311.

existing realization of desire."[31]   The locus of all value is in mind, and personality is the highest of all values. God is postulated as the eternal mind in which the absolute values (norms) have their repose.

But since we must be empirical in our approach to God, we ought not permit ourselves to define him in a way which embarrasses us in the face of the evidences. God is absolutely good; this is not contested. If God were not perfectly good, he would not have taken pleasure in creating a world in which other persons are given an opportunity of growth in value. He would have refrained from this expression if the slightest jealousy had obsessed him. But the empirical facts of nature preclude the postulation of omnipotence in God. Brightman (with Plato) says that God is the author of the good only.

Evil is a fact of our experience. Observe "the cruel and irrational waste and seemingly aimless futility which evolutionary studies have revealed. The evidence of such facts points toward the purposeless, the dysteleological, in short, surd evil. Chance rather than reason seems revealed in these facts."[32]   Evolution points to purposive advance, on the one hand, while suggesting that purpose labors under difficulties, on the other. The temptation is to stress either side of the evidence to the exclusion of the other.

> Thus the evidence of evolution is seemingly contradictory. It points toward purposeless waste and futility; and it points toward purposeful creation and value. Center on one half of the evidence, and you become an atheist. Center on the other half, and you become a theistic absolutist. Take both together without any explanatory hypothesis, and you become a skeptic. [33]

The explanatory hypothesis which Brightman deduces from the conflicting facts is that there is a struggle in the universe

---

31. Edgar Sheffield Brightman, *A Philosophy of Religion*, (New York: Prentice-Hall, Inc., 1945), p. 88.
32. *Ibid.*, p. 316.
33. *Ibid*, p. 317.

between God's purpose in creation and an opposing power of limitation. "The hypothesis which these facts force on us is that of a finite God."[34] The fact that God is achieving desired ends in creation is proved by the present fecundity of personality in the world and the almost infinite ways personality values are increasing. The recalcitrance of limitation is never final, therefore. An *élan vital* power, like a gushing mountain stream, can be thwarted only for a moment; then it either breaks through the dam or turns to one side and rushes off in another direction.

Plato remained unclear on the question of the origin of the time-space receptacle. If there was no time before creation, how can we speak of a creation in time? "To this difficult problem we have to grope for our own answer, since Plato does not consider the problem."[35] In contrast to this ambiguity, Brightman boldly advances his theory of the *given*. The given is an uncreated condition in the divine nature which must be respected whenever God engages in the work of creation.

> The Given consists of the eternal, uncreated laws of reason and also of equally eternal and uncreated processes of non-rational consciousness which exhibit all the ultimate qualities of sense objects (*qualia*), disorderly impulses and desires, such experiences as pain and suffering, the forms of space and time, and whatever in God is the source of surd evil. The common characteristic of all that is 'given' ... is, first, that it is eternal within the experience of God and hence had no other origin than God's eternal being; and, secondly, that it is not a product of will or created activity. [36]

By assuming that God struggles with a given in the field of his own consciousness, and not a time-space receptacle out there, Brightman defends a position which he believes not only guards against dualism, but which also satisfies both the heart and the empirical evidences. It is a simple deduction from

34. Brightman, *op. cit.*, p. 318.
35. Demos, *op. cit.*, p. 107.
36. Brightman, *op. cit.*, p. 337.

cause and effect: Since the cause is all good, while the effect is not, the cause is not all powerful.

The values which flow out of the doctrine of the finite God are both practical and theoretical. As for theory: "The case for belief in a finite God may be summed up by saying that it is empirically adequate. If God is an eternal person, whose will is limited by the eternal laws of reason and the eternal brute facts of his experience, then the observed empirical nature of the world we experience can be understood."[37] As for practice: *First,* "there is the greater assurance of divine sympathy and love; if God is finite, he is not voluntarily imposing any unjust suffering or 'surd' evils on other persons, but is exerting all his power against such evils."[38] *Second,* "there is something awe-inspiring and favorable to mystical and 'numinous' experiences in the magnificent cosmic struggle of God against the 'fire of anger'. . ."[39] *Third,* "belief in a finite God furnishes those incentives to coöperative endeavor toward ever higher moral and social values. . . ."[40] *Fourth,* grounds are afforded "for belief in creative cosmic advance."[41] *Fifth,* "it is more natural to pray to a finite God, who may be moved by our infirmities, than to an Absolute, whose decrees are eternally fixed."[42]

The real crux of the matter for Brightman is the *surd,* that "type of evil which is inherently and irreducibly evil and contains within itself no principle of development or improvement."[43] If God willingly creates things characterized by an intrinsic worthlessness, such as idiots, he has a malice in his will which makes it impossible for men to call him all good.

---

37. Brightman, *op. cit.,* p. 321.
38. *Ibid.,* p. 327.
39. *Ibid.,* p. 328.
40. *Loc. cit.*
41. *Loc. cit.*
42. *Loc. cit.*
43. *Ibid.,* pp. 245-246.

B. *The Caution of the Existing Individual*

The case for the finite God lies in a different category than other options, since it comes *in the name* of the very values which the heart believes are alone worth striving for. It is proffered in the defense of a God who is good, personal, and deeply interested in our affairs, a God eternally devoted to the preservation of the same values which human beings respect.

Furthermore, the problem of evil *is* a problem. "If there is unity, order, organization, and rationality in the universe, why so many chaotic, apparently irrational elements? If objective purposiveness is at the heart of creation, how account for what appears to us as dysteleological? How can a good God allow war and disease germs and human suffering to continue, if He has control of things?"[44] We may balk, twist, turn, connive, circumvent, and define, but there it is: Evil remains. "Evil will not be gainsaid, argued away, made out to be something other than it is. Evil is evil, a standing contradiction to any thoroughgoing optimistic view of the world and life."[45] And what of the so-called surds?[46] These are all facts which must be respected. An hypothesis is valueless if it cannot stand up after being threatened by the facts.

In spite of the *prima facie* reasons why it is plausible to believe in a finite God, the heart must proceed with great caution. The Biblical writers were fully aware of the presence of evil in the world, yet they confidently affirmed that the heart will know full satisfaction only when it trusts in a God who has a sovereign right to do things which appear to be contrary to human well-being. Since these men were of mature counte-

---

44. Alfred Fisk, *The Search for Life's Meaning,* p. 130.

45. F. W. Camfield, *The Collapse of Doubt,* (London: Lutterworth Press, 1945), p. 39.

46. "Some of these evils can be shown to serve a good purpose that compensates for them or to be among the conditions within which certain values — for example, certain qualities of mind and character — can be realized. But there are certain ills, such as unmerited suffering and especially certain deformities of mind and body and the suffering of children, which do not seem to come under any of the rational explanations of evil." H. D. Lewis, *Morals and the New Theology,* (New York: Harper and Brothers, 1948), pp. 54-55.

nance and reflection, what can account for their universal rejection of finitism? This question must be answered, for it is from Biblical wisdom that we have thus far drawn guidance. If their point of view is suddenly found deficient, reasons must be discovered to account for this deviation.

C. The Probe

Can one yield to the finite God with complete and unrestrained submission, or is there a slight feeling that God would be more perfect if he were sovereign? If sovereignty is even *theoretically* more satisfying than finitude, there is reason to question whether our goal has been reached in the finite God.[47] The heart has thus far been guided by the conviction that when perfection is reached, no arrangement could be even *conceivably* better. So, here is the problem: Can I unite myself in marriage to the finite God without reservation, or am I obliged throughout the ceremony to dream of how perfect the wedding would have been if I *could* have joined with sovereignty?

In most candid terms, the heart *does* suffer an initial disappointment when it is informed that God is deficient in power, for the arrangement is not what man expected. In retreating from our own powerlessness it was presumed that in God perfection would be found. We indeed hoped that he would be infinitely efficient where we are infinitely inefficient. Finitism frustrates this hope.

One must judge for himself what such evidence is worth, but the fact of the shock he cannot deny. A man who has come to self-desperation is quite ready to accept the consolation that God possesses resources and power to do the whole

---

47. This argument is not that of wish thinking. Brightman is right: "*Every desire*, whether of religious believers or of unbelievers, *must be subjected to the dialectic of reason and fact.* Wishful thinking is not valid merely because it is widespread and has inspirational qualities." *Op. cit.,* p. 326. The point is that when the heart experiences a dissatisfaction with an option (however small it may be), the suspicion arises that there *may* be a perfection elsewhere; and that the cause of dissatisfaction is one's refusal to keep going long enough in his search for values. It would be axiologically foolish to accept a substitute for perfection. And if perfection is not found in God, where else is it?

counsel of his will. When there is frustration in God, disappointment is left in the human heart; for what we thought would be the end of our journey in striving against evil turns out to be but another (and everlasting) form of struggle. Greek philosophy, let us remember, brought no hope for the longing heart. Tragedy can be traced to the steps of heaven itself.

If God is in the same predicament we are, we need each other's help. The relation between God and man is no longer that of sovereignty and worship, but a mutual struggle against a common enemy. The thought of struggle may be heroic and noble, but it is exhausting to spirit. Love demands times of peace. Love is truncated as long as the lover must fight against forces which continually interrupt quietness and intimacy. He learns the final pleasure of fellowship only when nothing opposes the union of hearts in love. The girl and the boy do not interpret an endless flight from disapproving parents as "a noble and heroic taxation of spirit." Having already run so long to find love, they are now ready just to love. And so with God: If love in heaven is always at the mercy of the recalcitrance of evil, peace will be shattered. Weary men are tired of running; they want to love.

In examining the case for sovereignty, it is best to proceed through the very questions which finitism has raised. If these blocks in the way of believing can be removed, perhaps the heart can rest in its native witness. It knows that it would be better if God were sovereign, for love would then have a perfect environment for expression.

The first step in the recovery of faith in sovereignty is the dismissal of the so-called "rational given."[48] If God were not related rationally to man, one could no more have fellowship with him than he could with a communist who disregards the fundamental values of truth and justice. Should God disregard rationality, perhaps everything he says might mean its

---

48. Brightman, let us recall, has defined the rational given as "the eternal, uncreated laws of reason." Nothing tricky is meant by the word *reason*, either. It is simply the faculty of ratiocination.

contrary; so that the proposition, "I will save you," really means (in heavenly tongue) "I will damn you." There is no quicker way to destroy a meaningful relation between time and eternity than to suppose that since God's thoughts are *higher* than our thoughts, therefore they are *contrary* to them. Revelation would be sheer gibberish if there were not a univocal, rational element uniting the meaning of propositions entertained by both man and God.

There is room for debate on the question whether God might have informed this world with another type of logic — although many difficulties arise once the problem is stated this way.[49] How can we use logic meaningfully to describe a hypothetical universe in which another logic is used?

But what is crystal clear is that the present man — the only man we happen to know — can find no meaning in loving a God who follows other than the laws of logic when he speaks. God may have attributes which human personality cannot comprehend, but God is not a person at all if his propositions are not meaningful and trustworthy.

The rational given does not really support finitism, therefore. God can still be infinite in power and yet remain rationally related to his creation. God is genuinely finite only when he is deficient where he wishes he were efficient. If a horse has only four legs, it is not deficient. How many legs should a horse have? If the horse had bad legs, however, while futilely wishing it had good ones, then its will is frustrated. There is limitation only when the desire for realization is blocked. And this is not the case with God, for God

---

49. The reason why the Christian is willing to leave open this question of other logics is that though God is a person, *he may be infinitely more.* God is not just a large-sized man. He has infinite attributes. Now, in the endless number of ways in which God's glory surpasses man's, there may actually be many other methods of communication which are different from the conventional laws of logic we follow in our thought life. God abides by the laws of Aristotelian logic because of his immutable covenant to respect the conditions of fellowship which this type of a creation presupposes. But the laws of logic are still subject to God's sovereignty in that their *relevance* for this type of a universe was decreed by his will. The laws are uncreated—indeed. But the decision to declare their relevance rests in God alone.

has never *struggled* to be rational. The laws of reason are a medium of perfect expression, not a block in the way to perfection.

It is clear, therefore, that the troublesome point is the "non-rational given."[50] The "stuff" or environment which freedom must respect in creation has always been the ace in the finitist's hand. It is plausible that God might use the rational given to *think* of possible worlds he might create, and still not be finite; but if he wills a creative perfection which either the potentialities in his own nature or the time-space receptacle outside prevents, he is finite. This is true-blue finitism: God *wills* perfection in creation, but he is thwarted because the conditions with which he has to deal in creation get in his way.

This is a real difficulty! The heart hoped that one way God differed from men was in his power to control the *conditions* of creation as well as engineer creation itself. Men can mold and form; God alone can create. When one thinks of God as a large-sized artist doing the best he can, but not fully approving the stuff he works with, an element of uncertainty is injected into the heart. We came to God for relief from weakness, not to be introduced into a new and higher type.

Since we are not yet persuaded that the postulation of a non-rational given is necessary, however, hope remains that one may still trust a God who enjoys sovereignty over even human personality.

Let us approach the mysterious, inner problems of God's relation to nature by a study of *compossibility*. Is it "possible together" that God be perfectly good and that he create a universe out of which evil should come? This states the issue clearly. The Christian stands squarely on the side of affirmation. "And Jehovah said unto him, Who hath made man's mouth? or who maketh a man dumb, or deaf, or seeing or

---

50. The non-rational given, to refresh our minds, is the "eternal and uncreated processes of non-rational consciousness which exhibit all the ultimate qualities of sense objects (*qualia*), disorderly impulses and desires . . . the forms of space and time, and whatever in God is the source of surd evil."

blind? Is it not I, Jehovah?" (Exodus 4:11) Jehovah God *boasts* of his right to make some men broken, and others whole. "Has the potter no right over the clay, to make out of the same lump one vessel for beauty and another for menial use?" (Romans 9:11) In opposition to this, the finitist says that if God is genuinely a person, he *cannot* willingly create those things which frustrate human happiness. It is not possible together that God be infinitely good and that he create evil.[51]

The instant we speak of compossibility, however, complexities mount. Compossibility may be either rational or non-rational. As far as rational compossibility is concerned, it can be written off immediately; since it is only another way of saying that God is subject to the rational given — a topic already dismissed as irrelevant. Rational compossibility pertains to *meaning,* not to stuff; and the rule which governs it is the law of contradiction. For example, if by the term *created world,* God means "round world," it is not rationally compossible that it likewise means "non-round world." If *fire* means "stuff which burns," it cannot simultaneously and in the same sense mean "stuff which does not burn." *The meaning of any term excludes its own contradictory.* If *water* means "liquid suitable for drinking," it cannot at the same time and in the same sense mean "liquid not suitable for drinking." Rational compossibility is the rational given viewed from another perspective. Once God decides on the meaning of a term, to retain rationality he must stick with that meaning.

---

51. It is rather obvious that two different standards are in contest here. Is the ultimate good the increase and preservation of human personality, or is it the will and glory of God? Questions of compossibility are too frequently judged by criteria which are unconsciously assumed from the start to exhaust the possibilities. When we decide in advance that there is no good higher than human good, obviously God is not good until he casts his lot behind man. But if it should prove (as the Bible teaches) that the glory of God is more important than the preservation of man, is not the good determined by a consultation with God, rather than independently? We do not yet say where investigation will lead us to, but it is well to know the alternatives in advance.

Non-rational compossibility has to do with the possibility together of the *stuff* of creation and God's *intentions* in creation. Is the stuff a given with which God has to deal, so that when he seeks to learn what things can be created, the final list is determined by the environment he *finds* rather than the environment he *creates*? Does God enjoy dominion over the conditions of creation, or is he obliged to struggle with data which are inherent in the situation? Conflicting answers are given to these questions. Plato said that God has to do the best he can with the time-space receptacle; Brightman says that God has a given in his nature which his will must respect, but which it does not create. The Scriptures teach that God's will sovereignly decreed both the end and the means.

There is good reason to believe that non-rational compossibility is really a scapegoat for a more basic problem. The reason there are surds in nature is *not* the fact that natural law is a "given" with which God must gently deal. The idiot is made of exactly the same stuff as the normal child; hence, the cause of idiocy does not lie in the resistance of matter. Inasmuch as there *are* instances when matter has yielded to created overtures, one must conclude that the differences between the normal and the healthy must be traced to other than the natural properties of matter. Given the right tools with which to work, even scientists can reshape deformed minds and bodies. The conclusion must be that it *is* possible together that there be a universe without tornadoes, hurricanes, floods, and idiocy. No analysis of the possibilities of matter yields the truth of the following proposition: "The disproportionate is necessary." The ideal of science is grounded in the faith that, given enough time, matter *can* be made to follow the straight and narrow path. Hence, a universe in which types of being deviate from the normal was not forced on God. If the scientist can make the crooked straight, is there any meaning to denying that God can?

Where else can the reason for deviations in the universe lie than in the will of God? He decided what course matter should follow. The nature of matter itself did not force the direction, for it *is* compossible that matter be used and that the earth have no surds in it. The proof (as indicated) is the presence of the normal. If an inventor succeeds in making *one* good automobile out of steel, while all the rest are faulty, the conclusion is that the deficiency of the latter lies in the skill of the man and not the potentialities of the steel. The presence of the one perfect car proves what the matter is capable of. Likewise, the presence of normal men shows what the non-rational given is capable of. *The upshot is that the non-rational compossible does not solve the problem of the surds.*

But the sensitive mind is not surprised at this, for the objections to sovereignty run far deeper than the petty complaint about what matter can or cannot do. One must be humble about matter's possibilities, for it is capable of a lot more than we first thought; science shows this.

The *real* issue is *ethical* compossibility. All other arguments are but dust from the battle, for here is where the crucial conflict has to be fought. Because he labored under a preconceived notion of the good, Plato was forced to resort to the expediency of a time-space receptacle to save God's goodness. But it was Plato's idea of the good, not the impotency of matter to yield to God, which tied him all up in the *Timaeus*. The same is true with Brightman. Having decided on the other grounds (in short, not by consulting God) what the good is, God's nature is trimmed to fit an antecedent axiology. The conclusion of both philosophies — and of all other instances of finitism as well — is that it is *not* possible together that God be absolutely good and that he willingly elect a world which in part should decrease human happiness. But note that the objection is based on *ethical*, not non-rational compossibility.

It is highly questionable if Plato had any legitimate grounds for postulating a problem of evil at all. Since God was pleased to make being as full as possible, why should Plato complain when such things as storms and filth appear? Do they not contribute to the plenitude of being by their by very presence? Would not the hierarchy of being remain incomplete without their representation? Thus, what is evil about an idiot? Since it perfectly fulfills the essence of idiocy, it takes its rightful place in the fecundity of all being. In a philosophy of plenitude it would seem that the real evil is the *absence* of idiots.

In the case of the increase of personality, however, the issue is far more complex. Brightman says that personality is the only ultimate value. If God is a person, therefore, is it *not* possible together that he be infinitely good and that he deliberately create a universe which decreases the sum total of values.[52] If God *reduces* personality values in the universe, can he meaningfully be called good? Our quest thus far has been grounded in the presupposition that what promotes our personal happiness is the good, while what subtracts from it is the evil. We cannot suddenly reverse field and pretend that we now *prefer* a God who decreases our happiness.

The moment we commence to measure God according to criteria gained in society, however, a sheepish feeling of indecorousness arises. We have come to God with the white flag of surrender up, for without him we are consigned to hopeless contradictions in life. Are *we* in any position to dictate the terms of surrender? The heart has thus far only insisted that God is at least a person. Whatever reservoirs of attributes he may have in addition to this are reserved for him alone. Perhaps strata of purpose lie beyond those we are able to perceive.

---

52. Brightman ends up in trouble from another direction, however. If God is not good unless he is actively creating and preserving personalities, then it follows that there is a *necessity* in God for creation. God would become non-God the instant he left off creating persons, for he would then jealously prefer his own solitude to sharing life with others, which is evil. From an analysis of the term *God*, therefore, one finds the necessary existence of creation. This involves Brightman in a theory of eternal creation. And once eternity is conceived of as time stretched out real long, woe to the mind that has to work its way through this embranglement! There is no meaning to progress in an infinite history, for every end has already had infinite chances of being reached. And not being achieved yet, it will never be reached. The Greeks may have adopted a cycle theory of history, but let us hope that modern man does not have to.

We cannot long proceed with this kind of approach, however, for hardly have we outlined the argument but what James jumps to his feet and decries this as the monotonous old story of absolutism. Appealing to the "hidden counsels of God" to relieve us of the hard office of solving problems for ourselves is as good a way to describe indolence as we could want. James asserts that by the appeal to such an asylum of ignorance one can explain everything. Why are there idiots? Oh, the will of God! Why are six and six fifteen? Oh, the will of God! *Sub specie aeterni* is a favorite device for the ignorant.

D. *Probe Continued*

If one has carefully followed the argument thus far, he will perceive that the issue which separates the finitist from the absolutist is not the fact that imbecility is evil. Christianity is not Christian Science. The Christian concedes and laments the presence of real, objective evil in nature. The issue is, rather, whether the Christian is forced to admit that the imbecile is a surd. It does not serve *men* any good;[53] but does it serve God? The question may sound cavalier at first, for how can an evil thing ever become a means to the good?

At this point in the argument the existing individual must make what is probably the most crucial decision in the whole of the theological encyclopedia. *Is the good whatever God does, or is the good an objective standard which God must*

---

53. This proposition must be taken provisionally. If it turns out that the Biblical world view is plausible, then one may justifiably conclude that idiots *do* service to men in the sense that they remind them (a) of the grace of God that we too were not brought into such a fate — thus promoting thankfulness (as the Persian proverb which says that one complained about his shoes hurting until he saw a man without feet); (b) of sin, which has caused God to curse the earth for man's sake — thus promoting a feeling of remorse that one is indirectly an accomplice in the work of bringing the generic punishment for sin upon men. If there had been no sin in the first place, there would be no need for God to curse the earth for man's sake in the second. For this reason it is not possible to understand the idiot without first understanding the relation between generic sin and God's dealings with it.

comply with to be called good? This statement puts ethical compossibility in its sharpest possible form. The Christian says that the will of God is the final standard of good, and that what God wills is good because he wills it. Job, for example, was willing to be slain at the behest of the will of God. The finitist, on the other hand, protests that God is not good (no matter what his will decides) unless he first is obedient to the good. In Platonic philosophy, therefore, the gods glance out into the meadow each morning, taking their own inspiration from the good even as mortal men do. The good is a third order of being which gives harmony to both God and man. At this point the struggle between finitism and absolutism reaches its climax.

One can easily perceive that this is the end of the trail. *Is God's will our standard of good, or is the good an abstract principle which binds both man and God together? Does man learn from God what the good is, or do God and man both learn it from a third source? If the increase of personality is the good, then obviously the idiot is a surd. But if God has a sovereign purpose in willing that the deformed be born, then it is not a surd.*

The Christian confesses that there are no few problems connected with sovereignty, for (as James convincingly shows) the doctrine is subject to easy abuse. But the Bible resolutely testifies to the fact that God *is* sovereign over the increase and decrease of human personality. "And as he passed by, he saw a man blind from his birth. And his disciples asked him, 'Rabbi, who sinned, this man or his parents, that he was born blind?' Jesus answered, 'It was not that this man sinned, or his parents, but that the works of God might be made manifest in him.' " (John 9:1-3) And since the Bible is our only source of information about Christianity, the system stands or falls on what it says.

Perhaps the leading clue to the solution has up to this point been left hidden under a bushel. By way of a simple illustration, let us seek to show what is the essence of the *real* problem separating the finitist from the absolutist. If a husband walks down the street and happens to observe his wife get into a taxi with another man, he can do one of two things. He can use the good as an abstract rule and charge her with being unfaithful, thus challenging the integrity of her heart; or he can remember that he has already pledged his love to her, and that though the act *seems* to be wrong, it nevertheless is good because it has proceeded from a heart he trusts. In this case he refuses to identify the appearance with the motive of her heart. Now, let it be noted from this example that the problem of evil is solved by the employment of loving trust. The husband *believes* in his beloved. That is how love works.

Or, let us appeal to the very illustration which Christ chose. Taking a little child in his midst, he set him before the others as a perfect example of one who would be first to find pleasure with the Father in the kingdom. The child is characterized by a simplicity and abandonment in trust which knows no easy counterpart in adulthood. The trusting child never imputes evil motives to his parents. If the father turns out the lights, leaving the little one in the dark, *e. g.*, a loving child will be satisfied with the father's word that an apparent evil means is actually bringing the child a resulting good. When love binds hearts together all fear is dispelled.

Now it begins to grow plain why the heart feels a little uneasy when it tries to worship a finite God. Since it comes to God armed with a principle by which it can periodically check to see if God is still doing the good, it follows that one does not really trust the *person* of God. If one loved God, he would be willing to believe God when he says that the creation of evil is but an expedient; and that through such means a perfect plan conceived in the counsels of eternity, is being fulfilled.[54] The finitist can trust God only when he is assured that God is devoted to the good — otherwise he cannot. If God is ever

---

54. Observe that this solution does not reduce evil to an illusion. Both God and man agree that idiocy *is* an evil. The issue is whether or not God has the right to use evil as means to accomplish good ends. The Christian answers *yes*, for he trusts the person of God.

found deliberately doing things which seem to run counter to our abstract notion of the good (such as creating idiots), the finitist must politely inform God that since he suspects his integrity he cannot bow down to worship. Whenever God returns to his proper task of increasing personality potentialities, friendship is restored. But what kind of a fellowship is this?

Since there is a complexity here which must be respected, however, great caution must be exercised. As a matter of fact we *do* apply an abstract rule when judging whether a neighbor is good or not; and thus, it appears that the point being made breaks down. But what must not be overlooked is that once loving trust enters as the mediator between hearts, the procedure is reversed. Before the boy falls in love with the girl, he applies the rule of the good to make sure it is a good girl he is dating. But when love captivates the heart, the abstract rule is forgotten and the beloved's motives are patiently dealt with in the gentleness of forgiving love. The instant that motives are questioned, love begins to decay. Love which is perfect casts out fear. It bears all things, believes all things, hopes all things, endures all things.

And so with God: Since it is necessary that we first be assured that it is God, not the devil, that we are doing business with, we must apply the rule of the good to find God. But once the heart is satisfied that God is worthy of receiving loving trust, the abstract good is then set aside and the will of God becomes the standard of goodness. Whoever cannot say that he trusts God to the point of worshipping him is deficient in a perfection in fellowship. Our abstract conception of good is only a formal means by which we come through to trust. Should we continue to subject God to this rule after having met him, we only demonstrate the fact that we do not trust him. Whoever reserves a right to examine the motives of God trusts not God but the good. If God is our Father, his will automatically becomes the standard of the good. How else may we interpret the divine, save on the analogy of what constitutes the profoundest relation in our own experience? Fellowship *trusts;* it does not question.

Plato, let us remember, placed the good, not God, at the top of the hierarchy of being; for (so he reasoned) what good would God be if he were not first good? Since the wrench is good only as it participates in the goodness of wrenchness, the same must be true with God: God is good only when he does what coincides with the good. It follows, therefore, that Plato's trust lay not in the person of God but in the abstract rule which God and everybody else abides by. Plato could not worship God because he did not know the kind of love which is willing to let go and trust. As soon as one commences to worship God he will willingly put out of his mind any easy, objective calculation of the good; preferring rather to hold out his hand to receive whatever might come his way from the divine being, knowing that what comes will be perfect for the very reason that it comes from God. Distrust is characterized by a pride which seeks to challenge motives whenever the occasion calls for it.

Here, as perhaps nowhere else, the difference between Christianity and finitism can be summed up: *The Christian turns to God to find out what things are good, while the finitist turns to the good to find out if God is good. Christianity says that it is a contradiction in terms to test God for goodness, for the good is what he does and approves. Finitism says that God is not God until he first does the good.*

It appears, therefore, that finitism is actually a disguised form of higher immediacy, for it is more anxious to introduce men to trust in an abstract good than to trust in the person of God the Father. The finitist can respect God for his magnanimity in creation; he can cooperate fully with him in overcoming the good; *but he cannot worship God.* There is a generic difference between admiration and worship of God. In worship the whole heart is prostrated completely before the supreme being. The worshipper transfers all authority to the one sitting on the throne, so that God's will becomes his will.

Whatever God commands is just: whatever he wills is holy. To remain before the throne of God armed with an abstract rule of the good is as unsatisfying as it is blasphemous. If I feel sheepish when I am capable of giving selfless devotion to my fellow men, yet fail to be selfless. I feel wretched when I want to give myself in worship, yet cannot let go. Worship involves an unreserved abandonment in perfect trust and obedience. The worshipper so takes to himself the will of the worshipped that implicit, unquestioned, and instantaneous obedience is given to God's meanest behest.

This is extremely serious. We were driven from the immediacies into humanism because we could not live with them in perfect peace. We cannot express our freedom in lower terms than trusting devotion to other persons. But because we found resources of love within us which men could not satisfy, we were driven to seek God. And there is nothing more certain in the heart than this: Should God appear in the room, the only posture which the whole person could assent to is worship. Since two orders of being are being juxtaposed — creation and the Creator — decorum demands complete and abject prostration. When *men* try to elicit our worship, we remind them that they are dust even as we are; but when *God* demands it, we feel foolish to resist. If we are fully satisfied in our whole person only when we worship, therefore, it follows that finitism is a lower satisfaction than Christianity. We cannot worship a God whose powers we have had to whittle down as a result of coming to him through an abstract good. Having had a hand in manipulating his dimensions, we hardly feel that the distance between him and us is great enough to justify worship.

Since the only God it will finally do business with is one against whom the threatening stick of ethical compossibility may always be pointed, finitism leads to a pride of the flesh. No more convincing proof of this charge need be cited than the now famous outburst of John Stuart Mill. His finitism let him to the point where man's goodness is even *better* than God's.

> If in ascribing goodness to God I do not mean what I mean by goodness; if I do not mean the goodness of which I have some knowledge, but an incomprehensible attribute of an incomprehensible substance, which for aught I know may be a totally different quality from that which I love and venerate. . . .To say that God's goodness may be different in kind from man's goodness, what is it but saying, with a slight change of phraseology, that God may possibly not be good? To assert in words what we do not think in meaning, is as suitable a definition as can be given of a moral falsehood. . . . Unless I believe God to possess the same moral attributes which I find, in however inferior a degree, in a good man, what ground of assurance have I of God's veracity?
>
> If, instead of the 'glad tidings' that there exists a Being in whom all the excellencies which the highest human mind can conceive, exist in a degree inconceivable to us, I am informed that the world is ruled by a being whose attributes are infinite, but what they are we cannot learn, nor what are the principles of his government, except that 'the highest human morality which we are capable of conceiving' does not sanction them; convince me of it, and I will bear my fate as I may. But when I am told that I must believe this, and at the same time call this being by the names which express and affirm the highest human morality, I say in plain terms that I will not. Whatever power such a being may have over me, there is one thing which he shall not do: he shall not compel me to worship him.
>
> I will call no being good, who is not what I mean when I apply that epithet to my fellow-creatures; and if such a being can sentence me to hell for not so calling him, to hell I will go. [55]

In contrast to this, observe the humble satisfaction that attends those who have come to the point where they can worship a sovereign God. "But he knoweth the way that I take; when he hath tried me, I shall come forth as gold." (Job 23:10)   Or again,

---

55. *An Examination of Sir William Hamilton's Philosophy*, Vol. I, pp. 130-131.

Jehovah is my light and salvation; whom shall I fear?
Jehovah is the strength of my life; of whom shall I be afraid?
When evil-doers came upon me to eat up my flesh, even mine
adversaries and my foes, they stumbled and fell. Though a
host should encamp against me, my heart shall not fear:
though war should rise against me, even then will I be confident. [56]

Where could one find more incompatible expressions? Whereas Mill is nervous and uncertain when he approaches a God
who prides himself in having created the blind and the halt,
Job and David rejoice that they have been privileged to worship this very one. What is the resolution in these two attitudes?

E. Probe Concluded

Mill ended up where he did, and Job and David did not,
for unlike them he was blinded to the *real* problem of evil in
the world. It is interesting to note that a straight line can be
drawn through the finitists of all ages. *They all share the one
presupposition that natural evil, not sin, is the more pressing
problem.* Plato was concerned about the disproportionate;
Mill troubled himself about the maimed and the abortive in
nature; Brightman lists the surd as exhibit A. And in no case
is *sin* the chapter heading for the problem of evil.[57] How can
finitists possibly learn to love a sovereign God, when they remain blinded to the fact that fellowship can be restored only
after sin is dealt with? If love is God's law, and if sin is a
transgression of that law, a self-loving creature has not begun
to realize his own condition if he does not see himself as a sinner.

This is extremely crucial. When we break the bond of
fellowship among men, we must give an apology; and when
we break the bond of fellowship between man and God, we
must confess our sin. However, we can confess sin only to

56. Psalm 27:1-3.
57. While Brightman has one of the finest and most exhaustive indexes
available in a book on philosophy of religion, *sin* is not even entered as a
topic. Is this not a tragic commentary on the fact that sin is not important
for finitism?

a God whom we can worship. If God is only quantitatively different from us — a large-sized architect, perhaps — *confession* is not called for. Since we are both doing the best we can, let us pity each other.

A cursory reading of the Scriptures proves that God's covenant in history had but one purpose: It is to restore men to fellowship through the meeting of the problem of sin. Although man can be on speaking terms with God only when he loves God with all his heart, the power of self-love within us continually sullies this perfection. We are proud, self-righteous, self-loving creatures. "All are under the power of sin, as it is written: 'None is righteous, no, not one.'" (Romans 3:9-10) It is the conviction of the Christian, therefore, that the most *awful* datum for philosophy of religion is not the surd evil, but sin itself.

> I cannot entertain the thought of man's guilt, cannot feel the burden of it, without in the very act striking up against the reality of God. The more I am impressed by the fact that sin is a terrible reality, the more surely shall I know that God is . . . . It is just here that the spirits divide. The men of the Bible were, for the most part, more appalled by the fact of sin, by its guilt, than by those miseries which were the consequences of it. Therefore, so far from denying God, they were moved more seriously and solemnly to affirm Him. They knew that the logic of moral evil . . . led not to unbelief but to so serious a belief that atonement for sin was called for. [58]

Would it not be a singularly tragic mistake if the finitist is unable to work his way through to the living God because he made the initial mistake of confusing natural evil with the *real* ethical problem? If it happens that man can know God only after he first realizes his own sinfulness, the devotee of finitism lacks the very precondition for fellowship.

The trouble with the finitist is that he is going about the whole thing backwards. When one seeks to gain his way into the heart of another person (and so learn to *know* the person),

---

58. Camfield, *The Collapse of Doubt*, p. 29.

he does it by first disavowing his own desert. Love enters only
after pride exits. The boy who disclaims his worthiness of
the girl's love is the first to receive it.

It is a plain fact of experience that we do not learn the nature of another person by setting up a rational hypothesis
which accounts for empirical facts. The hypothesis will lead
us to the edge of personality, but one knows another only
through personal acquaintance. Try setting up a presupposition to understand the child! You will end up with an
animated thing, perhaps, but hardly a child. To know the
little one, a person must walk right up to him and so speak that
spirit enters spirit in friendship.

How then can the finitist ever have fellowship with God?
The coherent hypothesis may lead us to the perimeter of God's
personality, but only confession of personal unworthiness can
plunge the heart of man into the heart of God. Love is a gift
of God, and it will be given only to those who have come to
God through an admittance of their own personal guilt and
sin. Sin makes it impossible for a person to know God, for
arrogance always blocks the entrance of love. A rational
hypothesis may be necessary to assure us that there *is* meaning
in surrendering our hearts to God, but it is the surrender, not
the hypothesis, which sends us to the heart of the Father.[59]

Let the reader decide: *Shall we trust a God who is able to
take away our sins, or shall we trust a God who is nobly struggling against evil, but who has made no provision for the forgiveness of sins?* It is obvious, of course, that the answer
to such a question will depend upon how impressed an individual happens to be with his sinfulness. But it does seem

---

59. "He also told this parable to some who trusted in themselves that
they were righteous and despised others: 'Two men went up into the temple
to pray, one a Pharisee and the other a tax collector. The Pharisee stood
and prayed thus with himself, "God, I thank thee that I am not like other
men, extortioners, unjust, adulterers, or even like this tax collector. I fast
twice a week, I give tithes of all that I get." But the tax collector, standing
far off, would not even lift up his eyes to heaven, but beat his breast, saying,
"God, be merciful to me a sinner!" I tell you, this man went down to his
house justified rather than the other; for every one who exalts himself will
be humbled, but he who humbles himself will be exalted.' " Luke 18:9-14.

to one who has cautiously worked his way through humanism to fellowship with God, that the most important question which must be settled is the forgiveness of sin. The more sensitive the heart is to the rule of life, the less worthy does it feel to approach the living God. Just as one cannot face an offended friend without an apology, so we cannot face God without first meeting the terms of confession and contrition. But where is God, that we may confess? What are his terms?

> Martin Luther once said that the article about the forgiveness of sins is the most important article in the Apostles' Creed, for if this is not true, or seen to be true for me, what does it matter that God is the Almighty Maker of heaven and earth, or that Jesus Christ was born, or that he suffered, died, and rose again? It is because these things have a bearing upon my forgiveness that they are important for me. Otherwise the rest of the articles of the Creed would tell us only about a God and a Christ from whom we are cut off because of the gulf between their holiness and our sinfulness. [60]

When Plato finished the last sentence of his philosophy, he offered hope neither to the individual nor to history; for his world view ended up in a pathetic dualism where the eternal struggle between good and evil shows no signs of relief. God remains forever on the side of the good, and thus commands our respect; but there is no possibility of his ever gaining complete control over that good. The time-space receptacle will always be on hand to harass God's desires for perfection.

Brightman has sought to diminish the gloom of dualism by postulating an eternal history in God. History is an infinitely stretched out moral evolution. But one questions the satisfaction of this alternative. If the non-rational given is as ultimate a factor in God as the rational given, how can God overcome himself? Dare we conclude from the emergence of human personality that God is actually gaining control over the given? Possibly history is only a series of cycles; for a time God wins, and for a time evil wins. Perhaps Empedocles was

---

60. Alan Richardson, *The Gospel and Modern Thought*, p. 176.

right: The cosmic agents of love and strife exchange hegemony from time to time. First love brings the dissimilar elements together in mixture, then strife enters to separate them. If one were judging the meaning of the process from that point where love is in the ascendancy, he might be tempted to conclude that love is gaining final control over strife. But what he overlooks in his partial perspective is that the time of love's ascendancy is brief. Strife *will* inevitably re-enter.

In any case, there is a great suspicion that since God has not yet overcome evil — though he has had infinite opportunity to do so — *he will never do it.* Royce has stated the problem excellently:

> If you found a man shoveling sand on the sea-shore, and wheeling it away to make an embankment, and if you began to admire his industry, seeing how considerable a mass of sand he had wheeled away . . . you might still check yourself to ask him: 'how long, O friend, hast thou been at work?' And if he answered that he had been wheeling away there from all eternity, and was in fact an essential feature of the universe, you would not only inwardly marvel at his mendacity, but you would be moved to say: 'So be it, O friend, but thou must then have been from all eternity an infinitely lazy fellow.' [61]

At the end of the finitist's efforts to convince us that God will overcome the given, however, the heart is still concerned about the most important question of all. *When will God overcome our sin?* Even if finitism saves meaning for history, does it save faith for the heart?

Christianity assuages the heart with the assurance that after the problem of sin is settled, the problem of natural evil will solve itself. Jesus Christ, the eternal Son of God, took on flesh that he might become the sin-bearer of the world — and especially of them that believe. Through the revelation of his Son the Father has announced the terms which must be met if communion with heaven is to be enjoyed. The law of life must be met, for God is holy. Perfection in heaven must

---

61. Quoted in Lovejoy, *The Great Chain of Being,* pp. 330-331.

be matched by a perfection on earth — each after its own order of being. But the problem immediately arises how a self-
loving creature can turn to God for fellowship, for it was an
initial uneasiness with ourselves which drove us to the arms
of God in the first place. We cannot overcome our own sinfulness, since our nature has a defect in it. We need power
and resources from beyond ourselves to strengthen our own
fainting spirits. Our problem is not want of knowledge, for
we know the good; our difficulty is a want of spiritual resources to make this knowledge good.

God has provided a free gift of salvation by substituting a
perfection in our place. In Christ's life the law of our being
has been fulfilled; in his vicarious and atoning death on the
cross a payment for sin has been made. Since Christ has
satisfied justice in our stead, the love of God for men can reach
out in fullness to save. "For God so loved the world that he
gave his only Son, that whoever believes in him should not
perish but have eternal life." (John 3:16)

Christ is Immanuel: God with us. And the proof is an
examination of the life he lived and the death he died. When
we evaluate Christ with a sensitive, compassionate heart, we
cannot avoid the conclusion that he has fulfilled what we know
by intuition constitutes the duty of life itself. By comparing
ourselves with Christ, we immediately fall under judgment.
Christ loved with perfection. He healed the sick, had compassion on those who were out of the way, was kind to enemies,
and made his bed with the downtrodden. He did all the
things we admit we must do if we are fully to be at ease with
ourselves. He is the only one in history who could ask, *Which
of you accuses me of sin?* He alone could say, *I am the truth.*
He was truth in his own person. Therefore, either he is God
among us, or he is a remarkably consistent man. But we
know from an examination of history that Christ is not just
a man, for no man lived like this man. He lies in a different
genus. The instinctive response of the heart is that in Christ
God is with us. Other men may give assent to what Christ
taught and lived, but they lack the power to reflect that good-

ness in their lives. Christ has no competitor in all the world; there are none who have risen to his loveliness.

As a result of trusting in the Son as an atonement for sin, the heart of the sinner is flooded with peace. We are justified before the Father, *i.e.,* made free from the penalties of law against us, by the imputed righteousness of Christ. The righteousness which Christ merited in his life and death is put to our account. We are poor people whose immense obligations to the grocer are suddenly met by the wealth of a friend. Through his payment we are freed from indebtedness to the law. The grocer is the Father, and the friend rich in righteousness is Jesus Christ. By his stripes we are healed; through his death we gain life.

The instant reconciliation between God and man is accomplished, the problem of evil is permanently solved. The heart which trusts God for personal salvation will likewise trust God at all other points. That is the way love works. If God is so kind as to postpone felicity with his Son for a time that he might gain the fellowship of sinners, he is worthy of being trusted entirely. Greater love than this has never been known.

> There is a fountain filled with blood,
>   Drawn from Immanuel's veins;
> And sinners, plunged beneath that flood,
>   Lose all their guilty stains.
> E'er since, by faith, I saw the stream,
>   Thy flowing wounds supply;
> Redeeming love has been my theme,
>   And shall be till I die.

One cannot love part of a person. One either plunges into the heart and accepts the whole person, or he turns aside in want of love. We cannot accept salvation in Christ without completely trusting the person of the Father who sent him.

Thus, the loving child turns heavenward and inquires, "Father, why hast thou formed this earth as it is? why hast thou created the blind? why hast thou chosen these ways to exhibit thine everlasting hatred against sin?" And the loving Father, pleased with the concern of his children to understand the connections in his creation, tenderly responds, *"Because, my child, it has pleased me."* With bowed head the son confesses, "So be it, Father."

This resolution of the problem of evil is *not* an asylum of ignorance. It is the most satisfying solution possible because it has been won by a battle against the worst form of evil: sin. Once the child has learned to love God the Father, the abstract rule of good is thrown away. The good is what God does. Love will tolerate no other condition.

> Paul in the most famous of his passages characterizes it. It suffers long and is kind; it does not envy; it is not jealous; it does not boast; it is not self-assertive or rude; it does not insist on having what belongs to it; it is not easily provoked; it is made sad by evil and rejoices in good; it hopes and through its power seeks to create in the one it loves what it hopes for; it believes that this is possible; it bears delays and disappointments in the appearance of what it longs for in the one to which it attaches itself; it never ceases and never, discouraged, gives up. [62]

The profundity of this solution grows out of the fact that time and eternity are related according to the analogy of heart meeting heart in family love. Since love is the most perfect expression of life on earth, can less than that bind heaven and earth? When we turn to God for final satisfaction, dare we betray the satisfaction we have already gained through love among men?

But what if Plato *is* right? What if God has made no provision for the forgiveness of our sin? What then? "If there were no such forgiveness, one of three things would be forced upon us; the denial of the binding character of moral obligations, the attempt to deceive ourselves about our achievements, or self-despair."[63] Let us examine these three options.

Shall we deny the obligatory character of the law of love? Shall we seek escape from the predicament of freedom by pretending that we are not at our best when we love? Hardly.

---

62. Latourette, *The Christian Outlook*, p. 167.
63. Bennett, *Christianity and Our World*, p. 10.

The instant we try to live without love, that moment we introduce the virus decay into our spirit and progressive self-disintegration of the person sets in. The man without love is passing through a living death.

But dare we deceive ourselves about our achievements? Can a man put his hand over his heart and declare that he *has* matched the law of his life? Only the completely blinded can pretend self-righteousness. The vitiating and sullying powers of pride, avarice, lust, greed, selfishness, and malice seethe deep in the heart of every man. There is not a person who can walk up to Jesus Christ and justly declare his competitive worth. When evaluated by the Son of Man all other men are as worms fit for the fire. We grab, store up, and shield, when we should sacrifice, share, and offer. When we are favored with a glimpse of the holiness of God, therefore, we can only cry out with Isaiah, "Woe is me! for I am undone; because I am a man of unclean lips, and I dwell in the midst of a people of unclean lips: for mine eyes have seen the King, Jehovah of hosts." (Isaiah 6:5)

Shall we despair? Shall we return to the Greeks and declare that there is no meaning to history? Or shall we climb on the band wagon of positivism, crying that reality is a meaningless farce and that all we have striven for will some day be destroyed in the fires of the universe? We can despair only if we turn our eyes away from one person: *Jesus Christ*. Christ is our one hope that life has meaning. In his life and death eternity entered time to give a solution to history's contradictions. God the Father has prepared a redemptive deliverance for all who put their trust in the person of the Son. The righteousness of Jesus Christ is imputed to us through a judicial, forensic act of God. Though we remain sinful in ourselves, through Christ we are freed from the guilt of sin.

There is therefore now no condemnation for those who are in Christ Jesus. For the law of the Spirit of life in Christ Jesus has set me free from the law of sin and death. For

God has done what the law, weakened by the flesh, could not do: sending his own Son in the likeness of sinful flesh and for sin, he condemned sin in the flesh, in order that the just requirements of the law might be fulfilled in us, who walk not according to the flesh but according to the Spirit. [64]

As a result, the peace of God which passes understanding is ours, for the gift of the Holy Spirit is shed abroad in our hearts to confirm our adoption into the family of God.

Summary

The inadequacies of the immediacies whipped spirit on to find relief in devotion to man. But the program of humanism initiates many more problems than it has resources to solve. Therefore, the heart is driven from faith in man to faith in God. In joining with God, however, the heart cannot abandon the insights which it has gained through the venture of human love. God must be understood after the analogy of the highest values we know on earth; and these values are faith and love. But the instant we draw near to a holy person for fellowship, that moment we are driven back by a knowledge of our own sinfulness. God cannot look upon sin.

Philosophers have never succeeded in satisfying the heart because the gods they define are able to account for everything but the one thing needful. The problem of man is the uneasiness of guilt which gnaws in his heart. Unaware of their own unworthiness even to speak the name of God, therefore, philosophers tend to deprive themselves of the very precondition for enjoying fellowship with God. Love is a gift from God; but God will give it only to those who declare their complete unworthiness of it. The Lord resists the proud, but he gives grace to the meek and the humble. Would we expect a person to act any differently? Pride always forces love out.

In Jesus Christ the problem of fellowship is solved. Being love incarnate, he reveals both the love of God and the conditions which man must meet to receive such love as a gift.

---

64. Romans 8:1-4.

There is no thinkable progression beyond this point. If we leave Christ, we leave the very law which dignifies our person; and if we leave the Father of Jesus Christ, we depart from the only center and source of power which can transform life from a hopeless moral contradiction to a tingling pilgrimage of spiritual promise.

Part V

KINGDOM CLARIFICATIONS

IX

Justice and Mercy

SINCE the announced purpose of Scripture is to reveal the counsel of God in matters pertaining to his covenantal working in history, it follows that the Bible intentionally leaves many of the most profound philosophical-theological problems untouched. For example, it is hardly accurate to speak of a "Biblical definition of space, time, or predication." Such concepts are employed whenever they are relevant to the covenant of grace, but their essence is neither explored nor dilated. Being concerned with a limited topic, the Scriptures consistently stay with it. "These are written that you may believe that Jesus is the Christ, the Son of God, and that believing you may have life in his name." (John 20:31) For this reason the church has always confessed that not all things in the Bible are equally clear or plain.[1]

But there is one pronouncement in Scripture about which there is no ambiguity whatever. It is the consistent witness of all the writers that since the mercy of God is extended to man within a day of grace, the opportunity to embrace this mercy is limited to this life only. Death seals man's eternal condition. So ineradicable are the effects of present choices on the soul, that neither the prayers of all the church nor the tears of men in all eternity can blot away a single mark. Judgment is irreversible. "It is appointed for men to die once, and after that comes judgment." (Hebrews 9:27) At the day of judgment a man is everlastingly confirmed in either righteousness or unrighteousness, according to his acceptance or

---

1. "All things in Scripture are not alike plain in themselves, nor alike clear unto all." *The Westminster Confession of Faith,* I, vii.

rejection of the Father's gracious offer of salvation through the death of Jesus Christ.

The concept of the day of grace can be traced through the Old Testament in practically all of its major parts. In fact, the severity of Jehovah God is so unmistakably taught that no few minds have been forced to turn away from the Old Testament text to find a more satisfying structure elsewhere.[2] "And Jehovah said, My Spirit shall not strive with man for ever." (Genesis 6:3) "And Jehovah said unto Moses, I have seen this people, and, behold, it is a stiffnecked people: now therefore let me alone, that my wrath may wax hot against them, and that I may consume them." (Exodus 32:9-10) "For Jehovah thy God is a devouring fire, a jealous God." (Deuteronomy 4:24) The prophets do not deviate from this same warning that it is a fearful thing to fall into the hands of the living God.

In the Gospels Jesus Christ brought man into the most exalted conception of the Father by clarifying the law of love. But with every clarification of God's love he included a somber warning of the Father's wrath and vengeance against those who spurn that love.

> And some one said to him, 'Lord, will those who are saved be few?' And he said to them, 'Strive to enter by the narrow door; for many, I tell you, will seek to enter and will not be able. When once the householder has risen up and shut the door, you will begin to stand outside and to knock at the door, saying, 'Lord, open to us.' He will answer you, 'I do not know where you come from.' Then you will begin to say, 'We ate and drank in your presence, and you taught in our streets.' But he will say, 'I tell you, I do not know where you come from; depart from me, all you workers of iniquity!' There you will weep and gnash your teeth, when

---

2. "In the Old Testament, at least in the older parts of it, the power of God is exalted at the expense of his goodness. For it is simply impossible by any human standard and within any intelligible meaning of the words to regard Yahveh as wholly good. His cruelty is notorious and his capriciousness is that of an Oriental despot." Walter Lippmann, *A Preface to Morals*, (New York: The Macmillan Company, 1929), p. 214.

you see Abraham and Isaac and Jacob and all the prophets in the kingdom of God and you yourselves thrust out.' [3]

The Apostle Paul, whose chapter on love (I Corinthians 13) has been found definitive in all generations, avowed that his doctrine came from Jehovah God and that God's warnings to those of old are likewise warnings to men in all generations; for God changes not. "For the wrath of God is revealed from heaven against all ungodliness and wickedness." (Romans 1:18) "We must not put the Lord to a test. as some of them did and were destroyed by serpents; nor grumble, as some of them did and were destroyed by the Destroyer. Now these things happened to them as a warning, but they were written down for our instruction, upon whom the end of the ages has come. Therefore let any one who thinks that he stands take heed lest he fall." (I Corinthians 10:9-12) The beloved John, who leaned on the breast of Jesus and whose epistles are a model of *agape* love, balanced every sentence about God's love with a grave warning about his justice. "He who believes in the Son has eternal life; he who does not obey the Son shall not see life, but the wrath of God rests upon him." (John 3:36)

> And the sea gave up the dead in it, Death and Hades gave up the dead in them, and all were judged by what they had done. Then Death and Hades were thrown into the lake of fire. This is the second death, the lake of fire; and if anyone's name was not found written in the book of life, he was thrown into the lake of fire. [4]

While the teaching of God's wrath and severity may be hard to hear, the important observation to note here is that the Scriptures *do* teach the doctrine. Facts are facts, and one cannot alter them by an arbitrary *a priori*. If anything is known about Jesus Christ, it surely is his teaching that God's grace will not always strive with man.

---

3. Luke 13:23-28.
4. Revelation 20:13-15.

I. The Case for Universalism

Whether we can *rest* in what Jesus taught is another question, however. No few minds, having proceeded this far through the stages of value commitment, declare that it is impossible to accept such a view of God with the whole heart. They aver that the doctrine of universal salvation is axiologically preferable, appealing to an intuition within us which cries out against God's drawing an absolute discrimination between men. If love stands for anything, it means that the lover will never weary of seeking and saving the lost. Less than this is not love. If ninety and nine are safe, the shepherd will leave them and seek out the one which is lost, not resting until every lamb is protected. Can the heart assent to a doctrine which teaches that God will finally write off some men as a loss? Would God be shepherd if he remained content with the ninety and nine?

The issue is as delicate as it is important. It is delicate because it turns on values which are dearest to the human heart. Hitherto we have reveled in the thought that God is Father, Shepherd and Guardian. Must we now reverse our consolation and pretend that we are completely satisfied with a God who expresses his attributes of love and forgiveness in a manner unlike that in social relations? Must we now persuade the heart to believe in a God who does not match the highest we know in society? Our finest is expressed in the refusal of the lover to withdraw his willingness to forgive and forget the beloved. The issue likewise is important because it involves far more implications than may be detected on the surface. Let us remember that we have thus far understood the height of God only after the *analogy* of human relations. Analogies must not be pressed to the point where a complete identity of the objects in the relation is reached. When once the univocal point of identity is extended to include the entire object itself, the relation is no longer that of analogy. It is a relation of identity. God is God, not man. Two orders of being are being juxta-

posed, and we must not force on the other, conditions which
define normalcy in the one.

A. *The Negative Argument for Universalism*

The classical negative defense of universalism is, perhaps,
that of "the Apostle of Unitarianism," William Ellery Channing. His attack against New England Calvinism remains
to this day one of the most militant and convincing pieces of
polemical literature ever penned.

The fundamental objection which Channing had to Calvinism — and to all other forms of particularism — is that it defends a system of morals which is offensive to the disciplined
moral intuitions of man. Christianity is true only in proportion to its obedience to what a sensitive conscience must live
by. "Christianity, we all agree, is designed to manifest God
as perfect benevolence, and to bring men to love and imitate
him."[5] The Scriptures are indeed a record of God's revelation to man,[6] but being written by and to men, they must be
interpreted in the light of the same moral and rational norms
which guide us into a critical understanding of everything else.
God has not revealed himself in a disrespectful way. Therefore, whenever something appears in Scripture which seems to
run contrary to either morality or rationality, it must be understood according to the higher, not the lower, principle.

> In other words, we believe that God never contradicts, in
> one part of Scripture, what he teaches in another; and never
> contradicts, in revelation, what he teaches in his works and
> providence. And we, therefore, distrust every interpretation
> which, after deliberate attention, seems repugnant to any
> established truth. We reason about the Bible precisely as
> civilians do about the constitution under which we live; who,
> as you know, are accustomed to limit one provision of that

---

5. "The Moral Argument Against Calvinism." *The Works of William E.
Channing,* (Boston: American Unitarian Association, 1869), Vol. I, p. 238.
6. "We regard the Scriptures as the records of God's successive revelations to mankind, and particularly of the last . . . by Jesus Christ." Channing, *Unitarian Christianity,* (Boston: American Unitarian Association,
1945), pp. 18-19.

venerable instrument by others, and to fix the precise import
of its parts by inquiring into its general spirit, into the intentions of its authors, and into the prevalent feelings, impressions, and circumstances of the time when it was framed.
Without these principles of interpretation, we frankly
acknowledge that we cannot defend the Divine authority of
the Scriptures. Deny us this latitude, and we must abandon
this book to its enemies.[7]

It might be convenient for a prophet to preface his utterances with the usual formula, "Thus saith the Lord," but
these words are hardly sufficient to persuade rational men that
whatever the prophet happens to say is automatically the mind
of God for men. Moral and rational men are interested in
truth. The prophet can no more convince them of the doctrine of particularism than he can that two times two are eight.
If we cannot submit to rational inconsistencies without prosti-
tuting our dignity as free men, why should it be supposed that
moral contradictions can pass the bar of the heart? Unless
God can serve us for good, he is of no service to us at all.

We cannot bow before a being, however great and powerful,
who governs tyrannically. We respect nothing but excellence,
whether on earth or in heaven. We venerate, not the lofti-
ness of God's throne, but the equity and goodness in which
it is established. We believe that God is infinitely good,
kind, benevolent, in the proper sense of these words; good
in disposition, as well as in act; good, not to a few, but to
all; good to every individual, as well as to the general
system. [8]

Channing buttresses his appeal to the highest moral disposition
in God by pressing the analogy between God and a father's
relation to his own children. As long as strength within him
remains, the father is lovingly ready to forgive the child, never
abandoning the little one in his waywardness, never showing a
final preference for one child against another. The only con-

7. *Op. cit.*, pp. 24-25. One can quickly detect the similarity between this
type of argument and that encountered in the deistic controversy.
8. *Ibid.*, p. 52.

dition which must be met by the prodigal is sincere repentance, for the father is always ready to forgive and forget. Dare we think of God in lower terms than this? In frankest response, we cannot.

> To give our views of God in one word, we believe in his Paternal character. We ascribe to him, not only the name, but the dispositions and principles of a father. We believe that he has a father's concern for his creatures, a father's desire for their improvement, a father's equity in proportioning his commands to their powers, a father's joy in their progress, a father's readiness to receive the penitent, and a father's justice for the incorrigible.[9]

If anything is intrinsically immoral, therefore, it is the doctrine of hell; since it is the embodiment of a moral condition which absolutely offends the disciplined conscience.

Calvin rebuts that the creature has no right to remonstrate with God on matters pertaining to either morality or rationality. When God speaks, debate is out of order. The will of God is the supreme standard of heaven and earth for the very reason that there is no authority beyond it.

> In the first place they inquire, by what right the Lord is angry with his creatures who had not provoked him by any previous offence; for that to devote to destruction whom he pleases, is more like the caprice of a tyrant than the lawful sentence of a judge; that men have reason, therefore, to expostulate with God, if they are predestined to eternal death without any demerit of their own, merely by his sovereign will. If such thoughts ever enter the minds of pious men, they will be sufficiently enabled to break their violence by this one consideration, how exceedingly presumptuous it is only to inquire into the causes of the Divine will; which is in fact, and is justly entitled to be, the cause of everything that exists. For if it has any cause, then there must be something antecedent, on which it depends; which it is impious to suppose. For the will of God is the highest rule of justice; so that what he wills must be considered just, for this very reason, because he wills it. When it is inquired, therefore, why the Lord did so, the answer must be, Because he would. But if you go further and ask why he so determined,

9. *Ibid.*, p. 54.

you are in search of something greater and higher than the will of God, which can never be found.[10]

When submitting to the doctrine of God's sovereignty over man, Calvin not only fails to experience any derogation of his moral sense, but he also takes great satisfaction from it.

Channing, on the contrary, is persuaded that a disciplined moral sense screams out against believing in a God who withdraws mercy at his will. The God of Calvin exhibits a "most merciless despotism,"[11] filling "our minds with a horror which we want words to express."[12]   Nature, conscience, and the merciful declarations of Jesus Christ join together in manifold witness that the fatherhood of God means just that: the fatherhood of God. If God as Father is not at least what we mean when we use the term in family relations, he is hardly Father at all.

The quickest way to corrupt pure religion is to take from it the mild and warming vitalities which bind spirit to spirit in trusting fellowship. Calvinism, says Channing, is guilty of this very corruption.   "By shocking, as it does, the fundamental principles of morality, and by exhibiting a severe and partial Deity, it tends strongly to pervert the moral faculty, to form a gloomy, forbidding, and servile religion, and to lead men to substitute censoriousness, bitterness and persecution for a tender and impartial charity."[13]

Calvin then inquires whether it is not presumptuous for man to sit in judgment on God, and whether decorum is not broken whenever unreserved obedience is withheld from the divine being.   To support his position, he quotes from Paul.

> You will say to me then, 'Why does he still find fault? For who can resist his will?' But, who are you, a man, to answer back to God? Will what is molded say to its molder, 'Why have you made me thus?' Has the potter no right over the clay, to make out of the same lump one vessel for beauty and another for menial use?[14]

10. John Calvin, *Institutes of the Christian Religion*, III, 23.2.
11. *Unitarian Christianity*, p. 56.
12. *Loc. cit.*
13. *Ibid.*, p. 57.
14. Romans 9:19-21.

Channing quickly retorts by denying that it is either presumptuous or sinful for man to inquire what constitute the attributes of God, proposing instead that it is sinful to do otherwise. It happens to be an attribute of our freedom that we can, and must, canvass the evidence before we submit to an option. Only a fool would accept a proposition because it *claims* to come from God. We must test the spirits to see if they be of God or not.

> 'But is it not presumptuous in man,' it is continually said, 'to sit in judgment on God?' We answer, that to 'sit in judgment on God' is an ambiguous and offensive phrase, conveying to common minds the ideas of irreverence, boldness, familiarity. The question would be better stated thus: — Is it not presumptuous in man to judge concerning God, and concerning what agrees or disagrees with his attributes? We answer confidently, No; for in many cases we are competent and even bound to judge. And we plead first in our defence the Scriptures. How continually does God in his word appeal to the understanding and moral judgment of man. 'O inhabitants of Jerusalem and men of Judah, judge, I pray you, between me and my vineyard.' [15]

Is it meaningful to say that we honor God, when we deliberately use our God-given moral faculties to believe things which are contrary to morality? "God, in giving us conscience, has implanted a principle within us, which forbids us to prostrate ourselves before mere power, or to offer praise where we do not discover worth."[16]

While the universalist says that it is a contradiction in terms for God to be Father and yet extend the arm of his mercy only

---

15. "The Moral Argument Against Calvinism," p. 231.
16. *Ibid.*, p 232. "If God's justice and goodness are consistent with those operations and modes of government, which Calvinism ascribes to him, of what use is our belief in these perfections? What expectations can we found upon them? If it consist with divine, rectitude to consign to everlasting misery, beings who have come guilty and impotent from his hand, we beg to know what interest we have in this rectitude, what pledge of good it contains, or what evil can be imagined which may not be its natural result? If justice and goodness, when stretched to infinity, take such strange forms and appear in such unexpected and apparently inconsistent operations, how are we sure, that they will not give up the best men to ruin, and leave the universe to the powers of darkness?" *Ibid.*, pp. 236-237.

within a day of grace, Calvin replies that any discrepancy between what we might have expected of God and what we actually discover in revelation to constitute the case is only apparently paradoxical. Our duty is to *submit* to the revelation, not question it. When the veil is lifted and the scales of the noetic effects of sin finally drop away, we shall then realize that what we thought was a contradiction is actually a harmonious relation. In other words, what now appears black will ultimately turn out in heaven to be white. Channing immediately fires a powerful salvo against this pretentious refuge. His argument is as convincing as his literary powers are beautiful.

> It is no slight objection to the mode of reasoning adopted by the Calvinist, that it renders the proof of the divine attributes impossible. When we object to his representations of the divine government, that they shock our clearest ideas of goodness and justice, he replies, that still they may be true, because we know very little of God, and what seems unjust to man may be in the Creator the perfection of rectitude. Now this weapon has a double edge. If the strongest marks and expressions of injustice do not prove God unjust, then the strongest marks of the opposite character do not prove him righteous. If the first do not deserve confidence, because of our narrow views of God, neither do the last. If, when more shall be known, the first may be found consistent with perfect rectitude, so, when more shall be known, the last may be found consistent with infinite malignity and oppression. [17]

If we are so bold as to use our moral sense when judging the worthiness or unworthiness of other religions, on what ground shall we be denied that same right to judge the worthiness and unworthiness of Jehovah God?

It is evident that no easy decision can be made between the arguments of Channing and Calvin, for the existing self wavers sympathetically between both truths. Channing is correct that man has a duty to search for a God who is related to the heart in the most excellent moral sense, for God is at least that beyond which nothing greater or more perfect can

17. *Op. cit.*, p. 234.

be conceived. And yet Calvin is assuredly correct that once the heart is persuaded that it *is* God who speaks, debate is then out of order and the good is what God does. There is no higher court of appeal that man may seek than the will of God.

How then can these two emphases be reconciled? It might seem that the solution is to call in an infallible third party to judge the matter — perhaps a subordinate god or a high-ranking angel — but such an expediency would only push the problem back one step; for we would then be obliged to judge the moral worthiness of the new mediator. Our problem is only doubled. If reconciliation is to be found, the individual must find it for himself. He, not his neighbor, must face the issue.

But since the evidence is not all in, the matter is yet not ready to go to the jury. There is more to the case for universalism than Channing's negative rejection of Calvinism.

B. *The Affirmative Argument for Universalism*

One of the reasons why Calvinism has historically enjoyed the success that it has, is that it, unlike universalism, has fortified its view of God with a *Weltanschauung* sufficiently closely knit to commend itself to philosophic minds. As a result, minor internal inconsistencies are supported by the strength of the system's broader beams and girders. Calvinism has withstood attacks because of the gross weight of its system. Over against this, universalism has tended to live a fragmentary existence, drawing its theological nourishment from particularism but refusing to launch a unified philosophy of its own. The result of this refusal is an eclectic philosophy which fails to stimulate the imagination of system-conscious thinkers.

Channing illustrates this weakness perfectly. After brilliantly defending the primacy of the moral sense and the right of man to judge what attributes are consistent with God, a foggy and unsatisfying theology is drawn up in support of these insights. As a result there is a swift dissipation of gains. On even so crucial a question as soteriology, for example, the mist of ambiguity hovers everywhere. "We believe that he (Christ) was sent by the Father to effect a moral or spiritual deliverance of mankind; that is, to rescue men from sin and its consequences, and to bring them to a state of everlasting purity and happiness."[18]   The pages in this context simply bristle with problems.   Who, precisely, is Christ?   What is his metaphysical relation to the Father?   What is his generic relation to man?   How is his death different from that of Socrates?   What is a "moral deliverance" of mankind?   Exactly what are the mechanics involved in Christ's moral deliverance?   What are the precise causal connections?   These questions are unsatisfactorily answered.

In recent days, however, the case for universalism has been taken up again, and this time it is protected by a rigorous philosophical-theological system. We have reference to the various forms of *agape* theology: Neo-orthodoxy, crisis theology, dialectical theology, and realistic liberal theology. *E. g.*, Karl Barth teaches that election reaches to all individuals. "Before His eyes from eternity God keeps men, each man, in Him, in this One; and not only before His eyes but loved and elect and called and made His possession.   In Him He has from eternity bound Himself to each, to all."[19]   Reinhold Niebuhr teaches that the difference between the righteous and the unrighteous, while significant both in history and at the final judgment, is but provisional only, since the righteous are set apart from the unrighteous only by their relative degree of sinlessness.   God takes the full sin of the world into and upon himself at the cross of Christ.   Since God is love, he performs the whole duty of his office in the salvation of men.

One of the most challenging philosophical expressions of *agape* theology, and thus an able defence of universalism, is that of Nels F. S. Ferré.   Epistemology, metaphysics, and philosophy of history are skillfully blended together in the service of the thesis that God, being *agape*, will pursue all men

---

18. *Unitarian Christianity*, pp. 58-59.
19. Karl Barth, *Dogmatics in Outline*, (New York: Philosophical Library, 1949), p. 91.

with his call to repentance until all are saved. The love of God will empty hell.

Ferré is not hesitant to admit his indebtedness to Anders Nygren of Lund University, and especially to his classic work *Agape and Eros; a study of the Christian idea of love.* From Nygren's studies comes a summarization of Christianity's uniqueness. "The uniqueness of Christianity lies in its basic motif, in its picture of God as *agape*. *Agape* is God's way to man; *eros* is man's way to God."[20] The reason why we hitherto have not arrived at a satisfactory view of God is that we have been more anxious to interpret him according to the mutuality of *eros* than the selflessness of *agape*. God desires only fellowship, and the means which he employs in directing men to the fellowship is spontaneous, unmotivated, creative love. *Agape's* distinguishing feature is the selfless way it reaches out its arms of intimate concern; it takes no thought of the intrinsic worth of the object as a motive in love. God loves by nature, seeking neither gain nor compensation, but only fellowship. "There is no relation whatsoever between *agape* and its object, except the free overflowing of creative love, which by the power of its purity, is productive of the highest fellowship."[21] *Eros* is particularistic and selective. It is a love which is compounded with man's urge for personal betterment.

Agape love is so rare and so hard to comprehend, that even the Biblical authors themselves fail at times to comprehend its purity. Ferré, in short, says that one must come to the Scriptures "critically," *i. e.,* armed with the highest category we know: *agape.*[22] Even in Jesus Christ himself we must proceed critically. When he teaches and lives *agape,* he is the Son of God; while when he fails in that role, he is only a great religious teacher. When Christ teaches the parable of the

---

20. Ferré, *The Christian Fellowship,* (New York: Harper and Brothers, 1940), p. 71.
21. *Ibid.,* p. 72.
22. "In view of the varied contents of the Bible, to call it equally and infallibly inspired seems something of idolatry." *Ibid.,* p. 38.

Prodigal Son, we see God; but when he teaches the doctrine of hell, we see a religious teacher who was a child of his times. A form of monarchianism results.

Agape is not a perspective which one chooses arbitrarily. On the contrary, it alone defines that ultimate in both experience and reality which gives completeness to the religious life. A man is religious whenever he gives a concerned response to reality over against him, for religion is simply the binding of man to reality. And the more adequate and concerned the response is, the more right is the religion. "Right religion is our fully positive whole-response to the complete combination of what is most important and most real."[23] To respond wholly is — in the words of Kierkegaard — to respond *existentially, i. e.,* as an existing person concerned over the responsibility of what it means to be an individual. Since we respond wholly only to what we make our highest interest, whole-response engages the whole man. The intellect seeks consistency, while the emotions and will seek depth and adequacy. The result of whole response is right reason. "Right reason is always *the whole man* thinking rightly. Wrong reason is reasoning apart from the needs and the situation of the whole man."[24] There is nothing illicit about making the individual and his needs the touchstone of truth, for it happens that the individual person is the one seeking the truth in the first place. How can a man be concerned with things which are of no concern? What affects us is the real; what affects us most of all is the most real.

> We know, then, that what is truly out there is related to some extent in the form of need to what is within us. Need is the organic interrelation between ourselves and that on which we depend. Needs bind us (*religare*) to the universe beyond the fact, and more intimately, that we simply are in the universe and have nowhere else to go.[25]

23. Ferré, *Faith and Reason,* (New York: Harper and Brothers, 1946), p. 4.
24. *Ibid.,* p. 12.
25. *Ibid.,* p. 33.

Since neither science nor philosophy is able to direct its method in such a way that the depth interests of the existing individual are placated, the perspective by which all else is finally to be interpreted cannot be extracted from either. Only an adequate religion can satisfy the whole man.

Religion is adequate when it measures up to the demands of the following five criteria. First: *The selective ideal.* "By this term we mean that religious truth is to be understood in terms of the highest instance of the good within actuality."[26] Such an ideal must (a) serve as a solution to the meaning of the universe, (b) contain an adequate guide in practical matters, and (c) embody a sample of history's highest and finest fruit. Second: *The selective actual.* The ideal must be actual if it is to be the cause of concerned response. The concrete, the incarnate, is always more persuasive, more satisfying than the hypothetical or abstract.

> It must possess the power of actualization and the organic relatedness and direction of concretion if later it is to solve our problems of actualization and concretion even indicatively, signifying even by its partial fulfillment of process, because of its representative character in its organic, fulfilling relation to the rest of process. [27]

Third: *The existential ultimate.* Only an ideal which is at once most real and most important can elicit whole-response. Since all we are is at stake in the commitment, we must act as an *all* in religious commitment. "No matter what we do we must react to that as the strongest, the most important, the most real, the most true. Whatever we do, in service or rebellion, our basic decision is with respect to that ultimate."[28] Whatever we are willing to live and die for *is* our existential ultimate. Fourth: *Reflexive superspective.* "The reflexive superspective is our perspective at the center of the selective ideal when this, in turn, is taken to be the center of all purpose and

26. *Op. cit.*, p. 145.
27. *Ibid.*, p. 148.
28. *Ibid.*, p. 149.

all processes."[29] Since the most high serves as a regulative pattern for the interpretation of process, the individual is preserved from confusing the whole with the significance of a part. By means of the reflexive superspective we take the highest ideal and make it our standard in evaluating the parts. What accords with the most high is true and permanent, while what fails so to comply is accidental and partial.

> It is the seeing of the right blueprints for our present process and at the same time the seeing of our present building, both right and wrong, in the terms of that [sic] blueprint. It is the existential seeing of the most high as the prospectively realized center of all coherence, as the kind of condition universally understood and accepted, as God ruling in a perfectly good and willingly accepted sovereignty in the midst of His people — and the anguish of heart, consequent on such seeing, that this condition is now far from us. [30]

Fifth: *Dynamic self-verification.* When the whole person proceeds in a given direction long enough, an option under test will exhibit a progressive self-verification or self-refutation. Only that which enriches and integrates the individual when dynamically tested with whole response, on the one hand, while providing the social mind with new powers of transformation, on the other, is whole truth. "The dynamic self-verification of religion depends on the truth that only by going according to the direction of its nature, according to the purpose prescribed for it, can the conditions of process become satisfactory."[81]

Ferré is persuaded that selfless love is the only adequate perspective from which to construct a wholly satisfying, depth interpretation of reality and history. *Agape* is both the most real and the most high. "Our perspective alone is ultimate. Our Christian perspective is God as Agape."[82] Through Jesus Christ God is actively related to his creation: he is sovereignly

---

29. *Op. cit.,* p. 151.
30. *Ibid.,* p. 152.
31. *Ibid.,* p. 155.
32. Ferré, *Evil and the Christian Faith,* (New York: Harper and Brothers, 1947), p. 3.

seeking to bring about a fellowship between himself and men and between men and their neighbors. The only end God has in view is the fellowship, for fellowship is the highest value both in heaven and on earth.

The framework which God has employed to bring many sons into glory is outlined in a skillful study of the problem of evil. Obviously the presence of evil in the universe must be explained, since this is the very thing which thwarts fellowship. Ferré does not contest the fact of evil in the universe: Evil is anything which resists the fellowship. His problem is to show the adequacy of *agape* when critically exposed to all the facts — including evil.

The first step in vindicating *agape* as the most high is the dismissal of the hedonistic and aesthetic perspectives. Since men are free, and since the highest things in life can be gained only after a struggle, it follows that suffering is an essential part of life. When we prefer one another in love we must sacrifice those immediacies which jeopardize the expression of that love. For the sake of the child's health the mother often must suffer a threat to her own physical security. Suffering *per se* does not speak out against *agape*, therefore, since God uses only moral means in bringing free men to sonship. The fellowship cannot be gained apart from suffering, for suffering is the very stuff of life itself.

> The most high judges our desire for perfect pleasure and demands that we find truth on a higher level where suffering is not inconsistent with the experience of the best that this life has to offer. When this best is also our highest standard of truth, God's Agape fellowship, the problem of evil has shifted perspective radically from that of the natural man whose one demand of life is that there be no suffering, that all be pleasure, or else God must be limited. [33]

Since the cross of Christ is the locus in which moral suffering was the greatest, it embodies the most high in a concrete historical act.

---

33. *Op. cit.*, p. 25.

It is God's will that every man freely pass through the requisite conditions of sonship. Since a man will suffer only for that which he reaches out to, but does not yet possess, it follows that an appreciation of God can be enjoyed only when a person has antecedently experienced the pain of heart which comes from *rebellion*. We choose only what we are first objectively related to.

> To become really free we must act in rebellion against others; we must act distinctly as separate individuals; we must sometime or other go contrary to their decisions.... Rebellion against God is necessary at some point in our lives if we are to become free sons, glorifying Him out of love and gratitude. The time has come when we choose for ourselves, judging even God.[34]

As long as the child is kept within the bonds of the home, being obliged to conform his own will with that of his parents, freedom is not yet perfect. It is when the child asserts his individuality and looks objectively upon the parents in rebellion that he is in a position freely to choose them in fellowship.

The picture of the whole world is that of people struggling through stages of suffering, rebellion, and fellowship. God has closed all the world up to the law of *agape* love, making rebellious sons out of all men in order that all individuals, coming to themselves as prodigals eating the husks of the swine, might some day choose God freely. God has set all men under the severity of the law of love, that he by love might give the fellowship as a gift. Sin is "the failure of the finite being to fulfill an infinite responsibility of which by nature he is qualitatively incapable."[35] Sin disintegrates, disappoints, frustrates, and decays. A person cannot continue in sin forever. At some point in the rebellion he will realize that the height of freedom in him is incompatible with anything lower than selfless love. By making each sin an absolute guilt — though committed by a finite person — God has ushered men

---

34. *Op. cit.*, p. 33.
35. *Ibid.*, p. 43.

into a despair of themselves that, forsaking law, they might receive the fellowship as a free gift. "God makes the law impossible in order that being convicted by it we may find no way to live by it."[36] The Father has set forth Jesus Christ as the way back to himself. God himself suffers for the righteous, taking the sins of the world upon himself in Christ. Fellowship is given as a gift to all prodigal sons who, weary of trying to live without the Father, freely choose God by repenting of their rebellion. All evil in the world is directly or indirectly compounded with suffering and rebellion.

The patience of God will remain until all men finally despair of law and self and return to the Father through a confession of their sin and a sorrow over their rebellion. Ferré rejects all sentimental forms of universalism, however. God "will perfect with all certainty that which He has here barely begun,"[37] but he will never relax the conditions which must be met for sonship. Here or beyond the grave *men must repent*. They will never be saved either because God is too meek to standardize the requisite conditions for fellowship or because man is too inherently righteous to be damned. Throughout eternity of eternity the law will be the hound of heaven to track down sinners and bring them to self-despair. But God *will* save all men; otherwise we have departed from the perspective of *agape*. To say that *agape* is ultimate and that God's mercies operate only within a day of grace is to employ contradictory terms. We must not mix perspectives.

On the grounds of our total analysis of truth, moreover, our existential ultimate requires that all be saved, or else Agape is not ultimate. Otherwise the most high is not fully the most real. . . . If one creature is to be eternally tormented, Christ's compassion declares that it were far better that there had been no creation . . . . If hell were eternal, furthermore, heaven would be an eternal place of mourning. All those truly in the Agape fellowship would identify their lot with the lost. The fuller the love, the deeper the suffering in

36. *Op. cit.*, p. 45.
37. *Ibid.* p. 106.

sympathy with the irrevocably and irreparably lost. That is why we have said elsewhere that heaven can be heaven only when it has emptied hell. [38]

Hell, however, continues to serve as a valid symbol of the condition of those yet outside of fellowship. God leaves men in hell until, recovering from their recalcitrance and rebellion, they accept the offer of the fellowship. "Yet hell does exist. Hell is the insurmountable barrier between heaven and the hardened heart. . . .No one can get to heaven apart from complete self-despair. God will never, to be sure, force direct surrender. To paraphrase an old Gospel song. He will not compel us to go against our will; He will just make us willing to go."[39]

God would not be God if he said to a single created son, "My mercy no longer reaches out to effect your salvation from sin." If human love suffers *long,* then God's love will suffer *eternally.* Christ will be preached to men until every prisoner is freed from the captivity of sin outside the fellowship. God's spirit *will* always strive with men. The provisional distinctions made between the saved and the lost at death will finally yield to the permanent condition of universal salvation.[40]

II. The Problem of Intrinsic Objection

The issues in the problem are adequately laid out before the existing individual by this time: *Does God possess a right to withdraw his mercy and yet remain agape love? Or does an analysis of the term agape force one to the necessary conclusion that all men will be saved?* The issue is extremely serious for if the Biblical writers are correct in their claims, the difference between gaining or losing Christianity hangs delicately in the balance.

---

38. *Op. cit,* pp. 118-119.
39. *Ibid.,* p. 120.
40. Even the animals will be saved. "We wonder if the child notion of animal heavens is as childish as the sophisticated sneer of the denier. If pain is real, God must have a purpose with it or the highest claim of religion is palpably false. That purpose, too, must apply to every individual that experiences the pain. We can accept no less a solution." *Ibid.,* p. 62.

The first question to be examined is whether a Christian particularism is a contradiction in terms. Obviously, if the term *agape* excludes *ex hypothesi* the doctrine that God's mercy operates within a day of grace, there is nothing further to seek; for one cannot accept with his heart what his head finds to be a contradiction. It surely *is* a contradiction for a father on earth to say he loves with perfection, while in the same breath warning that if his wandering son does not repent by dusk he will be disinherited forever. There are minimal qualities of human love which must be respected if the term is to have any significance whatever. But is *agape* theology accurate in saying there is no other way to understand the Father's love than that his mercy remains forever accessible to those who repent? Are we involved in a contradiction in terms to teach that God — who in both *agape* theology and the Scriptures is declared to be absolute love — has the privilege of withdrawing mercy from potential children of light? Is this a square circle? The universalist says *yes;* the Biblical writers say *no.* Which shall the contemporary mind decide for?

Although the settlement of this dilemma must, of course, be rationally satisfying (for by the mind we test for consistency), a full solution cannot be gained by a simple rational analysis alone. The reason for this is that crucial values are at stake, and values must be weighed by the whole heart, not by formal reason exclusively. If a satisfaction is to be enjoyed, the whole person must squarely face the whole problem. Basic interests are at stake in this controversy.

A. *Decorum*

The self-evident reason why the problem of particularism is not easily reduced to a square circle is that two orders or realms of being are being juxtaposed — time and eternity, the finite and the infinite, created order and the creating. If the scientist cannot as much as measure the length of a string because of the inaccessibility of the string, how much less can we measure God's relations to man without suffering from a great plus and minus of variable error in our conclusions?

First, note the *metaphysical* distance separating the finite and the infinite. Much as the mind may stagger when it contemplates the immensities of the created universe, it feels completely shattered at the thought of the created order drawing near, or being juxtaposed beside, the Author of this gigantic world of matter and spirit. When standing beside God, the existing individual instinctively realizes that he is out of his natural elements — not a fish out of water, perhaps, but at least a finite creature out of his finite setting. The wider the gap becomes between one person and another, the less comfortable does the lower in rank feel in the presence of the higher. While the mayor of the town receives applause, a hush of respect and obedience falls over a group when the president or king of the land enters the room. And who would not tape his mouth and sit quietly in the farthest corner if the greatest of persons in all history should parade across the platform: Plato, Aristotle, Confucius, Mohammed, Luther, Washington, or Lincoln. But if the announcement is made that the finite individual is to be favored by the presence of *Almighty God,* maker of heaven and earth, the everlasting repository of all light, power, wisdom, holiness, goodness, justice, and love, the contrast between the two orders so humbles the creature and so exalts the creator that the finite individual lacks hands with which to cover his face. Well do the Scriptures warn that no man can see God and live, for the light from the throne is too blinding.

We speak, of course, only of those who, having had good breeding, recognize decorum. Just as the uncouth would speak frivolously before the president of the land, forgetting that they but display their own want of manners, so some smile at the thought of being afraid of standing in the presence of Almighty God. But the manners of the ill-bred do not invalidate the conditions of propriety which men of rank respect.

Second, note the *moral* distance separating the finite and the infinite. The relation is not that of perfect man to perfect

God; it is that of sinner to absolute holiness. Man happens to have a defect in his nature which weighs his preferences on the side of pride and self-sufficiency. Having assented to more than the involved self can ever make good through living, the free self is harassed by the pangs of a guilty conscience and a sinful heart. We have not come to God out of an intellectual curiosity, as if we are measuring rabbit heads or classifying bugs; we have come as lost sinners whose broken hearts cannot be mended until they are received back into fellowship by the author of all reality, God. Fellowship *does* constitute our richest conceivable value, for fellowship is highest of all. The picture, hence, is that of the sinner reaching out for crumbs of forgiveness and mercy to fall from the table of a God assuredly known to be all holy and all powerful. In this relation the accused has thrown himself to the mercy of the court, having neither righteousness in himself to use as leverage for bargaining nor an outside defense attorney who would dare take his case before God. Sinner cannot defend sinner. Therefore, if mercy does not proceed from the judge himself, all is lost.

The finite person who does not understand the meaning of these two relations does not yet understand both the power of sin in his own life and the awfulness of that sin in the sight of a holy God. Whoever believes that he has a claim on God's mercies only heaps sin to sin. If presumption before man is a social odium, presumption before God is heinous sin.

For this reason a sensitive spirit is more than willing to exercise caution when coming to a final conclusion about the extent of God's mercy. He realizes that a decision in favor of universalism may itself be based on antecedent sinful preferences. It is easy for freedom and reason to collude about things which the sinful heart wishes were true. This may prove nothing more than that there can be no dogmatism on the issue of universalism and particularism. But this is sufficient for the time being, since the possibility of particularism at least is left open.

B. *Problems of Justice*

It is a recognized part of critical experience that it is far easier to *state* an abstract definition of justice than it is to reduce that definition to sharp propositions detailing justice in live situations. "This, then, is what the just is — the proportional."[41] There is no question about man's native endowment of a sense of justice and injustice, for the equilibrium in our social life is made possible because of this primitive intuition. Whether or not he is taught by his parents how to apply it skillfully, the child enjoys as part of his moral equipment an immediate sense of the just and the unjust. Whoever denies this should watch children at play.

The problem, however, is translating our intuition into an exact administration of justice in concrete situations. Observe how quickly the mind is forced to retreat to generalities and probabilities when determining precisely what comprises the balance of justice in specific instances. Suppose a person steals a registered Guernsey cow. What is the exact measure of punishment which he deserves for this type of a crime? A brief scolding? One lash on the back? A fine of five dollars? A thousand dollars? Three thousand? The obligation to pay back a cow? Two cows? Serving four days in prison? A year? Life? Suffering the guillotine? And suppose that *two* cows, not one, have been taken. Does the punishment reflect justice if the intensity of infliction is raised in direct ratio to the number of cows taken? And what if one cow dies and the other is returned? What is justice in this instance?

In short, *there is no exact, objectively measurable sliding scale to which one can appeal when proportioning justice to the crime.* The presiding jurist can not enjoy the same accuracy in court decisions that the physicist does when measuring theoretical distances. There is no place where crucial decisions are made with less precision than in the civil courts. The deliberating jury has a feeling that justice *must* be done,

----

41. Aristotle, *Nicomachean Ethics*, 1131b.

and it trusts that when the foreman announces its verdict that justice *has* been done; but the jury is never perfectly certain that its trust and act are coincident.

An *a fortiori* emerges which the modern mind would do well to face. *If we cannot ascertain the exact and proper proportions which define justice in concrete cases in society — situations in which the factors are relatively controlled — how much less can we know in advance what shall constitute the exact specifications when infinite holiness is sinned against?* We are men and not God. Only *God* can measure justice in such an instance, since he is the offended one. Whenever a man tries to anticipate what he would do if he were God, he overlooks the fact that he is deficient in the very moral rectitude needed to understand what it means to be sinned against. Man's finite standards are deficient when applied to an infinitely holy being. Criteria which are valid in a sinful framework cannot be transferred to conditions which prevail in an atmosphere of absolute holiness.

C. *The Ratio of Mercy and Humility*

In any situation where the guilty must face the offended, the latter extends mercy to the former only in proportion to the offending party's denial that he is deserving of mercy; for once the offender presumes upon the hospitality and clemency of the offended, demanding in the name of his rights that forgiveness be given, mercy is withdrawn and naked justice imposed. When the wayward husband returns to the wife and disclaims all right to receive her forgiveness, he is the very one who quickly receives mercy. But when he arrogantly demands to be forgiven on the ground that justice stands on his side, mercy is quenched.

Since love always gives the other the benefit of the doubt, refusing to justify itself in the presence of the offended, love never demands mercy; it only inquires patiently whether there be mercy or not. And if it turns out that there is no mercy, the lover will accept the verdict as what it knew all the while it deserved. Love seeks not its own.

When a sinner comes to God for mercy, therefore, the most that he may dare hope for is that there is mercy. The instant hospitality is presumed upon, that moment clemency is throttled and the full weight of the law is applied. The sinner can ask no more of God than that mercy unto salvation be prepared, since beyond this is further sin. God is *agape* if he has graciously arranged a way of escape for those completely undeserving of it; he is *agape* if he forgives the unworthy.

The obvious danger of presumption is that it will kill off the mercy which has already been put at our access. "Therefore it says, 'God opposes the proud, but gives grace to the humble.' Submit yourselves therefore to God." (James 4:6-7) Jesus said that the least in the kingdom shall be the greatest; and the least is he who not only confesses that God *may* send sinners away from his presence forever, but also that he himself ought to head the list of any receiving such condemnation. He is *first* in the kingdom because the Father gives the kingdom to those who believe themselves least deserving of it. That is the way love functions.

If God announces that his mercy is extended only within a day of grace, therefore, the sole issue involved is whether or not we can trust God in such a pronouncement. And the man who takes sin seriously *will* trust him, for he is so occupied considering the awfulness of his own offense against heaven that he does not permit himself to speculate long on what the precise terms of justice might be. He will leave such matters to the one handing down the decision. Love confesses that if there is mercy at all, it comes from grace, not necessity. Should the lover be informed that chronic sinning is so awful in the eyes of God that only everlasting separation from his presence can define justice, he will humbly submit to the verdict, remembering that only mercy spared him a like condemnation. If we cannot trust God when he condemns men, we cannot trust him when he saves men; for trust takes in the whole person, never a part only.

D. *Indolence*

The universalist argues that man possesses an inward moral suasion that God will never withdraw his offer of mercy and forgiveness. One must question the actual truth of this claim, however. Once a sinner understands the magnitude of his turpitude, not only is he not surprised to learn that God has set a time limit for his mercies, but in all honesty he would have been taken back to learn anything different. The easy optimism which teaches that God will postpone justice forever and forever is too congenial with what sinfulness wishes were the case for the sensitive heart to accept at its face value. It reminds one of the story William James used to tell his philosophy class: If a small country boy came to school one day with his face clean, his pants crisply pressed, his shirt and tie immaculate, with the pungent odor of Eau de Cologne all about him, one large suspicion would immediately rise: *It is too good to be true.* If a vote were taken whether or not sinners *want* universalism, there would not be a dissenting voice. But the pleasant results of that poll would not cancel out the more basic fear within the heart that sinners will actually not fare that well in the hands of a just God. Nothing could corrupt the tension of moral struggle quicker than the announcement that there is no time limit for repentance. If one has eternity in which to perform, why watch and act?

In all social relations we must set a time limit for decisions; otherwise the impulse for vigilance is enervated. The mother may love the child, but that does not prevent her from respecting the universal rule, "Now is the acceptable time; behold, now is the day of salvation." (II Corinthians 6:2) As she prepares dinner for the children, *e. g.*, she warns them that unless they are home from play by six o'clock they will miss the dinner. They *must* be in by that hour, for the food will be put away then. Now, suppose in answer to the child's question how long the food will be kept warm in the oven for him, the mother responded, "My little one, I shall stand vigil over your dinner plate forever and forever." Doubtless the child would wonder if his mother were not beset with some illness, for he would perceive that there would be no meaning to moral responsibility if decisions are not made within specified temporal limits. The university student might be delighted to hear that he has forever to hand in his term paper for a course, but he will experience real trouble in his heart trying to assimilate this glad announcement. Both he and the professor know that a term paper which may be prepared throughout eternity is a term paper which will never be prepared. Moral inertia can be overcome in the university only when a time limit is set to assignments, examinations, and the meeting of requirements for graduation. There is no exception to this rule. Even the prodigal son had to stir himself up to return to the father before the elder died. His return was not uncompounded with a fear of losing the inheritance through indolence.

If after approaching the throne of God Almighty and inquiring how long sinners will patiently be dealt with before they are called to a final judgment, one is told, "My son, you have *forever* to repent"; to put the matter candidly, the sinful heart suspects that a caricature, not the real God, is giving the verdict, for it is too good to be true. The heart cannot believe that God will keep the platter of his mercies warm until the individual, leisurely making his way through the truncation of being without fellowship, decides that it is about time to turn back to God for repentance. If everything else worthwhile can be appropriated only within a day of grace, why should the principle suddenly break down when the most important value in life is in question?

Since it is universally characteristic of sinfulness to postpone moral decision, it is questionable whether an eternity of opportunities to repent would be any more effective than the temporal overtures God now makes on the heart. If for three score and ten years men casually say, "Tomorrow, Father, tomorrow," what new element in eternity will alter the monotony of their refrain? We now have the evidence of salvation clearly before us; Christ was openly crucified, and the Spirit plainly works in our hearts. "For this was not done in a corner." (Acts 26:26) Experience teaches that the more a man resists righteousness, the more hardened his own heart becomes. Willingness to repent is one urge which must be given priority over all others, for once it vanishes it may never come back again.

III. What Am I Left With: Option One

Inasmuch as there is no intrinsic contradiction involved in believing that God's mercies are extended to sinners only within a day of grace, but that on the contrary suspicions mount that there is no meaning to a moral decision which does not oblige men to face a time limit, it is now in order to test the gains or losses which the heart experiences if it chooses one option over against the other. It is hardly fair to draw a decision between universalism and particularism until the implications in choosing are known.

Let us call universalism *option one.* Does the heart gain or lose values in choosing it?

The gains of universalism are self-evident. It is far from easy to imagine how God can remain *agape* love and yet willfully withdraw his mercy according to his own standards of justice. It is very ennobling to conceive of the Father after the analogy of an earthly parent who will receive the prodigal back home as long as strength lasts. Likewise, universalism is a comforting doctrine, especially to those who have seen unrepentant friends die. The mere thought of everlasting separation from God is so awful that the mind reels before it. If we could be assured that God will put an end to hell and that all will come to repentance, relief would immediately be felt. As Ferré so convincingly puts it, how can heaven be heaven as long as one soul remains outside of the fellowship?

When one seriously weighs the *losses* which attend universalism, however, he immediately questions the axiological wisdom of leaving the Biblical perspective. These deprivations must be faced if the whole person is to be satisfied, for no hypothesis is valid until it has been subjected to the damaging, as well as the supporting, data. Let us now examine the values with which one must part when turning from Scripture to universalism.

A. *Loss of Faith in the Person of Christ*

If words mean anything, the *real* enemy of universalism is Jesus Christ himself. "Just as the weeds are gathered and burned with fire, so will it be at the close of the age. The Son of man will send his angels, and they will gather out of his kingdom all causes of sin and all evil-doers, and throw them into the furnace of fire; there men will weep and gnash their teeth." (Matthew 13:40-42) *Christ* is the one who denies that God will always accept the repentance of men. When the foolish virgins rap to gain entrance to the feast, Christ responds, "Truly, I say to you, I do not know you." (Matthew 25:12)

> Jesus Christ is the Person who is responsible for the doctrine of Eternal Perdition. He is the Being with whom all opponents of this theological tenet are in conflict. Neither the Christian church, nor the Christian ministry are the authors of it. The Christian ministry never would have invented the dogma; neither would they have preached it in all the Christian centuries, like Jeremiah, with shrinking and in tears, except at the command of that same Lord God who said to the weeping prophet, 'Whatsoever I command thee, thou shalt speak.' [42]

Jesus Christ the very redeemer of mankind, *agape* incarnate, announced, reiterated, and clarified the distressing doctrine of endless separation from God. While the warning that the Spirit will not always strive with man is implicitly taught in the whole of Scripture, only in the words of Jesus Christ — plus apostolic commentary on these words — is the teaching explicitly defended. If *anything* is known about the Jesus of history it is that he personally believed in the doctrine of hell.

---

42. William G. T. Shedd, *Dogmatic Theology,* (New York: Charles Scribner's Sons, 1888), Vol. 2, p. 680.

"And do not fear those who kill the body but cannot kill the soul; rather fear him who can destroy both soul and body in hell." (Matthew 10:28) "And if your eye causes you to sin, pluck it out; it is better for you to enter the kingdom of God with one eye than with two eyes to be thrown into hell, where their worm does not die and the fire is not quenched." (Mark 9:47-48)

What this means is that the universalist must place the abstract rule of *agape* above the person of Jesus. Instead of learning the meaning of love by examining everything which Christ consisted in — believing, in short, that in his very person he is absolute love incarnate — the universalist must critically test Jesus by the rule of *agape*. And since Jesus is evaluated by *agape* and not vice versa, it follows that the person of Christ is not our most high. There is something or someone beyond Jesus. While we may be grateful to Christ for his life and death, we cannot worship him. If Christ were God in the flesh, and if universalism were the truth, Christ would never have been responsible for teaching the doctrine of eternal perdition. Would not omniscience know better?

> To threaten with 'everlasting punishment' a class of persons described as 'goats upon the left hand' of the Eternal Judge, while knowing at the same time that this class would ultimately have the same holiness and happiness with those described as 'sheep upon the right hand' of the judge, would have been both falsehood and folly. The threatening would have been false. For even a long punishment in the future world would not have justified Christ in teaching that this class of mankind are to experience the same retribution with 'the devil and his angels,' for these were understood by the Jews, to whom he spoke, to be hopelessly and eternally lost spirits. [43]

Whether Christ knew no better, or whether, knowing different, he deliberately contrived a falsehood, makes no difference for this first step in the argument. *The fact remains that*

---

43. Shedd, *op. cit.*, p. 676. Both the Shammai and the Hillel schools taught the doctrine of eternal punishment.

he was incompetent in his teaching. Therefore, we cannot commit our destiny to him. We may appreciate what he has done, even as we may thank Aristotle for his satisfying insights into metaphysics; but we cannot worship him. If there is a most high, we shall have to find it beyond the historical Jesus. The heart feels sheepish to be near Christ, for it is never perfectly certain whether *agape* or non-*agape* is being revealed at a given time. One moment Christ teaches the parable of the Prodigal Son — and thus is *agape* — while the next he teaches the story of the rich man in hell — and thus is not *agape*. Therefore, when the universalist is asked whether Jesus can be trusted, he must answer, "Well, the last time I saw him he could; but I am not responsible for what he may be teaching just now."

It is rather evident that universalism is either seeking final satisfaction in an abstract rule of *agape*, and so reduces to another immediacy, or it must press beyond Jesus to the person of the Father as the final hope of mankind. Thomas said: "My Lord and my God," for he rested in the person of the historical Jesus. The universalist, not trusting the person of Jesus, must say: "My Lord and my God — that is, whenever you are revealing *agape*."

B. *Loss of Faith in the Person of the Father*

The universalist has never concealed his rejection of the consubstantiality of the Son and the Spirit with the Father. "Jesus Christ is a being distinct from and inferior to God."[44] The point is that our faith is in *God the Father*, not in the historical vessel through which his revelation has come. Jesus at times may be modalistically identified with God, but it is the Father, not Jesus, who is God over all. Christ is ontologically subordinate to God.

The more one ponders the attempt to retain trust in the Father's person, while rejecting it in the case of the Son, how-

---

44. Channing, *Unitarian Christianity,* p. 50.

ever, the more suspicious he becomes of this type of solution. Regardless how high or low a view of the Biblical text a thinker might hold, he cannot deny that the bond which united Father and Son in the plan of salvation is that of absolute trust. In the entire gamut of religio-philosophical literature one could find no more perfect a pledge joining two persons than that which united the heavenly Godhead in revealing *agape*. The Father planned salvation; the Son merited it; and the Spirit applies it. Devoid of all jealousy, each looks away from himself to the other, for love seeks not its own. Therefore, while (on his own testimony) remaining ontologically equal with the Father, Christ gladly subordinated his claim to this equality for the sake of the Messianic office which the Father had appointed him to. Christ's perfection consisted in an absolute obedience to the Father's will. "Jesus said to them, 'My food is to do the will of him who sent me, and to accomplish his work.' " (John 4:34) "Jesus said to them, 'Truly, truly, I say to you, the Son can do nothing of his own accord, but only what he sees the Father doing; for whatever he does, that the Son does likewise. For the Father loves the Son, and shows him all that he himself is doing.' " (John 5:19-20) Christ claimed to be the author of no truth, for whatever doctrine he preached, he received it first from his Father in heaven. He took all his strength from the Father (Luke 22:42-43); he taught others to pray to the Father (Luke 10:2); he said nothing of himself, but only the things the Father taught him (John 8:28). Even his body was prepared by the Father (Hebrews 10:5).

In the entire corpus of Christian revelation there is no evidence to support any other conclusion than that the Father chose the Son from everlasting to be the sin-bearer. The selection of Christ was no last-minute expediency, no second best, as if the best were wanting. The word of the Father is ever, always, "In my Son I have found complete and absolute perfection." This unreserved satisfaction with the Son is illustrated here and there throughout the gospels when the voice of the Father thunders down out of heaven with absolute authority to punctuate all that the Son says and does. "And a voice came from heaven, 'Thou art my beloved Son; with thee I am well pleased.'" (Mark 1:11) "And a cloud overshadowed them, and a voice came out of the cloud, 'This is my beloved Son; listen to him.'" (Mark 9:7) After a trying day of teaching and healing, the Son resorted to prayer with the Father, for in this fellowship he found absolute satisfaction for his soul. The office of Messiah was completely rewarded by nods of approval from the Father.

If there were any time when we should expect the Father to express disappointment with anything the Son said or did, it surely was when the Son checked home as the Messiah to have the Father clear his fitness for the office. But the records tell us that the Son was completely pleasing to the Father at every point of his work. Not until the Son hung on the cross — a separate, and awful, incident — was flawless fellowship between heaven and earth disrupted.

The moment one appreciates this identity of purpose in both Father and Son, that instant he will blush to think that he could retain worship of the Father but not of the Son. If the Father deliberately guided the Son when the latter taught the doctrine of eternal retribution (and Christ reiterated over and again that he did), then the Father is an accomplice with the Son in the same teaching. Even if we preserve the moral integrity of the Son by saying that he taught things which *he* thought were true (but which the Father knew were not), we only all the more destroy the basis of worshiping the Father; for if the Father cannot be trusted in family relations, how can he be trusted by those who are outside? The *best* in a person is expressed when he is dealing with his own children; and in the case of the Father his best includes a deliberate revelation of untruths to the Son. Jesus was led to believe that everything he taught was veracious, when as a matter of fact (if universalism is true) his message is such a mixture of truth and error that modern man is forced to come to him "critically." At one moment he speaks *agape;* the next he is but a child of his times.

The seriousness at this point is not so much the actual error which Christ taught (though that would be sufficient to remove faith in his divinity), but rather that he solemnly announced it all as having been revealed to him from the Father. In the Parable of the Vineyard, *e. g.,* it is the *Father* who decrees punishment to the wicked servants. "He will put those wretches to a miserable death." (Matthew 21:41) It is the *Father* who is to be feared because of his power to cast men into hell (Matthew 10:28). The same one who sent the Son into the world is the one who will take vengeance against all who treat the Son with shame.

Is it possible for us to trust a Father who deliberately encouraged his own Son to believe and teach things which he himself disapproved? If the Father realized that the Son was speaking a falsehood, why did not he call it? *It is this complicity which destroys the Father's integrity.* We may exonerate a human Christ on the grounds that, being finite, he knew no better; but who can exonerate God the Father Almighty? Can we worship the Father when he permits — nay, *commands* — the Son to speak things in his name, which *de facto* are lies?

Even if a person seeks refuge in the unsatisfactory hypothesis that the Father had a "hidden purpose" in playing along with the Son, permitting him now and then to teach things in his name, but not approving of all that was said — as if the love of the Father *could* possibly express itself by holding truth back from the Son — there is a further reason why it is impossible to worship the Father if we cannot first worship the Son.

Since the creature cannot leave its limitations to probe fully into the meaning of God's relation to man, there are many mysteries connected with the divine economy. For example, we are never told all the criteria which the Father employed when choosing this type of world through which to reveal his glory. The text simply indicates that it pleased God to create the universe. But there is one thing of which there is no doubt: Regardless what mysteries may hover about the divine being, *God is not God apart from the attribute of holiness.* An unholy God is genuinely a square circle. The very thought of God smoking a black cigar and exchanging questionable jokes in a hotel lobby is so completely revolting to the heart that even the mention of such a situation is offensive to good taste.

If there is any being in heaven or on earth whose name is to be revered, protected, and adorned, it is the name of God Almighty, for a person's name stands for all that the person is. "A good name is rather to be chosen than great riches." (Proverbs 22:1) Throughout the Scriptures, therefore, the patience of God terminates when men corrupt the integrity and holiness of his name. Jehovah God is said to be "jealous" about his name, meaning that he intends to employ every means needed to insure its purity and integrity. The Ten Commandments commence with the holiness of God, therefore. "I Jehovah thy God am a jealous God . . . . Thou shalt not take the name of Jehovah thy God in vain; for Jehovah will not hold him guiltless that taketh his name in vain." (Exodus 20:5-7) A person with a questionable name is a person with a questionable character. For this reason men struggle to keep their name free of all calumny and scandal.

The quickest way that we can destroy our confidence in both God and his name is to learn that he cares so little about the dignity of being God that he frivolously permits others to usurp privileges and glories which belong to him alone. Suppose, for example, that God now and then permitted the devil to use his official stationary, to wear his signet ring, to promenade in the temple with heavenly robes of splendid hue, to sit on the throne and enjoy the laudatory cries of the seraphim and cherubim, to take shifts in receiving and answering prayers — in short, to receive worship; would not spirit be constrained to withdraw from its heavenward venture with an inward groan of shock and disappointment? If God carelessly permits others to usurp prerogatives which belong to him alone, he suffers from a character deficiency which prevents the heart from worshiping him. And once we believe that irresponsibility sits on the throne, the last vestige of trust in God vanishes. If God cannot be relied upon to keep his own name impeccable, he cannot be trusted for anything else.

It makes no difference who the being is that God permits to share in his prerogatives. As long as it is non-God, the usurper may be devil or perfect man; for any grade below God is infinitely less than deity. A God who respects his name will condemn usurpation in both the high and the low. None are exempt from the standing rule that worship belongs to God alone.

Here is the point: The documents of Scripture (to which both universalists and particularists must appeal) decidedly teach that *the Father deliberately chose, encouraged, appro-bated, and had fellowship with one — Jesus Christ — who not only spoke doctrine in the name of the Father but who also re-ceived worship from men.* Unless we are deliberately to falsify the clear words of the Bible, one must conclude that whoever Jesus Christ was, he was at least one who deliberately approved the reception of worship. When men fell down to worship him, he not only failed to check their postures, protesting that he was only a man, but he also went beyond that to bless them for their faith.

Search the entire Old and New Testaments and nothing can be found to parallel the conduct of Jesus Christ. When Cornelius met Peter and fell down to worship him, e. g., Peter, utterly shocked at the mere thought of usurping prerogatives which God alone may claim, shouted, "Stand up; I too am a man." (Acts 10:26) When the people of Lystra sought to make Barnabas and Paul into gods, so holy was the indignation which shot through their hearts that they swiftly countered, "Men, why are you doing this? We also are men, of like nature with you." (Acts 14:15) After the Apostle John had received so exalted a revelation from the angel on the Isle of Patmos, he felt that surely this being was close enough to the throne of God to be worshiped. But the guardian of the heavenly glory charged John to cease. "You must not do that! I am a fellow servant with you and your brethren the prophets, and with those who keep the words of this book. Worship God." (Revelation 22:9)

But the great exception is this one person in history, Jesus Christ. The leper worshiped Jesus; the ruler worshiped him; the disciples worshiped him; the Canaanitish woman worshiped him; *et al.* In these, and other instances which Scripture records, Jesus uttered not a syllable of protest against those bowing before him. Not only was Jesus a Jew who believed that God is one, but those who were worshiping him were likewise monotheists in the strictest sense of the term. And yet as they bowed graciously before him, he received their worship, as if the reception of worship were his rightful possession. When Thomas called him his God, Jesus blessed him for his faith. Christ taught men to pray in his name, trust in his person, repose in his power and authority, and wait for his coming in power and glory. This is the person that the Father chose to be his vessel in the revelation of *agape*.

Let us presume that the univeralist is right in his view that Christ is not the ontological son of God. Being non-God, Christ's channeling of worship to himself makes him an unspeakably awful person. We might sympathize with the Father's choice if Jesus were guilty only of making errors in coherence, for all sinful beings are subject to the frailties of finitude and personal interest. But Christ is guilty of infinitely more than this. He nonchalantly announced that he was so intimately related to the throne of God that he had a right to sit upon it. He dared to pretend that his nature was consanguineous with that of the everlasting Father, making no effort to check the ambitions of those who worshiped him.

One cannot escape from this predicament by a philological study of the word *proskuneo* for the problem does not turn on it. The word assuredly means just what it says, however: worship. The incontrovertible proof that Christ deliberately announced, and purposely intended his hearers to believe, that he had a right to be treated as God in the flesh, is that he was finally condemned by the Jews on the charge of introducing polytheism into their religion. The Jews were quick to see that one cannot be a Son of God without being equal with God, for the Son enjoys all of the privileges of the family. Therefore, the Jews could not stand to hear his doctrine, for this was a blasphemy which made fornication and murder seem trivial. "The Jews took up stones again to stone him. Jesus answered them, 'I have shown you many good works from the Father: for which of these do you stone me?' The Jews answered him, 'We stone you for no good work but for blasphemy; because you, being a man, make yourself God.' " (John 10:31-33) "This is why the Jews sought all the more to kill him, because he not only broke the sabbath but also called God his Father, making himself equal with God." (John 5:18) Jesus made no effort to gainsay their interpretation of his claim to deity. Rather, he took the occasion to teach his oneness with the Father in terms which could be mistaken by none.

The attempt of the universalist to retain faith in the Father, while rejecting the full deity of the Son, therefore, is freighted with insoluble difficulties. Once we realize that the Son deliberately acted as God in human flesh, our respect for the Father diminishes by the moment. It is plausible that the Father might tolerate one to come in his name and not have his philosophy quite straight (although this itself is almost impossible to conceive), but when he tolerates non-God to take privileges which belong only to God, there is an end to all propriety. *How can we respect God when he has no respect for himself?*

This is what Christ said: I and the Father are one; I am the eternal Son of God; I am returning to the glory which was

mine with the Father before the world was. If these statements are false, then the Father is an accomplice with one telling lies. We pity a pretender of Napoleon; we are shocked
at dictators; but we are outraged when non-God claims equality
with God.

The Father was not forced to employ Christ in his revelation. Why was not Socrates used? The maieutic method of
the Athenian sage may have suffered from many deficiencies,
but it at least did not exhibit the blasphemies and pretensions
of usurping worship. Socrates disclaimed knowing even what
mortal virtue was, let alone daring to pretend that he was the
ontological Son of God in the flesh. On the premise of universalism, he had more moral qualifications to be God's word
to men than Christ.

The conclusion is that with the loss of faith in the person
of Christ we lose faith likewise in the person of the Father.
Since the Father knew in advance the implications involved in
choosing Christ to reveal *agape,* we can only conclude that it
pleased him to be an accomplice in deception and frivolity.
With such a character deficiency, however, we can no longer
trust our destiny to the Father. Whoever is not moral when
dealing with his own children will hardly be moral when doing
business with neighbors.

Our excursion is finished, and the results are clear. When
we try option one, *i. e.,* when we provisionally accept the state·
ment of the universalist, that Christ was in error when he
taught the doctrine of eternal retribution, we emerge with a
loss of fellowship with God altogether.

In sum: My respect for Christ is destroyed because he made
claims which are contrary to fact; and my respect for the
Father is destroyed because he deliberately entered into collu-
sion with the Son in these claims. He played along with
Christ's mission, encouraging the Son to believe that he was
equal with the Father and was thus worthy of worship. Never
once did the Father register displeasure of Christ's usurpation
of divine prerogatives. If the moral vitalities which bind

Father and Son together are so shaky, therefore, where shall
the sinner stand when he comes to the Father for forgiveness?
Having placed *agape* above the person of Christ, universalism leaves us with a new form of immediacy. Our highest is
agape, not the person of God. The instant we subordinate
the historical Jesus to the abstract rule of *agape* we lose God's
fellowship altogether, for the Father placed his approval
upon all that the Son did and taught as embodying the perfection of his will for man.

When fellowship with God is destroyed, however, to whom
shall we turn? We are catapulted once again into the humanistic predicament, for we cannot trust God to supply us
moral resources beyond ourselves to make good the law of our
life. Universalism, in short, has left us with axiological
skepticism.

IV. What Am I Left With: Option Two

The instant we cease manipulating the historical Jesus, accepting instead a friendly reliance on his own testimony, the
heart experiences a flood of refreshment surging through it;
for one sensed a bit of sheepishness trying to convict Jesus
Christ of sin. His finger has too often written a list of our
own sins on the fresh sand. Christ so excellently met the law
of our nature that the heart shies away from seeking more
perfection in the rule of *agape* than in the person of Jesus
Christ himself. Christ alone had a right to say, *I am the truth*.

Let us assume for the sake of argument that the Scriptures
are veracious when they review for us both the offer of salvation and the promised consequences which attend either an
acceptance or rejection of it. It is only fair that the Biblical
authors themselves be given a full opportunity to speak.

A. *Preparation: Reminder of the Two Genera*

The first proposition which the Scriptures defend is that
one errs if he transfers to heaven the moral conditions which
prevail in earthly matters. While it is true that human love

asks for no more than a humble attitude upon the part of the one seeking forgiveness, one cannot justifiably conclude from this that God can overlook sinfulness with equal ease. There is a *toto caelo* difference between God's moral condition and that of man. Whereas God is without transgression, all men are full of transgression. Since the wife who forgives is in need of forgiveness herself, the guilt of her offending husband is only relatively different from her own. No more than mere contrition is required for the payment of guilt among members of a family.

To assume that God will expunge sin as easily as men erase misdemeanors is to commit the fallacy of converting an analogical into a univocal truth. When an earthly father forgives his son, he is not a sinless being forgiving sin. He is a sinner forgiving the misbehavior of another sinner. He must be clement because he is guilty himself. But this is not true with God, for God is perfection in his own person.

God indeed requires contrition when forgiving sin, for a not-caring-whether-or-not-men-repent God is another square circle. The minimal conditions for the restoration of personal fellowship must prevail in all realms. Otherwise there would be no analogy between God and man, and the use of the term "person" in reference to both God and man would become an equivocation.

But the issue is whether simple contrition *exhausts* the conditions which must be fulfilled if God is to forgive sin. Does a sinless being require only what a sinful creature does? Is fellowship gained this easily? One may want to answer these questions in the affirmative, but he would do well first to ask himself where the evidence for this conviction is obtained; for the Scriptures clearly indicate that the price to forgive sin was dear. And since we have agreed to permit the Biblical writers to speak, nothing is gained by branching off into *a priori* ventures.

What is often overlooked by those who are indisposed to sympathize with the Biblical view is the rather axiomatic law of jurisprudence that the guilt of an act is measured according to the dignity of the object against which it is committed, and not solely by the person committing the deed or the intrinsic nature of the act itself. Because God is an infinite person, therefore, sin is an infinite evil.

> Those who deny the position that sin is an infinite evil forget that the principle upon which it rests is one of the commonplaces of jurisprudence; the principle namely, that crime depends upon the object against whom it is committed as well as upon the subject who commits it. The merely *subjective* reference of an act is not sufficient to determine whether it is a crime. The act may have been the voluntary act of a person, but unless it is also an offence against another *person,* it is no crime. To strike is a voluntary act; but to strike a post or a stone is not a culpable act. Furthermore, not only crime, but *degrees* of crime depend upon the objective reference of a personal act. Estimated only by the subjective reference, there can be not only no culpability, but no difference in culpability. Killing a dog is no worse than killing a man, if merely the subject who kills, and not the object killed, is considered . . . . Now this principle of jurisprudence is carried into theology by the theologian. The violation of the moral law is *sin* and *guilt* only when viewed objectively in reference to God primarily, and to man secondarily . . . . One and the same act may be simultaneously an offence against an individual, a family, a state, and God. Measured by the nature and qualities of the offender himself it has no degrees. But measured by the nature and qualities of these moral objects against whom it is committed it has degrees of turpitude. As the first three are only finite in worth and dignity, the culpability is only certain degrees of the finite. As the last is infinite in worth and dignity, the culpability is infinite also. [45]

Since sinners can never experience what it is like to be a holy being who has been sinned against, it is impossible for them to calculate in advance specifically what a just God must demand before he can receive transgressors back into the family of fellowship. They can only wait until an announcement from heaven is made.

---

45. Shedd, *op. cit.,* p. 740, n.

B. *The Lamb of God*

When a person puts away the sentimentality of an easy forgiveness and focuses his attention on the record of what at least claims to be God's self-disclosure, he is brought to his knees in humility.

First, there is the fact of sinfulness itself. Sin is as universal as it is heinous. Sin is any want of conformity unto or transgression of the law of God. Sin is lawlessness, and the law to which all men are subject is the rule of fellowship. Since the defect of self-love in every man corrupts our efforts to live lovingly for others, every pretension to holiness is shattered. "For there is no distinction; since all have sinned and fall short of the glory of God." (Romans 3:22-23) The only person who can deny his own sinfulness is he who flies in the face of the law of fellowship, for whoever realizes the height of the law of love, plus the power of pride within him, will be the first to smite his own breast.

The heinousness of sin against God is proved by the fact that God can justly deal with it only by issuing the decree of capital punishment. "For the wages of sin is death." (Romans 6:23) And a careful study of the Biblical documents shows that death is twofold, physical and spiritual (or the second death). Physical death is the separation of soul and body, while the second death is separation of the whole person from fellowship with God. Since true life is fellowship, true death is want of fellowship. "And this is eternal life, that they know thee the only true God, and Jesus whom thou hast sent." (John 17:3)

Second, there is the incalculable price which God had to meet when atoning for the sins of men, that the fellowship might be restored. God *has* had mercy upon us, but only at a cost which challenges the imagination to conceive. Since the price of sin is death, and since death includes both the shedding of blood and the conscious separation of the spirit from fellowship with God, it follows that whoever atones for sin is obliged to suffer in both body and soul. "Without the shedding of blood there is no forgiveness of sins." (Hebrews 9:22)

But who can meet these conditions? Who can pass through death in order that he might gain life? An absolute impasse is reached in human wisdom, for the transgressor is too sinful to offer up a sacrifice for himself. Can the guilty felon effect his own release from guilt? We are obliged to pass through death as a *punishment* for sin, not as a means by which God can find a vent for his mercy.

When one carefully probes into the Biblical record of how God finally provided a sacrifice for sins, he must stand back and gasp for breath, so unexpected and appalling is the solution. While the way out is exactly what love had planned from all eternity, it was the last expedient that sinful humanity could have anticipated. In the eternal counsels of the world, before e'er the first man walked the meadows fair, God the Father had entered into a covenant with God the Son. The Son offered his own person as the Lamb of God to be slain for the sins of the world. "For God so loved the world that he gave his only Son, that whoever believes in him should not perish but have eternal life." (John 3:16)

Let not the modern reader's fond prejudices blind him to what the Scriptures actually teach about the person of Jesus Christ. He is God of very God, co-eternal and consubstantial with the Father and the Spirit. The Old Testament prophesied that a child was coming, and that his name would be called Wonderful, Counsellor, The Mighty God, The Everlasting Father, The Prince of Peace. (Isaiah 9:6) The New Testament catches up the prophecy and declares that in Jesus Christ the very Godhead is present. "In the beginning was the Word, and the Word was with God, and the Word was God." (John 1:1) Christ is the Word. Christ is "the image of the invisible God, the first-born of all creation; for in him all things were created, in heaven and on earth, visible and invisible... — all things were created through him and for him. He is before all things, and in him all things hold together." (Colossians 1:15-17)

Christ "reflects the glory of God and bears the very stamp of his nature, upholding the universe by his word of power." (Hebrews 1:3) Christ is Immanuel — "which means, God with us." (Matthew 1:23) Thus, Christ testified "Before Abraham was, I am." (John 8:58) "I and the Father are one." (John 10:30)

This one — the eternal Son of God — united to his person true human nature and died on the cross as a substitute in our stead. As the Lamb of God he bore the second death to take away the sins of the world. He alone could represent both the guilty and the offended.

> Man or angel would have been too low in respect of God: and an unveiled God would have been too high, in respect of sinful men, unable to bear intercourse with such heavenly Majesty. Wherefore the Son of God, that he might be fit to mediate, as he, being God equal with the Father, was high enough in respect of the party offending, by his becoming man. [46]

The Old Testament depicts the bloody sacrificial system as an adumbration of the good things to come in Christ, for Christ offered *himself* up without spot and blemish as the final and perfect sacrifice for sins. "When Christ appeared as a high priest of the good things that have come...he entered once for all into the Holy Place, taking not the blood of goats and calves but his own blood, thus securing an eternal redemption." (Hebrews 9:11-12) Sinners receive full pardon by turning away from themselves and looking to Jesus Christ as the atoning savior of the world. Salvation is a free gift, purchased by Christ and bestowed by love. "They are justified by his grace as a gift, through the redemption which is in Christ Jesus, whom God put forward as an expiation by his blood, to be received by faith." (Romans 3:24-25) "Great indeed, we confess, is the mystery of our religion:

---

46. Thomas Boston, *A View of the Covenant of Grace*, (London: J. Chalmers, 1742), p. 71.

He was manifested in the flesh,
vindicated in the Spirit,
    seen by angels,
preached among the nations,
believed on in the world,
    taken up in glory."[47]

C. *He Descended into Hell*

Nowhere in all literature can one find a more tender, yet more awful, scene than that which attended the passion and death of Christ. Plato's description of the death of Socrates is moving; but the Biblical account of the death of Christ is heart-rending. Neither feared the physical side of dying, and in this feature one discovers a common heroism. Socrates drank the hemlock, and Christ received the nails, without murmur or repine. But what Jesus Christ feared, and what Socrates knew nothing about, was the spiritual death he was soon to pass through. Because he was the sin bearer of the world, yet being without sin himself, Jesus in the garden cringed before the thought of such a death. "And being in an agony he prayed more earnestly; and his sweat became like great drops of blood falling down upon the ground." (Luke 22:44) But mindful of the office which he had come to fulfill, Christ left the garden determined to drink the cup of divine wrath. As he hung on the cross he bore the physical pain without complaint, for it was not this death which he feared; only as the moment drew near for him to pass through spiritual death did he cry out from the inner depth of his heart in unspeakable pain, "'Eloi, Eloi, lama sabachthani?' which means, 'My God, my God, why hast thou forsaken me?'" (Mark 15:34)

One will have slighted the real essence of the atoning work of Jesus Christ if he confuses physical suffering with the spiritual agony of the second death through which the Son of God passed. The cup which he feared to drink was the

---

47. I Timothy 3:16.

second death; and the second death is hell. Therefore, the Apostles' Creed confesses, "He descended into hell."

We tend to be blinded in our grasp of the meaning of the second death by crude notions of burning limbs and shrieking voices which so many, like Dante, have depicted. "Fire" in Scripture may be but an earthly analogy for the burning pain which one experiences when fellowship is ruptured. When the lover loses his beloved, does he not feel a fire in his spirit? "The worm dying not" may be but an analogy for the endlessness of pain which attends the loss of fellowship. As long as love is wanting, the worm lives. The best way to imagine the meaning of hell is to contrast it to the meaning of heaven. If heaven is that place beyond which nothing more perfect can be conceived, hell is that place beyond which nothing more awful can be conceived.

But what is the most appalling sorrow we can imagine? Is it physical pain? Is it suffering in the body? There is no question of the fearfulness of bodily agony. It is an unforgettable experience. But since we will endure this if we can have peace of spirit, it follows that sorrow in the soul is worse than discomfiture in the body.

Then is it the spiritual pain of seeing a loved one die? Is it the grief of standing beside the dead frame of one to whom we have so recently united our hearts in devotion? The loss of a friend is crushing to spirit, as all will testify who have passed through the experience. When love is lost, all is lost. But if one will but reflect for a moment about the whole of life, he will quickly see that there is pain worse than this.

Is there any grief greater than that which spirit experiences as it is united to the heart of a loved one who is dying a slow, inevitable death? What intensity of sorrow and anguish do the children experience as they watch their cancer-infected mother writhe on the bed in pain, knowing that she is doomed to die? Or, what agony does a mother pass through as she stands by helplessly and watches her small son waste away with an incurable brain tumor? Night and day the elder dies in the place ot the younger. This surely is the most awful form of suffering. Death is a benignity to those who, while ultimately doomed to death, are now consigned to life. Euthanasia *is* a pressing social problem.

However, there is yet a severity of suffering beyond all of these mentioned, a form of pain so incisive in its slashing of spirit that it forms the only persuasive analogy of what the condition of the second death is like. In plain language, *the most unbearable pain a person can endure is to sever the bonds of love and trust because of his own personal guilt.* Since there is no sweeter meaning to life than the joining of hearts through personal integrity, there is nothing more acrimonious than the rupturing of such love through a want of personal integrity. Whoever has known this pain has already known by analogy the meaning of the second death.

Suppose, for example, that a father descends lower and lower into the sins of sexuality, until one day he rapes and murders a minor to gratify himself. He is now brought face to face with a series of sorrows, the most awful of which is the knowledge that he has destroyed the conditions of trust and fellowship through his actions. There is embarrassment during the court trial; shame upon hearing his sentence; and pain and grief in physical incarceration. But these sorrows are minor compared to that of having to face his own family and know that their faith in him has been spoiled by his own lewdness; or having to stand before the parents of the murdered girl and realize that they have lost love as a result of his own character deficiency. When a person breaks the heart of another because of his own turpitude, his sorrow is indescribably awful. He can never forget the disappointed faces of his family as they stare at him, the criminal, during the court trial. He cannot blot out of his memory the moistened eyes of his wife when she says she never wants to see him again.

Observe the principle which is at work here. When the father is morally strong and the bond of the family is secure through that integrity, his ego is most secure. But when he is morally incapable, and a decay in family relations sets in because of his failures, the ego is least secure. In the one case self-dignity is retained, while in the other it is lost. The man who brings home his weekly pay is happy; the man who is addicted to alcohol and cannot make provisions for his own is unhappy. When a loved one dies from physical causes, love is taken away by forces which lie outside of one's control. But when the cause is a deliberate betrayal of those dignities which make a man a man, then there is sympathy neither inside nor outside, for love has been lost by default. The fellowship lies just outside of the reach of the guilty party, but his own inherent baseness prevents it from being realized.

It was this type of sorrow which Jesus Christ passed through as he bore the pains of the second death. When the sins of the world were laid on the Son, the Father was obliged to turn away, crying, "You are morally blameworthy; I cannot look upon you." For this reason the Son cried out in agony, "My God, my God, why hast thou forsaken me?" The loss of the Father's fellowship was infinitely painful to the heart of the Son.

> Surely never sorrow was like unto that sorrow which extorted such a complaint as this from one who, being perfectly free from sin, could never be a Terror to himself; but the heart knows its own bitterness. No wonder that such a complaint as this made the earth to quake, and rent the rocks; for it is enough to make both the *ears of every one that hears it tingle,* and ought to be spoken of with great reverence. [48]

The Son, who from everlasting was the object of the Father's supreme pleasure, empirically felt what it meant to have that fellowship cut off on the ground of the guilt which he had taken upon himself as the Second Adam. As in the Old Testament, where the priest laid his hands upon the head of the goat, making it the scapegoat for the sins of Israel (Leviticus 16:21-22), so "For our sake he made him to be sin

---

48. Matthew Henry, *A Commentary on the Whole Bible,* (New York: Fleming H. Revell Co.), Vol. 5, p. 246.

who knew no sin, so that in him we might become the right-eousness of God." (II Corinthians 5:21)

The spirit within man quivers at even the thought of the Son of God passing through the agony of hell, that he might redeem a holy church unto himself. We must put our hands over our eyes to keep from being blinded by this sacrificial splendor. At the moment Christ endured the second death, the only person the Father could see on the cross was one full of sin — sin which was not Christ's own, but of which none-theless he had become the vicarious agent. The sword in the heart of the Son was the withdrawal of the Father's fellowship. In the instant when the guilt and transgressions of the world were transferred to his cross, the Son (as it were) beheld the tears in the eyes of the Father. There was guilt in the heavenly family.

Abraham had raised the knife to slay Isaac, but he was spared the grief of the lad's death because God supplied the ram. But in the case of Christ, the Father was pleased to sacrifice his Son, for love knew that only through Christ's taking sin upon his cross could justice flow from God to the race of sinful men.

It was with a *loud* cry that Christ released the agony of his heart, not just a mild registration of uneasiness. He bore the scourging with equanimity; the spitting and the nailing were taken in course; but when the Father withdrew fellow-ship on the grounds of the Son's guilt, the pain was too great to be contained. The Son of God shrieked in sorrow.

In sum, *Christ descended into hell.* Nor was it simply a passive want of the Father's fellowship which made the fury of hell unbearable; it was also that the hatred of the Father for sin was personally directed against him, so that in his own heart he felt what it meant to be opposed by heaven, having the breath of an angry God on him.

> The forsaking of God is also *positive.* God is directly send-ing the torments of hell against the Christ. A cry of pain surges up in His soul: lead me not into temptation, but

deliver me from evil. And when God fails to hear this prayer, and persists in the failure to answer it (thus negatively withholding Himself, Psalm 22:3), Christ knows with immediate certainty that the representation of an inactive, and negatively withholding God by no means exhausts the truth. God is also actively busy in this inactive supervision .... It is God who looses the devils against Him, the devils and the four winds of the earth. The spirit of Christ, as it battles against the forces of hell for three hours, sees the devils rising up against Him, and as He sees it, God is taking the role of the supervisor in the arena, and it is God who releases the lions, the bulls and goats and cattle of Bashan, and it is God who releases the dogs (Psalm 22) against the great martyr with an agonizing calmness. It is God who lifts the doors of the cages. [49]

No man can be certain how long Christ endured the torments of hell. But what is certain from the data of Scripture is that he did so endure. Whether brief or long, it matters not, for the dignity and sinlessness of his own person gave infinite worth to his endurance; so that through his vicarious suffering all men of faith may be spared the decree of passing through the agony of hell themselves.

D. *Peacefulness in Submission*

When once the searching heart understands the meaning of Christ's passage through the second death (and what other meaning can we rest in, save that which the eyewitnesses themselves have sworn to?), an overwhelming feeling of ingratitude surges up for having ever questioned the Father's prerogatives in offering and withdrawing mercy at his will; for the price which the Father paid in sacrificing his Son on the cross was so unthinkably painful to heaven, and so in-

---

49. K. Schilder, *Christ Crucified*, (Grand Rapids: Eerdmans Publishing Company, 1944), p. 404. "He was in hell as a perfect stranger. He did not belong here, He could not acclimate Himself to that place. There was not a single reality of hell which He did not gainsay. His strangeness over against hell was not something negative, but something positive. He was a stranger in hell, because He remained a son and member of the family of heaven, because He remained theocentric in His thoughts, words, and deeds." *Ibid.*, p. 419.

comprehensible for the sinful heart on earth to perceive, that one can only marvel that God has made mercy available to man even *within* a day of grace. To conclude that God is morally obliged to extend mercy to sinners beyond that which he promised to the Son who bore hell for men, is but to add sin to sin, ingratitude to ingratitude, disobedience to disobedience. When a sinner questions the impropriety of decisions which proceed from the source of mercy itself, words fail to express the ingratitude for what mercy has already done. Love never demands mercy; it only patiently waits to see if mercy is there.

Submitting our wills to God's justice is the key to happiness. Once the heart yields to the Biblical doctrine of atonement with the same unreservedness that it yields to its account of the law of love, a perfect satisfaction with both Father and Son displaces confidence in an abstract *agape*. God rightfully and properly is our most high, for in worship the finest in man is exhausted. When we believe that the gospel is true, Christ can be worshiped; for he is now God in the flesh, the savior of the world, not a finite individual who took worship which did not belong to him. The Father likewise can be worshiped, for instead of being an accomplice in a fraud, he is tenderly bound to the sin-bearer with the cords of loving perfection. Rather than feeling sheepish in the presence of either Father and Son, therefore, the heart feels an urge within it to seek out their fellowship.

When once we have learned to trust God's person, we will trust him when he says that his mercy will be extended to men only within a day of grace. Since hell is simply a further form of the problem of evil, it is solved in exactly the same way that the difficulty of the surds was met. When *God* (not an abstract rule of good) is our ultimate, the good is what he does. Should a person complain against God, charging him with injustice when he does not extend his mercies to sinners forever, he only proves that it is not God, but a formal criterion of good, which is his trust; for whoever trusts and worships God will make God's own will the final norm of justice and goodness.

The issue once more is whether we shall become quagmired and embrangled in another immediacy, or whether we shall press on to genuine fellowship. Because of its rejection of Christ's will and word, universalism catapults the heart into a new, but no less disturbing, immediacy. Since we cannot have fellowship with *agape, agape* cannot be our most high. *God* is our final objection of trust.

But the universalist replies: "Is not God a God of love? And do we not mean by love the virtue of forgiving and forgetting as long as strength lasts?" God *indeed* is love, for the Scripures say that nothing short of *agape* can exhaust perfection in personality. But love never extends forgiveness until the antecedent conditions of justice are met. Even as a wife will not forgive the husband until contrition has been shown, so God will not forgive sinners until contrition for sin has been shown. But contrition before God includes the confession that because sin is so awful, those who perpetrate it *deserve* to suffer the second death. It includes the admission that sin's heinousness sent Christ to the cross, there to pass through the second death for sinners. *True* humility before God is always primed by a penetration into the appalling nature of sin. God indeed is love, but the Scriptures *never* speak about the arm of God's love apart from the Father's pouring out judgment upon the Son as the bearer of the second death. If the Son had not borne the justice of God in death, God's love would never have been known. Scripture warns that salvation comes only to those who accept Christ's passage through death as the very justice which they themselves should have met.

An *a fortiori* emerges: *When a man denies God's right to punish recalcitrant sinners in hell, he likewise must reject the Father's prerogative to punish his own Son through the second death on the cross; for the agony which Christ suffered in one moment is infinitely more awful than could be collectively endured by all sinners in an eternity of separation from God's fellowship.* The more perfect the love is, the more awful is the separation; and there is no perfection of love beyond that which God has for the Son. God the Father, Son, and Holy Spirit express absolute affection one for the other.

If Christ did not make atonement for sins, however, how shall guilt be put away? The only knowledge one has of God's love is in God's self-disclosure through Christ; and the Scriptures declare that there is no other way of escape from sin but by the endurance of the second death. It may be fashionable for modern man to shun the Biblical doctrine of atonement, but who can answer this question: "How shall we escape if we neglect such a great salvation?" (Hebrews 2:3) Philosophers cannot help us, for they all died as sinners. The great religious leaders cannot help us, for they have only bequeathed to us *systems* of thought, not personal fellowship with God. Only Christ is able to state the law of our life; and only he is qualified to meet that law both for himself and for all who know what it means to sin.

> O sacred Head, now wounded,
>   With grief and shame weighed down;
> Now scornfully surrounded,
>   With thorns, Thine only crown;
> O sacred Head, what glory,
>   What bliss till now was Thine!
> Yet, though despised and gory,
>   I joy to call Thee mine.
>
> What language shall I borrow
>   To thank Thee, dearest Friend,
> For this Thy dying sorrow,
>   Thy pity without end?
> O make me Thine for ever;
>   And should I fainting be,
> Lord, let me never, never
>   Outlive my love to Thee.

There is a penal element in the nature of God which must be satisfied if fellowship is to be restored.

The real question therefore, is whether God ever *punishes*. That he chastises, is not disputed. But does he ever inflict a suffering that is not intended to reform the transgressor, and does not reform him, but is intended simply and only to vindicate law and satisfy justice, by requiting him for his transgression? Revelation teaches that he does. 'Vengeance is mine; I will repay, saith the Lord,' Romans 12:19. [50]

The love of God has expressed itself by *punishing* Christ on the cross, for, as the Scriptures say, "it pleased Jehovah to bruise him." (Isaiah 53:10) When we seek to revise the meaning of God's love according to the way love expresses itself between sinners here on earth, we simply confuse genera. The documents which tell us "the greatest story ever told of the greatest life ever lived" assure us that if the vicarious death of Christ did not intervene on our behalf, the wrath of God would long since have consumed us. If we leave these documents, we leave the Christ; for they are our only access to both the statement and the fulfillment of the law of our life.

Because of the dust and smoke of battle between the universalist and the particularist, an important observation has been left unstressed. The contemporary mind ought to concentrate on one thing only: *The day of grace, during which God's mercies are extended to all in Christ, is with us yet*. Whatever may be the consequence of speculation about things which may not be, the glorious fact remains that the good news of salvation is yet ours. In this, rejoice!

The Christian Gospel — the universal offer of pardon through the self-sacrifice of one of the Divine Persons. . . should silence every objection to the doctrine of Endless Punishment. For as the case now stands. there is no necessity, so far as the action of *God* is concerned, that a single human being should ever be the subject of future punishment. The necessity of hell is founded in the action of the *creature*, not of the Creator. Had there been no sin, there would have been no hell; and sin is the product of man's free will. And after the entrance of sin and the provision of redemption from it, had there been universal repentance in this life,

---

50. Shedd, *op. cit.*, p. 721.

there would have been no hell for man in the next life. The only necessitating reason, therefore, for endless retribution that now exists, is the sinner's *impenitence*. Should every human individual, before he dies, sorrow for sin and humbly confess it, Hades and Gehenna would disappear. [51]

Summary

Just as the heart was on the verge of resting trustfully in the person of Jesus Christ as the solution to the problems of impotence and guilt raised in the venture of humanism, a golden apple of discord was suddenly thrown across the path by the universalist. Even as Plato preferred the abstract idea of good to faith in the person of God, so the universalist prefers the formal concept of *agape* to faith in the person of Christ. Therefore, the argument of the universalist is not unlike that of the finitist: God is not God unless he does the good. In the case of universalism the good is defined according to the analogy of forgiveness and love in human fellowship. God is good by continuing his overtures of forgiving mercy until every sinner, rescued from the jaws of hell, is firmly planted within the fellowship.

Although the problem of the day of grace is not generically different from other forms of the problem of evil — for universalism has turned against the Biblical documents on the ground that hell is a surd — it nevertheless is more difficult to face. What must the reality of the second death be like if the mere projection of it is so unsettling?

But a careful analysis of the problem shows that one solves nothing by resorting to universalism. Since the doctrine of the day of grace is so unequivocally taught in Scripture, and since Scripture is our only epistemological source of information about *agape*, it follows that once we reject Christ's veraciousness at this point we destroy our faith in his person altogether. An ignorant man cannot be our source of trust. Furthermore, if Christ is non-God, we instantly lose our faith

---

51. *Op. cit.*, p. 749.

in the Father; for the Father is an accomplice with the Son by encouraging him to take privileges which belong to God alone. If the Father has so slight a regard for his own dignity, that he shares his prerogatives of worship with non-God, we cannot trust him with the commitment of our immortal souls to his care. A God without self-respect will hardly respect the faith of others.

When the heart sets aside its prejudices and remembers that only God can tell us what constitutes justice in the punishment for sins, we learn the astounding fact that in the death of Christ the second death (hell) was endured on our behalf, and that personal exemption from God's wrath is now freely offered to all. Upon perceiving the immense price which Christ paid for sins, one recoils from further disputation with the Father as to his prerogatives in mercy.

Despite its brilliant efforts to clarify our relation to the love of God, universalism can only offer the hungry heart a very complex immediacy. We are taught what *agape* is; we have had the system of fellowship explained; and we are instructed about the theoretic superiority of a God whose justice does not demand the death penalty for sin. But what we are never taught is the precise way to fellowship. One can no more remain satisfied with an abstract *agape* than he can with sex, money, fame, wisdom, or devotion to mankind. The instant a person is juxtaposed with a thing, love is destroyed. We crave fellowship with the Father; we crave fellowship with the Son; we crave fellowship with the Holy Spirit. But universalism dashes all of these hopes to the ground by interjecting *agape* between the sinner and the freedom of God.

If the doctrine of hell is a hard doctrine to hear, universalism is even harder. And when the modern mind seeks to know whether it is better to suffer for the person of Jesus Christ or formal *agape*, it must remember that the gaining or losing of an absolute fellowship hangs in the balances. *Nothing less than this perspective can do justice to the axiological issues involved in the collision between universalism and particularism.*

X

The Primacy of an Institution

THE Scriptures teach, and the heart has leaped with joy to learn it, that since the body is the temple of the Holy Spirit, nothing can stand between the soul and God. The Spirit of God is immanent in creation, convicting, beseeching, and saving the hearts of men. "When the Spirit of truth comes, he will guide you into all the truth; for he will not speak on his own authority, but whatever he hears he will speak, and he will declare to you the things that are to come." (John 16:13) Since the issues of salvation are intensely private, the Spirit of God stands ready to hear the groanings of a lonely heart, teaching it when and how to pray. Just as confession is privately addressed to God, so in private God regenerates the heart, pouring out the gifts of salvation. No third party may stand between man and God to arbitrate the terms of spiritual surrender.

As one carefully studies the book of Acts, he learns that not even the church has power to intervene between the heart and God. Men who have been called out by the Spirit of God are asked to gather themselves together for the preaching of the gospel and the administration of the sacraments. This fellowship of believers is the church, for where two or three are gathered in his name, the Lord is there in the midst. The church is the mystical body of Christ, the organic union of all who are spiritually joined to Christ the head. The church may sow and water the seed, but only Christ can give the increase. God alone, never the church, can save or anathematize a soul.

If this structure were not true, the heart would suspect that God is not related to man according to the highest value we

experience on earth. In all relations of love *nothing* intervenes
between the heart of the lover and that of the beloved. The
mere thought of channeling affections through a third party
is chilling to love. Fellowship is the one virtue which can
exist only when heart leaps into heart with perfect directness.
Love which is obliged to express itself through a third party is
truncated.

Perhaps the most exasperating feature of man's quest for
axiological security, however, is that the closer he draws to
the truth, the more complex the picture becomes. It is not
enough that one labor his way through to the gates of Christianity; hardly has he pitched his tent and turned to enjoy the
fruit of his labors but what a powerful collective ego stands
in the way, warning him with a double-edged sword in its
right hand that not one red grape may be plucked until the
individual first pledges obedience to its power. The disappointment one faces is not unlike that of the weary traveler
who, having slashed his way through miles of steaming jungle
in a desperate search for water, discovers, upon locating the
streams of refreshment, that a foreign power holds monopolis-
tic rights over the land. Unless he submits his will to this
power, giving up his right to freedom, he cannot drink.

I. The Plausibility of Roman Catholic Authority

The individual who has not at one time or another cast a
glance of wonder toward the magnificence and weight of the
Roman Catholic Church is an individual who has hardly come
to full, critical selfhood; for to countless millions of people
the arguments which undergird the claims of the church of
Rome are so compelling that one's lapse into dissatisfaction
and error can be measured by the distance he recedes from
Catholic teachings. Wherever one travels, there he finds the
vigilant eye of the church; wherever learned men gather, Rome
has her able and honored representatives. Turn left, turn
right, and the ubiquitous church follows. To escape the dynam-

ic of Roman Catholicism, one must verily go out of the world itself.

A. *The Natural Step*

When the existing individual is brave enough to approach the door of a Catholic Church, inquiring of the resident apologist why he ought to pledge himself to the visible church, the cleric finds the indicia of Catholic truth so manifold and multifarious that he is temporarily embarrassed to know quite where to begin. Since he believes that the arguments for Catholicism form a perfect circle, it is inconvenient to break into this exactness for the expediency of teaching. The Catholic is so satisfied that his church has the whole truth, in fact, that he must pass through a brief time of self-discipline before he can even sympathize with those yet outside of the fold. Even to question Rome's ability to satisfy the whole person is a derogation of God's plan of salvation.

After learning of the axiological hardships that spirit has endured thus far in its quest for certainty, the Catholic apologist graciously congratulates the individual, pointing out that pilgrims who are so concerned with matters pertaining to the soul are rare and praiseworthy. Noting the obvious weariness of the visitor, the Catholic gestures toward the church, assuring his guest that his pilgrimage was directed by providence. He bids him to kneel before the Sacred Heart of Jesus, there to find everlasting rest for the soul. After its rough and dangerous voyage through shark- and reef-infested waters, the individual finds it easy to enter — oh, so easy. Even the walls of that stained marble edifice seem to chime out that this is the final haven for the soul. The steps leading to the church are cupped and worn from the shoes of the thousands of devotees who have passed in and out of the sanctuary of worship — some pausing only for a moment of prayer before commencing the day's toil, others entering for a full morning of meditation and worship. As the immense, leather-covered doors swing shut, the inquiring heart is very glad that the way was thus opened up.

Quite persuaded that if the penitent is directly exposed to the grandeurs of the Catholic faith he will take his own step toward truth, the apologist — after assuring the individual he will promptly return within a half hour — leaves the pilgrim behind to meditate and pray in the vast church. As the be-friended one watches the cleric exit through one of the side doors, he feels that he has been shown a kindness which is as unique as it is excellent. This gentleness is precisely what the heart would expect if it were making contact with those who know and hold the truth. The whole incident was so dramatic and inspiring, yet done with such little effort on the part of the Catholic leader, that the individual finds it easy to believe that providence has indeed led his way.

It is very easy to pray, for the entire milieu was designed for God's meeting of sinners through the repeated sacrifice of Jesus Christ on the altar. As the individual bows his head, joining the hundreds of others about him, a spirit greater than his seems to force its way into the heart, enveloping it with the persuasion that the ubiquitous presence of Christ is here expressed in a different and intense way. The spiritual ex-perience is almost ineffable in its grandeur.

Far too curious to offer a long prayer, however, the search-ing individual sits tall in the pew and looks around. While the actions of the priests and altar boys in the front of the sanctuary are mysterious and unclear, there is something solemn and deliberate about their every gesture. They seem to mean serious business with God as they chant and sing — turning to the laymen first, then reaching up to heaven, then kneeling before the sacred Scriptures and the tabernacle in the center of the altar. Likewise, it is hard to understand why the laity respond as they do — first genuflecting, then rising again — but one cannot mistake the earnestness and under-standing on the faces of those about him. The obedient re-sponse on the part of the laity is a convincing commentary on the apparent wholehearted satisfaction with the Catholic religion enjoyed by those who enter it to win.

If aesthetic experience is equivalent to fellowship with God, the heart has nothing more to crave. The ceiling above the main altar is covered with painted works about the very heavenly splendors towards which it ascends. From the upper reaches of the cathedral a pencil of light spears down toward the pure white altar below, bearing (as it were) perpetual approbation to those about the altar who are keeping the watch of perpetual adoration. Never before has the heart felt its insignificance in such a strange and inexpressible way. The individual is nothing — yet everything — in the immensity of that edifice. The walls of the cathedral are banked with blue and red prayer candles, the stations of the cross, three auxiliary altars, symmetrically spaced, mahogany confessional booths, and a large quantity of canes and crutches in one corner — apparently discarded by those who had been miraculously healed. With the ending of the mass, priests and nuns, obviously confident of themselves and the high office they represent, enter and exit from time to time through the many doors leading from the church to the sprawling adjacent property housing the educational and administrative plant of the seat of the bishop. One cannot take his eye off them, for their habit is as neat as the stance they maintain.

Before he has even been asked to become a Roman Catholic, therefore, the penitent feels the drawing power of this great church within him. Having come this far in the venture of suffering, is not the next natural step that of Catholicism? Or to state the matter another way, how *can he avoid becoming a Catholic?* One feels like a slender piece of straw being drawn into the vortex of a roaring hurricane. Resistance seems completely futile.

B. *The Step Made Easy*

At the end of the designated period, the apologist — true to his word — invites the penitent into one of the side offices of the church, there to discuss the basic virtues of Catholicism. The easygoing manner of the priest sets the individual at ease. Before the inquirer has even had a chance to become nervous, the Catholic is casually working his way through a moving defense of the oldest, biggest church on earth.

The strategy of the cleric is to prove that whatever any other Christian body can offer, the Catholic Church can match with interest; wherever deposits of religious truth have been made, the church has had a hand in their formulation. The self is so impressed with this list of proofs that it begins to wonder what need there is to hear more. This *must* be the answer.

When the penitent again reviews his long struggles through the lower and higher immediacies, the apologist verbally applauds, insisting that the Catholic mind is in complete agreement with this axiological progression. The only thing wanting now is to drop anchor and put to use the cargo of axiological experience gained through the dangerous venture. The church is needed as the custodian of spiritual things, lest they be dissipated through inattentiveness.

At the very mention of the first century the heart spins with curiosity, for whoever was present then was near the Master himself. Upon perceiving this interest in first-century things, the apologist calmly informs the penitent that the Roman Catholic Church dates back to Matthew chapter sixteen, when Christ gave Peter the keys of the kingdom and founded the institution against which the gates of hell would never prevail. Peter was the first bishop of Rome; and since Peter's day the church has been spiritually shepherded by an unbroken succession of popes, acting in the office of vicar of Christ.

Four authoritative sources fortify Catholic claims: The Papal bulls, the Tridentine standards, the Vatican standards, and Canon Law. These, the Catholic apologist assures the heart, form the most imposing bloc of authority in the entire world. They give assurance and peace to all who are weary of wandering through the sects and the isms.

This is a solid epistemology, for in all matters pertaining to faith and morals the living pope is authorized to speak infallibly. The doctrines which the church now teaches were handed to Peter in the first century, and from Peter through the living mind of the church to all generations as long as the world lasts. The Roman Catholic Church says she teaches the same doctrines, ever, always.

Rome claims to offer the searching heart everything taught in the Bible — plus a substantial body of tradition by which to interpret Scripture. She teaches the existence of the Triune God: Father, Son, and Holy Spirit. She teaches the incarnation of Christ; his redemption of sinners through a vicarious and atoning death; the sufficiency and objectivity of Scripture as God's self-revelation; creation, the fall, the covenant, the second coming of Christ, and the condemnation of the wicked at the final judgment. There is no topic of importance relating to the pilgrimage of the soul but what the Roman Church has already pronounced upon it. There is a Catholic view of labor, marriage and divorce, politics, science, etc. Just as the Spirit of God brooded over the waters in creation, so the church now broods over all the earth, preaching and interpreting the mind of Christ for men. In sum, the church is the extension of Christ's incarnation, for whoever sees the true church has already seen Christ. The body and the head form one organism.

The Catholic instructs the inquirer, warning him that the only alternative to the order and authority of the church is spiritual chaos. Once the individual becomes his own authority in Biblical interpretation, the logical conclusion is a welter where there are as many interpretations as there are persons themselves. And to undergird this contention the Catholic apologist points to the hundreds of competitive Protestant denominations, each one averring that its own doctrines have been received from the Holy Spirit. Things pertaining to the soul are far too delicate to be entrusted to private interpretation, since they involve matters of life and death.

The church watches over the spiritual condition of her children from the cradle to the grave, extending to all, rich and poor alike, the plenary resources of her custodianship. Entrusted by Jesus Christ with authority to purvey saving grace to lost souls, the church controls the power of the seven sacraments. Baptism washes away the stains of original sin and cleanses the soul for heaven; confirmation steps up grace by preparing the soul for its warfare with the world; the eucharist offers the feast of the body and blood of Jesus Christ; confession removes the mortal stains of sin on the soul; and extreme unction prepares the soul for its final and last journey. The sacraments of orders and marriage supply stores of grace to all entering such vocations. Wherever there is a spiritual need, there the shepherding arm of the church will be found — consoling, protecting, feeding, and calming.

The priest has no family save that of the parish itself. He is the "father" of them all. Married to Jesus Christ, the nun devotes herself unstintedly to the work of the church — and especially to the education of the little ones entrusted to her care. Tirelessly, the priest and nun work side by side, bringing the message of the crucified Christ to a lost and dying world. Until death halts their labors, each is seeking to fulfill the Great Commission of Christ.

When he inquires where he may find some literature defending the church, the penitent is deluged with answers. The embarrassment of the apologist is to know which of the immense tomes on a given subject would be best suited, and in what language. For every volume defending Protestantism, the church can point to an entire library of ancient documents to fortify her own claims. Scholars in every age — men with the finest mental equipment — have risen to the defense of the church. Although such minds as Thomas Aquinas and Robert Bellarmine may tower above other Catholic authors for their voluminous contributions in both theology and philosophy, the Catholic finds it inconvenient to speak of "official" writers in the church. Roman doctrine seems to have germinated within the inner bowels of the church herself, being the result of generation after generation of spiritual fertility. And standing guard over this gigantic corpus of changeless truth is the contemporary, *living* church. She is a watchful mother, supplying her own with both the medicine of life and the free gift of immortality.

If ecumenicity is to be found anywhere, it is in the Roman Catholic Church. Knowing little of the limitations of race or color, the church has standardized the mass on every continent. Wherever the Catholic finds himself, there he is at home in the church. Set as a beacon light on a tall hill that all may see her, Rome's perpetuity seems guaranteed. If *anything* will endure to the end of time, it is the church. She has met and conquered the Goths, Vandals, Huns, Visigoths, Lombards, Mohammedans, Nestorians, Eutychians, Arians, Reformation Schismatics and Materialists. Her organizational unity is a political wonder of the world. Through a complex maze of vows and pledges, each Catholic subordinate is united in confident trust to his superior, and that one to his superior, etc., with all pledged to absolute obedience to Christ's earthly vicar, the pope. So incontestable is the church's authority at this hour that no international move is made without direct or indirect consultation with the Vatican.

Measuring her age by the century, the church is in no hurry about anything. Whether today, tomorrow, or a century from tomorrow, it matters not; the guiding faith of every devout Catholic is that the church will some day enjoy the hegemony of spiritual world dictatorship. Her flow is like hot lava; men may rush from its path, divert it for a time, but in the end the power and might of flowing mass is irresistible. All must succumb to Roman Catholic authority.

The church is the repository of the fine art of the ages. Her cathedrals are mountains of granite and marble, wonders of architectural achievement — vast, luring, museum-like. Compared to the modest adornments of the Protestant edifice, the Roman church sings out like the peals and swells of a mighty baroque organ in competition with the feeble twittering of distant sparrows.

And if all this is not enough to bring the penitent to a quick decision, the Catholic apologist closes the conversation with a volley of questions which throw a complete haze over non-Catholic options. Without aid from the mind of the church, how can one know for certain that the Bible is a reliable document? Since the church wrote the Bible, she alone knows what it contains. And what church was there prior to the Reformation, save the one which dates back to the Master? Who, thus can be more equipped to fathom the mind of Christ than that institution which has been in the business of salvation for almost twenty centuries? Through every experience she has learned more truth, and all of the truth is free to all who join her ranks. Is it possible that Rome could be in error, when she has been defended by so many brilliant minds for so many centuries, men from every branch of learning?

Confident that there is a necessary, inner dialectic which will lead the inquiring mind safely into the fold of the church, the apologist leaves the matter there, bidding his good friend farewell and encouraging him to read widely on the subject — especially the life of John Henry Newman. The priest is prudent enough to perceive that no decision for the church is significant until it has first passed through that period of maturation and inquiry which converts curiosity into a stable conviction.

II. The Real Issue

When seeking to evaluate the axiological worth of suffering for an institution, the heart is beset with a situation it has not yet had to face. Hitherto it presumed itself natively qualified to investigate an option without the assistance of a third party. In the case of the Roman Catholic Church, however, the very *raison d'être* of the institution herself pivots on the inadequacy of the individual to be his own interpreter. If man were competent to know God's will privately, the antecedent ground for an infallible church would be destroyed. The church is a mediator in matters of salvation.

The existing individual must by-pass this issue, however, relegating it to the same limbo that he did the positivist's argument that one is not competent in matters of meaning until he first accepts the chart of positivism. If the inquirer is not competent as a private interpreter, how can he ever ascertain whether or not it is advantageous to accept Catholicism? Channing has already convinced the heart that it *is* licit to inquire into divine things, judging their agreement or disagreement both with coherence and with our own moral sense. Should Catholicism deny us this prerogative, let not the Roman apologist be offended if we smile broadly at his overtures toward converting us to the church. Since we are not qualified to judge such things, we can hardly be blamed for turning aside from Catholicism. What we are incompetent to evaluate remains a *je ne sais quoi.*

A. *Independent Research*

Whether qualified or not, the penitent cannot betray the dignity of his own freedom by accepting the witness to a church which he has not first evaluated by private interpretation. And the more he reasons out the issue, the less cogent does the over-all Catholic apologia become. Take, for example, the datum of antiquity. Can the age of an institution establish its truth? Since people can perpetuate error just as easily as they can truth, there is no *intrinsic* merit in antiquity. When one reads the epistles carefully, he finds that the churches which the apostles founded quickly lapsed into doctrinal heresy. Possibly the Catholic Church has for all these centuries been reciting some of these early errors. Who knows? At least the criterion of antiquity cannot disqualify such an hypothesis.

Or, take the consolation of Roman authority. When one asks how corrupt popes could have been speaking the mind of Christ, he is told that Catholics do not defend the *person* of the pope; the vicar speaks the mind of Christ only when he is the official interpreter in matters of faith and morals. Thus by one sweep all of the papal abuses are brushed aside.[1] When the individual next inquires who is to determine when a pope actually speaks *ex cathedra*, the answer is, the living pope. But how do we know when the living pope is acting officially and when he is but voicing his own opinion? Since he does not raise his right hand every time he is speaking infallibly, one cannot tell. But suppose he *did* signal to the world whenever he was about to speak in faith and morals, what then? His words would have to be interpreted, would they not? Who would infallibly interpret this interpretation? A third-man problem results. At some point the individual must exercise his private right of interpretation, or no meaning is conveyed. Where, then, has our unique authority gone? Probability, as Butler sagaciously observed, is the guide of life.

One by one the external criteria defending Catholicism dissolve. Which piece of evidence can establish the claim of the church that she is the continuation of the incarnation? *Unity?* Hardly, for people can — and more often do — unite around error. Great men, like Elijah, have had to stand alone in their defense of the truth. *Universality?* Skepticism, atheism, and general carelessness have always been more universal than truth. If truth were ascertained by counting heads, Christ long ago would have been displaced by his blasphemers. *Power?* A neutral value capable of either good or evil. *Grandeur?* An irrelevant criterion. If one is *near* heaven in the Catholic cathedral, he is *in* heaven in the sumptuous lamasery; for whereas the former uses common marble and paint, the latter employs pure gold, precious stones and lavish inlaid work. But what relevance is there between the architectural

---

1. For a rather competent proof of the fallibility of the popes, see David S. Schaff, *Our Fathers Faith and Ours*, (New York: G. P. Putnam's Sons, 1929), pp. 274ff. Popes endorsed errors, espoused heresy, condemned truth as error, made submission to their will a matter of salvation, lived corruptly, destroyed scholarship, fulminated and cursed with virulence, repudiated each other, endorsed witchcraft, sanctioned wars, annulled civil laws, and pronounced scientific opinion heretical.

structure of an institution and its claim to truth? The Son of God had no place where to lay his head. He was at home in the tent or the lean-to, for the Father's immensity could not be localized in so small a space as a temple or synagogue. The true worshipers worship the Father in spirit and in truth.

As the existing individual commences to come to himself, therefore, he is smitten in heart at the way his own sinfulness brought on axiological blindness. Since the moment he walked into the Catholic cathedral in his search for deeper insights into truth, he has been as a pig with a ring in its snout. Under the spell of ancillary evidences the heart lost sight of everything it had already learned through its costly venture in axiology. Since the mountain-high pile of evidences for the infallibility of the Roman Catholic church are, whether taken separately or collectively, but mere subtle immediacies, the self is ashamed to think that it could have been impressed by the lure of institutional security.

After reading the venturesome life of John Henry Newman, the penitent reaches the conclusion that there is only one way to find peace within the church, and that is by a clear persuasion of her divine authority. Once he believed that the Catholic Church is the oracle of God, Newman had no difficulty accepting all the doctrines of the church. *This is the real issue*. The Roman organization is making claims to divinity, and *it is in reference to such a pretension that her veraciousness is to be evaluated*. As the hands of the priest elevate the host on the altar, the church exercises a power to manipulate God Almighty. All which Christ did, she can do. She has the authority both to forgive and to withhold forgiveness of sins; the power to communicate and excommunicate both individuals and nations; the power infallibly to interpret the will of God for men.

It is obvious, therefore, that there is *one* issue at stake in this question of becoming a Catholic. *Is the church a continuation of the incarnation?* When I see the church, do I see Jesus Christ in his saving ministry? When I am instructed by the church, am I instructed by the Holy Spirit? Do I hear the voice of the Father breaking through into history, saying, "This is my beloved church, hear you her." If this question can be settled, all else will fall in line, for everything else revolves about it.

B. *Research Continued*

Now that the self has regained axiological balance, it may lose no time in applying this crucial test to Catholicism. If anything is certain to the heart, it is that the clearest mark of truth is the fellowship of love; for the law of our being is exhausted in love. This is how the heart was able to recognize that Christ is God in the flesh, for God is love. Since the Catholic Church comes in the role of a perpetual incarnation, therefore, we should expect to learn from Roman doctrines and actions a perfect statement of the law of love. And if such love proves to be wanting, one can conclude that the continued incarnation is wanting likewise. "If I [or the Catholic Church] have prophetic powers, and understand all mysteries and all knowledge, and if I have all faith, so as to remove mountains, but have not love, *I am nothing.*" (I Corinthians 13:2)

Perhaps the most expeditious way to understand Rome's relation to the law of love is to examine what she has done with the doctrine of imputed righteousness. Both Scripture and experience have thus far led the heart to realize that when the law of love is our standard, the only way a final righteousness before God can be attained is by a gracious imputation of the righteousness of Jesus Christ. Self-love and pride make personal attainment of righteousness impossible. God, therefore, has determined to save men by grace, never by good works. All glory belongs to his Son, and none to the generations of mankind. "For by grace you have been saved, through faith; and this is not your own doing, it is the gift of God — not because of works, lest any man should boast." (Ephesians 2:8-9) When once we learn what Roman theologians have to say about imputed righteousness, we will immediately know what they likewise think of the primacy of the law of love.

If the existing individual has hitherto been shocked in his long venture into axiological suffering, the greatest recoil has yet to be experienced. Upon carefully examining the authoritative sources of Roman theology, the heart finds that Catholicism — which comes in the name of Christ — is not only *based* upon a system of good works, but that it is vitriolic in its rejection of the Biblical doctrine of imputation. This means that the ground of Christian hope is undermined in favor of institutional primacy.

> If any one saith, that men are justified, either by the sole imputation of the justice of Christ, or by the sole remission of sins, to the exclusion of the grace and the charity which is poured forth in their hearts by the Holy Ghost, and is inherent in them; or even that the grace, whereby we are justified, is only the favour of God: let him be anathema. [2]

The Scriptures teach that men are saved through the free mercy of God, while the Roman Catholic Church declares that this is the one way nobody is saved.

> When the goodness and loving kindness of God our Savior appeared, he saved us, not because of deeds done by us in righteousness, but in virtue of his own mercy, by the washing of regeneration and renewal in the Holy Spirit, which he poured out upon us richly through Jesus Christ our Savior, so that we might be justified by his grace and become heirs in hope of eternal life. This saying is sure. [3]

This affirmation is as persuasive and clear as is the Catholic denial of it. "If any one saith, that justifying faith is nothing else but confidence in the divine mercy which remits sins for Christ's sake; or, that this confidence alone is that whereby we are justified: let him be anathema."[4] How shall this disparity be resolved?

If the doctrine of imputed righteousness were taught sporadically — here and there (as it were) in Scripture — the heart might have reason to believe that the contradiction between

---

2. *The Canons and Decrees of the Council of Trent,* Sixth Session, Canon 11.
3. Titus 3:4-8.
4. *Council of Trent, ibid.,* Canon 12.

Catholicism and the Bible arises out of an incompetency upon the part of the interpreter himself. But the fact is that justification by faith in the finished work of Christ is the *only* soteriology taught in Scripture.

Ironically, the book of Romans was written to a church which was already confused about justification by faith. Could it be that Rome, not heeding Paul's letter, has for all these centuries been teaching the very error that the apostle tried to straighten out? The hypothesis has great plausibility. Paul taught in the first two and one half chapters of Romans that there is no difference between men: All are under sin. The law is so demanding in its absoluteness that either with the help of the grace of God (as in the case of the Jews who were entrusted with the oracles of God) or without it (as in the case of the Gentiles, born outside of the Israelitish faith), "None is righteous, no, not one." (Romans 3:10) God shut up all men within the severity of law that he might justify them freely through faith in Christ. The following is a crisp summary of Biblical soteriology:

> Now we know that whatever the law says it speaks to those who are under the law, so that every mouth may be stopped, and the whole world may be held accountable to God. For no human being will be justified in his sight by works of the law since through the law comes knowledge of sin. But now the righteousness of God has been manifested apart from law, although the law and the prophets bear witness to it, the righteousness of God through faith in Jesus Christ for all who believe. For there is no distinction; since all have sinned and fall short of the glory of God, they are justified by his grace as a gift, through the redemption which is in Christ Jesus, whom God put forward as an expiation by his blood, to be received by faith . . . . What becomes of our boasting? It is excluded. On what principle? On the principle of works? No, but on the principle of faith. For we hold that a man is justified by faith apart from the works of law.[5]

---

5. Romans 3:19-28. "Why then the law? It was added because of transgressions, till the offspring should come to whom the promise had been made." Galatians 3:19. "The scripture consigned all things to sin, that what was promised to faith in Jesus Christ might be given to those who believe." Galatians 3:22.

Unless one deliberately destroys the rights of language itself, he cannot deny the Biblical teaching of imputed righteousness.

What can account for Roman Catholic impatience with justification by faith? Observe the unpersuasive way that Catholic writers dismiss this doctrine as but a fabrication of Luther to justify a torpid and carnal way of life.

> The Catholic doctrine on this point is in direct opposition to the strange theories of Protestantism. Faced by his failure to control his violent and sensuous character, Luther evolved a theory which is a combination of pessimism and easy optimism . . . . For Luther taught that if only we will have complete confidence that the merits of Christ are actually applied to us, our sins are ignored, as it were, by God; our souls remain indeed hideous in themselves, but God covers them over with the merits of Christ so that these are looked upon by him as being ours; our sins are not 'imputed' to us, but the merits of Christ are.[6]

Nothing could be less scholarly and less in accord with the facts than this indictment against Luther.[7] Why not put the blame on the Apostle Paul where it belongs? He devoted both Romans and Galatians to the doctrine of imputed righteousness.

The impatience of the church with the Pauline teaching becomes clearer when one probes into the soteriology of Catholicism. At this point the outlook of the pilgrim passes into sheer wonder, for Catholic theologians have deliberately removed the absolute law of love — declaring it too difficult for a man to fulfill in this life — and in its place substituted a more domesticated code of ceremonies. The exchange is authorized by what is called "Pelagianism," the theory that a law has no demands on a person unless he is capable of fulfilling it. And since our nature suffers from a defect which inclines us toward selfishness, it follows that we cannot meaningfully be

---

6. George D. Smith (Ed.), *The Teaching of the Catholic Church*, (New York: The Macmillan Company, 1949), Vol. I, p. 550.

7. See David Schaff, *op. cit.*, pp. 503ff for a convincing answer to this baseless charge against Luther.

responsible for the law of love. An obligation which man cannot meet constitutes no true obligation at all.

> The Catholic observes: Either it is possible for man,
> strengthened and exalted by the Divine aid, to observe the
> moral law, in its spirit, its true inward essence, or it is im-
> possible to do so. If the former be the case, then, undoubt-
> edly, such observance cannot be too strongly urged; and
> every one may find a proof for its possibility in the fact, that,
> on every transgression of the law, he accuses himself as a
> sinner: for every accusation of such a kind involves the sup-
> position that its fulfillment is possible, and even, with assist-
> ance from above, not difficult. But if the latter be the case,
> then the cause must be sought for only in God and in such a
> way, that either the Almighty hath not framed human nature
> for the attainment of that moral standard which He proposes
> to it, or He doth not impart those higher powers, which are
> necessary to the pure and not merely outward, but internal,
> compliance with His laws. In both cases, the cause of the
> nonfulfillment lies in the Divine will; that is to say, God is
> represented as not willing that His will should be complied
> with, which is self-contradictory. But in any case, there could
> be no conceivable guilt in respect to this non-obedience to the
> law, and, accordingly, there could be, notwithstanding the
> non-observance of the Divine precepts, no obstacle to the
> attainment of eternal felicity.[8]

It should be noticed that the argument here outlined by Möhler
fails to include the Biblical alternative, namely, that it has
pleased God to close men up to the performance of a law higher
than they can meet, in order that he might redeem them freely
through grace. This omission is extremely significant.

The Pelagian position is successful only as a rationally conceived *a priori,* not as a carefully defined hypothesis to account
for the data of both Scripture and our daily experience. Evaluated in isolation of experience, it is as persuasive in fields of
morals as Zeno's arguments against motion are in the realm
of philosophy. It appears to be a truism that law cannot bind
us unless we have the capacity of living in accord with it.

---

8. John Adam Möhler, *Symbolism; or Exposition of the Doctrinal Differences Between Catholics and Protestants,* (New York: Edward Dunigan,
1844), p. 250.

Is the blind man responsible for seeing color, or the deaf man for hearing harmonies? Do not civil courts function on the presupposition that there is no guilt when there is no power to observe the law? Why, then, should we suppose that God's moral economy operates independently of this principle?

Catholic divines are unambiguous in their denial that it does. "If any one saith, that the commandments of God are, even for one that is justified and constituted in grace, impossible to keep: let him be anathema."[9] "If precepts are impossible, they oblige no one, and hence the precepts are not precepts. Neither is it possible to devise wherein any one sins in respect to that which is impossible to avoid."[10]

The first response of the heart — though by no means the most telling in its effect — is the advice, Physician heal yourself. If one is to take the Pelagian argument seriously, he cannot at the same time take Roman Catholicism seriously; for the former defends a principle which, if true, cancels out the very *raison d'être* for the latter. Observe, if you will, the reason for baptism. Catholic theology teaches that everyone born of woman receives the inherited stains of Adam's sin in his nature and thus, in his unbaptized condition, is lost and undone. So important is baptism, therefore, that even non-Catholic nurses are encouraged to sprinkle water on a newborn child which may die. And should there be forced a choice between the death of the mother or that of the infant, consistent Catholics choose the mother's decease every time. She has had a chance to be baptized, while the child has not. Death in an unbaptized state hurls the child into limbo. Even baptism by stealth is better than letting the infant fall short of the

9. *Council of Trent,* Sixth Session, Canon 18. "In modern times, some men have endeavoured to come to the aid of the old orthodox Lutheran doctrine, by assuring us that the moral law proposes to men an ideal standard, which, like everything ideal, necessarily remains unattained. If such really be the case with the moral law, then he who comes not up to it, can as little incur responsibility, as an epic poet for not equalling Homer's Iliad." Möhler, *op. cit.,* p. 251.

10. Bellarmine, *De Justificatione,* iv. 10.

glories of heaven.[11] But what could be more obviously contradictory than a simultaneous affirmation of the following
propositions: (a) There is no precept unless that precept can
be kept; (b) All infants are responsible for the sin of Adam.
If one accepts the presuppositions of Pelagianism, how can
he believe at the same time that the infant, whose tiny fingers
are yet incapable to grasp a bottle of warm milk, is responsible
for sin and can be justly condemned to limbo by God on that
ground? This seems close to complete nonsense.

> A sinfulness which is as much that of the race as of the
> individual, which depends on a freedom quite different from
> the power to choose between good and ill, which is 'intro-
> duced into the human situation' and made inevitable by a
> 'force of evil prior to any human action,' is devoid of rele-
> vance to the conduct of individual lives; and for that reason
> alone it must stand discredited at the bar of ethics. [12]

Therefore, since she rejects the proposition that a person can
be held responsible for precepts which he cannot meet, it follows that the Roman Church is sawing off the very limb she
is sitting on. If there is no meaning in holding the race responsible for a sinful tendency which Adam initiated, it follows that mankind is relieved of any need for remedial grace.
What call is there for the sacraments of the Roman Church?
Obviously, there is none.

> Against the doctrine that the best works of the believer are
> imperfect, the Romanists are especially denunciatory. And
> with good reason. It subverts their whole system, which is
> founded on the assumed merit of good works. If the best
> works of the saints merit 'justam opprobrii mercedem' (i.e.,
> condemnation), they cannot merit reward. Their argument
> on this subject is, that if the Protestant doctrine be true
> which declares the best works of the believer to be imperfect;
> then the fulfillment of the law is impossible; but if this be so,

11. See Paul Blanshard, *American Freedom and Catholic Power*, (Boston: The Beacon Press, 1949), p. 120.
12. H. D. Lewis, *Morals and the New Theology*, p. 68. "It does seem to
me beyond the range of reasonable controversy that no man can answer for
another's sins or be guilty of it." *Ibid.*, p. 76.

then the law is not binding; for God does not command im-possibilities. To this it may be answered . . . that the ob-jection is inconsistent with the doctrine of the Romanists themselves. They teach that man in his natural state since the fall is unable to do anything good in the sight of God, until he receives the grace of God communicated in baptism. According to the principle on which the objection is founded, the law does not bind the unbaptized. [13]

Catholic moral theory is artistically enmeshed with the Thomistic philosophy of "natural law." This law represents the sum total of those inclinations inherent in, and proper to, all objects in the created world. Creatures participate in the "eternal law" to the extent that they own an essential tendency toward the species imprinted in them by God. This participa-tion generates urges in a thing toward the fulfillment of its own essence — such as sexual relations, propagation of off-spring, and the nourishment of the young.

Out of the axiom of natural law emerges a basic moral dic-tum: *Good is to be done and evil is to be avoided.* There is a tendency in all natural beings toward the "good." The good is the sum total of those realizations which form the essence of a thing. Striving is good or bad in direct proportion to its realization of, or subtraction from, essentiality. The good is the natural; to oppose nature is to oppose the good.

Armed with this concept of morality, the Roman Catholic easily justifies a "natural" ground for selfishness, thus negat-ing *agape* as the abiding law which alone can exhaust the es-sential man. Observe the following way philosophy prepares for a theological vindication of selfishness:

Out of right love come a right will and good deeds; perverted love and distorted preferences are an offense against the universal moral order . . . . All things are good, but they are not equally good. The higher must be preferred to the lower, and on the pinnacle of the order of love is God, the highest good and the common good of all . . . . With respect to the order of love that affects persons, *man must love himself more than his neighbor.* This is simply the order of nature:

13. Charles Hodge, *Systematic Theology,* Vol. 3, p. 233.

that a thing first perfects itself and then shares its own perfection with others. The order of love is built on the order of nature which it perfects. Self-love comes before the love of neighbor for another reason: if self-love is based on self's participation in the divine goodness, then the neighbor is also to be loved because he is joined to this divine goodness. The neighbor is to be loved according to his proximity to God, *i.e.*, according to his perfection. Divine justice demands that we wish for everyone happiness according to his degree of perfection. *The neighbor is to be loved more intimately the more closely he is related to us,* and persons are closer to us the more they have an essential and not only an accidental relation to us. *Therefore blood relatives are to be loved more affectionately and are to be supported more than strangers, friends are to be loved more than enemies, the common good of many more than the private good of one individual,* provided this good is in the same sphere . . . . With respect to the object of the love, *the father is to be loved more than the children because of his greater resemblance to God,* since he is the procreating principle; but with regard to the closer union, *the children are to be loved more than the parents* . . . . As the effective and forming principle in procreation, *the father is superior to the mother, who is only the passive principle providing the formless matter.* Viewed objectively, the parents as principles are to be loved more than the spouse. [14]

The Catholic theologian is injecting on the moral level what the universalist introduced on the theological plane and the finitist on the cosmological. In all three cases a rational *a priori* is used to ascertain in advance the meaningful limits within which God must abide if he is to command our respect. The finitist says that God may not will to create idiots for his glory; the universalist denies that God may consign poten-

---

14. Hans Meyer, *The Philosophy of St. Thomas Aquinas,* (London, W. C., 1946), pp. 380-381. (Italics mine) Since the "natural man" is really not natural, but seriously depraved—for he is born into the world in a defective condition (Romans 5:12ff.)—the Herculean effort of Aristotle and Thomas to erect a natural theology upon a description of man's present tendencies rests on a false foundation. The inclination of man to love his friends more than his enemies, and close friends more than distant friends, is, Biblically, *sinful.* Our natural estate was destroyed with the fall of man. In heaven, where the truly natural will be expressed, we will love all men without discrimination.

tial sons to hell; and the Catholic rejects God's right to employ responsibility for *agape* love as that moral means by which men are reduced to humility and abjection before him. As can easily be seen, we are catapulted back into the problem of compossibility all over again. Pelagianism involves a disguised form of the problem of evil. Is it compossible that God be just and moral, and yet declare that we are responsible for keeping a law which we cannot fulfill? The Catholic is emphatic in his negation. God would be a square circle if he utilized such means. We can have confidence in God only to the extent that he is continuous with those rational and moral categories which we respect in nature.

Short work can be made of this Catholic rejection of *agape*. Having been redeemed from sin by the precious blood of Christ, Christians are ushered into a "filial" relation with the Godhead. As adopted children, we now *trust* God; he is our Father. To trust God means to transfer all loyalty, all devotion, and all obedience from ourselves to him alone. Applied to compossibility, trust means the following: Since God decrees that he is pleased to create blind men, the Christian rejoices in the perfection of the Father's will. Since God warns that those who trample his Son under foot will be cast into the lake of fire, the Christian, moved by a sense of the dignity of God's unalterable justice, agrees with God. And since God is pleased to bring many sons to self-despair by consigning them to a moral contradiction from which they cannot liberate themselves, the Christian meekly bows in respect. It *is* compossible that God be infinitely just, and yet that he oblige what we cannot do. Since we have God's word for it that he has closed us up to a law which we cannot fulfill, we *trust* him. *What God does is good because he does it.*

Pelagianism forces us to decide between the person of Jesus Christ, on the one hand, and a new immediacy, on the other. We may repose either in the persuasion of a rational *a priori* or the person of Jesus Christ. Let us not neglect to observe who is the real opponent of Pelagianism. *That one is Jesus Christ,* "You, therefore, must be perfect, as your heavenly Father is perfect." (Matthew 5:48) Even as it is Christ who supported the dogma that the Father may create both blind and deaf to his glory; even as it is Christ who solemnly warned that God will cast unrepentant sinners into hell; *so it is Christ who announced in the name of the Father that the rule which defines the essential man, and hence the code by which all men will be judged, is the law of selfless* love.   The *locus classicus* is Mark 12:28-34:

> And one of the scribes came up and heard them disputing with one another, and seeing that he answered them well, asked him, 'Which commandment is the first of all?' Jesus answered, 'The first is, "Hear, O Israel: The Lord our God, the Lord is one; and you shall love the Lord your God with all your heart, and with all your soul, and with all your mind, and with all your strength." The second is this, "You shall love your neighbor as yourself." There is no other commandment greater than these.' And the scribe said to him, 'You are right, Teacher; you have truly said that he is one, and there is no other but he; and to love him with all the heart, and with all the understanding, and with all the strength, and to love one's neighbor as oneself, is much more than all the whole burnt offerings and sacrifices.' And when Jesus saw that he answered wisely, he said to him, 'You are not far from the kingdom of God.' And after that no one dared to ask him any question.

Christ teaches that the *true* natural law is that rule of love which makes no distinction among men. We are to love our enemies as ourselves, thus expressing the high moral rectitude for which we were created.

Jesus *commended* the scribe for his submission to the rule of selfless love. The scribe knew in his heart of hearts that he dare not resist a morality pitched on the premise that all self-ishness is immoral.   He realized — as we have suggested elsewhere — *that one cannot argue for the privilege of being selfish without having a red face.* Conscience rhythmically beats its tom-tom sounds, warning that the instant we break from *agape* we retreat from the only dignities able to preserve self-hood. Since pride is *qualitative* stuff, it follows that the justification of any amount of it involves the vindication of all of it. Selfishness possesses an inward tendency to extend its own rights to infinity. The only way to restore a challenging moral ideal is to poison Pelagianism at its roots, denouncing all forms of pride and self-love as evil. Rather than speak of self-love as "natural," it would be far more Biblical — not to mention vastly more satisfying morally — to denominate it "sinful."

On the strength of this thought, the Christian quickly discards the optimistic attempt of Pelagianism to erect a parallel between a blind man's responsibility to see and a sinner's obligation to live selflessly. There is something within the soul which *obliges* us to admit that only perfection in love can define our free, moral possibilities. A spiritually sensitive man knows that he is at less than his best when he gives way to any pride, selfishness, or indifference. The blind man's defection is quite different from that languor which abides in the heart of a sinner. A blind person is inwardly conscious of no power which morally obliges him to see. There are no throbbings of responsibility in his breast.

Since it is the solemn duty of excellent philosophy to explain — not explain away — the data of critical experience, it follows that Pelagianism is not even good rationalism. Coherent philosophy must correlate the following complex facts of our experience: (a) We cordially assent to the full terms of the law of love; (b) We acknowledge there is a defect in our nature which prevents us from realizing this ideal; (c) We yet admit we are responsible for performing the ideal, for freedom is always capable of more charity than it ever fulfills. Whatever progress we have made toward perfect selflessness, freedom acknowledges its ability to reach yet higher expressions. The degrees of perfection in the assignment of love are infinite. And since we can always act more selflessly than we ever have done in the past, it follows that nothing short of absolute love can summarize our ideal obligations. If our duty is defined by a denominator lower than perfection, we once again face the questionable arrangement where men destroy morality by legalizing the privilege of being selfish.

These are the facts of our experience, and no philosophical *a priori* can alter them. "Facts are worth more than theories. If logic says that facts are not facts, there is something wrong with the logical argument. The facts of history must not be explained away out of deference to a theory which cannot fit them into itself without breaking."[15] Pelagianism is an *a priori* theory, not an *a posteriori* structure gained from a careful appraisal of the actual data experienced in life. Pelagianism must be rejected as detrimental to morals, therefore, since it encourages men to claim a right to be selfish.

We are actually forced to make a decision between the authority of Jesus Christ and that of a Pelagian church. And for the person who has already met the one who passed through the pains of the second death on his behalf, the decision is extremely easy. We gladly trust the means which God employed in effecting our salvation, for we ourselves have been saved through them. We have experienced the self-despair which results from assenting to a law more demanding than we can ever meet; and out of this desperation the saving arm of grace has come. When the end achieved is so satisfying, a regenerated heart is grateful to the one who so wisely chose the means. By what finer means could the fellowship be gained? Personal self-despair must always precede the rendering of an apology. The law has taught us both the limits of what we are able to do and the perfection of the one who finally fulfilled the law's measure. "Now before faith came, we were confined under the law, kept under restraint until faith should be revealed. So that the law was our custodian until Christ came, that we might be justified by faith." (Galatians 3 :23-24)

> Loved with an everlasting love,
>   Led by grace that love to know;
> Spirit, breathing from above,
>   Thou hast taught me it is so!

15. Richardson, *The Gospel and Modern Thought*, p. 75.

Oh, this full and perfect peace!
Oh, this transport all divine!
In a love which cannot cease,
I am His, and He is mine.

Those who have experienced the love of God in their hearts, rather than *objecting* to God's pleasure in using the means of the law to bring us to Christ, have jointly cried, "Thanks to God for his inexpressible gift!" (II Corinthians 9:15) If we are not subject to blame for the whole law, then Christ did not take the fulfillment of the whole law upon him on the cross. But Christ in fact did; and since he performed in our stead, he accomplished what we were responsible for doing but failed so to do.

What consolation is there to gain the authority of the Roman Catholic Church after losing the authority of our Savior, Jesus Christ? Holiness, like water, can rise no higher than its source. If Christ is not veracious when he tells us that we are responsible for fulfilling the law of fellowship, then he is incompetent to be the founder and head of the church. How can a church be the incarnation extended, if there was no incarnation in the first place? A Christ who speaks untruth at one point is infinitely less than God at all points.

III. Catholic Perfection

Only he who has felt the heavy sword of the law hanging over him has learned to confess, "Christ my righteousness." The Roman Catholic, befogged by a Pelagian view of responsibility, can never come to complete self-despair. He can only cry, "Christ *part* of my righteousness."

A. *The Root of Perfection*

Whereas the Biblical writers consistently assert that the perfection of a justified man resides in Christ alone, Catholic divines are pleased to define justification as the infusing of grace into the sinner, thus constituting such an one a perfect person. In Roman theology to justify means not "to *pronounce* righteous," but "to *make* righteous." While it may seem to the untutored that this distinction is but a case of theological logomachy, the fact is that in this slight terminological variation lies the difference between a system of faith and a system of good works. Catholic soteriology is built upon the hypothesis of infused, rather than imputed, righteousness.

It is the uniform experience of all who have come to Christ for saving mercy that *in Christ* they are sinlessly perfect, while *in themselves* they remain unclean. Since the heart of a Christian has been regenerated, he enjoys holy affections. Yet, a defect in his will remains, for though he cordially assents to the mind of Christ, he finds that it is not possible to match that decision with perfection in act. And since absolute perfection is a good will coupled with good actions, it follows that saving goodness resides in Christ, not in the Christian.

Both sides of this experience are reiterated in Scripture. On the one hand faith brings an absolute perfection in Christ: "There is therefore now no condemnation for those who are in Christ Jesus. For the law of the Spirit of life in Christ Jesus has set me free from the law of sin and death." (Romans 8:1-2) "No one born of God commits sin; for God's nature abides in him, and he cannot sin because he is born of God." (I John 3:9) On the other hand the regenerated individual remains imperfect in himself: "If we say we have no sin, we deceive ourselves, and the truth is not in us." (I John 1:8) "For I know that nothing good dwells within me, that is, in my flesh. I can will what is right, but I cannot do it. For I do not do the good I want, but the evil I do not want is what I do. Now if I do what I do not want, it is no longer I that do it, but sin which dwells within me." (Romans 7:18-20)

A perfect moral tension results: All *attainment* is achieved by Christ, while all *attaining* is accomplished by the regenerated individual out of a love for what Christ has already done. Until the day of his death the Christian seeks to die daily unto sin and live unto righteousness; and all out of a love for Christ and a holy desire to do his will. Righteousness *in fact* belongs to Christ alone, while righteousness *in principle* belongs to all men of faith. "But far be it from me to glory except in the cross of our Lord Jesus Christ, by which the world has been crucified to me, and I to the world." (Galatians 6:14)

Even if we did not gain a knowledge of this moral tension through special revelation, we could come very close to it through a study of our daily experience. If we do not assent to the law of love, we corrupt our own self-dignity; for we acknowledge we were made unto fellowship. And if we do assent to that law, we face the impasse of having committed ourselves to something which we can never in actions match; for there is a flaw in our will which makes it impossible to quench self-love. We cannot, so to speak, jump out of our skins. As the forms of time and space are to Kant's epistemology, so self-love and personal interest are to our decision life.

In sum, neither the Scriptures nor the heart knows of any possessed perfection save that found in Christ. *A good will is not perfection.* We are perfect only when we mediate the law of love with infinite exactness in our daily lives. We are holy *in fact* only when we live according to the same law to which we give assent in our will. No wonder the followers of Christ cried, "Who then can be saved?"

The Roman Catholic, however, knows of *two* loci of perfection. The one is in Christ and the other is in the recently baptized Christian. "The Council lays it down that we become just before God not through a non-imputation of sin but by an interior renovation which blots out sin. This is effected by sanctifying grace, which is explained as a reality poured forth upon us and inhering in us."[16] "Justification is an act of God declaring and *making* a person just."[17]

> The Council of Trent. . .represents justification as a renewal of the inward man, by means whereof we become really just, as inherent (*inhaerens*) in the believer, and as a restoration

---

16. George D. Smith (Ed.), *op. cit.*, p. 551.
17. Donald Attwater (Ed.), *A Catholic Dictionary*, (New York: The Macmillan Company, 1949), p. 272.

of the primeval state of humanity. On this account, the same synod observes, that, by the act of justification, Faith, Hope, and Charity, are infused into the heart of man; and that it is only in this way he is truly united with Christ, and becometh a living member of His body. In other words, justification is considered to be sanctification and forgiveness of sins, as the latter is involved in the former, and the former in the latter: it is considered an infusion of the love of God into our hearts, through the Holy Spirit; and the interior state of the justified man is regarded as holy feeling — as a sanctified inclination of the will — as habitual pleasure and joy in the Divine law — as a decided and active disposition to fulfil the same in all the occurrences of life — in short, as a way of feeling, which is in itself acceptable and well-pleasing to God. When God declares man to be just and well-pleasing to Him, he really is so.[18]

A Catholic is perfect if his reigning dispositions form a holy feeling.

But one problem remains: If both Christ and the baptized Catholic are perfect, what is the moral difference between the two? If the latter died on the cross for our sins, would it be a perfect sacrifice? The answer to this is surprising. Although both Christ and the baptized Catholic are perfect in themselves, *each is perfect according to his own order of being*. In other words, Christ perfectly fulfilled the law of *agape* love, and thus attained absolute perfection; while the other attains only to "Christian" perfection, a holiness commensurate with the abilities of Adam's original nature. Thus, Pelagianism and justification join hands to form a perfection which is really not perfection.

When describing the state of a justified-sanctified person, the Council of Trent is referring to Christian, rather than absolute, perfection. Christian holiness is based, not on the law of love, but upon the Pelagian axiom *pro hujus vitae statu*. Since it would be contrary to rationality for God to require more of human nature than it is capable of attaining, God

---

18. Möhler, *op. cit.,* pp. 188-189.

defines perfection according to our abilities. The outcome
of Catholic theology is a law which has been trimmed down
in its demands to fit our powers, a code of charity and good
works which all Christians may, even as many do, fulfill. *God
declares a man just who has done all that can "justly" be required of him.* And so a straight line can be drawn from
Bellarmine to Channing, for each has reinterpreted Biblical
doctrine according to a rationalism gained independent of
careful exegesis.

Beyond this generic Christian perfection lies a "religious"
perfection gained by the saints. The saints are so perfect, in
fact, that virtue from their good works flows over into the
"treasury of merit" in the church; from which point it is
rationed out (for a financial fee)[19] either to those in life who
are on the way to complete sanctification or to the writhing
souls in purgatory who, regretfully, were unsolicitous about
the temporal punishment of their sins.

> The Roman system teaches that good works in excess of
> what the Gospel requires may be performed and thereby
> extra merit secured. These works, which are called works
> of supererogation from the Latin word meaning 'more than
> is demanded,' have in themselves grace. It is as if a school-
> boy were marked 100 plus, that is, perfection and something
> more.[20]

But this saintly perfection is still not to be confused with the
perfection of Jesus Christ, for it likewise is measured only by
a law commensurate with human nature, and not the absolute
law of fellowship in Mark 12. A canonized saint is a *sinner*
when judged by the absolute law, though *more than perfect*
when measured by the law of good works. Catholic theology
results in the equivocation that perfect men are fully perfect
by one law, but want in perfection by another. A man would

---

19. "For a Mass with the name announced, the fee in Brooklyn in 1948
was $5; for a Mass with one priest singing part of the Mass the fee was
$15; for a High Mass with three priests, $35; for lights at different altars,
$5 at each altar"; etc. Blanshard, *op. cit.,* p. 37. This is somewhat different
from the Master, who gave out the water and the bread of life *freely.*
20. David Schaff, *op. cit.,* pp. 506-507.

not be just if he were not just in fact; yet it is the justified man who is still a sinner.

> If anyone denies, that, by the grace of our Lord Jesus Christ, which is conferred in baptism, the guilt of original sin is remitted; or even asserts that the whole of that which has the true and proper nature of sin is not taken away; but says that it is only rased, or not imputed; let him be anathema . . . . But this holy synod confesses and is sensible, that in the baptized there remains concupiscence, or an incentive, (to sin) ; which, whereas it is left for our exercise, cannot injure those who consent not, but resist manfully by the grace of Jesus Christ . . . . This concupiscence, which the apostle sometimes calls sin, the holy Synod declares that the Catholic Church has never understood it to be called sin, as being truly and properly sin in those born again, but because it is of sin, and inclines to sin.[21]

The spiritual anatomy of the baptized Catholic, therefore, is that of a holy will sitting in judgment over the lower tendencies in the nature. If enough grace is solicited, the will can perfectly resist all of the overtures to yield to these tendencies, and so continue to enjoy the perfection gained through baptism. The perversity of sensuality, thus, is independent of the will, for the will can look objectively on sensuality, weighing, evaluating, and deciding either for or against it. Concupiscence is but the temptation, the tendency to sin; the sin is the decision to yield to its overtures. "If, accordingly, there be no consent, then there is no sin."[22] When Potiphar's wife tried to seduce Joseph, for example, he was able to retain his integrity by leaving his garment in her hand and fleeing. (Genesis 39:12)

The difficulty with this psychology of sinning (as Joseph would be the first to testify) is that in recoiling from temptation the will is never perfectly pure. The man who turns aside from the woman asking him to lie with her does so only after an antecedent moral struggle in his own nature. He may have fled from the act of fornication, but when he is safe in

---

21. *Council of Trent*, Fifth Session, Decree Concerning Original Sin.
22. Möhler, *op. cit.*, p. 192.

the fields he must admit that it was a narrow escape. So prone is man to indulgence that a wise person will deliberately turn aside from scenes of nakedness, fearing lest sinful desires temporarily seize the hegemony over his reigning spiritual affections. The will *never* disaffiliates itself from temptations with perfect moral purity. And the proof of this is the urgent cry upon the part of the will for balancing powers in grace. If a sinful power in the will did not already incline us to sin, there would be no struggle within the individual to overcome sin. Jesus Christ, whose will was pure (since his nature was completely holy), resisted sin in his human nature with a perfect revulsion, being completely upset by sin's disgustedness. But no man can honestly assert that he resists sin with that same perfection. We *resist* sin, indeed; and thanks be to God for enabling us to do it. But too often our triumph in holiness is a photo finish, for we emerge from severe temptations with beads of perspiration on our brow, so close was our brush with sin.

If the will in the regenerated man is not defective in part, why is it such a struggle for him to perform the will of God? Study the following proposition, for example:

> He said also to the man who had invited him, 'When you give a dinner or a banquet, do not invite your friends or your brothers or your kinsmen or rich neighbors, lest they also invite you in return, and you be repaid. But when you give a feast, invite the poor, the maimed, the lame, the blind, and you will be blessed, because they cannot repay you. You will be repaid at the resurrection of the just.'[23]

Who has ever willed to follow out this precept in actions? *Let him speak up.* And if there be a lone voice to break the evening silence, let him remember that when he gave one of these famous dinners his motives were not purely moral; for compounded with his presumed outward charity was the warm and comfortable (sinful) feeling in the heart either that he had performed all righteousness before God or that the ap-

23. Luke 14:12-14.

plause of men was received. Whenever we lavish our table with rich food, a turpitude within us fights violently against inviting other than those whose social status will reflect on the security of our ego. We do not naturally favor feting those outside the circle of our friends. Whoever holds a repast for the outcast in the community does so only after an inner moral struggle.

But if the will is not defective, why the conflict? Why is it not natural for us to perform this high service of charity? Why the preparatory discipline? Why the feeling that we are deploying our opportunities imprudentially if we do not favor those who can favor us? And why, when we do perform Christ's will, do we seek the favor of men in addition? Observe the proud bishop who once a year washes the feet of a poor member of his parish: He washes the feet, to be sure, but only after reporters from the local paper have been advised of his unprecedented piety. The act is always much easier to perform when one knows that a large release will appear in a syndicated news column.

The deficiency of Catholic psychology is its gross oversimplification. Our moral struggle is a wretchedly complex affair. We seem to have two wills, in fact (though there is but one); one which assents affectionately to the word and will of God, and another which assents affectionately to the persuasions of sin. The reason why it is easy to hypothesize the existence of two separate wills is that, though our reigning affections are for God, they are never heeded independently of the voice of the minor, evil affections holding the power of veto in the soul. A man often comes to the very edge of sinfulness, confessing that his reigning affections lie on the side of righteousness and that he hates both himself and his actions; yet finally yielding to the lure of the minor will by capitulating to the temptation. This ambivalence is experienced every day in the hearts of all who are struggling with a besetting sin. And whom does this category exclude? Never once do we triumph over sin but what we glance over our left shoulder with a very slight — but nevertheless real — regret that we cannot remain holy before God and enjoy our sin, too.

Actually there is but one will, for it is the whole man who sometimes commits sin and sometimes prays for pardon for sin. But the point is that the will is not a neutral directive power which mysteriously hovers midway between the inner recesses of the heart and the opposing powers of concupiscence — a sort of uniformed moral engineer having the responsibility of turning valves off and on. The ego *is* the will; the will *is* the ego. In the nature of the person surrendered to Christ, therefore, the reigning feelings lie on the side of the right; while a minor, but powerful, set of affections lie on the side of sin. And since these two sets of powers *are* the ego, and not something in addition to it, it follows that the will is likewise composed of these elements. We choose whatever our nature prefers; we act in preference to whatever affections are dominant in the heart at a given instant. In other words, we will holy things because we are holy; even as we will outlets for pride and greed because we are sinful. We are both holy and sinful.

Except during revival moments of prayer and contrition, there is no time in our conscious life when we are exempt from the ambivalence in our will to favor the good while yet flirting with evil. Even when we draw apart from the world to break the force of sin within us completely, we only add sin to sin. The law of life is not quietism; it consists in the active expression of selflessness through a positive love both to God and to man. Since we prove our faith by active charity, faith without works is dead. But the moment we turn to such charity, the powers of self-love within us rise to ascendancy and we realize once again that we are not acting out of purely moral motives. When the priest performs his office before the laity, *e. g.,* his acts are never initiated solely by a will to glorify God. There is the prestige of the flesh which acts as a catalytic agent, inducing finer and more precise actions. This is proved by the fact that the sermon is always easier to give, the gospel always easier to read, when the church is full. And the ease is not simply due to better acoustics. As with every actor, the ego is more secure when more eyes are upon it. Likewise, when the laic drops a dollar into the plate, either the name is put on the envelope, so the ego can get full credit on the church books for this extremely generous act; or, if no envelope is used, the bill is so held that not only is the left hand able to see what the right hand is doing, but the whole pew can in addition. And if the bill is hid from the others, then the individual is proud of his own humility. Every committee chairman is replete with pride over the good work he is doing for the cause — though the actual facts are never able to support this boastful contention.

> The actual situation is that man may be redeemed from self-love in the sense that he acknowledges the evil of it and recognizes the love of God as the only adequate motive of conduct, and may yet be selfish in more than an incidental sense. The pride of a bishop, the pretensions of a theologian, the will-to-power of a pious business man, and the spiritual arrogance of the church itself are not mere incidental defects, not merely 'venial' sins. They represent the basic drive of self-love, operating upon whatever new level grace has pitched the new life. Pure love is 'by faith' in the sense that only when man, in prayer and contemplation, is lifted beyond himself does he have a vantage point from which self-love does not operate. In action the power of self-love is mixed with the new power of the love of God which grace has established.[24]

In the Catholic catalogue of evils one finds a simple distinction drawn between mortal and venial sins (not to mention the "peccadilloes"). However, neither Scripture nor experience can support this easy division of evil. Except for blasphemy against the Holy Spirit (Matthew 12:31), the Scriptures recognize no grades of sinfulness. Since all transgression is directed against infinite holiness, each sin deserves death. The difference between thinking about fornication and actually committing the act, is but quantitative, for guilt is present in both cases. In the list of sins which Paul draws up, thus,

24. Reinhold Niebuhr, *Human Destiny*, p. 137.

nothing is mentioned even to hint that self-love is a venial and murder a mortal sin. *All sins are mortal.*

> They were filled with all manner of wickedness, evil, covetousness, malice. Full of envy, murder, strife, deceit, malignity, they are gossips, slanderers, haters of God, insolent, haughty, boastful, inventors of evil, disobedient to parents, foolish, faithless, heartless, ruthless. Though they know God's decree that those who do such things deserve to die, they not only do them but approve those who practice them.[25]

"For men will be lovers of self, lovers of money, proud, arrogant, abusive, disobedient to their parents, ungrateful, unholy, inhuman, implacable, slanderers, profligates, fierce, haters of good, treacherous, reckless, swollen with conceit, lovers of pleasure rather than lovers of God." (II Timothy 3:2-4) In this enumeration of sins no difference is drawn between a sin unto, and a sin not unto, death; for *coram deo* all sins are deadly. The only way one can divide sins into venial and mortal is by overlooking the fact that inward pride and self-love — which cannot be processed by the machinery of the confessional because of their infinite shades — are actually our worst sins, being the breeding ground for all other sins. If it were not for self-love, there would be no murder or fornication. Catholicism cannot take self-love seriously, however, otherwise its program of Christian and religious perfection would collapse; for it would immediately understand that the most strenuous act of charity is compounded with the sullying powers of pride and egocentricity.

The conscience which has been enlightened by Jesus Christ refuses to accede to a perfection within sinfulness, for the law which we are obliged to keep is the law of love; and not keeping it perfectly, we have no claim to perfection. We must be perfect in the same way that our Father in heaven is perfect. And God is not perfect because negatively he does not murder or commit adultery; he is perfect because he is love in his very person. In like manner, man is perfect only when he — in his

---

25. Romans 1:29-32.

own order — has destroyed inordinate pride and self-love by a perfect love to God and a selfless devotion to man.

> Beloved, let us love one another; for love is of God, and he who loves is born of God and knows God. He who does not love does not know God; for God is love. In this the love of God was made manifest among us, that God sent his only Son into the world, so that we might live through him. In this is love, not that we loved God but that he loved us and sent his Son to be the expiation for our sins. Beloved, if God so loved us, we also ought to love one another.[26]

In no act do we ever resist sinfulness with perfection. There is always an element of pride in the will which toys with an option before sin is fully defeated. This is our experience. And it is not just a "sinful tendency." *It is sin. We are responsible for its presence because we never disaffiliate ourselves from it with the consistency of which we are capable.* We fraternize with pride, incompletely resisting it, and thus in no instance is the will ever exempt from the charge of responsibility. We always have greater potentialities for selflessness than we ever utilize.

In other words, our experience testifies — in agreement with Scripture and in disagreement with Catholic theology — *that we sin because we are sinners. We are not sinners because the will elects to sin.* Our nature has sin in it; our will is an accomplice in its performance. The transcendent self cordially assents to the law of love, but the involved self never expresses complete selflessness in act; for no act is ever uncompounded with the perverse powers of self-love and pride. Because our hearts condemn us, therefore, Pelagianism cannot persuade us that we are not responsible for what we cannot help doing. It happens to be true to experience that we *are* responsible for the present attainment of a moral perfection which *de facto* can be reached only by infinite degrees. Perfection in love *is* a possibility which we assent to as commensurate with our own nature.

---

26. I John 4:7-11.

> We cannot be required to do what is impossible because of
> the limitation of our nature as creatures, as to create a world,
> or raise the dead; but to love God perfectly does not exceed
> the power of man as he came from the hands of his maker.
> It is not absolutely, but only relatively impossible . . . to us
> not as men, but as sinners.[27]

Because it encourages us to become self-satisfied, Pelagianism
serves as a perfect framework for the sins of pretension. The
instant a moral relativity is crowned as a moral finality, that
moment the partial is converted into the integral, and new and
more boastful prides and pretensions are generated. Is there
anyone more intolerably haughty than the self-righteous man
who, quite without justification, believes he has attained moral
and spiritual perfection? His sinfulness is particularly unbounding because it is protected by a facade of religiosity.

B. *The Fruit of Perfection*

When the existing individual examines the outworking of
the Catholic theory of law, the last prospect vanishes that the
Roman Church is an extension of the incarnation, the repository of the mind of God and the immanent soul of the Holy
Spirit. Having already met Jesus Christ, it would be a step
backwards in the journey of suffering to transfer loyalty from
him to a visible institution. When we examine Christ, we
see the Father; but when we examine the church, we do not
see Christ. We see only an institution which claims, both for
herself and for those who rule, exemption from the absoluteness of the law. Thus, prides and pretensions are given institutional protection. By being more interested in the perpetua-
tion of a church than the exaltation of fellowship and love
through Jesus Christ, Rome exhibits a self-sufficiency and
haughtiness which, while characteristic of all earthly totalitarian systems, was quite unknown to the incarnate Son of God.

> The heresy of Rome is that it is fundamentally self-regard-
> ing. It is more concerned with the success of an institution

---

27. Hodge, *op. cit.*, pp. 233-234.

than with the creation of a single redemptive fellowship. Its heresy is that it identifies too simply a fallible and proud human institution with the Kingdom of God.[28]

Take, for example, the attribute of *holiness.* It is curious to watch anyone discuss his own piety, for the clearest attribute of a righteous man is that he never talks about his holiness. He is kept busy smiting his breast in lamentation over the piety of which he is deficient. Even Christ disclaimed to speak of his own holiness saying (on the grounds of his economical subordination to the Father and not of a want of perfect righteousness in himself) that there is only one who is good, the Father. The Catholic Church, however, edits volume after volume of apologetical material adorning the attribute of holiness.

It is true that out of Catholicism a steady stream of pious individuals has proceeded, and for this one can greatly rejoice. The church as an institution, however, has little right to pretend righteousness, for she has pursued ways of bloodshed, pride, intolerance, history, hatred, and will-to-power which hardly have a parallel. Rome's bloody inquisitions against heretics form pages in one of the most unhappy chapters of man's tragic history. Self-love thrives with too unchecked a virility and robustness within the Roman institution for her to claim the glory of being the incarnation of Christ continued throughout history. If *Christ* had come to earth bearing the characteristics which Rome now bears — dealing with non-conformists with the same totalitarian tactics — the heart would scorn him as a blasphemer and impostor; for no man can claim to be consanguineous with God unless at the same time he exhibits a flawless perfection of love in his own person. Natural light is sufficient to teach a man that human nature is complete only through fellowship and love.

When an institution which mediates the judgment of God upon all the ambiguities of historic existence claims that it has escaped those ambiguities by this mission, it commits the

---

28. Trueblood, *Alternative to Futility,* p. 44.

same sin which the prophets recognized so clearly as the sin of Israel. This sin becomes particularly apparent—and intolerable—when it expresses itself in political will-to-power; and it is mitigated only slightly by the achievements of universality which the historic church and papacy have to their credit. A 'Vicar of Christ,' who represents one among many competing social and political forces in history, cannot be a true representative of the Christ, who was powerless in history and in whom no particular cause or force in history triumphed or was vindicated. The fact that the papal-ecclesiastical power actually achieved a measure of impartiality and transcendence over warring nations and competing social forces and was thereby enabled to play a creative role in the history of the Western world may be recorded with gratitude. But it does not prove that the church was able to escape the mixture of creativity and corruption which characterizes all historic striving.[29]

Because she arrogates to herself prerogatives of judging infallibly, while at the same time claiming exemption from divine judgment, the church of Rome is able to define the good as whatever promotes her security. At no point in history can one detect purely moral motives in Catholic negotiations; for compounded with every spiritual crusade is a thirst for world domination. Rome's defense of the feudal-agrarian economy as containing the will of God for society is never purely moral; it is always commingled with sinful pledges to dominate, control, and subordinate. The end she seeks is not a loving fellowship among Christians with Jesus Christ as the mystical head, but a subordination of all men to the visible head, the pope. Catholic orders are united to advance *Catholicism,* not brotherly love and kindness to all.

Even in the contemporary picture — and in so unsuspecting an environment as America — convincing evidences are conspicuously on display that the Roman Church is concerned only with the security of Catholicism, not with the weightier things of the law: justice, mercy, faith. It is not without significance that Paul Blanshard's volume, *American Freedom and Catholic*

29. Niebuhr, *op. cit.,* p. 145. Cf., Paul Blanshard, *Communism, Democracy, and Catholic Power,* (Boston: Beacon Press, 1951).

Power, has become a "must" on the list of great modern books. Its documentation of Catholic ambitions to undermine our traditional religious freedom is so incontestable that reprisal and boycott are feared. The American press today is no longer free.

> American priests habitually use their pulpit to condemn any newspaper that publishes material critical of the Church, and they are particularly vehement in condemning any editor who publishes facts unfavorable to priests and nuns. Whenever a newspaper prints a news-story reflecting upon the character of a priest, local Catholic organizations, directed by priests, write, telephone and telegraph vigorous protests to the editor, and frequently approach the business office of the newspaper with threats to boycott the paper's advertisers. As a result of this policy of seige and boycott, very few publishers in the United States are courageous enough or wealthy enough to deal frankly with Catholic social policy or stories of priestly crime.[30]

The 1944 Archbishop Mitty case illustrates Catholic negotiations perfectly. Because the San Francisco *News* printed a true story about a priest who was arrested for drunken driving, Mitty sent out a dictatorial warning that if this antagonistic and bigoted press did not cease such activities, more strenuous means would be resorted to. Because the church claims to be the custodian of God's oracles, she pretends exemption from all judgment. She forgets that judgment must *begin* with the house of God.

Blanshard proves that the Roman Catholic Church is consciously seeking the religious control of America. By overseeing education, marriage, politics, the press, movies, and social-economic centers, the church has already worked herself into a position of advance prestige in this country. The Catholic goal is a final, religious totalitarianism where the state employs its power and finances to support and defend "the true religion." If the Catholic hierarchy should gain the powers it is aiming for — and it assures all that it will, either tomorrow or a century from tomorrow — a dictatorial system will so overlord our life that wholesome fellowship in Jesus Christ would

---

30. Blanshard, *American Freedom and Catholic Power,* p. 195.

be as difficult to enjoy then as it would be if communism gained the hegemony. Communism is more explosive than Catholicism, for it not only claims exemption from the law of love (as does Catholicism) but also from all law. The Christian heritage in the Catholic Church acts as a salt of conservativism to keep the program from early spoilage. But one would be very deluded if he supposed that fellowship under Catholic domination would be easier than under a secular dictatorship. The aim of the Vatican is to bring every national government under its control, until in the end Catholicism is the only tolerated religion in the world. The church does not plan to wait until the angels separate the tares and the wheat at the end of the age; she seeks to keep the garden well hoed as she goes along.

> In any Catholic state, schools receiving public funds would be either entirely Catholic or operated under Catholic moral supervision. Vituperative attacks on the clergy would be suppressed, and all books directly attacking the hierarchy or its doctrines would be forbidden. Non-Catholic sects would probably be permitted if they were relatively quiet and confined their ceremonies to their own property. The Church would have sole authority over the marriage and separation of Catholics, and complete veto power in censoring all books, magazines, newspapers and films. The Vatican would be the chief organ of international peacemaking and the Pope would be the world's highest arbiter. In each nation the Church would play the leading role in mediating between the propertied classes and organized labor.[31]

The pope often calls for schismatics to come home and rest within the fold of the true shepherd; but he obviously over-

31. Blanshard, *op. cit.*, p. 270. "Whenever any issue arises in Congress which may or might affect Catholic interests, a seasoned lobbyist in priestly garb is likely to appear in a Congressman's office, reminding the legislator that 26,000,000 Catholics in America feel such and so about this matter. Even when the legislator knows perfectly well that the opinion is actually that of a handful of top-ranking bishops, acting on orders from Rome, he may swallow his convictions and say 'Yes, yes,' because he knows that in American Catholicism the bishops speak for Catholic power. He knows also that Catholic pressure can be morally effective in swinging any close election against him." *Ibid.*, p. 29.

looks the fact that the heart has already met Jesus Christ and the true law of our being. Once the Son of God has announced the terms of both life and death, no earthly institution can alter them. To accept the primacy of an institution which claims to mediate the terms of salvation, but which itself refuses to be judged according to the divine law, involves more than a step backwards in the journey of suffering; it entails a deliberate betrayal of the person of Jesus Christ himself. Having already received his sure word, we would simply be telling the Son that we cannot trust him. And this the existing spirit once and for all refuses to do.

> We would be more secure if the Roman Catholic Church were anxious with us under the divine judgment and not so anxious about us. We would be willing to dispense with the assurance of its fatherly forgiveness toward us if we were certain that it sought divine forgiveness with us for the evils in which we have been jointly involved.... The Roman church has a favorite explanation of all the ills of modern life. They are due to mankind's departure from 'God's Plan' as incorporated in the church. We have an equally plausible explanation, not for all the ills of the modern world but for a serious aggravation of all our difficulties. The animosities of modern men are exacerbated on the one hand by the priest-kings of a secular religion who make ridiculous pretensions of omniscience and omnipotence from the Kremlin; and on the other hand by priests of a true religion who give the final glory to God but meanwhile are too certain that they are privy to his counsels and the sole dispensers of his grace.[32]

The urge for institutional security is basically sinful. Under the old economy, for example, God promised his covenant children that he would guard over them directly. But the Israelites, lusting after a security which was quantitatively measurable, demanded that they be given a king like unto that of their neighbors. Refusing God's invisible guidance in the heart, therefore, they brought down a pot of boiling water upon them.

---

32. Reinhold Niebuhr, "The Pope's Domesticated God," *The Christian Century*, January 18, 1950, p. 75.

It took the form of a tyrant who was prone to use God's law to judge everybody but himself. From that time Israelitish history was a sequence of sorrow and trouble.

One need be no prophet to realize that the spirit of a God-fearing man will be brought into no small vexation as a result of exchanging the invisible Lordship of Christ for the measurable security of a church which claims exemption from judgment. *When an organization pretends that there is no voice of divine condemnation against its own sins — be it communism or Catholicism — one must take care. There is no sinfulness quite so intolerable as that which pretends to enjoy divine approval.*

The incongruity which subsists between Jesus Christ and the Catholic ideal can be perfectly illustrated from one of the religious street scenes during the Reformation. The skit is in two parts. In the first there rides a poorly dressed man with a kindly face — humble, meek, sitting on the back of a shabby donkey, and exchanging loving glances of sympathy and pity of all.

"Pray, who can this one be?" demanded a bewildered bystander, clutching his own rich clothing in shame. The sight of such love incarnate brings him under swift judgment.

"This is the Son of Almighty God."

In the second scene there appears a breath-taking setting of gorgeous medieval splendor. A color guard precedes the gaily adorned, highly borne chair of inlaid jewels and gold, draped with the finest tapestries and silks obtainable. High and elevated above those bearing him — that all might understand his incontestable exaltation among men — sat a heavily robed, richly crowned lord. It was the pope.

"And sir, who can this one be?" inquired the bystander again, feeling a relief from judgment at the sight of one who apparently lived in the gaudy splendor he did.

"This is the Son's earthly representative."

IV. From Sympathy to Righteous Indignation

If ever the penitent must fall to his knees for prayer, praying God to give him grace that he may be loving and tolerant, it is now. We were assured that we would find peace and truth in the Roman Church, but what we finally received was a caricature of the mind of Christ. Patience may tolerate many errors and mistakes; but when a church excuses herself from divine criticism on the ground that she is the custodian of the whole counsel of God, spirit explodes within. Whoever uses the name of Christ to foster his own privileges and securities has crucified the Son in a new and unspeakably awful manner.

A. *The Supreme Example: Jesus Christ*

Just as the heart is about to cringe in shame over this posture of indignation, challenging the propriety of such impatience altogether, it suddenly awakens to the fact that the Master himself set a pattern of indignation. There may be a comfort in his example.

Since Christ bore all manner of spitting, mocking, scourging, and physical torture without raising a hand to defend himself, his example of tolerance and patience is a monument to holiness. When others lost their temper and rose to self-defense, Jesus Christ — mindful of his Messianic office — resigned himself to the will of the Father. "For to this you have been called, because Christ also suffered for you, leaving you an example, that you should follow in his steps. He committed no sin; no guile was found on his lips. When he was reviled, he did not revile in return; when he suffered, he did not threaten; but he trusted to him who judges justly." (I Peter 2:21-23) Regardless how awkward sinners were in their approach, how vile their language or repulsive their physical condition, Christ was always ready to love and receive them. When those about him reached for stones with which to kill, he forgave and blessed. The disciples were proud, blundersome, quick tempered, forgetful, easily provoked to jealousy, sensitive, and often given to discouragement; but Jesus never condemned or scolded them. Rather, he used their shortcomings as leverage to teach them the more perfect way of forgiveness and love.

On two separate occasions, however, the text of the gospels tells us that Christ, unable to restrain his holy reaction to sinful pretentiousness, released the surgings of righteous indignation. Let the contemporary mind note this well, for Christ (we must remember) was the one in whom the Father had perfect pleasure.

The first incident was after our Lord discovered that the Jews had converted God's holy temple into a merchandizing mart. He used physical force against the gear of the money-changers, deliberately overthrowing their tables and seats, crying, "It is written, 'My house shall be called a house of prayer'; but you make it a den of robbers." (Matthew 21:13) Note the ingredients which make up the incident: There were those who stood between the people and the free mercies of God, using spiritual things as a basis for augmenting their own sinful securities.

The second, and more moving, occasion, was when Jesus collided with the scribes and Pharisees. Immediately prior to the giving of the Olivet Discourse and the making of final preparations for the pains of the second death, Christ resorted to barbed denunciations to express his inner feelings.

> But woe to you, scribes and Pharisees, hypocrites! because you shut the kingdom of heaven against men; for you neither enter yourselves, nor allow those who would enter to go in. Woe to you, scribes and Pharisees, hypocrites! for you traverse sea and land to make a single proselyte, and when he becomes a proselyte, you make him twice as much a child of hell as yourselves . . . . Woe to you, scribes and Pharisees, hypocrites! for you tithe mint and dill and cummin, and have neglected the weightier matters of the law, justice and mercy and faith; these you ought to have done, without neglecting the others. You blind guides, straining out a gnat and swallowing a camel! Woe to you, scribes and Pharisees, hypocrites! for you cleanse the outside of the cup and of the plate, but inside they are full of extortion and rapacity . . . . Woe to you, scribes and Pharisees, hypocrites!

for you are like whitewashed tombs, which outwardly appear beautiful, but within they are full of dead men's bones and all uncleanness . . . . Fill up, then, the measure of your fathers. You serpents, you brood of vipers, how are you to escape being sentenced to hell?[33]

As one examines the entire account in Matthew — together with the parallel passages — so scathing are Christ's invectives against the scribes and Pharisees that one is forced to ask himself whether it is still the life of Christ he is reading. What can account for this sudden explosion in the heart of him who always turned the cheek? Jesus did not act this way in the presence of those who were guilty of murder and fornication. He did not react in such a manner even when dealing with those who, having blasphemed the Holy Spirit, committed the unpardonable sin. Atheists and skeptics were treated with gentleness and kindness. What had the scribes and Pharisees done which was so intolerable?

The problem becomes even more complicated when one studies the exalted mission and doctrine of the Pharisees. Rather than being hoodlums who ruthlessly plundered the poor or deliberately defended violence, the Pharisees (on their own profession) were the custodians of God's eternal law, the authoritative interpreters of the faith, and the indefatigable defenders of truth. They believed in Jehovah God's self-revelation through Moses, the writings, and the prophets. So exemplary was their zealousness for the covenant faith that the Apostle Paul, subsequent to his conversion, boasted of his Pharisaic zeal. "According to the strictest part of our religion I have lived as a Pharisee." (Acts 26:5) "A Hebrew born of Hebrews; as to the law a Pharisee." (Philippians 3:5) The Pharisees defended monotheism, resisted the Hellenization of their culture by the Greeks, sought spirituality, promoted individualism, vigorously supported the program of the synagogue, encouraged missionary activity, and preached future life. They stepped up the place of womanhood by relaxing the laws of purification and cleansing; placed the interpretation of

33. Matthew 23:13-33.

Scripture into the hands of the average man; and strove valiantly to make the symbols of the Jewish religion intelligible to the common people. And to insure a complete acceptance of the individual by God, they brought every phase of man's conscious activity under meticulous, ceremonial observance. Why, then, did Christ disapprobate the Pharisees so strongly?

The answer is found in the text: "The scribes and the Pharisees sit on Moses' seat." (Matthew 23:2) Whereas Moses had *reluctantly* accepted God's appointment to mediate the will of Jehovah to his people, the Pharisees, eager to augment their own prestige, were self-appointed successors to the job. They arrogated to themselves the right to mediate between the people and a holy God by infallibly interpreting the word of revelation to the people. They did not seek to add to revelation; they only claimed authority to give an infallible interpretation of the corpus of revelation already given. They were "vicars of Moses" on earth, in short. They represented a continuation of the authority of Moses in all generations.

The wrath of Christ was raised against them because they took the law — which was given to bring men to despair, that they might be justified by faith — and converted it into a basis of self-righteousness; thus cancelling out an antecedent need for the death of Christ. "If justification were through the law, then Christ died to no purpose." (Galatians 2:21) Moses gave a severe law in order that men, seeing how lost and undone they are before God, might know that the just shall walk by faith. "For all who rely on works of the law are under a curse; for it is written, 'Cursed be every one who does not abide by all things written in the book of the law, and do them.' Now it is evident that no man is justified before God by the law; for 'He who through faith is righteous shall live.'" (Galatians 3:10-11) The purpose of the law was to make men thirsty, that they might drink freely from the water of life; hungry, that they might eat freely of the living bread. The law was given to destroy self-righteousness in men, for God had elected to redeem men, not by works, but by free grace.

"Christ redeemed us from the curse of the law, having become a curse for us — for it is written, 'Cursed be every one who hangs on a tree.' " (Galatians 3:13)

This is what roused Christ's righteous indignation. Whereas he was soon to pass through the second death for the salvation of the world, the Pharisees so fragmatized and corrupted the severity of the law that faith in Jehovah was displaced by a meticulous obedience to a troublesome, petty series of regulations, which, when met, supposedly made a person righteous in the eyes of God.

Ignoring the fact that God applies salvation directly through the Holy Spirit, the Pharisees concluded that if the people needed a mediator during the days of Moses, they likewise needed one now. Since salvation is a life-and-death matter, there should be no risks or probabilities when men decide. To insure safe passage to heaven, therefore, the Pharisees drew up a body of tradition as an authoritative interpretation of Moses. In the Jewish Mishna we are informed that Moses handed the law to Joshua, Joshua to the elders, the elders to the prophets, and the prophets to the men of the Great Synagogue. The net result was a bulky volume of laws and regulations designed to explain the meaning and application of the original 613 laws in the Pentateuch. When once it was believed that Moses could be improved upon at some points, it was no problem for a skilled polemicist to argue that everything in God's self-revelation must be processed by the minds of living authorities.

By the time Jesus Christ came, Pharisaism was the dominant religion of the people. Sitting in the seat of Moses, the Pharisees shackled the masses with a childish formalism that stood in the way of God's free grace reaching men and of man's heart-sacrifice returning to God. Whichever direction a person turned, there the Pharisees were on hand to regiment conduct according to the mind of Moses. The sacred ritual was defined so minutely that the verve of spiritual religion was quenched. Reading like a rulebook governing prisons, rather

than a codified statement of the will of God for free man, the
Mishna is a monument to self-righteousness. Men are permitted to light certain types of candles with certain types of
wicks, but only at specified times and with specified lighting
instruments. To deviate from this procedure is to sin against
God. Such matters as the consumption of eggs laid on a festi-
val day, or the distance one may lawfully depart from his home
on the Sabbath, became ponderous theological questions which
engaged the energies of the great doctors of the day. Before
the grace of God could reach the heart of man with free salvation, therefore, it had to work its way through this maze of
trite legislation.

Unless this self-appointed mediatorial office is understood,
one will miss the point of Christ's impatience with Pharisaic
practices. "So, for the sake of your tradition, you have made
void the law of God. You hypocrites! Well did Isaiah proph-
esy of you when he said

> 'This people honors me with their lips,
> but their heart is far from me;
> in vain do they worship me,
> teaching as doctrines the precepts of men.' " [34]

Not only did the Pharisees claim exemption from divine judgment because they were the interpreters of the law, but they
kept the common man from reaching the word and will of the
true God. Whenever God's love reached out to man, it was
speedily converted into new forms of ceremonial obedience.
The hypocrisy of the Pharisees grew out of the disparity between their profession and their conduct. While they were
meticulous in tithing mint and dill and cummin, they overlooked the weightier matters of the law: justice and mercy
and faith. The net result was a proud and fleshly heart. The
Pharisees were so self-satisfied through their possession of
righteousness that they became completely blinded to the real
criterion of holiness. God judges the heart of man, not his

---

34. Matthew 15:6-9.

formal, external actions. "You blind guides, straining out a gnat and swallowing a camel!" (Matthew 23:24)

The locus of Christ's righteous indignation must be appreciated. Being near the end of his earthly ministry, he was already anticipating the grief of the second death. It was here that he collided with those who were deliberately seeking to overthrow the effectiveness of his Messianic ministry. The incongruity of the situation could only call for a burst of indignation in answer. His work was so sacrificial and holy, while the Pharisees' condemnation was so bitter, that divine wrath (as it were) leaped out of its context to bring an eternal judgment upon men in time. While Christ was weeping for Jerusalem, the Pharisees were gathered together in a corner scheming ways to dispose of him. And the unspeakably awful part of the arrangement was that the authority so to act was declared to have come from God. Exemption from divine judgment, under the pretension of being Moses' earthly vicar, was a perfect cover for pride and will-to-power. The elements in the relation were so unthinkably blasphemous, therefore, that the Son of God, no longer containing his vexed spirit, vindicated the righteousness both of his Father and of his Messianic ministry by releasing barbed scorn upon the imitators of Moses.

Freedom is incapable of conceiving a more awful, more moving cause of righteous indignation, than to have sinful vessels pretend a release from divine judgment, while at the same time retaining the right to judge those subordinate to them. Just as the meanest person among men is he who takes advantage of another's self-sacrifice to augment his own security, so in the eyes of the Father there is nothing more intolerable than the use of the sacrifice of the Son as an occasion to increase fleshly pomp and circumstances.

B. *Application*

After reviewing the reaction of Christ to the pretensions of the Pharisees, the heart feels a decided relief; for it is now able to explain why it felt so strange after its recoil from Catholicism. Roman Catholicism, "sitting in the seat of Peter," is guilty of arrogating to itself a power to impose a code of ceremonial law between God's free offer of grace and the longing hearts of sinners. Instead of teaching the people that true religion consists in a heart of humility and love — for love exhausts the need for all law — it offers a substitute codification of petty moral precepts which makes it more moral to perform the Catholic ritual than to exemplify personal selflessness. The issue is whether a person eats meat on Friday or whether he has attended mass at least once a year; not whether there is fleshly pride in his heart because he is not numbered among yonder unrighteous Publicans (Protestants). The issue is whether one is guilty of attending a non-Catholic worship service, not whether he has bitterness in his heart for those who are non-Catholic. The issue is whether he supports Catholic charity, not whether he has charity in his own heart toward Christ's persecutors. The perfect Catholic is the one who implicitly absorbs the doctrine, ritual, and prescriptions of the church in every phase of his life; not the one who, renouncing all virtue, reflects a life of humility and love which is a reasonable counterpart to the perfection of Jesus Christ.

Although the heart quickly restores a feeling of love and sympathy toward the persons of those already won to the Catholic Church, it cannot but feel toward the *system* of Catholicism as Christ did toward the system of Pharisaism: By a tradition of men the law of God has been made void. Because the Catholic Church is exploiting the sinner's best friend to increase her own power, the heart is estranged from fellowship with such an institution.

Retired from the work of showing how the absolute law of love applies to the lives of men in complex social relations, therefore, the Catholic theologian (like the Pharisee) can shun the weighty matters of the law to discuss the minutiae of these trivial ceremonial observances which a man must fulfill if he is to be holy. Since the Council of Trent has frozen Catholic doctrine, it is already a settled datum that a person is not justified by the imputed righteousness of Christ. Hence, the problem of the Catholic divine consists in defining the specifications of the substitute ceremonial righteousness by which men are actually saved. Since Catholics earn merit by not consuming meat on Friday, rather than by devoting Friday to a day in which to do deeds of kindness to heretics, the problem which the theologian must solve is not the relation of the law of love to modern living, but rather, the more weighty matter of how Friday's meat shall be defined. What is meat, anyway? This is extremely important for Catholic piety. The dictionary defines meat as the flesh of animals. But as any competent scientist knows, it is almost impossible to tell where animals leave off and plants begin, or what constitutes an animal at all. If one drinks a glass of water with all the small animals swimming in it, has he broken his Friday fast and brought desecration on the holy sacrifice of Christ? After a volume or two have been written on this topic, then research must be made into such problems as that of lobsters. Are they animals? Is their flesh meat, or is it not? To taste it one would surely say it was meat —- and delicious meat, at that. Was not life taken when the squirming creature was tossed into the boiling water, and is not the taking of life a sacrifice?

Compared to the weighty tomes which the Catholic Church produces to solve such ponderous problems as what happens when a mouse eats part of the body of Christ or whether a church is still consecrated after it has been used as a morgue during a disaster, the Mishna is exceedingly terse. The things that really count for Catholicism are discussions about contraceptives, the saliva at baptism, the crucifixion picture at the beginning of the canon, when a deacon may or may not bless with the hand, the order of handling the sacred vessels, preaching costumes, rites, vows, and the reconsecration of altar stones. With the world standing on the edge of chaos because men refuse to take the law of love seriously, Catholic divines continue their inquiry into the trivialities of ceremonial observances. The following is a fair sample of this activity:

LIP-STICK AS A THEOLOGICAL PROBLEM

Question 1: Is there any reason to fear that lip-stick will break the eucharistic fast?

Question 2: If the lips of a woman who is receiving Extreme Unction are coated with lip-stick, is there any danger that the anointing of the mouth will not be valid?

Answer 1: The danger of breaking the eucharistic fast to which the question refers might seem to some to be present if a portion of the paste which women use for reddening their lips is dissolved by the tongue and swallowed. However, according to the interpretation of theologians, this would not break the fast, since it would be consumed *per modum salivae* (Aertnys-Damen, *Theologia Moralis*, [Turin, 1939], Vol. II, n. 156). Accordingly, it is not conformable with theological teaching to warn women against the use of lip-stick before receiving Holy Communion on the ground that they are likely to break their fast.

Answer 2: If there is a thick coating of lip-stick on the lips, there would be grave danger that the anointing of the mouth performed on the lips would not be valid; and in that event the validity of the sacrament would be doubtful. If a priest encounters a case of this kind, the practical solution would be to anoint on the skin above or below the lips, not colored by the lip-stick. This would eliminate all danger of an invalid anointing.[35]

After one reads this pathetic attempt to make the gospel of Jesus Christ relevant to modern man, he is not surprised to hear the feet of the Son of God softly approaching behind him. With a sadness in his eyes from observing the way men turn from faith, mercy, justice to the tithing mint and dill and cummin, one can hear him say to those who "sit in the seat of Peter," *"You blind guides, straining out a gnat and swallowing a camel!"*

Summary

After freeing itself from the long shadow of universalism, the weary heart believed that now, at last, it could lie down to rest, there to worship God and be a servant to fellow

---

35. *The American Ecclesiastical Review* (a monthly publication for the Catholic clergy in America), November, 1944, p. 395.

men. This aspiration was swiftly challenged, however, for the disturbing weight of the Roman Catholic Church was seen looming on the horizon. Unable to remain disinterested, the penitent quickly entered the doors of the greatest organization on earth. On learning that absolute security could be enjoyed within institutional authority, the heart experienced immediate relief. After the resident apologist enumerated some of the basic proofs of Catholic authority, the existing individual was less and less inclined to wander. Rome is too vast, too old, too wise to be wrong. She has been in the business of salvation for so long that none can effectively compete with her. As the heart began to yield to Rome's overtures, thus, it felt that it was coming into port after a rough sea.

Pledged to balance all options by the rule of whole perspective coherence, however, spirit determined to conduct a private investigation on its own. And after this research was completed, the heart was shocked with indignation to think that it could have been drawn so close to what is so far from whole truth. More impressed with an *a priori* Pelagianism than with the plain revelation of Jesus Christ, Roman divines have displaced the absolute law of love by substituting a domesticated code of ceremonies. Thus, the Catholic is able to work his way to heaven with the initial help of, but in the final analysis independent of, the righteousness of Jesus Christ. Since she denies that we are saved by faith, therefore, Rome is guilty of the sin of the Pharisees. She is a self-appointed mediator by "sitting in the seat of Peter." Through her authoritative program she interposes a burdensome code of ceremonies between the free mercies of Christ and the thirsting heart.

Catholicism has appealed to the earning of merit as a catalytic agent in the sinner's sanctification, fearing that imputed righteousness might lead to either quietism or license. But her substitution is as pathetic as her fear, for whoever loves Jesus Christ will perform good works — not as a ground of justification, but as a proof of love. As in marriage, the legal bond only opens the way to new and more fecund expressions of devotedness; it does not kill off fellowship. Whoever storms heaven by good works is guilty of denying both the absoluteness of the law of love and the redemptive substitution which Jesus Christ performed in the sinner's behalf.

The heart shuns any tampering with Christ's definition of law, for it not only confesses that it is *capable* of this height (for with every stage of love, there is yet room for improvement), but also that in rejecting the law one spurns the authority of Jesus Christ himself. And since it was *Christ* who died for our sins, and not the Roman Catholic Church, primacy belongs to him alone. Rome leads to another complex immediacy by blocking to the way to wholehearted fellowship with our Lord. Since Christ announced a law which we cannot be responsible for, our Lord (in plainest language) spoke a lie. Rome forces us to destroy fellowship with the Lover of our souls, and such a price is too great for any axiologically sensitive person to pay.

But will not Rome conquer the world? And are not those who defy surrender to her demands doomed to obscurity as a forgotten sect? The answer, in all Christian truth, is *no*. Not only will the sovereign Christ prevent an organization from swallowing up his true body, but also (as history proves) Catholicism itself is subject to an optimum point of efficiency in any nation. People will tolerate less than the full measure of self-dignity for a time, perhaps, but sooner or later freedom will rise above premature holiness and demand a perfection which is perfection indeed. Pelagianism encourages men to argue for the right to be selfish. But sensitive men find that when they articulate the privilege of excluding others from selfless love, they instantly undermine their own self-dignity, bringing opprobrium on spirit.

Regardless how vast the Catholic Church may become, how immense her coverage over the earth, let no true believer in Jesus Christ tremble before institutional prestige. If Christ is an authoritative revelation of the Father's will, Catholicism is anti-Christ. That much is lucidly clear. The gospel according to Christ and the gospel according to Rome cannot, in a rational universe, simultaneously be true. Romanism *will* fail.[36]

> Not the labors of my hands,
>   Can fulfill Thy law's demands.
> Could my zeal no respite know,
>   Could my tears forever flow,
> All for sin could not atone;
>   Thou must save, and Thou alone.
>
> Nothing in my hand I bring,
>   Simply to Thy cross I cling;
> Naked, come to Thee for dress,
>   Helpless, look to Thee for grace;
> Foul, I to the fountain fly,
>   Wash me, Savior, or I die!

---

36. For those who may wish to supplement this axiological study with a thoroughgoing *rational* analysis of the inconsistencies of Roman Catholicism, there is nothing finer in any language than the work by George Salmon, *The Infallibility of the Church*. First printed in 1888, this masterpiece of Protestant polemics remains to this day the definitive refutation of the Roman Catholic Church.

XI

The Loci of Truth

THE imminent danger one faces in revolting from an all-embracing absolute such as Roman Catholicism is that, having tasted the elixir of independence and freedom, one may become completely drunken with his own autonomy. It is perfectly proper that one resist any form of objective authority which threatens to corrupt the potentialities of spirit, lest a spurious guardian of the soul throttle brotherhood and fellowship. But it is hardly sagacious for the free self to pursue independence at the cost of defying those objective forms which define rational evidence itself. Unless faith is supported by a genuine authority, it will soften into an ephemeral expression of inwardness.

In no instance do the Scriptures encourage the penitent to believe that by a subjective "leap" of faith he may atone for a deficiency in objective authority. On the contrary, cordial trust in Jesus Christ is always grounded in reasonable evidences. When Thomas refused to release perfect faith until he put his hands in the nail wounds of Christ, e. g. our Lord both obliged in his request and blessed him for asking. The faith of Thomas was augmented in direct proportion to the witness of the rational evidences. If faith were grounded in a subjective "leap," Thomas would have had greater faith if Christ had not obliged him, in the first place, and the greatest faith if there had been no Christ at all, in the second.

Love is so characterized that unless it accurately terminates upon the person for whom it is intended, its expression is truncated. But in the dispersing of such love one can recognize the presence of the other only after the evidences have spoken. Knowledge by acquaintance is still an act of rationality. The prudent woman does not lavish her affections upon the first person she sees approaching. She carefully weighs the data, and then, fully persuaded in her mind that it is her lover in the distance, releases trust and faith. In like manner, one can do justice in his love for God only when he first is rationally convinced that it is *God* whom he is fellowshiping with.

When addressing the heart, therefore, the Scriptures use rationally intelligible propositions. Spirit can be led to the God worthy of being worshiped only through the avenue of objectively veracious evidences. If our knowledge of God were discontinuous with good scientific-philosophic inquiry, we would never know God at all. Faith in God is not generically different from faith in either another individual or in the body of scientifically veracious knowledge. Generic faith is a resting of the mind in the sufficiency of the evidences. Saving faith may go beyond this general expression, but it does not exclude it. Whoever does not first have generic faith can hardly be said to possess the richer form. Even the highest surgings of spiritual ecstasy own no powers which are free from the veto of the understanding. "I will pray with the spirit and I will pray with the mind also; I will sing with the spirit and I will sing with the mind also." (I Corinthians 14:15) If Biblical Christianity rested on rational paradox or absurdity, it would quickly reduce to foolishness.

I. The Third Locus of Truth

A. *The Limitations of Philosophy*

Conventional philosophy divides the species of truth into two general types. *First,* truth is the sum total of reality itself. The trees in the rear yard are *truly* trees; the man approaching my friend is *truly* a foreigner. *Second,* truth is systematic consistency or propositional correspondence to reality. If a person states a proposition which, when tested by experience, does not frustrate our expectations, we conclude quite properly that he speaks, or has, the truth. And by "experience" we do not mean simply the witness of the five senses; we imply the

total conscious life of man, inside and outside. As indicated
elsewhere, man is a participant of a double environment. The
soul has more eyes with which to see than the body.
Philosophically, hence, truth has only two loci. When a
Ph.D. candidate is examined for his knowledge of the *Eudem-
ian* or *Nicomachean Ethics* of Aristotle, his interrogators are
concerned only with his ability to compose answers which
correspond to the data in Aristotle's system. Whether or not
the student is ethical in his own person is hardly a matter
which directly concerns the philosophy department. In the
same manner, the professors are hired to teach, not witness
to, the truth. If an instructor persuasively teaches the evils
of divorce, for example, it is irrelevant to the university if he
himself happens to be a divorced man.

But suppose that the mother of the Ph.D. candidate is on
hand. Since she is related to her son personally, she is concerned with another species of truth. Thought can only prepare for the type she is looking for; it is not an end in itself.
She wishes above all else that her son *be* the truth, namely,
that he reflect goodness and honesty in his own character.
What worth is a theoretical knowledge of morals if he is lewd
and predaceous in his social relations? The mother does not
disparage the theory; her only concern is that the boy live in
accordance with the morals he learns.

Since it is what men look for every time they seek fellowship, there is nothing intrinsically mysterious about the third
locus of truth. A person may *truly* be a human being; he may
comprehend formal truth after memorizing a world view; but
he *is* the truth only when he is kind, humble, and gentle in his
own character. A truthful person is a trustworthy person.
For positions of responsibility, the employer hires only men of
character; the girl trusts only the boy who is good in his own
person; the father rejoices only when he observes expressions
of obedience and kindness in the lives of his own family. A
person who has come to critical selfhood will quickly realize
that whoever acquires the whole world at the expense of losing
his own self-respect, has lost everything and gained nothing.

A mother would many times over prefer a son with a low mental acumen, but with a good heart, than a shifty Phi Beta Kappa behind prison bars. She would rather have her boy *be,* than *comprehend,* the truth.

It is this third locus of truth to which Christ refers in his sweeping claim to self-revelation. "I am the way, and the truth, and the life. . . . Have I been with you so long, and yet you do not know me, Philip? He who has seen me has seen the Father." (John 14:6-9) One may ransack the archives of philosophy and he will uncover no counterpart to this stupendous claim. No philosopher has ever dared to announce that he achieved the mediation of truth in his own person. The world's philosophers have been far too occupied constructing rational systems to trifle with such an insignificance as personal witnessing to the truth. Whoever attempts to compete with Jesus Christ will find himself in the embarrassing plight of claiming what is false. A barbed conscience exposes our exiguous virtue and our sinewy vice. Being guilty of pride and self-love, we are untruth in our own person. Only Jesus Christ has meaningfully been able to say, "I am the truth." So morally exact was his life that a revelation of the Father's essence is reflected in the kindness of his face. By taking note of what Christ said and did, one may reach a perfect statement of the law of love.

Christianity places a premium upon the third locus of truth — truth in the heart — because man is related to God personally; and in all personal affairs fellowship rests upon trust. "Without faith (cordial trust) it is impossible to please him." (Hebrews 11:6) Just as there is no perfection of knowledge beyond acquaintance, so there is no perfection of truth beyond the truthfulness of a good heart. The lovers say little during their honeymoon, not because they have forgotten the art of conversation, but because they are so absorbed in the perfection of love. Since each presentationally enters into the truth of the other, no pleasure is wanting. Their fellowship is so consummate that all suspicion, jealousy, and distrust are cast aside. And so in worship with God: When the heart is completely committed to Jesus Christ, fellowship is absolutely sweet because perfect trust and truthfulness reign.

B. *The Balance of the Loci*

The Christian philosophy of truth may be summarized as follows: (a) Reality "out there" is the truth. This universe is *truly* God's creation. (b) Truth is a property of a judgment or proposition which corresponds to reality. The mind of God forms a perfect system of truth. "Thy word is truth." (John 17:17) Finite minds approach this perfection only by degrees, by systems of thought, in short. Since their systems are never complete, however, propositional truth can never pass beyond probability. (c) Truth in the heart is a quality of personal character which coincides with the law of love. God is perfect truth because his nature is pure love. Love is the stuff which forms the character of God. Men become the truth as their character becomes good.

God has so tempered truth together that no locus may say to another, I have no need of you. Truth as reality makes up the environment for fellowship; truth as propositional correspondence to reality defines the criteria of true fellowship; while truth as goodness of character is the fellowship itself. These loci must act tunefully if the whole man is to be harmoniously related both to the universe over against him and to the totality of his own person within.

The faculty of reason has been authorized as the responsible guardian of the third locus of truth, for apart from its council the heart would never fully recognize when the conditions of inward truth have been met. For this reason the will has no authority to lead the heart into a commitment until it has first cleared with the understanding. Only the understanding can finally test for error. Truth as inwardness may be more important for fellowship than truth as a rational system, but apart from the guidance which inwardness receives from such a system it is a rudderless ship on a shoreless sea. Through the faculty of reason freedom is able to project if-then hypotheses to classify and correlate the meaning of the multifarious data which constantly bombard the whole person. If this power to test for truth and error is ever tampered with in an effort to protect the autonomy of the third locus of truth, skepticism and subjectivism will lurk near the door of the heart.

Realizing that the heart has no independent rights, therefore, the Scriptures place a great premium on rational teaching. Subsequent to relieving emergencies, the first task of the missionary is to translate the Bible into the native tongue. Unless the understanding digests the propositions of the gospel, the gospel cannot be believed in the heart. Faith does not germinate *in vacuo*. The Great Commission is fulfilled only when we *teach* all nations.

> But how are men to call upon him in whom they have not believed? And how are they to believe in him of whom they have never heard? And how are they to hear without a preacher? And how can men preach unless they are sent? . . . So faith comes from what is heard, and what is heard comes by the preaching of Christ.[1]

Rising to challenge this theory of mutual dependence among the loci of truth, however, is a new philosophical-religious mood called *existentialism*.[2] Existentialism has spurned the conventional method of understanding the meaning of reality in favor of a reading off of life from the perspective of the existing, passionate individual himself. Rather than reduce the meaning of life to a rational system, therefore, existentialism has preferred to ask what life's meaning is when evaluated through the eyes of a person desperately trying to be a responsible individual. Truth as rationality, therefore, is dealt with

---

1. Romans 10:14-17.
2. "Existentialism, we suggest, is thought which endeavors to become self-authenticating by including the trial of suffering within its own domain. This thought begins with a negation. It denies reason's power to provide meaning. But since we cannot live without meaning, the result is despair. Such is the trial of suffering for the thinking mind. No thought is authentic unless it has traversed despair, the Existentialist claims, and he offers himself as an expert guide through those bleak regions." Helmut Kuhn, "Existentialism — Christian and Anti-Christian," *Theology Today*, October, 1949, p. 317.

cavalierly. The idea is that existential truth — truth which men gain through inward concern — bears its own criteria of validity and may be accepted on its own rights. In the instance of a collision between inward truth and truth as propositional correspondence to reality, the latter must go. A body of logical propositions is too colorless to have the power of veto over heart-truth.

Let modern man rise to this final decision in the stages of suffering: *Is the heart equipped with criteria of verification which may be obeyed independently of, if not in opposition to, the witness of logic; or are convictions of the heart, like everything else meaningful, subject to the authority of rationality?* The Bible says that we can pray or sing with the spirit *only* when we can at the same time pray or sing with the mind. Existentialism responds that since logical forms are impotent to reach down into the rich, paradoxical complexity of life, they therefore may be abandoned whenever necessary.

Before one can adequately speak to the issue, however, it is necessary that a cursory study of the rise and meaning of existentialism be pursued. The reader must gird his loins for an exceptionally difficult task, however, for existentialism is as complex as it is alluring. It is complex because it resorts to the data of our inner life as a basis for its *Weltanschauung*; and it is alluring because it is directed toward times of despair.

II. Fountainhead: Soren Kierkegaard

While it is true that the mood of existentialism can be traced back through philosophy to the venerable sage of Athens, Socrates, the mysterious patience of time waited until the nineteenth century for the appearance of a person endowed with just the proper acumen and personal temperament required to give existentialism its classical formulation. This one destined to be the focal point of reference for all future existentialism is Sören Kierkegaard.

The Danish philosopher, Sören Kierkegaard, 1813-1855, was the man from whom either directly or indirectly, every major stream of so-called Existential thought is derived. Both in his religious and in his philosophical works, Kierkegaard showed himself to be in contradiction to the basic attitudes of the nineteenth century, and kept insisting in a variety of ways that the meaning of experience must be related back to the meaning of the personality of the experiencing man. In other words, the distinctive contribution of Sören Kierkegaard was his insistence that every question about the meaning of existence was in the last analysis a question about the meaning of the existence of the man who was asking the question. [3]

Through the expedient of a series of topics, let us seek to probe into the essential features of this new philosophy of religion.

A. *Kierkegaard's Vocation in Life*

After observing the prevailing conditions in both the universities and his native city, Copenhagen, Kierkegaard concluded that man's chief sin is his confusion of logical and existential systems. The logical system is a rational anticipation of reality. The existential system is the willing, passionate individual in the process of becoming. In Berlin, therefore, students supposed they gained truth by the simple exercise of memorizing Hegel's thought; while in Copenhagen men were Christians either because they had been reared that way or because they had some objective proof to rest on, such as their baptismal certificate or the recitation of church creeds. The result of this confusion was the destruction of existential truth. Men sought everything but the glory of *being* the truth. Kierkegaard, thus, appointed himself a contemporary Socratic gadfly to nettle people into taking the existential assignment seriously. "My purpose is to make it difficult to become a Christian, yet not more difficult than it is, nor to make it difficult for stupid people, and easy for clever pates, but qualitatively difficult, and essentially difficult, for every man equally, for essentially it is equally difficult for every man to relinquish his understanding

---

3. Charles D. Kean, *The Meaning of Existence,* (New York: Harper and Brothers, 1947), xiii.

and his thinking, and to keep his soul fixed upon the absurd."[4]
When understood as an existential assignment, "Christianity
simply does not exist."[5] The number of professing Christians
in Copenhagen almost equaled the total citizenry itself, indeed, but this unanimity was only possible because an easy objectivity supplanted the dangerous venture of witnessing to
Christianity. "It is not my fault that the age in which we live
has reversed the relationship, and transformed Christianity into a philosophical doctrine that asks to be understood, and
turned being a Christian into a triviality."[6] In former days men
risked everything on professing the Christian life, while today
men need courage to renounce it.

Kierkegaard, it can be seen, is a powerful apologist of the
third locus of truth. Demanding that Christianity be interpreted as a living truth rather than a system of thought, he
set a fresh pace within philosophy of religion. Swenson calls
it a "veritable Copernican revolution "[7] Rather than permitting
a highly self-satisfied *Privatdocent* to cross-examine existence,
Kierkegaard reversed the field and cross-examined the *Privatdocent* by existence. No man has a right to claim truth until he
first *is* the truth.

B. *Kierkegaard's Anthropology*

Central to existential literature is the individual. It is imperative, therefore, that men heed the Delphic epigram, "Know
yourself!" for how can they appreciate the meaning of existential truth if they do not first recognize its locus? The
existential assignment is an inwardness.

Swiftly by-passing the obvious facts that man is formed of
both body and rationality, Kierkegaard concentrates on the
essence of human nature as spirit or freedom. Man is body and

---

4. Kierkegaard, *Concluding Unscientific Postscript*, p. 495.

5. Kierkegaard, *Attack upon "Christendom,"* (Princeton: Princeton University Press, 1944), p. 277.

6. *Concluding Unscientific Postscript*, p. 339.

7. David Swenson, *Something About Kierkegaard*, (Minneapolis: Augsburg Publishing Press, 1941), p. 126.

soul carried away by freedom. "Man's essential idea is spirit."[8] Spirit is the power of self-transcendence. "Man is a synthesis of the soulish and the bodily. But a synthesis is unthinkable if the two are not united in a third factor. This third factor is the spirit."[9] Another way of expressing the synthesis is to classify man according to his potentialities. In this case "man is a synthesis of the infinite and the finite, of the temporal and the eternal, of freedom and necessity, in short it is a synthesis."[10]

The synthesis confines man within the milieu of both time and eternity. Freedom reaches out and grasps the rule of duty (eternity), while necessity limits the mediation of this duty through temporality. Man *is* the truth, *i. e.*, he has risen to the existential assignment, only when he reflects the eternal in time. Spirit is freedom, and freedom is choice. The eternal *becomes* time, therefore, only in the *instant* that passionate, inward decision materializes. When the eternal is made temporal, man exists as, or becomes, a spiritual being. "Existence is the child that is born of the infinite and the finite, the eternal and the temporal, and is therefore a constant striving."[11] *Truth* comes into being only when the individual existentially decides for the eternal in time. Where there is no locus as its receptacle, there obviously can be no truth. Even as the flower "becomes" through growth, so the individual becomes through ethical decisions. "To exist means to express the eternal in time, to translate the eternal content of the human self into a living reality in time."[12]

---

8. Kierkegaard, *Either/Or*, (Princeton: Princeton University Press, 1944), Vol. I, p. 52.

9. Kierkegaard, *The Concept of Dread*, (Princeton: Princeton University Press, 1944), p. 39.

10. Kierkegaard, *The Sickness Unto Death*, p. 17. "The synthesis of the eternal and the temporal is not a second synthesis but is the expression for the first synthesis in consequence of which man is a synthesis of soul and body sustained by spirit." *The Concept of Dread*, p. 79.

11. *Concluding Unscientific Postscript*, p. 85.

12. E. Geismar, *Lectures on the Religious Thought of Sören Kierkegaard*, (Minneapolis: Augsburg Publishing House, 1938), pp. 45-46.

C. *Stages on Life's Way*

Freedom is not only able to ascertain the conditions which comprise the existential assignment but it can also measure the stages of commitment which lead up to, and finally include, truth as inwardness. "There are three stages: an aesthetic, an ethical, and a religious."[13] The stages are ranks of existence, and "All interpretations of existence rank in accordance with the degree of an individual's dialectical apprehension of inwardness."[14]

> What serves to mark the thoroughly cultivated personality is the degree to which the thinking in which he has his daily life has a dialectical character. To have one's daily life in the decisive dialectic of the infinite, and yet continue to live: this is both the art of life and its difficulty. Most men have complacent categories for their daily use, and resort to the categories of the infinite only upon solemn occasions; that is to say, they do not really have them. But to make use of the dialectic of the infinite in one's daily life, and to exist in this dialectic, is naturally the highest degree of strenuousness: and strenuous exertion is again needed to prevent the exercise from deceitfully luring one away from existence, instead of providing a training in existence.[15]

The aesthetic stage is pure immediacy. It is made up of all who, caught in a decisionless round of living, betray spirit by destroying its powers of self-transcendence. Time means nothing to the aesthete, for the experience of satisfaction is gained within the present moment. The aesthete suffers for nothing; spirit is dormant; there are no contradictions for the will to resolve through passionate decision. Since the aesthete sees no responsibility in living, thus, he risks nothing. He just *is*; he never *becomes*.

In the ethical stage spirit soars to eternity and interprets the assignment of life as a response to eternal duty, thus introduc-

---

13. *Concluding Unscientific Postscript*, p 261. "In an exceptional degree, this man's thought was shaped by his life. For him, as for Hosea, reality was what he himself had passed through." H. R. Mackintosh, *Types of Modern Theology*, (New York: Charles Scribner's Sons, 1937), p. 220.
14. *Concluding Unscientific Postscript*, p. 506.
15. *Ibid.*, pp. 79-80 n.

ing a challenging ground for the exercise of spirit. "When an individual abandons himself to lay hold of something great outside him, his enthusiasm is aesthetic; when he forsakes everything to save himself, his enthusiasm is ethical."[16] Since "only absolute either/or is the choice between good and evil,"[17] it follows that ethics is quite capable of introducing strenuousness into the life of spirit.

The difficulty with the ethicist, however, is that he is blinded to the nature of the existential assignment. When the discussion turns from the *theory* to the *living* of ethics, "the comedy begins,"[18] for the ethicist only snivels in the face of such an arrangement. "Even to listen to such talk is unethical, is something for which ethics has neither *time* nor *opportunity*."[19] But a man who lives dialectically, rather than speculatively, is a man who realizes that there is no good until the individual himself is good. He understands that ethical *living* is the only ethic there is.

Once the ethical assignment is converted into a program of duty to God, one then leaps from the ethical into the religious stage. At this shift, genuine passion is injected into existence, for what the ethicist haughtily dismisses as an inconsequential inconsistency is now seriously understood as sin. Sin is: "*Before God, or with the conception of God, to be in despair at not willing to be oneself, or in despair at willing to be oneself.*"[20]   *Being* a self involves the mediation of eternity in moments of temporal decision; sin is the failure so to do. Whoever boasts that he is truth is guilty of sin, because he fails to see that the existential assignment cannot be fulfilled; and whoever is in despair over the existential assignment, recoiling from the task of being an individual, is untruth through indolence. Sin cannot exist in the realm of thought. Being

---

16. *Ibid.*, p. 350. "He who lives ethically . . . lives dynamically . . . he lives in and by the enthusiasm, but also, by the effort and strain of an essential and profound becoming." Swenson, *op. cit.*, p. 167.
17. *Either / Or*, II, p. 141.
18. *Concluding Unscientific Postscript*, p. 451.
19. *The Concept of Dread*, p. 15.
20. *The Sickness Unto Death*, p. 123.

another name for untruth, sin is an existential determinant. It comes into being whenever the individual passes out of truth. "Its idea is that its concept is constantly annulled. As a state (*de potentia*) it *is* not, whereas *de actu* or *in actu* it is and is again."[21] The individual is the locus of both truth and untruth. Truth is the witness in time to an eternal duty, while untruth is the failure of such witness either through want of humility or want of resolution.

Since Socrates believed that man's problem is ignorance (not sin), it follows that the sage of Athens never arrived at the most strenuous form of inward passion. Socrates remained in *Religiousness A*; Christianity presses on to *Religiousness B* Because he perceived that one does not have the truth until he is the truth, Socrates is not far from the existential kingdom. Yet, he always defended the covert optimism that, given time and opportunity, man could make his way back to eternity through reminiscence. Because of this undialectical conception of mediation, he was unable to penetrate to the full meaning of existential self-despair. Religiousness B closes the gate to reminiscence by making truth an existential determinant, a truth which exists only when the individual himself ethically exists. Reminiscence is a thought, not an existential process. "The more difficult it is made for him to take himself out of existence by way of recollection, the more profound is the inwardness that his existence may have in existence; and when it is made impossible for him, when he is held so fast in existence that the back door of recollection is forever closed to him, then his inwardness will be the most profound possible."[22]

Spirit is ushered in to its highest office only within the tension of paradoxical religiousness. Although man is metaphysically discontinuous with eternity, he is not yet a man until the eternal univocally enters time through passionate decision. Freedom brings sinfulness, therefore. Freedom simultaneously reveals both the sanguine responsibility of the in-

21. *The Concept of Dread*, p. 14.
22. *Concluding Unscientific Postscript*, pp. 186-187.

dividual to be truth and the gloomy impossibility ever of realizing it.

> Let us call the untruth of the individual Sin. Viewed eternally he cannot be sin, nor can he be eternally presupposed as having been in sin. By coming into existence therefore (for the beginning was that subjectivity is untruth), he becomes a sinner. He is not born as a sinner . . . but he is born in sin as a sinner. This we might call *Original Sin*. But if existence has in this manner acquired a power over him, he is prevented from taking himself back into the eternal by way of recollection. [23]

Kierkegaard assigns the locus of original sin to freedom itself. Whenever the eyes of freedom are opened, the want of existential truth makes man a sinner. Sin is untruth and its abode is the deciding person.

The picture of Socrates standing in the fields gazing up to heaven, expresses the height of passion which can be attained in Religiousness A. Such a form of inwardness only *looks* to the eternal; paradoxical religiousness strives to *be* eternal in time.

> Religiousness A makes the thing of existing as strenuous as possible (outside the paradox-religious sphere), but it does not base the relation to an eternal happiness upon one's existence but lets the relation to an eternal happiness serve as basis for the transformation of existence. From the individual's relation to the eternal, there results the how of his existence, not the converse, and thereby infinitely more comes out of it than was put into it.[24]

Spirit can discover no more thinkably decisive an assignment than to *be* eternal in time. There is no passion beyond this passion. Since *existence itself* is a contradiction, all possibility of complacency is driven out. The dialectic of truth/untruth is inward, essential, and perpetual.

---

23. *Concluding Unscientific Postscript*, p. 186.
24. *Ibid.*, p. 509.

In a remarkably concise passage Kierkegaard sums up the findings of spirit as it soars dialectically into the alternative commitments of freedom:

> *Immediacy, the aesthetic,* finds no contradiction in the fact of existing: to exist is one thing, and the contradiction is something else which comes from without. *The ethical* finds the contradiction, but within self-assertion. *The Religiousness A* comprehends the contradiction as suffering in self-annhilation, although within immanence, but by ethically accentuating the fact of existing it prevents the exister from becoming abstract in immanence, or from becoming abstract by wishing to remain in immanence. *The paradoxical religiousness* breaks with immanence and makes the fact of existing the absolute contradiction, not within immanence, but against immanence. There is no longer any immanent fundamental kinship between the temporal and the eternal because the eternal itself has entered time and would constitute the kinship.[25]

D. *Truth and Decision*

If the third locus of truth is the individual himself, truth is concerned existence. Truth is: *"An objective uncertainty held fast in an appropriation-process of the most passionate inwardness."*[26] While it may seem confusing to hear Kierkegaard speak of truth as "subjectivity," what he actually means is the subjective state of ethical decision, not that odious subjectivity which characterizes skepticism. Subjectivity is infinite passionate concern; it is the being of becoming, the attaining of the existential assignment.

> Decision is no mere consequence of recognizing truth, it is a living and essential factor in apprehending it. To think subjectively—and no other kind of thinking matters here—is to act upon a risk. Cool detachment is an atmosphere in which we cannot believe, as the New Testament accounts believing.

---

25. *Concluding Unscientific Postscript,* pp. 507-508. By *immanence* is meant any optimism that man, through a resolute extension of resident potentialities, can overcome the contradiction of existence and convert untruth within him to consistent truth.

26. *Ibid.,* p. 182.

. . . When Kierkegaard said that truth is subjectivity, then, he bade men recollect that personal Christianity without *decision* is nothing better than a phrase. We are set, each of us, in the inescapable presence of God; and to live and think as if it were not so, is in fact not to think or live at all.[27]

Truth (like sin) comes into, and passes out of, being in direct ratio to the inward concern of the individual. "Man has the truth and what is more becomes the truth to the extent to which, according to the covenant of God and the image of God, he becomes pure subjectivity, a spiritual person."[28]

When he examines the stuff of decision itself, Kierkegaard's insights reach heights of magnificence. He employs the New Testament concept of *agape* love, making it serve as the link between time and eternity. Love is the very content of truth itself, for to be inwardly truthful is to love. "What is it which connects the temporal and the eternal, what except love, which just for this reason is before everything, and which abides when everything else is past?"[29] Not only is love the only vital existential determinant — for it comes into, and passes out of, being as the individual is either truth or untruth in his person — but it also is so inexhaustive in its demands that in it spirit meets a rule which completely taxes it. Spirit swims in dizziness (dread) when it understands both the height of love and the simultaneous responsibility and impossibility of spirit to fulfill it. Man is to love his neighbor, not a great deal, not energetically, *but as himself.* "If the commandment about loving one's neighbor were expressed in some other way than by the use of this little phrase, 'as thyself,'

---

27. Mackintosh, *op. cit.,* pp. 224-225. "The language of the existentialists affords an opportunity of expressing the prevailing sense of being a *survivor,* a survivor who has but a short time to debate the issues of suffering and death before they overtake him also, a survivor who must find his freedom and self-realization in some terrible personal decision of the will, a survivor whose only chance to do a noble act in defiance of a monstrous world might be to anticipate the end by suicide." B. Moss, "This Existentialism," *The Church Quarterly,* Vol. 146. 1948, p. 197.

28. Haecker, *Sören Kierkegaard,* p. 24.

29. Kierkegaard, *Works of Love,* (Princeton: Princeton University Press, 1946), p. 6.

which is at once so easy to use and yet has the tension of eternity, then the commandment would not be able thus to master the self-love."[30] With every attempt to live selflessly before one's neighbor, one experiences the throbbing of pride and egotism within him, thus canceling out truth and in its place putting sin (untruth). "Certainly no wrestler can get so tight a clinch upon his opponent as that with which this commandment embraces the selfishness which cannot stir from its place."[31]

Coupled with this limitless duty to neighbor is an infinite duty toward God. Here the horizontal potentialities of spirit join with the vertical, bringing man into a possibility/impossibility dialectic beyond which it is not possible for spirit to pass.

> There is only One whom a man may with the truth of the eternal love better than himself, that is God. Therefore it does not say, 'Thou shalt love God as thyself,' but it says, 'Thou shalt love the Lord thy God with all thy soul and with all thy mind.' A man must love God in unconditional *obedience* and love Him in *adoration*. [32]

Love makes inwardness absolutely strenuous by joining an infinite impossibility with an infinite necessity. The duty is impossible because eternity cannot become time; man is man, not God. But it is infinitely necessary because self-dignity rests on love. Until the day spirit is separated from body in death, man must strive to be a man. The chain of dialectical tension is endless. If there were an end, it would not genuinely be dialectical.

> In the Christian sense no human being has ever accomplished the highest in love; and even if it were possible, this impossibility, there would at that very moment, from the Christian standpoint, be a new task. But if there is immediately a new task, then it is impossible to have time to know

30. *Op. cit.*, p. 15.
31. *Loc. cit.*
32. *Op. cit.*, p. 17.

whether one has achieved the highest or not; for at the moment when one would get to know it, he is engaged in accomplishing the new task, and hence, is prevented from knowing anything about the preceding moment, for which he has no time.[33]

E. *Kierkegaard's Break from Reason*

Once Kierkegaard accelerated this tremendous momentum in the direction of inwardness, he was unable to stop until he had dislodged every potential stumblingblock from the path of subjectivity. Troubled by a ubiquitous portent that the natural man might drive a wedge of spiritless complacency into the task of subjectivity, he set up an electrically charged fence around the gains of Religiousness B. And one of the first pillagers to be snared on the barbed wires was, quite regretfully, reason. The reasonable is the leaven of complacency in the shewbread of *Existenz*.[34]

One would be guilty of inaccuracy if he supposed that Kierkegaard disparaged reason *per se*. "All honor to philosophy, all praise to everyone who brings a genuine devotion to its service."[35] Far from turning aside from the use of reason, the Copenhagen philosopher was a master dialectician himself. Nevertheless, by restricting reason's domain, Kierkegaard *in fact* turned aside from reason. Reason reads off the implications of logical relations in order that spirit (for that reason) might not believe them. "A Christian. . .uses understanding

---

33. *Works of Love*, pp. 152-153.

34. "Existenz is an attitude of the individual to himself, which is called forth by such concrete situations as the necessity for choice of profession or a conflict in love, a catastrophic change in social conditions, or the imminence of one's death. It leads immediately to sublime moments in which a man gathers his whole strength to make a decision which is taken afterwards as binding upon his future life. Furthermore, Existenz never becomes completed, as does life through death. In its different manifestations it is only a beginning which is faithfully followed or faithlessly forgotten. Moreover, Existenz is not real in being known, it is real only in being effectuated, in the remembrance of it, and in resolutions for the future which are taken as absolutely binding." Werner Brock, *An Introduction to Contemporary German Philosophy*, (Cambridge: Cambridge University Press, 1935), pp. 83-84.

35. *Concluding Unscientific Postscript*, p. 54.

... to make sure that he believes against the understanding; ... he makes so much use of the understanding that he becomes aware of the incomprehensible, and then he holds to this, believing against the understanding."[36] Whereas Christian epistemologists hitherto thought that faith is grounded in the reasonable, Kierkegaard reversed the order, demanding that faith derive its energies from the infinite passion of objective uncertainty. When relations are rational and easy, passion is chilled. Spirit is aroused only in the face of frightening contradictions. Since one may calmly assent to formal truth, while at the same time remain offensively untruth in himself, it follows that logical relations simply feed the appetite of sinfulness. Thus, they cannot be a ground for faith.

Faith is a "higher understanding." It goes beyond the formal connections of rationality by gaining insights directly. "Because an individual gives up his understanding for faith and believes against the understanding, he should not think meanly of the understanding, nor suddenly arrogate to himself a glittering distinction within the total compass of the understanding; for after all a higher understanding is also an understanding."[37]

Behind this spectacular reversal in Christian epistemology is Kierkegaard's dread of Hegelianism. Hegel aroused the Dane through his attempted identification of historical becoming with the immanent movement of logical categories. Kierkegaard realized that if history is the quest of the infinite *Geist* for freedom, then the existential assignment of finite spirit is corrupted; for process and becoming are generated by the juxtaposition of logical contraries, not by the decision experiences of the individual.

Kierkegaard lashed back at Hegelianism, protesting with scathing diatribe that logically necessary relations, being *necessary*, cannot become; otherwise they are not necessary. What must be, always has been; it does not suffer change. "Media-

36. *Op. cit.*, p. 504.
37. *Ibid.*, p. 501.

tion can have no place in logic, since it presupposes transition, which is a transcendence that logic excludes. The transition-category is historical, not logical"[38] Logical relations form an eternally necessary *IT IS*, just as the person of God forms an eternally necessary *I AM*. To become is the prerogative of will only; and since the individual alone straddles both time and eternity, it is the existing individual which mediates time and eternity. "The individual through strain and suffering becomes what he becomes."[39] It is unspeakable existential blasphemy to farm out to logic what inwardness is responsible for. "Personality will protest in all eternity against the proposition that absolute contradictions can be mediated . . . it will repeat its *immortal* dilemma through all eternity: to be or not to be, that is the question."[40] To *be* is not to occupy space; to *be* is to mediate absolute love through an infinite passionate decision. The logical and the becoming are as far apart as darkness is from the light.

> In the construction of a logical system, it is necessary first and foremost to take care not to include in it anything which is subject to an existential dialectic, anything which is, only because it exists or has existed, and not simply because it is. From this it follows quite simply that Hegel's unparalleled discovery, the subject of so unparalleled an admiration, namely, the introduction of movement into logic, is a sheer confusion of logical science; to say nothing of the absence, on every other page, of even so much as an effort on Hegel's part to persuade the reader that it is there.[41]

Since thought directs itself backwards, only the decision life of the individual can creatively carve out a future. The philosopher can formulate a complete system of rational connections, but never anything which faintly resembles either be-

---

38. Swenson, *Something About Kierkegaard*, pp. 118-119.

39. *Ibid.*, p. 119.

40. Kierkegaard, *Journals*, (London: Oxford University Press, 1938), §286.

41. *Concluding Unscientific Postscript*, p. 99.

coming or the future. "I get no reply, for philosophy mediates the past and has its existence in it."[42]

But if reason is utilized that faith may believe against reason, how is Christianity brought into the picture? Kierkegaard has a ready answer. Christianity is the final religion because it is based on the most thinkably offensive paradox. Since the more offensive the objective becomes, the stronger faith is, passion is accented maximally when it reaches that logical contradiction beyond which it is impossible to pass. And this paradox is the incarnation of Christ, an absolute contradiction in the strictest sense of the term. Paradox is present whenever time and eternity are juxtaposed;[43] and only by the earnestness of his faith can the individual bring about a union of these two realms. In the instance of the incarnation of Christ, however, the eternal God became a finite individual. "Behold where he stands — God! Where? There; do you not see him? He is God; and yet he has not a resting-place for his head, and he dares not lean on any man lest he cause him to be offended. He is God."[44] When judged by the canon of contradiction (declares Kierkegaard), the incarnation is complete nonsense. "The paradox consists principally in the fact that God, the Eternal, came into existence in time as a particular man."[45]

But how does faith know that Christ is God in human flesh? Flesh we see, yes, but where is God? Jesus is the full measure of God because of the absolute existential truth (love) which

---

42. *Either/Or*, II, p. 144.

43. "Because we are dealing with existence, and not with formal logical patterns produced by the intellect, we are dealing with paradox, with absurdity. Existence itself is a paradox (it is full of antinomies), as it is in the nature of God to be a paradox (He is immanent and transcendent), and of Christianity to be a paradox (for one has the interruption of the temporal process by the eternal). In one's choice, therefore, one has to accept the dialectic, the paradox, the absurdity of existence and choose nevertheless. Faith by virtue of the absurd, cries Kierkegaard. Faith is a recoil from the utter despair of unbelief." Leslie Paul, *The Meaning of Human Experience*, p. 175.

44. Kierkegaard, *Philosophical Fragments*, (Princeton: Princeton University Press, 1936), p. 25.

45. *Concluding Unscientific Postscript*, p. 528.

he mediated through his own person. Christ *is* the truth. For an historical person to love perfectly is as impossible as a door with one side; but it happened nonetheless.

> His meat was to do His Father's will; thus He was one with the Father, one with every demand of the law, so its perfecting was a necessity to Him, His sole need in life. The love in Him was perpetually active; there was no moment, not one single instant in His whole life when His love was merely a passive feeling which seeks expression while it lets time pass; or a mood which produces a self-satisfaction and dwells on itself while the task is neglected. No, His love was expressed in perpetual activity; even when He wept, was this not redeeming the time?[46]

In deciding for Christ, one gains only in proportion to his willingness to break with the congeniality of reason. The more reasonable the incarnation is made, the less is a place left for the passion of decision.

Kierkegaard therefore launched a galling attack against all who bestrew complacency by making Christianity acceptable to reason. When the sting of offense is taken away, the faith of inwardness is corrupted. "For the defense wishes out of the goodness of its heart, to take the possibility of offense away. . . . Take away from Christianity the possibility of offense . . . and then lock the churches, the sooner the better, or make them into recreation centers."[47] The mistake of Christian apologists consists in their going at the problem retrogressively. Instead of adorning the splendor of the paradox, showing the great cost involved in believing, they try to reduce the offense, making acceptance of Christianity easy and painless. "Oh, these proofs which are advanced for the truth of Christianity, these devilish learned and profound and perfectly convincing proofs."[48] There is no speedier way to decompose Christianity's uniqueness than to melt down the absoluteness of the paradox. "They sought by reasons to prove the truth

---

46. *Works of Love*, pp. 81-82.
47. *Ibid.*, pp. 162-163.
48. *Attack Upon "Christendom,"* p. 145.

of Christianity, or to adduce reason in support of it. And these reasons — they begat doubt, and doubt became the stronger. For the proof of Christianity really consists in 'following.' That they did away with. So they felt the need of reasons; but these reasons, or the fact that there are reasons, is already a sort of doubt — and so doubt arose and thrived upon the reasons."[49]

Totally apart from its destruction of faith, furthermore, proofs for God are rationally futile. There is nothing quite as humorous as to watch a finite demonstration of the Almighty. "If God does not exist it would of course be impossible to prove it; and if he does exist it would be folly to attempt it."[50] Kierkegaard dismissed the ontological argument as a tissue of fallacies:

> For if God is not really conceived as existing in the first part of the argument, the argument cannot even get started. It would then read about as follows: 'A supreme being who does not exist must possess all perfections, including that of existence; *ergo*, a supreme being who does not exist does exist.' This would be a strange conclusion. Either the supreme being was non-existent in the premises, and came into existence in the conclusion, which is quite impossible: or he was existent in the premises, in which case he cannot come into existence in the conclusion.[51]

But if the incarnation is a total offense to reason, why accept it, anyway? Why not veer to the side and believe something else? The answer is that one cannot spurn love incarnate without spurning everything which comprises self-dignity in the individual. Whoever admits that he is responsible for doing what he cannot do (and thus rejects Pelagianism) has already committed himself to Christianity. By parting with rational coherence he gains infinite satisfaction — eternal happiness. It is happiness because spirit is taxed to full capa-

---

49. Kierkegaard, *For Self-Examination and Judge for Yourselves!* (Princeton: Princeton University Press, 1944), p. 88.
50. *Philosophical Fragments*, p. 31.
51. *Concluding Unscientific Postscript*, p. 298.

city; and the happiness is eternal because the dialectically directed life is in harmony with the essential order of reality itself.

> And so I say to myself: I choose; that historical fact means so much to me that I decide to stake my whole life upon that if. Then he lives; lives entirely full of the idea, risking his life for it: and his life is the proof that he believes. He did not have a few proofs, and so believed and then began to live . . . . That is called risking; and without risk faith is an impossibility.[52]

If Christ is the revelation of the law of eternity, *then believe;* for further time spent questing after proofs and evidences only increases the vigor of sin. We are untruth as long as we abide in complacency.

Kierkegaard's astounding conclusion is that faith is not only obliged to shun the advices of reason and objective evidence, but it also is empowered with authority to create its own object of devotion. "Freedom is the truly wonderful lamp; when a man rubs it with ethical passion, God comes into being for him."[53] Whatever causes a man to be passionate is a valid object of commitment, for it is the commitment which is truth indeed. The object is simply the occasion for the decision of inwardness. Away with Scripture; away with scientific proofs; away with apologetics; away with doctrine; away with systems. It is more than enough that faith confidently clings to the isolated proposition, "God became an individual." Beyond this is sinful complacency.

> If the contemporary generation had left nothing behind them but these words: 'We have believed in such and such a year God appeared among us in the humble figure of a servant, that he lived and taught in our community, and finally died,' it would be more than enough. The contemporary generation would have done all that was necessary; for this little advertisement, this *nota bene* on a page of universal

---

52. *Journals,* §1044.
53. *Concluding Unscientific Postscript,* p. 124.

history, would be sufficient to afford an occasion for a successor, and the most voluminous account can in all eternity do nothing more.[54]

III. The Initial Difficulty

There can be no question but what Kierkegaard has given a profoundly convincing defense of the third locus of truth. What Christianity has always assumed, Kierkegaard made explicit. "For I desire *goodness,* and not sacrifice." (Hosea 6:6) "I appeal to you therefore, brethren, by the mercies of God, to present your bodies as a *living* sacrifice, holy and acceptable to God, which is your spiritual service." (Romans 12:1) "I by my *works* will show you my faith." (James 2:18) Saving faith is not simply an intellectual assent to objective facts. Faith is cordial trust; it is a concerned, inward response to the person and work of Jesus Christ. Until the end of time, therefore, men who remember what it means to be a person will defend the supremacy of truth as inwardness. God sent his Son to make us *good,* not simply to make it possible for us to recite the creeds of the church.

But what must be questioned is the prudence of Kierkegaard's attempt to secure inward truth by opposing it to objective evidences. It is from *his* lips, not those of the Biblical writers, one learns that faith must believe what the understanding finds contradictory — and for that very reason. Scripture's healthy balance of the loci of truth has been upset by Kierkegaard. Rationality was bequeathed by Jesus Christ as a light by which men may penetrate the darkness of error. "The true light that enlightens [gives a spiritually rational nature to] every man was coming into the world." (John 1:9) Being a rational creature, thus, man must proportion his spiritual commitments to what the mind can conscientiously clear. Apart from this distribution of authority edification is impossible.

---

54. *Philosophical Fragments,* p. 87.

Therefore, he who speaks in a tongue should pray for the power to interpret. For if I pray in a tongue, my spirit prays but my mind is unfruitful. What am I to do? I will pray with the spirit and I will pray with the mind also; I will sing with the spirit and I will sing with the mind also. Otherwise, if you bless with the spirit, how can any one in the position of an outsider say the 'Amen' to your thanksgiving when he does not know what you are saying? For you may give thanks well enough, but the other man is not edified.[55]

Saving faith germinates only after the mind is first convinced of the sufficiency of the evidences. If Christ taught plain logical nonsense — such as *Homntrecn beibdt rushll* — a balanced man would turn aside from him as one to be pitied, not trusted. The reason why we are able to trust Christ is that he spoke and lived in a way which is congenial with our axiological expectations.

A. *Faith and Reason in Daily Life*

There is nothing offensive about the Scriptural insistence that faith be based on a co-operative activity of spirit and mind, for it is the very arrangement we are obliged to respect in all conscious activity. We commit ourselves in faith to — that is, we act with concern over — only what is reasonable. The faculty of intelligence is the guide of our lives. By its word we conclude that since the alarm has rung it is time to arise; that this hallway leads to the bathroom; that this is our toothbrush in front of us; that these are our children with us at breakfast; that the driveway is clear as we back our automobile out; that the signals in traffic mean what they say; that the building ahead contains the office in which we must labor for the day, etc. *And in no case do we act passionately in defiance of the report of reason.* The only way a person can maintain both social respect and personal sanity is to proportion his commitment to the veraciousness of the evidence which the understanding processes. When reason assures us that our automobile is the blue one parked just beyond yonder sign, we

---

55. I Corinthians 14:13-17.

dare not passionately believe against the understanding that the brown car over to the left belongs to us. Suppose that a person, having generated enough passion to act in opposition to the understanding, concluded: "My understanding tells me that this is a porcupine, but I passionately believe that it is my loving wife." If he existentially acts upon this urge, the results will be interesting. The porcupine will be perplexed, the wife greatly resentful, and the individual filled with quills. In any case the terminal value could hardly commend itself to a person who remembers he is made in the image of God.

If our conduct in life is able to suggest any axiom, it is the following: *The native person — the one unaffected by corrupting philosophic presuppositions — is at his best, and is most ideally a man of faith, when he obeys, rather than defies, the report of a critically developed understanding.* If my understanding assures me that I cannot drive through the darkness ahead because a bridge has been washed out, I come to grief when I permit my inward passion for crossing to go in defiance of the evidences. Faith may *remove* mountains, but it cannot declare mountains to be non-mountains.

B. *The Controversial Exception*

At this point Kierkegaard interrupts to say that the above discussion is entirely beside the point. Not only does he himself grant that *nous* is part of the *imago dei* — and thus is the daily guide in our practical affairs — but that all praise belongs to the understanding for the regal authority of its office. There is only one realm in which reason must be defied, and that is when our eternal happiness is at stake. Whenever time and eternity intersect, paradox results. It is at this point that objectivity brings offense to the understanding. The finite cannot assimilate the infinite without facing paradox. To seek to construct a rational bridge between time and eternity is to assume the very attitude of sinful detachment and disdain which is characteristic of existential untruth. The very *desire* to meet God on congenial, rational terms is sinful. If the brideto-be is offended to see her bridegroom calmly collect rational evidences to prove her existence, God is slashed in heart to have his own children leisurely move about the world, using strength supplied from him, to accumulate evidences which make it rationally respectable for them to believe there is a God.

Kierkegaard appears firmly convinced that a faith which reposes in objectively veracious evidences is not a faith at all. Faith rises and falls in proportion to the risk the will must take in the leap of decision. One has no faith when doing mathematics, since all venture is missing; but infinite faith is generated when approaching God, for the proof of God's existence is the commitment itself. Any bridge to eternity apart from the existential witness is untruth.

> In this objectivity one tends to lose that infinite personal interestedness in passion which is the condition of faith, the *ubique et nusquam* in which faith can come into being. Has anyone who previously had faith gained anything with respect to its strength and power? No, not in the least. Rather is it the case that in this voluminous knowledge, this certainty that lurks at the door of faith and threatens to devour it, he is in so dangerous a situation that he will need to put forth much effort in great fear and trembling, lest he fall a victim to the temptation to confuse knowledge with faith. While faith has hitherto had a profitable schoolmaster in the existing uncertainty, it would have in the new certainty its most dangerous enemy. For if passion is eliminated, faith no longer exists, and certainty and passion do not go together.[56]

Once Kierkegaard restricted his revolt from logic to time-eternity relations, he greatly strengthened his case. Not only is it true that we have moved into a new genus, but also the individual himself is so concerned to learn of God that he would be the last to follow a method which might jeopardize his success. Since everything turns on God's mercy toward us. a wise man will always seek to maintain proper decorum before

---

56. *Concluding Unscientific Postscript*, p. 30.

the Almighty. If it is indecorous to seek out rational evidences for God's existence, then let the evidences go.

With all candor, however, one finds it impossible to concede Kierkegaard's thesis that in matters of eternal happiness we may — nay, *must* — go against the understanding. The obvious difficulty is that in our approach to eternal things — whether we follow either analogy or dialectic — we doom our venture to defeat the instant we turn aside from a mindful respect of the degrees of objective evidence. If there is any realm where we should expect to rally all our faculties for one harmonious thrust toward truth, it is at the point where our eternal happiness is at stake. If the witness of daily life has another axiomatic insight to teach us, it is the following: *The obligation of the will to clear with the verdict of the understanding rises in direct ratio to the importance of the value at stake.*

Unless the point has been missed, Kierkegaard appears to be instructing men to do quite the opposite of what they are natively obliged to respect if they are to live integrally both with themselves and with others about them. He counsels that in inconsequential situations we may act in complacent conformity to logical coherence; but when the supreme value of eternal happiness is in question, it is necessary that we break with reason and believe against the understanding. In the real affair of living, however, we proceed in inverse order. The things which are of no significance may be believed against the understanding, while the values which count for the most must not. Suppose, for example, that as I lounge on the front porch during my summer vacation my eyes chance to fall on a patch of green in the distance. Since it is of no concern to me what the color might represent, I can legitimately employ the prerogative of believing against the understanding. Perhaps it is a colony of blithe fairies dancing around a green fire; or perchance it is a vernal forest of cookies and candy. My hypotheses would hardly stand up under scientific investigation, of course. But no worry; no investigation will be undertaken. Nothing matters whether the green is a golf course, a repulsive dragon, or an illusion of distant water. Under these circumstances — *if anywhere* — one may believe against the understanding.

Observe, however, that as the things which are of concern to us come into focus — the values about which our personal happiness revolves — a man comes to grief the instant he is careless in his dealing with rational evidences. Recently a fireman rushed into a burning building to save a small girl trapped in one of the rooms. In his anxiety to save the frightened child he mistakenly seized a life-sized doll lying on the bed near the little one. The doll was saved from the fire, while the child perished. Notice the cause of his error: Because of his great passion to preserve happiness, he momentarily lapsed into a state of careless respect for the report of the understanding. He did not *intend* to believe against the understanding, but in his actions he finally did. If he had been scrupulous in his employment of rational coherence, he would have known that the evidences which he faced pointed in the direction of doll, not child.

The principle illustrated here holds in every conceivable circumstance where the valuable is in the balance: The more a value increases, the more our concern should respect the report of reason. When a fleeing man comes to a fork in the road, knowing that one path leads to life while the other guides to death, he will critically examine the evidence and then act in harmony with the report of the understanding. Suppose he said, "My understanding tells me that if I go to the right I will find life; but in passionate faith I shall act against the understanding; for I will be complacent in my decision if I follow objective truth." One would label him unbalanced. *Worthy passion is aroused by the nature of the value in question, not the strength or weakness of the evidences which support it.*

And when the supreme value is brought into the discussion, namely, faith in God, the heart can think of absolutely no reason why the axiom which guides us in all other axiological situations should now suddenly fail. If God's existence is of infinite concern to us, we ought to express infinite determination to obey, rather than defy, the understanding. Since the gods of the heathen, like the poor, are with us always, it behooves a rational man to be exceedingly cautious when he worships deity. In his enthusiasm to find Christ he might wind up worshiping non-Christ, and so lose all through his rational mismanagement. Does one adorn his faith to say, "My understanding assures me that the historical Jesus is the revelation of God's *agape* in the flesh; but since I experience less passion if I respect objective evidences, I passionately believe that God has revealed himself through a motley land turtle"?

Kierkegaard says that a heathen who passionately worships an idol has more truth than the Christian who is complacent. This is a questionable statement — very questionable, indeed. If the name of God means anything, God must be jealous that worship be given to him alone. Feeble worship directed to him is far preferable to strong worship of a false god, therefore. In all personal relations it is infinitely important that the intention of the person coincide with the reality of the one being loved, for love cannot be accomplished by proxy. Is the wife consoled to learn that though her husband is embracing another woman, he actually believes that it is she he is with? Hardly. The passion of his intention does not compensate for his responsibility to terminate his amorous overtures upon her person. An imperfect husband who at least lives with his wife is much to be preferred to the one who passionately distributes his affections to everyone who in faith he thinks is his wife. In like manner, the Father of Jesus Christ does *not* take consolation from observing the heathen worshiping non-God, even though they worship with more existential earnestness than the Christian who mildly chooses Christ.

Therefore, Kierkegaard's advice that we believe against the understanding cannot commend itself to a person who still respects the fact that he is made in the image of God. Rationality is so integral to our nature that when we betray it in favor of a higher understanding, we corrupt our own person. If rationality tells us that two and two are four, we cannot passionately live as if they total seven. All of the existential heat in the world cannot alter facts *in rerum natura*. Once a warfare is declared between the head and the heart, the inner balance of man is endangered. The will and the understanding were tempered together to act as teammates in a global struggle against common enemies; they must not revolt against each other in mutiny.

IV. The Problem of Error

No religious or philosophic thinker has ever turned to the complexities of epistemology without noticing the omnipresent specter of the problem of error on the edge of every page of argument. How can we be sure our conclusions are justified? What is a valid argument? If we cannot test propositions for error, we can never exclude the possibility that the particular statements we believe are themselves instances of the very error we cannot test.

If the problem of error is urgent in philosophical matters, it is desperate in religious situations. There are hundreds of conflicting religions in the world, each presuming to have the whole truth, yet each teaching doctrines which logically exclude the verity of the other religions. And if anything is clear from an examination of the history of the Christian church, it is the somber warning that the farther theologians recede from an objective test for error, the more deeply the religious life of the church descends into fanaticism. Responsible thought is corrupted whenever heart and reason are related discontinuously.

This danger could be exemplified many times over from the early passages of Quaker history. A zealous young preacher named Farnsworth proposed a preaching tour on a diet of nothing but spring water and Scripture. Richard Sale, a constable, felt moved to go through Chester barefoot and bare-legged, in sackcloth and ashes, flowers in his right hand and 'stinking weeds' in his left; this was supposed to be a sign. He felt moved also to walk through Eastgate Street, London, carrying a lighted candle as a testimony against worship by candlelight. A Quakeress named Susanna Pearson was convinced she could bring back to life a young man who had drowned himself; so she had his corpse unearthed, lay on it, and prayed; unfortunately it had to be reinterred. Fox called this a 'mad whimse,' but Fox himself did not escape the dangers of this sort of spirit that controlled men 'not in partnership with their own faculties, but independently and infallibly.'[57]

Religion often pretends an easy excuse for carelessness in logic on the premise that its cause is promoted "in the name of the Lord." But such an attitude erroneously regards God as one who disrespects rational connections. Should it be that God is not related to men rationally, it would be impossible for thoughtful men ever to know his will; for everything he promises might mean its exact opposite.

A. Kierkegaard and the Problem of Error

Whenever one asks Kierkegaard how a man of faith can test his own decision life for error, he is told that he should be so occupied by commitment that he has no occasion to lapse into such complacent inquiry. Speculation vitiates *Existenz* by calmly substituting rational problems for the vitality of commitment itself. "The crucial thing is not deliberation but the baptism of the will which lifts up the choice into the ethical."[58] The half-truth here is that one can only learn experiential truth through an experience itself. No one has ever denied that. There is a greater presentational richness in plunging into the pool of water than in speculating over what it would be like if the dip were actually taken. Out of commitment comes the knowledge of what it means to be committed. The issue is, rather, why one ought to commit himself to this or to that in the first place. How can advices leading to commitment be screened for error? Perhaps it is not prudent to learn by commitment — as in taking poison into the stomach or placing

57. Brand Blanshard, "The Inner Light," *Harvard Divinity School Bulletin,* March 10, 1946, p. 57.
58. *Either / Or,* II, p. 143.

one's head under a moving drill press. It is far better to have the paltry theoretical knowledge of what it might be to suffer an agonizing death than to learn its richness through actual decease. Better it is to be a live rationalist than a dead existentialist. And so with becoming a Christian: What standard shall one employ to ascertain whether he gains or loses values through commitment? Both the Christian and the non-Christian declare that one can learn the truth only in commitment. For which shall an axiologically sensitive man decide? Is an experiential knowledge of Christianity worth-while?

Kierkegaard is very clear when describing the values one gains in commitment: In Christianity one enjoys a perspective from which existence itself can be explained. The existential task keeps the individual dialectically suspended between the rule of truth and the impossibility of ever realizing it. The individual is untruth by virtue of existence itself. There is no possibility of frustration to those who live dialectically, for they always have the eternal before their minds. They suffer no crisis of disappointment, for they are in a crisis every moment.

The question remains, nevertheless, how one can test this commitment for error. How can one determine that this expression of the dialectic, rather than another, best yields the unfrustrated life of tension? At this point Kierkegaard's aversion to reason counsels him to amalgamate the irrational with the test of error itself. The more risk faith takes, the truer it is. Because becoming a Christian involves the greatest risk of all, it therefore is the truest form of faith.

> Without risk there is no faith. Faith is precisely the contradiction between the infinite passion of the individual's inwardness and the objective uncertainty. If I am capable of grasping God objectively, I do not believe, but precisely because I cannot do this I must believe. If I wish to preserve myself in faith I must constantly be intent upon holding fast the objective uncertainty, so as to remain out upon

the deep, over seventy thousand fathoms of water, still preserving my faith.[59]

In broadest terms, Kierkegaard takes his stand in the Thomistic tradition. Catholic philosophers teach that it "is impossible that one and the same thing should be believed and seen by the same person."[60] When one knows something, he does not believe it; when he believes it, he does not know it. Aquinas sought to safeguard this bifurcation of faith and reason by saying that though faith goes "beyond" reason, it does not go "against" it. Kierkegaard, however, is firmly persuaded that if believing is not equivalent with knowing, then the farther faith is removed from reason the more pure it becomes. "Anything that is almost probable or extremely and emphatically probable, is something he can almost know, or as good as know, or extremely and emphatically almost *know* — but it is impossible to *believe*. For the absurd is the object of faith, and the only object that can be believed."[61] Because the reasonable is able to address the mind congenially, it leaves the ego undamaged. If eternity is to cut across our complacency, it must completely shock our expectations. It must leave us gasping and shaken. Only then are we passionately engaged.

The outcome of this epistemology is a sliding scale of faith values. One can measure the quality of his faith by the intensity of the absurd he has courage to face. Since "without risk there is no faith,"[62] it follows that the greater the risk is, the more faith develops; until in the end one shows his perfection in Christ by believing that which completely offends the intellect. *"The absurd is precisely by its objective repulsion the measure of the intensity of faith in inwardness."*[63] A simple application of concomitant variations results: As objective repulsiveness increases, the intensity of the existential commit-

59. *Concluding Unscientific Postscript*, p. 182.
60. Aquinas, *Summa Theologica*, II, Q. 1, Art. 5.
61. *Concluding Unscientific Postscript*, p. 189.
62. *Ibid.*, p. 188.
63. *Ibid.*, p. 189. (Italics mine)

ment increases; as incoherence diminishes, faith diminishes.
"The less outwardness, the more inwardness."[64] People who refuse to commit themselves to foolish things can enter the kingdom only with great difficulty. Ignorant men may easily find
their way to kingdom truth because they yield, rather than inquire. "The greater a man's equipment of knowledge and culture, the more difficult it is for him to become a Christian."[65]
There is little wonder why the act of becoming a Christian was
the most fearful thing in the world for Kierkegaard, for whoever would pass through the kingdom gates must first check his
understanding outside. "When faith requires a man to give up
his reason, it becomes equally difficult for the cleverest and the
most stupid person to believe, or it becomes in a sense more
difficult for the clever."[66]

But if the rationalist's vomitive is the existentialist's nutri-
ment, pray, then, what is the place of reason in the test for
truth? Kierkegaard answers: Reason has the assignment of
searching out what things are offensive in the first place, and
of exhibiting how absurd the offensive really is, in the second.
"To explain the paradox would then mean to understand more
and more profoundly what a paradox is, and that the paradox
is the paradox."[67] Here is the final test for truth in Christianity: The incarnation is the most objectively absurd thing in
all the world. "What now is the absurd? The absurd is —
that the eternal truth has come into being in time, that God has
come into being, has been born, has grown up, and so forth,
precisely like any other individual human being, quite indistinguishable from other individuals."[68] Freedom lives in the
aura of paradox whenever it faces eternity in time, for two
separate orders of being are juxtaposed. But when the whole
God becomes an individual man, freedom swoons and the intellect is crucified. The passionate man "merely thrusts the

---

64. *Ibid.*, p. 341.
65. *Ibid.*, p. 342.
66. *Ibid.*, p. 337.
67. *Ibid.*, p. 197.
68. *Ibid.*, p. 188.

understanding away in the interests of inwardness in exist·ing."[69]

> That God has existed in human form, has been born, grown up, and so forth, is surely the paradox *sensu strictissimo*, the absolute paradox. As such it cannot relate itself to a relative difference between men. A relative paradox relates itself to the relative difference between more or less cleverness and brains; but the absolute paradox, just because it is absolute, can be relevant only to the absolute difference that distinguishes man from God, and has nothing to do with the relative . . . . But the absolute difference between God and man consists precisely in this, that man is a particular existing being . . . while God is infinite and eternal.[70]

The inescapable difficulty of this test for error is that, when taken to its full logical conclusion, Biblical Christianity itself vanishes. Since it happens that there is a univocal point of identity binding the eternal God and a finite individual together — for both God and man are *persons* — is it not true that the incarnation is an "absolute" paradox. The Christian church has always defended the doctrine that the entrance of the Creator into his image and likeness is not a derogation to the Divine majesty — humbling in dignity though the descent was. There could be no lovelier garment for God to robe himself with than unfallen human nature, a nature replete with righteousness, knowledge, and holiness of the truth. Since man is made in the image of God, therefore, the intellect is *not* completely offended to learn that God has taken on his own image. The incarnation may be received by rational minds without self-betrayal. Indeed, great is the mystery of the hypostatical union! But the mystery is not to be confused with objective paradox. If we are searching for *absolute* paradox, we must go beyond the incarnation. It is far more strenuous to believe in the whole God becoming half a man. for example, or half of God becoming a whole man. And it is most absurd to believe

---

69. *Ibid.*, p. 195.
70. *Ibid.*, pp. 194-195.

in the whole God becoming a common earthworm. Not being made in God's image, the worm is an altogether unfit receptacle for the holiness of God, for an infinite person is joining with a finite non-person. On hearing this, some cry out:

But what expressions of consciousness can God release through the organs of an angleworm? What passion for fellowship can a worm possess? And what consolation does faith receive from beholding deity incarnate in a writhing soft-bellied creature of the soil? *No matter!* Faith must not be blocked by objectively directed questions. We are to believe, not investigate. We are to be witnesses to the truth, not interrogators. Freedom is the wonderful lamp, which, when rubbed, brings God incarnate in a worm into being! To cavil whether or not this marvelous entrance of God into a worm ever took place is to retreat from faith to sinful, objective inquiry. "Here is God! Where? Over there! Can't you see? But all I can see is a naked, red worm retreating from fellowship with men to join the limbless creatures of the soil. But that *is* God! Though ruling heaven and earth, yet God has not a place where to lay his head. You cannot believe? But you must! Stake all on it! If you retreat from this offense you only throttle the powers of freedom and faith within you!"

What other conclusion can there be but that Kierkegaard's obsession to defend the third locus of truth drove him to the point where, if men were to pursue such a theory of knowledge, madness would result. "If a thinker without paradox is an inconsiderable fellow, the thinker who loves the absurd for its own sake is, in his own way, a questionable character, for he may easily turn out as much falsity as truth or as much nonsense as sense."[71] If "to accept the idea of a 'God-man' is much the same as accepting the idea of a 'round square,' "[72] there is no more *meaning* to believing in Christ than in a four-angled triangle. The only question which may rightfully be asked — without retreating to a theory of faith which Kierke-

---

71. Marjorie Grene, *Dreadful Freedom*, (Chicago: University of Chicago Press, 1948), p. 37.
72. Mackintosh, *Types of Modern Theology*, p. 247.

gaard has already spurned — is whether or not passionate inwardness follows from one commitment or another. If one is able to rest his eternal happiness in a God-man myth of a pagan religion, for example, the only test such a one must meet is the barometric reading of passion. It is the baptism of the will which is the important factor, not the object to which one commits himself.

Some have sought to rescue Kierkegaard from this slippery road to skepticism and nihilism, but all in vain. Observe the following as a typical instance:

> It is true that Adolf Hitler was an existential thinker, of sorts; so are most of the inmates of insane asylums. To this charge, so frequently brought against existentialism, there is a pragmatic answer—and another answer which applies to Christianity alone. The pragmatic answer consists simply in pointing out that the false 'ultimates' refute themselves in experience: they lead to the disintegration of a personality and not to its unification. The other answer is that Christianity by definition excludes irrationalism: the 'choice' here cannot possibly be arbitrary, because it is the choosing of Eternity in time.[73]

There are two rather convincing reasons why these comments cannot apply to Kierkegaard. Let us consider them in turn.

First, pragmatic fruits are themselves a species of objective consolation, a reward toward which men may set their sights: and *any* relaxation is a virus in the arteries of pure passionate inwardness. It was against this — and all other forms of refuge from dialectical tension — that the Dane fired his most telling ammunition, for the whole existential venture rests on the disavowing of all grounds of complacency. Furthermore, not only does Kierkegaard nowhere make health in the inner man a test of truth, but he consistently disavowed such integration in himself. The more existential he became, in fact, the more bitter and rancorous his own soul grew. This is proved by the vitriolic literature he penned toward the end of his life.

---

73. Robert Bretall (Ed.), *A Kierkegaard Anthology,* (Princeton: Princeton University Press, 1946), xxi.

His salvation lay within the dialectical tension of striving, never in possession. One searches in vain for the warm consolation of justification by imputed righteousness. A perpetual activism forced out the Biblical promises of possession of truth and hope in Christ. *Any* claim to possession is untruth, for existence itself is a contradiction.

> He was not able to find 'the freedom of the Christian man.' Salvation lay for him in the future; this life was hope and suffering, but hardly more. He remained to the end a Johannes Climacus, one who wished to be a Christian but was not yet one. Though in the last phase he seemed to have broken through to a decision, it was death which saved him from discovering how uncertain was the ground on which he stood.[74]

If the master neither sought nor found pragmatic fruits, where shall the disciple stand?

Second, nothing could be less a reflection of the actual case than the optimism that Christianity by definition excludes irrationalism. According to Kierkegaard, rather than *excluding* the irrational, Christianity is *based* on the absurd. "For the absurd is the object of faith, and the only object that can be believed."[75] If the object of faith did not engage the reason offensively, we would simply condone the entrance of another form of immanence and complacency.[76]

One can only wish that Kierkegaard's personality had not prevented him from submitting his manuscripts to friends for critical reading. His insights into both the nature of love and the third locus of truth are too inimitable to be united with

74. E. L. Allen, *Kierkegaard: His Life and Thought,* (London: Stanley Nott, Ltd., 1935), p. 306.
75. *Concluding Unscientific Postscript,* p. 189.
76. Chaning-Pearce is unconvincing: "The test of truth for Kierkegaard and all existential Christian thinking which accepts his dual premise is thus an existential decision or apprehension of the self when confronted with the objective reality of life and God." Donald Attwater (Ed), *Modern Christian Revolutionaries,* (New York: Devin-Adair Company, 1947), p. 23. If Kierkegaard has been correctly interpreted thus far, it follows that it is enough that one *think* the evidences are objective, whether they are thus or not. The value is the passion, not the accidental source instrumental in its rise.

a theory of knowledge which can justify neither the presence of truth nor the absence of error.

> Start with the assumption that what God says must at least make human sense, and we know what to think when some dervish from the desert or from Berchtesgaden raises his voice to claim guidance from above. Start from the assumption of Kierkegaard . . . that revelation must needs be an offence to our understanding, and what is to prevent us also from becoming blind followers of the blind?[77]

When common sense and reason must be betrayed to establish them, it is difficult to appreciate the central contributions of any thinker. Would not a communist hail with gusto Kierkegaard's doctrine that time and eternity are related paradoxically! If paradox has the power to establish love in one instance, it can with equal ease justify world hatred and revolution. How can we believe that vicious means can bring about good ends? How can we say that the sordid is another name for the pleasant? Are these not contradictions? *Believe!* for your eternal happiness hangs on it! Your understanding cannot help you, since it *is* logically offensive to destroy the world to make peace; but for this very reason believe it! Stake all on it!

Whatever guidance we may glean from Kierkegaard, we must draw the line at that point where reason is betrayed. The result of setting faith against logic is the loss of a test for error. "Suffice it to say that few men have offered to God such a sacrifice as he did, yet surely what he gave was that one sacrifice which God does not ask of his children, for it was a quenching of the Inner Light."[78]

B. *Contemporary Dialectical Theology*

The speed with which dialectical theology displaced the liberal theology of immanence is a partial tribute to the power of Kierkegaard to capture the imagination of great minds.

---

77. Blanshard, "The Inner Light," p. 63.
78. Allen, *op. cit.*, p. 22.

It is hardly possible to overturn a spadeful of soil without uncovering some of the rapidly spreading roots of this new theology. Although Continental expressions are more dialectical than those in America — for the Continent has faced the crisis of our hour more directly than its neighbor across the sea — both at home and abroad thinkers have joined together to celebrate Kierkegaard's insights. Amidst a sea of variations, one denominator is shared in common: *the real man is the existential man, and the relation between time and eternity is dialectical.*

A Herculean effort has been made by dialectical theologians to correct the extravagances in Kierkegaard, to be sure, and it must be admitted that great strides have been made. Nevertheless, since the third locus of truth is still supported by dialectical tension, rather than by a wholesome repose in objective, rational evidences, modern dialectical theology has not been able to slough off Kierkegaard's revolt against Aristotelian logic.

The skirmish between Barth and Brunner over the value and extent of the point of contact illustrates the unsettled conditions prevailing in the new theology. To what degree must revelation be an offense to our understanding? Barth denies all point of contact, while Brunner admits a small zone. While neither may have reached a definitive statement concerning point of contact, however, each is persuaded that whenever revelation does enter time it *must* offend rational categories. The Greek stands for the rational mind, and the gospel is "foolishness to the Greek." When Barth is asked if dogmatics is obliged to justify itself before the canons of philosophy, therefore, he replies with a dogmatic *Nein!* "It cannot be otherwise than that Dogmatics runs counter to every philosophy no matter what form it may have assumed."[79] If this is

---

79. Karl Barth, *Credo*, p. 186. "All our activities of thinking and speaking can have only a secondary significance and, as activities of the creature, cannot possibly coincide with the truth of God that is the source of truth in the world. The value of what theology has to say is measured by no standard except that of its *object*." *Loc. cit.* Barth, in sum, is a philosophic skeptic.

true, however, then dogmatics should not even use language in its expression; for words are based on the law of contra-diction. Brunner, not quite as dialectical as Barth — but nevertheless a devoted pupil of Kierkegaard — retains tension in the divine-human encounter by keeping the content of revelation qualitatively different from that in standard phil-osophic inquiry. "Revelation" knowledge is different from "rational" knowledge.

> The evidence for the knowledge of faith is no whit inferior to that of rational knowledge, but it is evidence of a different kind. It is a knowledge which takes place in the fact that the Spirit of God himself unveils to me the truth of the witness of the Bible to Christ, and so illuminates the eyes of my heart that I now can see for myself. It is not knowledge that I have gained by my own efforts, but it is that which I now have, which is neither capable of proof nor, indeed, requires proof. It is knowledge in the dimension of personal en-counter: God Himself discloses Himself to me. It is revelation . . . . For this truth is both trust and decision: *we must decide either for proof or for trust, either for rational evidence or for the evidence of personal encounter* . . . . *The Holy Spirit, as He who testifies to me the truth of the witness of the Scriptures, creates a 'knowledge' of a new kind.* [80]

If faith and dogmatics have no part with philosophy and rational proof, however, the heart is bequeathed a bifurcation in knowledge which renders the conventional laws of philos-ophy impotent to test for the truth of revelation. Then what test is there for a veracious crisis experience or divine-human encounter? Perhaps what we think is God overtaking us in Christ is either only an emotional disturbance or the by-product of a hidden disease. Since we use coherence to test for truth in all other realms, why should its power suddenly be ruled irrelevant where we need it most, namely, in the testing for revelation? These questions remain unanswered.

> The difficulty with a faith of this kind is that it . . . has thrown down the gauge to reason by insisting that the in-

---

80. Emil Brunner, *Revelation and Reason*, (Philadelphia: The Westmin-ster Press, 1946), p. 179. (Italics mine).

coherent may still be real. And so far as it takes that line, as some Barthians are apparently ready to do, theology is declaring war on philosophy and science. I think I know how such a war is bound to end. It will end in the annihilation of theology, as much by internal paralysis as by external attack. I will not argue this matter beyond quoting Dr. McTaggart to the effect that no one ever tried to break logic but what logic broke him.[81]

It may possibly be true that angels have a perfect intuition for divine things, but this faculty is sadly wanting in sinful humanity. Man can know that it is God, not the devil, speaking to his heart only when what he reveals is consistent (a) with itself and (b) with the total body of philosophic and scientific knowledge which we already have affirmed. If "revelation" knowledge forms a different order of knowledge, then the wedge is set for the defense of such revelations as make people do and believe foolish things.

Reinhold Niebuhr, least dialectical of all, is yet unable to relate Kierkegaard's psychology of sin to the conventional laws of logic without belittling the latter. Convinced that the essential relation between time and eternity is expressed in a dialectical tension created by freedom's apprehension of the law of ideal love, on the one hand, and the involved self's failure to match that height, on the other, (a tension which can obtain equally well on a non-dialectical Biblical structure), conventional laws of consistency are obliged to relinquish their rights whenever they cut across the religious experience of the race. Observe Niebuhr's study of grace "in" and "for" us, for example:

> It is not easy to express both these two aspects of the life of grace, to which all history attests without seeming to offend the canons of logic. That is one reason why moralists have always found it rather easy to discount the doctrine of 'justification by faith.' But here, as in many cases, a seeming defiance of logic is merely the consequence of an effort to express complex facts of experience.[82]

---

81. Blanshard, *op. cit.*, p. 62.
82. Niebuhr, *Human Destiny*, pp. 124-125.

A "seeming" defiance of logic lies so perilously close to an actual defiance, that it serves as a flag of warning for philosophers of religion to proceed with caution. The actual difference between a seeming, and real, defiance might be skillfully obliterated by a dictator armed with an intention to rule the world.

True to Kierkegaard, Niebuhr retains the "leap" in faith. For this reason he is anti-metaphysical. If Christianity were reduced to a rationally satisfying metaphysics, the leap would be destroyed and the Christian faith would be reduced "to metaphysical truths which need not be apprehended inwardly by faith."[83] Once again one fears the invasion of a bifurcated knowledge into religious epistemology. Such an emphasis encourages the unwary to suppose that there is a faculty of "inwardness" which recognizes a knowledge not subject to the canons of logic. While Niebuhr leaves the door ajar for paradox, he quickly closes it when Kierkegaard says that the final truth about life is a *complete* absurdity.

> The final truth about life is always an absurdity but it cannot be an absolute absurdity. It is an absurdity inasfar as it must transcend the 'system' of meaning which the human mind always prematurely constructs with itself as the centre. But it cannot be a complete absurdity or it could not achieve any credence. In this sense Kierkegaard goes too far.[84]

Niebuhr's difficulty (Kierkegaard would reply) is that he has not gone far enough in his dialectical thinking. By retaining an area of rational congeniality, he is making it somewhat convenient for sinful men to have faith. Existential tension is corrupted the instant faith tolerates a point of contact to which the natural man may appeal. Niebuhr is trying to tack between a Kierkegaardian psychology of sin and a form of liberal realism; and what the outcome will be is not yet clear.

---

83. *Ibid.*, p. 61.
84. *Ibid.*, p. 38 n.

But it does seem that some slack must be taken in from one side or the other, for he has already granted Kierkegaard too many of his reigning presuppositions to escape his distressing conclusions.

C. *The Truth about Faith*

It is extremely difficult to understand why it is necessary to antagonize faith's relation to rational evidences. Kierkegaard started off with a completely false prejudice in supposing that inwardness is jeopardized when the mind is satisfied with the consistency of objective evidences. It is *not* psychologically true that passionate concern increases in commensurate ratio to objective uncertainty. In our daily living we *proportion* our inward response to the certainty of the evidences. Suppose, for instance, a man of questionable character comes to me and swears that my house is on fire; rather than being passionate over such objective uncertainty, I only shrug my shoulders and pass my way. Why become excited over nothing? If in the next minute I see smoke rising from the direction of my home, I now become somewhat concerned, though not greatly, for the smoke may be from a passing train. The evidences are not yet sufficient. But if a trusted friend rushes up and gasps out the words that my property is actually on fire, I then become aroused to great concern, for the evidences at last are fully trustworthy. I now passionately act upon the truth of what has been told me, my whole person being satisfied with its coherence. Thus, a faith based on rational evidences is able to nourish a healthy inwardness. But if faith were a passion grounded in objective uncertainty, then I should exhibit my best faith when I have no house, when there is no fire, and (alas) when I myself am not.

There is no convincing reason why time-eternity relations should stand outside of the conventional connections of rational coherence. If rationality does not form a univocal bond of meaning which significantly relates these two orders of being, not only is the venture of faith made difficult; it is rendered impossible. When God is not rationally related to us, we cannot trust him for our salvation. Not only will we never understand what he says, on the one hand, but also we would never know whether he means to perform what he says, on the other.

There is no "leap" in faith. While faith may involve a cordial commitment of the whole man to Jesus Christ, it is a passion which is drawn out by objectively measurable evidences. Whenever spirit is satisfied that the evidences are sufficient, it rests in truth. One ought to repent, for example, only when he has been persuaded that it is an axiologically good thing so to do. Why repent if it is not worth-while? Why believe in Christ if it is not a coherent act? Why be obedient to God's law if it is absurd? Truth is one, not many. Plato long ago realized that the world of Ideas is useful only if it is continuous with rationality as philosophers in the academies know it. The Christian stands in this tradition. Jesus Christ is worthy of our faith — and consequently ought to receive it — because both his person and his doctrine are rationally continuous with the values which we have already accepted in ordinary experience. We do not think dialectically when we do geometry, operate a battery of drill presses, drive our automobiles, or converse with friends. Why, then, should we suddenly do it when we either perform God's will, struggle within the tensions of morality, interpret the Scriptures, or converse with the Father in prayer? There is no cause for a shift. The same Lord of truth is sovereign in both heaven and earth; his mind gives meaning to both natural and special revelation.

V. The Self Is Lost Altogether

Kierkegaard, like Rebekah, gave birth to two struggling children: Theistic theology and atheistic philosophy. And it is significant to observe in this Jacob-Esau struggle for existential hegemony that the philosophic offspring has the more consistent position to offer the modern mind — provided, of course, that one accepts Kierkegaard's thesis, "the less outwardness, the more inwardness." If Kierkegaard examined contemporary dialectical theology he would probably scorn all but Barthianism for returning to the fleshpots of objectivity. What he would think of philosophic existentialism is another question. If he remained consistent with his own teaching, he would be obliged to offer only commendation; for existential philosophy has taken anti-objectivity so seriously that it has made the existing, deciding individual both master and captain of his own salvation. It has swept the sky so clear of outside reference points that only the lonely, creative individual is left.

A. *The Argument for Atheism*

Kierkegaard never veered from his conviction that individuality is most effectively sustained, and freedom maximally accented, when the individual leaps beyond the universal to behold himself transparently in God. The individual is higher than the universal because he experiences the absolute in God. When duty flows from an absolute will, the last refuge of man in immanence is shattered and Religiousness B results. Existence itself is rendered a contradiction. Philosophical existentialists, however, are not moved to tears by this side of Kierkegaardian thinking. They are convinced, much to the contrary, that "transparency in God" is simply a further form of objectivity which stands in the way of full individuality and creativity. God is but a metaphysical crutch for an existentially lazy man to lean on.

> In the view of Sartre and, by Sartre's account, of Heidegger, it is the very denial of God's existence, not the search for him, that makes the inner odyssey of the self seeking the self philosophy's primary concern. The self that existentialism seeks is each person's individual self, which he must forge for himself out of such senseless circumstances, such meaningless limitations, as are given to him. This self-creation— the making of one's essence from mere existence — is demanded of each of us because, according to existentialism, there is no *single* essence of humanity to which we may logically turn as standard or model for making ourselves

thus or so. And there is no single concept of humanity, because there is no God. For the concept of *a* human nature, Sartre believes, was a by-product of the traditional idea of God the maker; and so, when God dies, the notion of an essence of humanity dies with him, leaving just these particular histories of these particular selves to 'live themselves subjectively' as best they can.[85]

Sartre makes several attempts to formulate an intellectual refutation of God's existence; but in the long run he rests his case on existential considerations. Arguments *against* God's existence, even as arguments *for* such an existence, are existentially irrelevant. Sartre, therefore, chooses atheism as the best framework within which to express individuality, even as Kierkegaard chose theism. Since God is an instance of antecedent reality with which man must deal — a metaphysical block to pure freedom — it follows that man would be more creative, more autonomous, and more inwardly passionate if there were no God at all. And thus, there is no God.[86] If Kierkegaard's magical lamp of freedom can bring God into existence, presto, Sartre's lamp can cancel that existence out.

If there is a transcendent being anywhere in the whole universe, it is the free individual who is doomed to existence. "Man is a being who is constantly oriented towards his pos-

85. Grene, *Dreadful Freedom*, pp. 41-42. "L'existentialisme athée que je représente, est plus cohérent. Il déclare que si Dieu n'existe pas, il y a au moins un être chez qui l'existence précède l'essence, un être qui existe avant de pouvoir être défini par aucun concept, et que cet être c'est l'homme ou, comme dit Heidegger, la réalité humaine Qu'est ce que signifie ici que l'existence précède l'essence? Cela signifie que l'homme existe d'abord, se rencontre, surgit dans le monde, et qu'il se définit après." Jean-Paul Sartre, *L'Existentialisme est un Humanisme*, (Paris: Nagel, 1946), p. 21.
86. The same observation was made by Nietzsche. "The death of God brings a profounder loneliness than man has yet known .... What am I? What shall I do with my life? We have to be responsible to ourselves for our own existence. Each of us knows that he is a unique person, but few have the energy, courage or insight to throw off the husks of convention and achieve a sincere realization of their potentialities, and no one can do that for us. But unless we do 'become ourselves,' life is meaningless." George A. Morgan, Jr., *What Nietzsche Means*, (Cambridge: Harvard University Press, 1943), p. 39.

498 A PHILOSOPHY OF THE CHRISTIAN RELIGION

sibilities; the existent is a being who *has* to exist."[87] Only in
an empty and lonely universe is it possible for man to be the
sole creator of his own destiny. When we stand alone — absolutely alone — we are the responsible agents of our own
being. Therefore, Sartre rejects all expressions of authority
which might give the individual an excuse for not being the
author of his own choices.

> He cannot stand any appeal to an authority beyond the indi-
> vidual's responsibility; his almost blatant atheism is an
> expression of his disgust at the reliance by some on values
> for which they themselves assume no immediate responsi-
> bility. His philosophy, consequently, is for lives that see
> themselves as desolate, forlorn, anxious. The man who
> chooses only what someone else has chosen for him is the
> man every existentialist distrusts; choices are dignified only
> by personal deliberation and ownership.[88]

If God existed, man would already be committed to limits
within which freedom may soar; whereas if God does not exist,
the individual is the sole cause of all his decisions. Theism
makes sinners out of individuals by giving them a ground for
indolence.

After scouring Kierkegaard's philosophy, atheistic existentialism found other data which threaten to destroy individuality. Take the value of freedom itself: Kierkegaard was
very thankful for freedom, for by its phenomenal powers he
could joyfully make his way through the stages on life's way
"The religious man has his satisfaction in himself."[89] It is
this "satisfaction in freedom" which Sartre looks upon
askance. Is it not a new form of complacency? Is it not a
sanguine threat to infinite passionate concern? If freedom,
like existence itself, is a curse, then the individual is inwardly
aroused to that point beyond which it is not possible to pro-

87. Jean Wahl, *A Short History of Existentialism*, (New York: Philosophical Library, 1949), pp. 16-17.
88. Ralph Harper, *Existentialism: A Theory of Man*, (Cambridge: Harvard University Press, 1948), p. 98.
89. *Concluding Unscientific Postscript*, pp. 515-516.

ceed. He must face absolute dread. And since the test of truth is inwardness, it follows that there is more truth if freedom is a bane. Kierkegaard, like Abraham, could delightfully lean on the blessing of life itself; for freedom leads to satisfaction. Sartre can lean on nothing — nothing save the indomitable determination to lean on nothing.

> Freedom reveals itself rather, when we screw up our courage to see it without pretense, in the dizzying collapse of external sanctions and universal laws, in the appalling consciousness that I, and I alone, have, absurdly and without reason, brought order out of chaos; that I alone, crudely and stupidly, without cosmic meaning or rational ground, have made a world out of nothing: and with that awareness my world itself totters on the brink of the nothingness from which it came.[90]

When one cries, What must I do to be saved? the existentialist replies (even as Kierkegaard did when men asked for a proof for God's existence) that one should be so busy *being* an individual that he is not ensnared by such complacent inquiries. To seek to be "saved" from something is but another way of refusing to stay put in the endless, meaningless labor of individuality. Salvation — if salvation there be — consists in the *renunciation* of salvation ambitions. We are saved the instant we strive to remain lost.

> Salvation, if it is possible for man to be saved, consists precisely in not regarding salvation as a problem; it consists in the act of decision by which he decides to assume the burden of his finite nature, without giving way to temptations arising from the world and from outside the world, and fulfills

---

90. Grene, *op. cit.*, p. 52. "Decadentism represents an irrevocable withdrawal of man into himself. Having severed the threads which unite human existence to the world of things and other men, and to the transcendency of God, man, confined to his own existence, detects its slightest vibrations, investigates its most secret preoccupations, and follows its obscurest movements. He sees before him existence, not as existence in general, but as the existence which is peculiar to him, as that centre of actions and reactions which is himself, and whose unique career he alone is in a position to explain and reveal." Norberto Bobbio, *The Philosophy of Decadentism,* (New York: The Macmillan Company, 1948), p. 22.

his own mission, unconcerned with saving himself in the eyes of history or in the eyes of God, attentive to no call other than that of inward sincerity, which urges him to regard salvation as a snare and a delusion.[91]

Observe the total grief that this theory comes to: Bobbio contends that we should remain attentive to the call of "inward sincerity." Indeed! But is this not another expression of objectivity? And should not a person be so infinitely occupied in the assignment of individuality that he is undeterred by such objective baits as "inward sincerity?" Thus (it seems) all we have left to do is to stand on a hill and scream at the top of our lungs. There is absolutely no meaning to the act, for to act out of considerations of meaning is once again to respect objectivity.

History's stern justice tends to beat questions out to their true issues. And however harmless Kierkegaard's theory of inwardness may have first appeared, the perspective of time proves that it contains the sting of death in it. Whoever takes up the sword of setting the heart against the head will perish by that sword. Existentialism has ended in complete metaphysical nihilism.

B. *The Peril of Morals*

If freedom can veto God's existence, it can also authorize the nonexistence of a changelessly valid theory of morals. One of the most neglected facets of Kierkegaardian existentialism (one which dialectical theology has not dared to fraternize with) is the hypothesis that the existence of the good is conditioned to the decision life of the one who wills the good.

---

91. *Ibid.*, p. 25. A strong resemblance to Nietzsche can be traced here. "For Nietzsche, indeed, all those mysterious and superhuman metaphysical entities which man has always believed to be without himself, and which he has reverenced under different names—'God,' the world of the 'Thing-in-self,' 'Truth,' the 'Categorical Imperative'—are merely phantoms of our imagination. The most immediate reality, the only reality which it is permitted us to know, is the world of our desires, of our passions." J. M. Kennedy, *The Gospel of Superman*, (New York: The Macmillan Company, 1926), pp. 115-116.

Kierkegaard does not wear the implications of his philosophy on his sleeve. While writing an entire book which presupposes an objective theory of morals (*Works of Love*) — as if love is *one* objectivity which swivels independently of the active life of the individual — Kierkegaard yet defends the skeptical moral theory that the good exists only for the fact that one wills it. There is no good until one desires that there be a good. "The good *is* for the fact that I will it, and apart from my willing it it has no existence."[92] If these words mean what they say — and they can mean no other if we grant the premise of existential activism — it makes no ultimate difference whether one chooses to follow either love or non-love. The point is that an earnest choice has been made, and that is all that counts. "In making a choice it is not so much a question of choosing the right as of the energy, in earnestness, the pathos, with which one chooses."[93] "It is, therefore, not so much a question of choosing between willing the good or the evil, as of choosing to will."[94]

What Kierkegaard feebly whispered in the middle of several bold paragraphs, atheistic existentialism has loudly shouted from the mountains. A changeless code of morals — be it *agape* love or otherwise — is as much an objective limit to creativity as the existence of a divine being to whom we are responsible. Since man is infinitely alone, he can ground his structure of morals in neither God, a collective ego, nor his neighbor. An absolutely free individual is the responsible author of the very order of values to which he at the moment is devoted. "Values are created, in other words, only by the free act of a human agent who *takes* this or that to be good or bad, beautiful or ugly, in the light of his endeavor to give significance and order to an otherwise meaningless world."[95]

Since every decision involves a revolution within the self (for infinite emptiness yawns on every side) every man who

92. *Either/Or*, II, p. 188.
93. *Ibid.*, *p.* 141.
94. *Ibid.*, p. 143.
95. Grene, *op. cit.*, p. 11.

is, is passing through hell — the hell of being. And he will remain in hell until the meaninglessness of death severs his powers of individuality.

What shall I do? "Next to nothing,"[96] responds Heidegger, following the teaching of existentialism to its full end. There can be no normative statement of a way to act, for such a code would only be another objective datum to obstruct autonomy. Man must stand infinitely alone in the solution of every problem. Individuality is lost the instant one goes beyond himself in decisions. "The very manner in which Kierkegaard defined these problems again so narrowed German existential philosophy that its inquiries ended by isolating the individual hopelessly from society, from humanity, from history, or any rational community of spirits."[97]

The logical conclusion to antagonizing the relation between inwardness and metaphysical objectivity is, as suggested, complete chaos. Even tough-minded Heidegger perfectly illustrates the ease with which an individual can pass from the enthronement of *Existenz* to the protection of a collective ego which sustains itself by destroying individuality. The transition is perfectly painless, for having already corrupted individuality in the meaningless taxation of existentialism, nothing is lost or gained in the transaction. "The conversion to Nazism seemed, in Heidegger, the fitting conclusion to a philosophy that described man as destitute of common loyalties and responsibilities, of humility and rational understanding."[98]

What shall I do? In answering this, Sartre adds to confusion by writing voluminously within a philosophic framework of hopeless chaos. Just as there is no changeless truth, so there is no changeless code of morality.[99] In the Sartrean literature,

---

96. Grene, *op. cit,* p. 69.
97. Frederic Lilge, *The Abuse of Learning,* p. 127.
98. *Ibid.,* p. 128. "In his peculiar language, pretentious and profound in an obscure way, he proclaimed not only his own self-abasement but the degradation of philosophy in general to a lackey of the new state." *Ibid.*
99. "Distrust in face of the establishment of all possible forms of systematic and universal knowledge, which is characteristic of existentialism, is encountered here also as distrust in face of the establishment of all possible forms of universally valid social morality." Bobbio, *op. cit.,* p. 28.

therefore, the heroes — Garcin, Mathieu, and Oreste, *e. g.* —
are judged solely by what each chooses within the situation of
his own freedom. There is no standard written in the nature
of either man or the universe by which conduct is evaluated.
This would involve a retreat from the existential gospel. The
free man is the dreadful man, the one who has found himself
by losing reality over against him.

Sartre, however, still possessing too much common sense
to carry existentialism out to its full end, has sought to counter-
balance some of the more cynical effects of moral individualism
by postulating a political theory based on reciprocal relations.
The free man is the genuine revolutionary; but a true revolutionary is he who, while acting in absolute freedom, acts both
for the oppressed and for all men in history. Without a system
of reciprocity within free obligations, revolution would be
simple chaos.

This token gesture to save significance for political action,
however, constitutes a raising of the flag of surrender; for it
proves that without converting himself into a mad ego the
existing individual *cannot* consistently accept Kierkegaard's
thesis that inwardness increases in proportion to objective uncertainty. Sartre *must* introduce objective certainty, or the
whole venture of *Existenz* will blow up. Grene summarizes this
observation crisply:

> Here we have the explicit statement of the oppressor-op-
> pressed subject-object equation. It is in terms of conflict
> and, as far as one can see, conflict only that the revolutionary
> recognizes the 'plurality of liberties.' But suddenly out of
> this grim picture 'one understands the revolutionary move-
> ment and its project, which is to make society pass by
> violence from a state wherein liberties are alienated to an-
> other state founded on their reciprocal recognition.' From
> what human situation, from what new and marvelous source
> in the depths of a subjectivity otherwise so lonely, so closely
> and so constantly endangered, does this balm of reciprocal
> recognition flow? Without it the whole theory of revolution
> as *the* philosophy of human liberty, as man's call 'to his
> total destiny,' collapses into unreality. Yet in the existential

view of the individual there is no place for such recognition and therefore, one is bound to conclude, no foundation on which to build the political theory which Sartre himself has sketched.[100]

In any act of speaking or writing one pays tribute to the objective rights of both language and logic — new forms of otherness which limit man's freedom. To be *completely* creative, therefore, one ought to by-pass the conventions of speech and join with Cratylus. He would not so much as talk to express his philosophy, but would only wave his hand. Yet even here existential problems abound. Since the hand itself is an objectivity with which freedom must deal, it consitutes an ontological limit to creativity. A hand can wave just so far, and just so long. In fact, the *real* shame is that man even exists at all; for in existing he is limited to existing.

C. *Conclusion*

After the inquiring individual supposed he had safely completed his exhausting hike through the dense forest of competing options, he must now face the worst shock of all. For a full week now he has struggled to find his way to shelter. But after obediently following every familiar sign — believing that beyond each hidden clump of trees an outlet would be discovered — he discovers, having walked in a circle, that he is back where he started from in the first place. There is the familiar growth of unhappiness from which he sought so hard to escape. But this is not all. Not only is he wanting in hope that he will ever find his way out of this forest alive, but also the existential guide at his side offers the dismal consolation that deliverance consists in being lost forever. Even the possession of a compass would constitute a form of objectivity to cool off the passion of inwardness. The only way to be saved is to remain lost every moment. The desire to find a warm cabin is itself an existential untruth, for it proves that the individual

100. Grene, *op. cit.*, p. 119.

is shrinking from the gloom of facing complete nothingness alone. But no worry: There are no cabins; there is no compass. All is lost!

The existential doctrine of salvation reminds one of the well-known story of the man who, when asked why he hit himself on the head with a hammer, responded that it felt so good when he stopped. But even this illustration is faulty, for the existentialist says that satisfaction comes, not in stopping, but in continual beating. Unless we perpetually strike ourselves with the mallets of atheism, moral relativism, and complete separation from all objective authority which sets a limit to creativity we suffer the corruption of decisionless existence.

Existentialism forces us to be unnatural. Because freedom stands under the impulsion of *rationes aeternae*, we must discipline ourselves to reckon with those objective forms which define the limits of legitimate creativity. Freedom *finds* the values of truth, goodness, and beauty; it does not create them. Let creativity be infinite; but let it be infinite *creativity*. Without transtemporal, trans-spatial criteria to serve as guides in our freedom, we shall so obliterate the difference between creative progress and destructive retrogression that all significance in life will be destroyed. Unless we are getting somewhere in our freedom, we are simply caught in the prison discipline of walking in a treadmill.

Summary

Because of the ease with which an objective structure of authority can swallow up human freedom, Kierkegaard concluded that the best way to preserve both Christianity and individuality is to set the subjective witness in opposition to the objective, proportioning the certainty of the former to the uncertainty of the latter.

It is very easy for one to sympathize with Kierkegaard's intentions, for it is too sadly true that an objective system often becomes an excuse for deferring individual responsibility. Whoever acts this way or that just because another has told him to, is bound in the same cuffs and chains as the girl in the harem or the boy in the slave market. Since God has made us free, free let us be.

But it is not easy for one to sympathize with the method Kierkegaard elected in preserving Christianity. A *healthy* inwardness must be guided by, and proportioned to, objective evidences. Once the subjective and objective loci of truth are set in antagonistic relations, the final result is the destruction of the free individual himself. If faith is based on the absurd, than it may soon be good faith to support dictatorial madness.

The proper solution to the problem is to distinguish between valid and invalid systems of authority. Submission to either Hegelianism or Catholicism is axiologically foolish, not because man becomes complacent in the presence of systems, but because a good system is able to show that these systems are bad. Submission to the system of Biblical Christianity is good, not because complacency is destroyed by absurdities, but because the system is able to support spirituality through its rigorous systematic consistency. If a man seeks to increase inwardness, therefore, let him *adorn*, not belittle, that metaphysical system which alone makes being an individual — or anything else — meaningful. The proof of faith is a defense of the truth.

The more firmly one is convinced that the Christian faith is true, the more eager one should be to provide himself and others with proof of that fact by disinterested examination of the evidences for his faith in hours of disciplined detachment. What is needed would seem to be not a life of passionate disregard of truth on the one hand and passionless indifference on the other, but a passionate search for the truth in which emotional experience will provide its full share of the evidence.[101]

The exhaustive effort of both dialectical theology and existential philosophy to make peace with Kierkegaard's dictum

---

101. Harold DeWolf, *The Religious Revolt Against Reason*, (New York: Harper and Brothers, 1949), p. 113.

simply adds proof that the principle itself is inadequate. There is no way to safeguard theology or philosophy as sciences apart from the presupposition that a single genus of knowledge envelops both time and eternity. If revelation is *one* type of knowledge and science and philosophy *another,* a hopeless bifurcation results in which there remains no universal and necessary test for error.

Russian Communism has become a roaring lion, seeking whom it may devour. Whether or not Western culture can survive this new challenge depends on the virility of the philosophy which undergirds it. And there is no more effective way to undermine the health of a culture than to impregnate it with a philosophy which, like that of Nietzsche,[102] conditions the rise of the *Ucbermensch* to the absence of any moral or metaphysical restraints over against him. When freedom is given license to wander independently of the support of a philosophy of life which is objective, rationally verifiable, and intelligently communicable, individual and social action will have no more meaning than the random gestures of the swine in the sty. How can we know if inwardness is either good, true, or beautiful except by judging it according to standards which the individual depends upon, but which themselves do not depend upon the individual?

If perchance Kierkegaard *is* correct in saying that truth as inwardness increases in proportion to the absurdity of the objective, then at least let all the universities and churches close their doors; for in their enthusiasm to make stable individuals out of those who come to them for learning they are in effect killing off individuality itself.

---

102. "The concept 'God' was invented as the counter-concept to life — everything harmful, poisonous, slanderous, and all deadly hostility to life, all bound together in one horrible unit.... The concept 'sin,' together with the instrument of torture appertaining to it, the concept of 'free will,' was invented in order to mislead our instincts, to render the mistrust of them man's second nature!" *The Philosophy of Nietzsche,* (New York: The Modern Library), p. 932.

Part VI

TO WHOM SHALL WE TURN?

XII

The Sum of the Matter

THE famous "idols" of Francis Bacon form a perfect commentary on the fact that one of the most powerful forces in life, and for that reason one of the most destructive, is *prejudice*. If the booty of all the professional thieves in history were weighed together, the resulting sum could not balance a fraction of the loot plundered by this crafty robber. Prejudice accomplishes its malicious work in the heart of the free individual by shutting out the light of sympathy, understanding, and appreciation. Through its power to control judgments of value it blinds an individual both to the person of others and to what they are doing and saying. Rare is that spirit which, resisting the suasions of personal prejudice, breaks through to an objective appreciation of the real facts in a situation. Most individuals go to their grave a seething mass of blinding opinions and prejudices.

I. Biblical Christianity

While each must judge the matter for himself, it is the conviction of the Christian philosopher that men turn from Biblical Christianity more by the leading of prejudgment than by light gained from critical hypotheses. It is easy to misunderstand the simple system of Biblical truth by confusing it with a dissatisfying denominational or institutional system which pretends to come in its name. Consequently, men comb the world for data with which to deliver them from the uncertainties of the present hour, while by-passing a copy of the Scriptures which may be purchased for a few cents in a variety store.

511

If one were to lay his finger on one of the most successful prejudices against the Biblical faith, it probably is the fear that Christianity is an authoritative system of dogma which threatens to reduce the total complement of values in a free individual. The hedonist fears reduction to a negative, Sunday School manner of a life; the lover of bread the choking off of material rights; the positivist the corrupting of scientific verification; the philosopher the imposition of an extra-rational revelation; the humanist the swallowing up of the dignity of man; the finitist the loss of goodness; the universalist the loss of love; the Roman Catholic the loss of authority; and the existentialist the loss of creativity.

One can only respond that these apprehensions are nourished by prejudice, not fact. Since Christ is the true shepherd, not the hireling, he has not come to rob us of anything. He has come to give us life and freedom — and that abundantly. Biblical Christianity defends the covenant of God as that stable framework within which man is permitted to express infinite self-creativity. There is no freedom apart from the protection of such limits. One is free to drive his automobile only after he submits to the system placed upon him by the traffic signals. Without these guides chaos would reign. The existentialist (let us recall) is not really free. Having seized autonomy by bludgeoning the very norms which keep both society and the heart free, he is clamped in the strongest of irons. He has nothing to strive for, nothing to gain or lose. Since there are no lines to cross and no goals to reach. the race is not exciting. Freedom enjoys progress only when there is a *terminus a quo* from which one departs and a *terminus ad quem* towards which one moves. When these permanent markers are confiscated and destroyed, creativity itself is dissipated.   Since the individual has chosen it with infinite independence, Sartre may believe that an ode to a belch is a fine illustration of creativity; but in actual truth such an ode is but the rattle of the heavy chains which shackle him hand and foot.   The links in the chains of existentialism were bright and gleaming when first forged, for freedom relished the labor of tearing down law and norms; but the bleeding ankles of the captives now tell their own tale of suffering.

Biblical Christianity outlines an epistemological and metaphysical framework which gives cosmic support to the virtue of love. The framework does not limit freedom; rather, it makes freedom possible by defining the normative conditions of creativity. The law of love offers a latitude within which freedom can never be exhausted. However perfect our love may be, however exhaustive our search for brotherhood in history, freedom can yet locate new and richer ways to love. Kindness, charity, gentleness, patience and forgiveness gain in fecundity as they are practiced. Because God so loved the world that he sent his only Son to be the propitiation for our sins, men are provided with a metaphysical ground for the virtue of love. Since we were loved by God when we were his enemies, we respond by loving those who are our enemies. Only this structure can protect the venture of love. The instant we depart from the cross of Christ we are catapulted back into the humanistic predicament. Why should we love those who lie outside our sphere of social influence? Once again the clanking of chains of bondage can be heard in the distance.

Biblical Christianity does not denounce those values which all men seek by nature. *Pleasure?* "The earth is Jehovah's, and the fulness thereof; the world, and they that dwell therein." (Psalm 24:1) The only Biblical rule is this: Love both God and man, and then go and live any way you want. *Economic-social security?* "If any one will not work, let him not eat." (II Thessalonians 3:10) Because man is made in the image of God, principles of thrift, industry, and justice become virtues of faith. Biblical Christianity puts a real dynamic into economic struggle, for to waste resources is a sin. Because he lives unto God, the thrifty man is the virtuous man. *Wisdom?* "Happy is the man that findeth wisdom, and the man that getteth understanding. For the gaining of it is better than the gaining of silver, and the profit thereof than fine gold." (Proverbs 3:13-14) When the scientific-philosophic enterprise is rooted in the covenantal revelations of Jehovah God, it is lavished with infinite dignity. Armed with great clues to the meaning of life, the thinker can then enjoy infinite self-expression by filling in the details — and all to the glory of God. A godless *Weltanschauung* leaves the systematizer without consistency. *Authority?* "You will know the truth, and truth will make you free." (John 8:32) Truth in Christ brings release from the bondage of sin, clearing up both mind and heart for clear vision in life's venture. Christ is the sovereign, mystical head of each Christian, and no individual or institution has a power to step in and destroy this fellowship. This is a satisfying authority for freedom. Until the day of death each man stands or falls before his own master.

There are blind spots in the Christian revelation — many of them. Therefore, whoever *wants* to find fault with Scripture will assuredly meet with no difficulty in his labor. But is this the course prudence dictates? Is not a rational man satisfied with that system which is attended by the fewest difficulties? Christianity at least explains man's predicament from the center of his heart, and that is accomplishing a great deal. Fairness at least requires that any substitute accomplish as much. *But to whom shall we turn?*

II. Terminal Responsibility

Because the Christian is seeking to bring men to decision, rather than entertain them through a series of sophisms, his work is less popular than that of the novelist. The novelist can unravel the plot in the course of the closing chapters, but the Christian cannot. At best, he is only a voice crying in the wilderness, seeking to make straight the way of the Lord. After he has cleared away some of the stones and debris which clutter the pathway to Christ, his authority terminates. He may show that one is better off leaving non-Christ for Christ, but there is no way that he can put saving satisfaction into the heart of that one. The satisfaction must come through personal trust. It is a simple case of the horse and the water. The

Christian may prove the power of the water to satisfy thirst, but he cannot take away the thirst. That comes only by drinking.

The final chapter in any book on a Christian philosophy of religion must be written by the individual himself, therefore. The only way to gain acquaintance knowledge of the person of Christ is to believe, for fellowship can never be generated by proxy. Heart must meet heart in personal love. Knowledge by inference must pass over into knowledge by acquaintance. In no other way can the values of fellowship with Christ be fully felt. Christian philosophy may be of service to show why God's love ought to be sought, and how spiritually emaciated a man will be who lacks that love, but it cannot make a satisfied lover out of the person. Only the Spirit of God can create a heart of love, and only the will of the individual can summon the Spirit. One can know of the meaning of any value only after he *wills* to know it.

Christian theologians have long debated whether we first *know* that we might believe, or *believe* that we might know. The truth is that we do both. First we know in order that we might believe; then we believe in order that we might know. Observe the following illustration: Before a sensible man will leap into a body of water, he will first rationally persuade himself that the blue patch beneath him is actually water and not just a sheet of painted concrete. Once he is rationally convinced that the water is safe and clear, he is then ready to commit himself to the pool. *First he knows; then he believes.* But this is not the end of the matter. Now he must act upon this belief. After diving into the pool he comes into the possession of a body of knowledge which could never be gained by an eternity of rational anticipation. He now knows by experience what it is like to be wet and refreshed. *After believing, he knows.*

The same principle applies in person-person relations. We first use our intellect to recognize the presence of the other person (thus believing by knowing); but only in the act of personal trust is the knowledge relation completed (thus knowing by believing). Fellowship can never be experienced apart from commitment. Love is such a strange — yet infinitely satisfying — datum that only the lover knows of its inner dimensions.

If it is impossible to enter the heart of another person independently of commitment, how much less can we know the love of God apart from faith? Who can comprehend the peace of sins forgiven, who save the man who has passed through the despair of the law? Who can realize what it means to feel the arms of God undergird him, who save the lonely heart which has lost its way?

Tasting Christ is (as suggested earlier) but another instance of pudding tasting. While the chef may show that the pudding is able to assuage the hunger of the body, the final proof is in the actual taste; and each man must do this for himself. Thus with Christianity: Are its premises able to satisfy the whole man? Is Christianity nourishing and clean? If it is not, then a rational man ought to pass it by in favor of a more satisfying option. But if it is, then to refrain from tasting would be foolish. "O taste and see that Jehovah is good." (Psalm 34:8)

This is the sum of the matter: *Since we must suffer for something, let us endeavor to suffer for the right.*

INDEX

INDEX